TRUE STORIES from the American Past

EDITED BY

WILLIAM GRAEBNER

STATE UNIVERSITY OF NEW YORK
COLLEGE AT FREDONIA

McGraw-Hill, Inc.

New York St. Louis San Francisco Auckland Bogotá
Caracas Lisbon London Madrid Mexico City Milan
Montreal New Delhi San Juan Singapore
Sydney Tokyo Toronto

This book was set in Plantin by The Clarinda Company.
The editor was Niels Aaboe;
the production supervisor was Louise Karam.
The cover was designed by Joseph A. Piliero.
Project supervision was done by Tage Publishing Service.
R. R. Donnelley & Sons Company was printer and binder.

This book is printed on acid-free paper.

TRUE STORIES FROM THE AMERICAN PAST

5 6 7 8 9 0   DOC   DOC   9 0 9 8 7 6 5 4

ISBN 0-07-023915-0

Library of Congress Cataloging–in–Publication Data

True stories from the American past/edited by William Graebner.
     p.   cm.
  ISBN 0–07–023915–0
   1. United States—History—1865-   I. Graebner, William.
E661.T78   1993
973—dc20   92-30973

ABOUT THE AUTHORS

George Chauncey Jr. is assistant professor of history at the University of Chicago. He has contributed articles to the *Journal of Social History*, *Salmagundi*, and several scholarly anthologies, and is co-editor of *Hidden from History: Reclaiming the Gay and Lesbian Past* (New York: New American Library, 1989). He is currently finishing a book, *Gay New York: Urban Culture and the Making of a Gay Male World, 1890–1970*, (New York: Basic, forthcoming), and is also at work on a study of the relationship between gender politics, anti-communism, and anti-homosexuality in Cold War political discourse.

Ellen Carol DuBois is professor of history at the University of California at Los Angeles. She is the author of *Feminism and Suffrage: The Emergence of an Independent Women's Movement in America, 1848-1869* (Ithaca, NY: Cornell University Press, 1978) and the editor of *Elizabeth Cady Stanton, Susan B. Anthony: Correspondence, Writings, Speeches* (Schocken, 1981). She is currently at work on a biography of Harriot Stanton Blatch, entitled *Generation of Power: Harriot Stanton Blatch and the Winning of Woman Suffrage*.

Wayne K. Durrill, assistant professor of history at the University of Cincinnati, is author of *War of Another Kind: A Southern Community in the Great Rebellion* (New York: Oxford University Press, 1990), and articles in the *American Historical Review*, the *Journal of American History*, and *Slavery and Abolition*. He has received fellowships from the American Council of Learned Societies and the Smithsonian Institution.

Michael Frisch is an American social historian who had recently completed graduate school when he joined the throng at the Woodstock Festival in 1969. Since then, he has been teaching history and American studies at SUNY Buffalo. His most recent book is *A Shared Authority: Essays on the Craft and Meaning of Oral and Public History* (Albany: State University of New York Press, 1990); forthcoming from Cornell University Press in 1993 is *Portraits in Steel*, an oral history of ex-steelworkers prepared in collaboration with documentary photographer Milton Rogovin.

James Gilbert is professor of American history at the University of Maryland and the author of several books including *Another Chance: America Since 1945* (Philadelphia: Temple University Press, 1981), *A Cycle of Outrage: America's Reaction to the Juvenile Delinquent in the 1950s* (New York: Oxford University Press, 1986), and, most recently, *Perfect Cities: Chicago's Utopias of the 1890s* (Chicago: University of Chicago Press, 1991).

William Graebner is professor of history at the State University of New York, College at Fredonia. He has written on a variety of aspects of twentieth-century American history. His books include *A History of Retirement* (New Haven: Yale University Press, 1980), *The Engineering of Consent: Democracy and Authority in Twentieth-Century America* (Madison: University of Wisconsin Press, 1987), *Coming of Age in Buffalo* (Philadelphia: Temple University Press, 1990), and *The Age of Doubt: American Thought and Culture in the 1940s* (Boston: Twayne, 1991). He currently serves on the editorial board of *American Studies*.

Walter LaFeber is Noll Professor of History at Cornell University. His recent books are *The American Age: U.S. Foreign Relations At Home and Abroad Since 1750* (New York, 1989), and *America, Russia, and the Cold War, 1945–1990*, 6th edition (New York, 1990). He currently serves on the editorial boards of *Political Science Review* and *International History Review*.

George Lipsitz is professor of ethnic studies at the University of California, San Diego and the author of *Time Passages: Collective Memory and American Popular Culture* (Minneapolis: University of Minnesota Press, 1990), *A Life in the Struggle: Ivory Perry and the Culture of Opposition* (Philadelphia: Temple University Press, 1988), and *Class and Culture in Cold War America: A Rainbow at Midnight* (South Hadley, MA: Bergin and Garvey, 1982).

Gerald Markowitz is professor of history and chair of the interdepartment of thematic studies at John Jay College of Criminal Justice, City University of New York. He is author of numerous articles on twentieth-century politics and culture in America. He has authored a number of books and collections including *Democratic Vistas: Post Offices and Public Art During the New Deal*. With David Rosner he has edited *Dying for Work: Workers' Safety and Health in Twentieth-Century America* (Bloomington, IL: Indiana University Press, 1987) and *"Slaves of the Depression": Workers' Letters about Life on the Job* (Ithaca, NY: Cornell University Press, 1987).

Elaine Tyler May is professor of American studies and history at the University of Minnesota. She is the author of *Great Expectations: Marriage and Divorce in Post-Victorian America* (Chicago: University of Chicago, 1980), and *Homeward Bound: American Families in the Cold War Era* (New York: Basic Books, 1988). She is currently working on a new book, *Barren in the Promised Land: American Identity and the Quest for Parenthood*.

Stuart Creighton Miller is professor of social science and history and director of the social science program at San Francisco State University. He is the author of *The Unwelcome Immigrant: The American Image of the Chinese, 1785–1882* (1969), the runner-up for the 1970 Bancroft Prize, and *"Benevolent Assimilation": The American Conquest of the Philippines, 1899–1903* (1982). His current research is on immigration history, focusing on cultural pluralism as a romantic quest.

W. J. Rorabaugh is professor of history at the University of Washington in Seattle. A graduate student at Berkeley in the early 1970s, he is the author of *The Alcoholic Republic* (New York: Oxford University Press, 1979), *The Craft Apprentice* (New York: Oxford University Press, 1986), and most recently, *Berkeley at War: The 1960s* (New York: Oxford University Press, 1989).

David Rosner is professor of history at Baruch College and the Graduate Center of the City University of New York. He is also adjunct professor of community medicine at Mt. Sinai Medical School. He has written extensively on the history of public health and medicine in America and is the author of *A Once Charitable Enterprise: Hospitals and Health Care in Brooklyn and New York, 1885–1915* (Princeton, NJ: Princeton University Press, 1986) and most recently, with Gerald Markowitz, *Deadly Dust: Silicosis and the Politics of Occupational Disease in Twentieth-Century America* (Princeton, NJ: Princeton University Press, 1991).

Ronald Story is professor of history at the University of Massachusetts at Amherst. Story's work includes *Generations of Americans* (New York: St. Martins, 1976), *The Forging of an Aristocracy* (Middletown: Wesleyan University Press, 1980), *A More Perfect Union* (Boston: Houghton Mifflin, 1984–1992), and, more recently, "The Country of the Young: The Meaning of Baseball in Early America" in *Baseball and the American Culture* (Westport: Meckler, 1991), *Sports in Massachusetts* (Westfield: Institute for Massachusetts Studies, 1991), and *Five Colleges, Five Histories* (Amherst: Five Colleges, Inc., 1992).

Alan Trachtenberg is Neil Gray, Jr. Professor of English and American Studies at Yale University. He is the author of *Brooklyn Bridge: Fact and Symbol* (New York: Oxford University Press, 1965), *The Incorporation of America: Culture and Society in the Gilded Age* (New York: Hill & Wang, 1982), and *Reading American Photographs: Images as History, Matthew Brady to Walker Evans* (New York: Hill & Wang, 1989).

Altina L. Waller is professor of history at the State University of New York at Plattsburgh. She received her doctorate from the University of Massachusetts at Amherst and has taught at West Virginia University and Rhodes College in Memphis, Tennessee. Her first book was *Reverend Beecher and Mrs. Tilton: Sex and Class in Victorian America* (Amherst, MA: University of Massachusetts Press, 1982). Her second book, *Feud: Hatfields, McCoys and Social Change in Appalachia, 1860–1900* (Chapel Hill, NC: University of North Carolina Press, 1988) is the basis for her story about the feud.

CONTENTS

PREFACE

True Stories is a special kind of reader. It consists of fifteen stories, each thoroughly researched and impeccably crafted by scholars who are authorities in their respective fields. Each story deals with a significant and compelling episode in the history of the United States since the Civil War. Every decade of that history is represented by at least one story.

In selecting the stories, I have been moved by the sense that the American past is too rich and varied to be bound and contained by the traditional and comfortable narratives with which most historians are conversant. Nonetheless, some of our stories—the story of the nation's imperial adventure in the Philippines, or the account of Francis Townsend's confrontation with Franklin D. Roosevelt's New Dealers over pensions for the aged—will be generally familiar to instructors, if not students. Other episodes, including the opening of Disneyland, the rock concerts at Woodstock and Altamont, and the Bernhard Goetz subway shooting, will have resonance for many Americans, yet are receiving their first serious historical treatment in this book. Still others—the story of the debate over an early artificial insemination, and the sex crime panic of the 1940s, concern issues and incidents that are not even mentioned in survey textbooks. I hope readers will appreciate the remarkable diversity of *True Stories*.

Together, the stories cover a wide variety of fields of historical inquiry, many of them new to the study of history in the last two or three decades. These include popular culture; the history of medicine, sexuality; rural life; youth culture; women's history; the history of African-Americans; crime and violence; the aged; urban history; and the history of science and technology. Most important, each episode was selected because it promised to make, well, a good *story*.

Why use stories to study and learn history? The idea is not as unusual as it might seem. We live in a culture steeped in stories: the myths of ancient Greece, Biblical narratives, bedtime stories, fairy tales, newspaper accounts, Hollywood epics, neighborhood rumors, one's personal account of the day's events after a hard day at school or at the office. Even the standard history textbooks are essentially stories—longer, more general, more familiar, and more generally accepted stories than the ones found in this book—but stories, just the same.

The accounts that make up *True Stories* are obviously not myths, or fairy tales, or rumors. They are a certain kind of story that we easily recognize as

vii

"history." Indeed, history might be understood as a set of analytical stories about the past whose authors think are "true." When we read an historical account, we expect it to be balanced, to be based on historical research and "facts," and to show respect for the past; by these standards, the stories in *True Stories* certainly qualify as history. But it is not quite the history one finds in a history textbook. *True Stories* features people who live and act in specific places and times and in precise historical circumstances. Its flesh and blood protagonists—some of them resembling mythic heroes or antiheroes—build bridges, march in parades, take money to throw baseball games, justify the marketing of hazardous substances, shoot people on the subway, speak from the big stage at the Woodstock Music & Art Fair—or, in one incredible case, artificially impregnate a woman without her knowledge. In short, one function of any story—and one purpose of *True Stories*—is to put people, and people's deeds, back into history.

There is another lesson to be learned from these stories, one that has to do with what a story is. Although the stories presented here often involve individuals acting in specific situations, they have significance that goes far beyond the setting or the actors. The people in *True Stories* (indeed, all of us) inevitably live their lives on the stage of history. The things that they do—even the odd, eccentric, or criminal things—are ultimately historical deeds, carried out within the economic, political, social, and cultural frameworks of a particular historical era. Therefore, a good story provides the insights of the traditional textbook, though in a very different form.

Sometimes it can be difficult to see the connections between a story and history, between the text and its context. When one sees a movie, or watches the 11 o'clock television news, one does not easily or automatically think of these "stories" as part of history; and making the connections between a specific event and the larger past can be more difficult when the event occurred decades ago. To help students make these connections, and to see the need for making them, each episode concludes with an interpretive section that pulls together the themes in the story and links the story proper with some larger and familiar historical context. For example, the epic hill-country feud between the Hatfields and the McCoys in the 1880s emerges as a product of industrialization and urbanization; and the Iranian hostage crisis that began in 1979 is shaped as a moment in America's decline as a world economic and political power.

Each episode, then, has two distinct parts. The first part is the narrated story. Our goal was to keep this story section as free as possible from analysis and interpretation, in the hope that students would fashion their own perspectives once freed, if only relatively and momentarily, from the learned authority of the historian. The second part of the episode is a shorter interpretive conclusion, where the authors have been given free reign to bring their considerable analytical skills to bear on the body of the story.

As students and instructors will discover, the attempt to separate narrative and interpretation has been only moderately successful. Even the most rudimentary collections of "facts" and the simplest narratives begin with preconceptions, proceed from moral and ethical premises, and imply interpretive frameworks. So do our "true stories." Despite our efforts to put these elements in the background, they inevitably appear in the stories. Indeed, one purpose of the collection is to draw attention to the inescapable subjectivity of historians. Nonetheless, we also believe that the effort made here to separate narrative and analysis can assist students in generating their own readings of the past and, by doing so, in becoming active participants in the complex process of understanding and creating their own history.

ACKNOWLEDGMENTS

The authors wish to thank John C. Chalberg, Normandale Community College; Anthony Edmonds, Ball State University; Gerald J. Goodwin, University of Houston; Robert Ingalls, University of South Florida; Stephen Kneeshaw, College of the Ozarks; Leon F. Litwack, University of California, Berkeley; C. K. McFarland, Arkansas State University; James M. McPherson, Princeton University; Sonya Michel, University of Illinois, Urbana-Champaign; David Nasaw, City University of New York, College of Staten Island; Alan Schaffer, Clemson University; Richard Schneirov, Indiana State University; Ken L. Wetherbie, Del Mar College; and R. Jackson Wilson, Smith College, for their helpful reviews of earlier versions of this book.

William Graebner

1

THE SOUTH CAROLINA
BLACK CODE

WAYNE K. DURRILL

In December 1865, South Carolina's all-white legislature passed a series of four acts known as the Black Code. Although the Code was almost immediately declared null and void by the commander of the Union military troops stationed in the region (8 months after the Civil War had ended), the Code was a landmark in the transition from a political, economic, and social system based on the enslavement of black people to one based only on their exploitation.

As Wayne K. Durrill's account of the origins of this document reveals, the South Carolina Black Code was a complex and sometimes contradictory law, the provisions of which reflected the disparate desires of the state's low-country planters, upcountry yeoman farmers, and merchants. These groups disagreed on the most basic issues—whether, for example, black people should vote, or own property, or be required by law to labor for others.

Because South Carolina's former slaves or "freedmen" could not vote and were not directly represented in the deliberations, they had much less influence over the final product than the various white constituencies. Yet they did have a voice, and they made it heard. From the summer of 1865 through the end of the year, the state's emerging black leaders reinterpreted the meaning of emancipation for their black audiences, challenged the racist assumptions that underpinned the arguments for legal control of the black population, and, in November, came together in a convention that demanded the right to vote and objected to the very idea of a separate code governing the rights and obligations of the state's black people. Most of all, they proclaimed the right of freedmen to a measure of economic independence: to own and farm land or, at the very least, to receive a share of the crop in return for tilling land owned by others.

The story of South Carolina's Black Code is partly the story of war, and of the dislocations and the social and political readjustments that followed inevitably from it. During the Reconstruction era, South Carolina's blacks retained and amplified the public voice they had found in the summer of 1865. Under laws pushed through the United States Congress by the Radical Republicans, they voted, held political office, and, in 1868, formed a majority in the legislature that wrote a new constitution for the state. Despite the violence and intimidation practiced by the Ku Klux Klan and other organizations, blacks played a major role in South Carolina government until 1876,

1

when the withdrawal of Northern soldiers made it unsafe for blacks to exercise their rights and effectively ended a period of experimentation and reform in race relations.

Yet there is another context in which to interpret the story, and it is one that involves neither war nor Reconstruction. When South Carolina's black people opposed the Black Code and scorned efforts to turn them into simple wage earners, their actions resembled and anticipated those of hundreds of thousands of nineteenth-century workers who in the following decades would lose their skills, their small businesses, their farms, and their independence to an organizational and technological revolution spearheaded by giant corporations. For the freedman, one threat lay in the past, in a reconstitution of the ages-old system of slavery. Another—the threat of new forms of exploitation, based on wages, rents, and contracts—signaled that the future might be dangerous as well.

By late July 1865, freedmen along the South Carolina coast had begun to wonder what this new thing—freedom—might mean. Some few thousands on the Sea Islands had gotten a taste of it during the previous 3 years. After the federal invasion of Port Royal Island in 1861, some former slaves on the cotton plantations there had divided the land among themselves, planted corn and other foodstuffs, and produced a living solely for themselves for the first time in their lives. Others not so lucky were drawn into government-sponsored cotton growing schemes that employed freedmen on large plantations for very low wages. But in the late spring of 1865 planters in South Carolina had begun to talk of returning to their plantations on the coast. What then would become of those freedmen and the crops they had just planted? On July 24, 500 or 600 freedmen on St. Helena Island gathered near an old brick church to hear a lecture given on that very question. The speaker, Martin Delany, was a major in the 104th U.S. Colored Troops, and he had been a free black man and a prominent abolitionist in the North before the Civil War. As such, he spoke with great authority when he addressed the former slaves at St. Helena Island.

Delany first informed his listeners that they were free, that slavery had been "absolutely abolished." He did not, however, attribute that fact to Abraham Lincoln and his Emancipation Proclamation issued in January 1863. Delany declared instead that emancipation "was only a War policy of the Government . . . knowing that the whole power of the South laid in the possession of the Slaves." Speaking as a black man (but not as a former slave), he went on to argue that "we would not have become free, had we not armed ourselves and fought out our independence." So important did he think this point that Delany repeated the sentence twice. In doing so, he laid claim to full citizenship for all black people in the United States. Many black men, after all, had given their lives to preserve the nation. And from that claim would flow a program to secure for freedmen in South Carolina all the rights due to any citizen.

Delany began with the question of how the economic rights of freedmen might be secured during the next few years. By June 1865, planters in South Carolina already had argued that freedmen were too lazy to work and, as Delany told the crowd, "have not the intelligence to get on for yourselves without being guided and driven to the work by overseers." "I say it is a lie, and a blasphemous lie," Delany exclaimed, "and I will prove it to be so." With that he launched into a lengthy account of slavery in the United States, showing that white men had turned to Africans for labor because the latter could stand work that Indians could not. From this Delany concluded that black people in America had always worked, otherwise whites would never have taken the trouble and expense to enslave them in the first place. Hence, there was no reason to believe that they would not work in the future.

But work for whom? Delany's answer: For themselves. "Get a community and get all the lands you can—if you cannot get any singly," Delany told the freedmen. "Grow as much vegetables etc., as you want for your families; on the other part of land you cultivate Rice and Cotton." In other words, freedmen should strive to become independent yeoman farmers who depended on their own labor to produce a subsistence and some surplus crops for sale in distant markets. The advantage lay in the fact that such farmers depended on no one else—including their former masters. They required no credit, accumulated no debt, and thereby retained their economic independence. Recognizing that not all freedmen would possess the financial resources to purchase land immediately, Delany said that those who had neither the money nor an opportunity to buy

After the Civil War, freedpeople in South Carolina attempted to establish themselves as independent farmers. The first step, even before renting or buying land, was to acquire two basic farming tools—an ox for plowing and a wagon for hauling the crop to market. (South Caroliniana Library, University of South Carolina)

or rent land should work for a portion of the crop. He informed the freedmen at St. Helena Island that the federal government had decided that "you shall have one third of the produce of the crops from your employer, so if he makes $3, you will have to get $1 out of it for your labour."

In making these proposals, Delany advocated self-reliance as the means to achieve economic independence. By contrast, he warned, freedmen who agreed to work for planters for wages would forfeit all chance to chart their own economic destiny. "Now I look around me," Delany told his audience, "and I notice a man, barefooted and covered with rags and dirt. Now I ask, what is that man doing, for whom is he working. I hear that he works for that and that farmer for 30 cents a day. I tell you that must not be. That would be cursed slavery over again. I will not have it, the Government will not have it. . . . I tell you slavery is over, and shall never return again."

After Delany concluded his speech, the "excitement" of the crowd "was immense," according to one observer. Groups formed to talk over what they had heard, and "ever and anon cheers were given to some particular sentences of the speech." One freedman commented: "That is the only man who ever told [us] the truth." Another vowed that the freedmen on St. Helena Island would "get rid of the Yankee employer"—men who had contracted with the federal government to raise cotton on abandoned plantations during the war. And one black man concluded that, in the future, planters would "have to work themselves or starve or leave the country—we will not work for them anymore."

This was exactly what South Carolina planters had feared would happen should the Confederacy be defeated. Some few planters who happened to be present at the meeting of freedmen "listened with horror depicted in their faces, to the whole performance," according to an army officer on the scene. "What shall become of us now?" the planters wondered, "if such a speech should be again given to those men, there will be open rebellion."

But there were other troubled listeners as well. Col. C. H. Howard, a post commander in the 128th U.S. Colored Troops, had sent two observers to report on Delany's speech. One of the men described Delany as "a thorough hater of the White race [who] tries the colored people unnecessarily," and was especially critical of Delany's "advising them not to work for any man, but for themselves." This statement contradicted what the observer believed to be government policy: "that all the [freed]men should be employed by their former masters as far as possible." He also worried that Delany had encouraged freedmen to act by force, if necessary, to preserve control over their own labor. "The mention of having two hundred thousand [black] men [in the U.S. Colored Troops] well drilled in arms—does he not hint to them what to do? if they should be compelled to work for employers."

This single meeting at St. Helena Island exemplified a debate that had emerged throughout South Carolina in July of 1865, a debate out of which would come the infamous Black Code. With slavery destroyed would black people in the South ever work for planters again? Or would freedmen gain access to land and become independent yeoman farmers? If so, the large plantations might break up and be replaced with tenant farms, and planters would become landlords, if they managed to hold on to their land at all. Or from the merchants' point of view: Would black people simply grow a subsistence crop of corn and hogs and cease to produce a cash crop such as cotton or rice entirely, as some had done on the rice islands during the war? If so, South Carolina's largest merchants would go broke. There would be no cotton for them to buy, insure, ship to New York, and sell for enormous profits as there had been before the war. Moreover, freedmen who ceased to produce a significant cash crop would have no money on hand to buy cloth and shoes from Northern factories. They would begin to produce those goods at home and the merchants' import trade would falter.

In the summer of 1865, it fell to the Union army to mediate the differences among planters, merchants, and freedmen, and that arrangement favored the former slaves at first. In May, General Quincy A. Gilmore, the federal commander at Hilton Head, had arrested the Confederate governor, disbanded the civil courts, and divided the state into nine military subdistricts with garrisons in each, although the Union troops, in fact, were spread thinly and unevenly. Many of the soldiers were black and, as the army mustered out white troops in June and July, some places were garrisoned entirely by black soldiers. At about the same time, Gilmore also established a network of provost courts wherever his troops were stationed. During the war, trials in these tribunals had ordinarily focused on infractions of military discipline by soldiers. But beginning in July of 1865 the provost courts also tried cases involving planters and freedmen, the charge usually being breech of contract by a planter. Freedmen living in communities supplied with black troops and provost courts had powerful friends to call on in their disputes with local planters.

Because South Carolina remained under martial law for several months, Union commanders also had no choice but to make the laws by which free labor would replace slavery. In March, General Rufus Saxton had issued the first general regulations governing the labor of freedmen. In his Circular No. 3, Saxton directed that "in making contracts with the freedmen to cultivate upon shares, the employer can make no claim to any of the crops except the cotton," and he could take only half of that. Moreover, the freedmen were "to be allowed the whole corn and vegetable crop they raise, for their own support, and no contract will be held valid that does not conform to this requirement."

These regulations were further strengthened by General Oliver O. Howard, who was Commissioner of the Freedmen's Bureau which had been established in March 1865 to distribute clothing, food, and fuel to freedmen and white refugees made destitute by the war. In late May, Howard directed from Washington that freedmen "must be free to choose their own employers, and be paid for their labor." He further required that all labor contracts be entered into freely and in good faith by both parties, and be approved by officers in the Union army or Bureau. To ensure enforcement of these contracts, Howard authorized Freedmen's Bureau agents to adjudicate all differences between employers and employees in places where local courts did not exist or where the courts failed to recognize the testimony of freedmen.

Despite such rules, planters and freedmen often disagreed. Consider, for example, the contract signed in late June 1865 by S. D. Doar and sixty-five of his former slaves on Fairfield plantation located near Charleston. The document committed the freedmen "to attend & cultivate" the lands on the plantation until December 31, 1865, "according to the usual system of planting rice & provision lands, and to conform to all reasonable rules & regulations as may be prescribed" by Doar. Doar reserved the "power to order & arrange the kind of business to be done & insist upon its faithful performance" and the right to dock any freedmen's pay for damage to tools or equipment. In return, the planter promised to compensate the freedmen with "half of the crop raised after having deducted the seed of rice, corn, peas & potatoes." Should any freed man or woman fail to "agree to the terms of this contract or breaks said terms," the planter could evict them from the plantation, thus rendering them both jobless and homeless. Not surprisingly, the army officer who witnessed the contract noted: "More trouble on this place than any other on the river."

Another officer, C. C. Bowen, who later investigated conditions on Doar's plantation, voiced "several serious objections" to the terms of this contract. According to Bowen, Doar claimed that the contract empowered him to send the freedmen "into the woods to cut wood . . . or into the rice fields to ditch, but they are paid nothing for their work, nor are they fed while performing it." Moreover, the planter insisted "that the freedmen must thresh out the old crop of rice which was made on the plantation when they were slaves, and put it on board of boats or flats for the owner to send to market. All this labor," the officer concluded, "is of no benefit to the freedman. He gets nothing for performing it, and has to furnish his own provisions or go without." It was, however, the clause requiring the freedmen to "conform to all reasonable rules & regulations" as prescribed by Doar that caused the most trouble. "It makes no difference," wrote Bowen, "how much they are abused, they cannot leave without permission from the owner." If they did leave, "it is claimed they have violated their contract and forfeited their share of the crop. Several cases of this kind have already arisen," Bowen explained.

In the South Carolina upcountry, planters exercised an even freer hand with freedmen because the Union army had stationed few troops there. In July 1865, for example, William Turns proposed to the freedmen working on his plantation in the Pendleton District that they "sign a contract for their lifetime," according to a Freedmen's Bureau agent there. When Robert Perry and his pregnant wife, Laura Perry, refused, along with all of the other freedmen, Turns drove them off the plantation "without food, or any compensation for their labor upon his crop." At that point, the Perrys and two other freedmen named Novel and Richard set out for Columbia. After walking about 25 miles, they were "overtaken" by two white men named Jolly and Dickenson who had followed them on horseback. Each carried a gun and had been sent by Turns to force the freedmen back to the plantation. The white men asked the freedmen where they were going and, after they had answered, Jolly and Dickenson tied Robert Perry and Novel "hands and feet to a tree . . . leaving the third to hold their horses." The white men shot and killed Perry and Novel, at which point Richard "ran to a creek some twenty yards distant, plunged in, [and] was shot at by Jolly, but succeeded in making his escape." Jolly and Dickenson "then took Laura, stripped her bare, gave her fifty lashes upon the bare back and then compelled her to walk back" to Turns's plantation. There, Turns rewarded Jolly and Dickenson "by giving them twenty yards of cloth, three bushels of clean rice, two bushels of salt and a government wagon." Laura, on the other hand, fared more poorly. Turns "put her at the plow by day and confined her in the dark house by night, for one week giving her nothing to eat."

But coercion through violence was a risky business for planters. It invited intervention by the Union army or retaliation in kind from freedmen. Indeed, planters in South Carolina firmly believed during the fall of 1865 that the state's freedmen had just such violence in mind. As the governor put it in a letter to the Union commander at Charleston, "There is an apprehension felt in many sections of the State that there will be some insurrectionary movement on the part of the colored people who were lately slaves." Planters expected freedmen to attempt to "drive off or murder the whites with a view to possess themselves of the lands and stock of the whites." In fact, fears of an insurrection proved groundless; freedmen engaged in no violent activity at all during the Christmas holidays in 1865.

But the possibility of pitched battles did exist during the division of crops and negotiation of contracts. Therefore, in the fall of 1865 planters in South Carolina sought to bring the power of the state to bear on the conflict over labor. They hoped that new laws governing freedmen—a Black Code—might compel them to work, laws that might be enforced by civilian courts dominated by planters themselves. But new laws could not be put on the books until the South Carolina civil government had been restored, and the current military regime disbanded. Hence, in early June 1865 a self-appointed delegation of ten planters and merchants from Charleston made their way to Washington, D.C. There they met with President Andrew Johnson and convinced him to appoint a provisional governor for South Carolina and to specify the conditions under which the state might be readmitted to the Union.

Johnson, who had risen to political power as a young man with the votes of yeoman farmers in east Tennessee, favored the early readmission of South Carolina, but only under conditions that would shift power in the state from low-country planters and merchants to yeoman farmers in the upcountry. The latter, he thought, would more likely support the Union as many had before the war and, Johnson hoped, the Republican party that he headed. To produce this dramatic shift in political power, Johnson directed Benjamin F. Perry, the provisional governor he appointed, to arrange a state convention that would rewrite South Carolina's constitution.

Meanwhile, Governor Perry attempted to undercut the Union army's power to intervene between planters and freedmen. In August, he met in Columbia with General Gilmore, by then military governor of the state, and General George Meade, commander of Union forces in the Atlantic states. The three men negotiated two questions crucial to the disposition of the labor of freedmen. Perry first requested that the army's provost courts be abolished on the grounds that the officers serving as judges were incompetent in matters of military law. These courts, in fact, had been quite effective in forcing planters to abide by the terms of the labor contracts they had signed with freedmen during the previous summer. In the end, the three men agreed that provost courts might still adjudicate all cases involving freedmen, while civil courts dealt with cases involving only white people. For the moment, the freedmen's labor contracts with planters remained enforceable by military law.

The other question involved black soldiers stationed throughout South Carolina. As white troops had been mustered out in July and August, companies of the U.S. Colored Troops had taken their place throughout the state. This was so in part because many black soldiers had been slaves before the war and they had no paying jobs or farms, as white soldiers often did, to which they were anxious to return. But the black soldiers remained on duty as well because they had taken on themselves the task of intervening on behalf of freedmen in disputes with employers. Jane Pringle, owner of several plantations on a sea island near St. Helena, reported that "all hope of inducing the freedmen to work has been lost since the arrival of the Negro troops" there. The laborers on one plantation had "declared they would not clean ditches" and on another plantation the freedmen now "refused to work at all, many coming out of the field." With great indignation, Pringle noted that "the negro troops openly encouraged them to stand up for their rights."

Benjamin F. Perry, a native of the Pendleton District in upcountry South Carolina, was a strong advocate of small farmers. Before the Civil War, he served nearly 30 years in the South Carolina legislature, and he vigorously opposed secession in 1860. (South Caroliniana Library, University of South Carolina)

The actions of black soldiers had begun to tip the balance of power in South Carolina away from planters and toward freedmen. To Perry and his political allies this was unacceptable. Therefore the governor demanded that all black troops be removed from the state. Although Meade and Gilmore both saw much wisdom in such an action, they remained short of soldiers. So, in the end, the generals decided to remove all black troops from the upcountry and confine them to duty inside several forts on the coast. The soldiers could be dispatched throughout the state if serious trouble arose, but in the meantime they could not intervene on behalf of freedmen in disputes with South Carolina planters.

The restoration of civil government in South Carolina which had been authorized by President Johnson in June began formally on September 13, 1865, when the state's constitutional convention met in Columbia. There the delegates wrestled over how the new civil government might be shaped and who might control it. Essentially the question turned on who might be counted as population for voting purposes. Planters now wanted to count all freedmen for voting purposes as they had with slaves before the war, but at the same time not allow them to vote. Not surprisingly, yeoman farmers from the upcountry objected vehemently. They owned few slaves and therefore wanted seats in the legislature determined strictly by the number of white persons in each parish or district in the state. In the end, the convention delegates worked out a compromise that permitted low-country parishes to count two-thirds of their black population for voting purposes, but without allowing black men to vote. That shifted some but not all power in the state to the upcountry.

But the compromise also left freedmen in South Carolina without any formal means to shape the civil laws that soon would govern their labor. This was a great concern because, in the fall of 1865, freedmen had gotten their first taste of how planters intended to deal with their new employees. After the harvest on S. D. Doar's plantation near Charleston, for example, the planter "stopped the rations on the one hand & on the other claimed very hard, very prompt & constant labor on thrashing *last year's* rice for market." When some freed men and women refused this uncompensated labor, the planter hung six of them up by their thumbs "for the space of three quarters of an hour, their toes barely touching the ground," according to a Freedmen's Bureau agent in the neighborhood. The freedmen argued that this work "ought not to have anything to do with the contract entered into for the raising of a crop this year." Moreover, "all clamor for *food* at least," the Bureau agent reported, "as long as they work, especially on last year's crop." In dividing the corn raised for subsistence on the plantation, Doar had taken most of it as his share for use as seed the next spring. That left the freedmen virtually nothing to eat for an entire year.

It also worried South Carolina freedmen that the convention had acted on two matters that greatly strengthened the hand of planters over their black employees. The first was a clause added to the state constitution that allowed the legislature to create "district courts" throughout South Carolina. These courts would have exclusive jurisdiction over cases involving freedmen and, South Carolina planters hoped, replace the army's provost courts. In such courts, planters would sit as judges and jurymen in place of army officers who operated the provost courts and, presumably, would rule against freedmen in cases involving a breach of contract. The second concern for freedmen was the proposed Black Code.

The convention had authorized Governor Perry to form a commission that would draft an extensive new set of laws "for the regulation of labor and the protection and government of the colored population of the State." The proposed Black Code was to be subsequently considered by the new state legislature in November. The purpose of the Code was not, however, only to "regulate" and "protect" freedmen, but also govern them in such a way as to strengthen the planters' position when conflicts arose. As Perry told legislators who later considered the Code, such legislation "will remove all pretense for military rule in the State," thus returning to the hands of planters and merchants the state's laws and courts. In September, the governor appointed two eminent South Carolina jurists and politicians, D. L. Wardlaw and Armistead Burt, to draft the new legislation. While working on the document, the two men drew on a furious debate then underway in South Carolina over the disposition of the labor of freedmen.

Planters such as Edmund Rhett wrote to Wardlaw hoping that the freedmen's labor would be "limited, controlled, and surrounded with such safeguards, as will make the change as slight as possible. In other words," the planter went on, "the general interest of the white man and of the negro requires that he should be kept as near to his former condition as Law can keep him—that he should be kept as near to the condition of slavery as possible." To accomplish this goal, Rhett suggested to Wardlaw that the Code should prohibit all freedmen "from ever owning Real Estate in South Carolina. Let the idea of their ever owning land pervade amongst them, and they will never work for the white man, or upon any land but their own," Rhett believed. Moreover, the Code should include a "stringent" act controlling "vagrancy" that would require every black person to show proof that "he is in the lawful employ of some white man."

Some South Carolina merchants, by contrast, argued that plantation agriculture had died with slavery and must be replaced with an independent yeomanry. They believed that planters ought to give up directing the labor of freedmen and instead rent small farms of forty or fifty acres to them. Such an arrangement, merchants argued somewhat disingenuously, would ultimately pay the landowner more than planting simply because it required that he invest nothing—hence there was no cost and little risk involved. (In fact, there was considerable risk because tenant farmers had no long-term interest in the property and hence were likely to exhaust the soil, let the barn fall in, and ignore unmended fences.) Meanwhile, freedmen would pay their rent in a marketable crop that would pass through the hands of merchants who might resell it in the North.

Freedmen contributed a third voice in the debate over labor. "The position taken by the laborers" at Georgetown, South Carolina, on the coast, explained an army officer on the scene, was "that they never intended to contract for anything beyond the harvesting and division of growing crops, that it was never explained to them that more than this was expected of them." Therefore, "they positively refuse to do more than this." Moreover, freedmen let it be known that they would refuse to contract in the new year when all current agreements expired. According to one report from the coast in November: "The impression that lands are to be given to the Freedpeople after the 1st of January is still generally entertained and interferes with the making of contracts for the next year."

In fact, there was to be no land distributed to the freedmen. In October, President Johnson had ordered the Freedmen's Bureau to restore all plantations to their antebellum owners. But freedmen had good reason to believe otherwise. General Saxton, by then head of the Freedmen's Bureau in South Carolina, had strongly advocated selling coastal plantations to freedmen earlier during the war. And in January of 1865, General Sherman had issued his famous Special Field Orders Number 15. This edict set aside all coastal lands in the state south of Charleston for freedmen, giving them "possessory" titles to abandoned plantations that they had occupied during the war. Despite Johnson's order, it was clear to freedmen that there were powerful white men who remained sympathetic to their desire to own land and farm independently.

About the same time, black men from throughout the state met to frame a formal response to the proposed Black Code. On November 20, 1865, more than fifty delegates, mostly from the low country, convened at Zion Church in Charleston for the first statewide meeting ever of black people in South Carolina. "The Colored People's Convention of the State of South Carolina," as the delegates called it, included prominent black men who had been free before the war, a few Northern free black men, several black non-commissioned officers from the U.S. Colored Troops stationed in the low country, and a few former slaves from the plantations. All of the delegates had been elected by the black communities in which they currently resided. If they could not vote and be represented in the legislature, South Carolina freedmen could at least attempt to influence the debate over labor in that body and any resulting laws.

The delegates began by calling on the state's white leaders to grant black men the right to vote. Allen Coffin, editor of the black-owned *South Carolina Leader,* explained that "a government based upon an oligarchy of the skin is not republican in form." Without suffrage, another delegate pointed out, "we will still have to be governed by laws that we have no voice in making," laws that would almost surely include an extensive Black Code.

Later in the week, the delegates turned to a consideration of the proposed Black Code itself. At that time, the four acts that constituted the Code were under consideration by the legislature. Hoping to help shape that debate, the delegates to the convention of freed blacks resolved: "That we hereby object to a 'negro code,' or any other class legislation by the State, considering as we do the same to be unjust and anti-republican. In our humble opinion, a code of laws for the government of *all,* regardless of color, is all that is necessary for the advancement of the interests and prosperity of the State."

Despite the freedmen's convention protest, South Carolina's legislature approved the Black Code in late December, 1865. It was a curious document indeed. On the one hand, several provisions encouraged freedmen to become independent yeoman farmers, as the state's merchants had hoped they would. Chief among these provisions was the act "To Establish and Regulate the Domestic Relations of Persons of Color." It legalized marriages between black men and women, whether they had begun in slavery or freedom, and legitimated their children. It also gave parents full control over the labor of their children. At the same time, the "Act to Establish District Courts" permitted black people to testify in all cases involving themselves and their property, and it extended to freedmen the right to will to their heirs property with the same law that applied to white people. The effect of these provisions was to create the legal basis for black ownership of land and personal property, and for the transfer of that property to heirs.

On the other hand, the Black Code included an extensive list of rules and regulations designed to subordinate freedmen to planters. It did so chiefly by requiring all black people to work for some employer. The Code defined "Vagrancy and Idleness" as "public grievances" that "must be punished as crimes." All black people without "some fixed and known place or abode, and some lawful and reputable employment" qualified as criminals under this definition. The crime of vagrancy also included those black men and women who had become petty entrepreneurs selling their surplus produce in crossroad markets—that is, those people found "vending, bartering or peddling any articles or commodities." Another section provided that no freedman could ply a trade as an artisan, mechanic, or shopkeeper without obtaining a license each year from the local district court judge—a difficult and costly prospect at best. In short, the Code left freedpeople no choice but to work as agricultural laborers for some planter. Those who attempted to avoid working for a white employer could be imprisoned or put to hard labor for up to 12 months. Hard labor consisted of being hired out to a local planter or to labor "on the streets, public roads, or public buildings" with all wages going to the state.

In addition to simply requiring employment, the Code closely regulated the actual work of black employees. It set the hours of labor "from sun-rise to sun-set." And the law required black employees to "feed, water and care for the animals on the farm, do the usual and needful work about the premises, prepare their meals for the day, and begin the farm work or other work" before sunrise. Failure to work at this rate was deemed "evidence of indolence." Moreover, willful disobedience of the planter, "want of respect and civility," or absence from work without permission could result in dismissal without any wages due for the entire year. The Code also provided that any child 3 years of age or older could be involuntarily apprenticed by a District Court judge if he found the parents to be "paupers" or "vagrants." In other words, a planter could secure the labor of any black child simply because his or her parents were poor or unemployed.

The story of the Black Code did not end with its approval by the South Carolina legislature. At the national level, the Code, and another like it approved about the same time in Mississippi, played an important part in shaping the federal government's efforts to reconstruct the Southern states. Republicans in Congress offered the Black Code as evidence to prove that Southern planters had not given up on slavery, and therefore should not be allowed to control the Southern state governments. In mid-November, 1865, the *New York Tribune* ran a story on the proposed Black Code under the headline: "South Carolina Re-establishing Slavery." And after its passage, Burton Cook, a Congressman from Illinois, argued: "Can we now place the freedmen in the uncontrolled power of their former masters? The Negro codes enacted by the reconstructed Legislatures of Mississippi and South Carolina are our sufficient answer." In the spring of 1866, the Code persuaded Congress to extend the life of the Freedmen's Bureau and to approve the first Civil Rights Act.

In South Carolina by contrast, the Black Code promised to give planters a free hand in securing the labor of freedmen. In late December, they refused, in fact, to contract with freedmen for the coming year. This was so because they

The Black Code made efforts by freedmen to market their surplus crops a crime. Here freedmen in Charleston sell their first harvest of watermelons in the summer of 1866, after the Black Code had been declared null and void. (Library of Congress)

hoped that the Bureau would disband in the early spring when its enabling legislation expired. They were also confident that the Union army would withdraw quickly now that civil government had been established. With the Black Code in full force and no one to intervene on behalf of freedmen, planters could then establish compulsory labor in a new form—forced wage labor. But events took a different turn than South Carolina planters imagined they might. On January 1, 1866, General Daniel Sickles, the new commander of Union troops in South Carolina, declared the Black Code null and void at the request of the state's governor, thereby ensuring the continuation of existing military regulations governing the labor of freedmen.

Sickles's decision in turn strengthened the resolve of South Carolina freedmen to seek independent livelihoods. In January of 1866 on some coastal plantations, freedmen "positively" refused, wrote the Freedmen's Bureau agent at Georgetown, "to make any contracts unless they have the control of the crop themselves, the planters to have little or nothing to say in the matter, but to receive a portion of the crop raised. They desire to lease the lands, repaying the planters the seed supplied by him, and giving him one-third of the crop." This was so because the freedmen there had concluded that "labor under a Contract is but a form of slavery." To achieve their goal, freedmen around Georgetown had formed "an extensive coalition" among themselves. "It is really wonderful how unanimous they are," noted the Bureau agent, "communicating like magic, and now holding out, knowing the importance of every day in regard to the welfare of the next crop, thinking that the planters will be obliged to come to their terms."

AN INTERPRETATION

Why did the Black Code attempt both to shackle freedmen and to protect some of their rights? The answer lies in the months of struggle and debate that preceded the drafting and approval of the Black Code. On the one hand, some of the Code's provisions responded to the plan for a new economy outlined by merchants. They wished to see freedmen become independent farmers, and that was possible only if blacks could own land and pass it on to their children. On the other hand, the Code also reflected the desires of South Carolina planters. They realized that plantations could not exist without extremely cheap labor, forced labor. Because the freedmen were no longer slaves, compulsion had to be produced in another way. Some planters simply resorted to violence or threats of violence. Others attempted to confine their laborers to the plantation, thus cutting them off from the power of the Union army and the Freedmen's Bureau. But some planters sought the power of the state and its laws and courts to compel freedpeople to work cheaply. The Code accomplished that purpose by making vagrancy a crime punishable by imprisonment at hard labor, and by specifying the many powers planters might exercise over their employees' work and social life.

The South Carolina Black Code then was not solely a triumph of planters over freedmen as it was portrayed in the Northern press at that time. It, in fact, represented a deadlock or perhaps a compromise between the state's planters and merchants. Regardless of which it was, we do know that the Code included something for both planters and merchants, but in doing so it failed to produce a coherent legal structure that would support and shape a new system of free labor. It encouraged freedmen, on the one hand, to seek land on which to produce a subsistence for themselves and some staple crop for sale in distant markets. On the other hand, it bound some freedmen closely to planters as forced laborers. Not surprisingly, this contradictory legal framework produced economic chaos when planters and freedmen began to spar over new labor contracts in December of 1865. Recognizing the failure of the Black Code to create a coherent legal basis for a new labor system and the tremendous hostility the Code had raised in the North, South Carolina's governor decided to cut the state's political losses and ask Sickles to void the Black Code.

In the end, the Black Code resolved nothing. It would be another several years before South Carolina planters breathed new life into the plantation system. They would do so, organized as the Ku Klux Klan, in a campaign of unprecedented violence against freedmen that would introduce new forms of compulsion onto South Carolina plantations. Yet something good and useful had resulted from the struggle over the Code. Freedmen in South Carolina had established their right to testify in court and thereby defend themselves and their property. And, by their refusal to contract with planters, they had forced the state's white leadership to back down in the effort to implement new forms of forced labor, at least for the time being. Martin Delany's insistence on self-reliance had made some headway afterall. He had not spoken in vain when he said to the freedmen at St. Helena Island: "I tell you slavery is over, and shall never return again."

Sources: The story of the Black Code has been told here from three very different sources. The reports, now housed in the National Archives, of army officers in South Carolina acting as local post commanders and as Freedmen's Bureau agents proved most useful. These men met on a daily basis with planters and freedmen both, and observed the actions of each closely. The other important sources were those that documented the debate between planters and merchants over the labor question—the unpublished letters of South Carolina planters writing to D. L. Wardlaw and Benjamin Perry in the Duke University Library, and the *Charleston Daily News,* now housed at the Library of Congress, in which the state's merchants held forth their views.

2

BUILDING THE BROOKLYN BRIDGE

ALAN TRACHTENBERG

It took 15 years to build, but when the bridge spanning 1600 feet of East River between Brooklyn and Manhattan was opened in 1883, it was undeniably one of the great engineering and scientific feats of the age—the equivalent, perhaps, of the development of the atomic bomb in the 1940s, the construction of the nation's system of interstate highways in the 1950s, or the drive to place a man on the moon in the 1960s. But while these were all entirely public projects, carried out by the national government with public funds, the Brooklyn Bridge was begun and partially built by a private company—chartered, to be sure, by the state government, as nearly all corporations were—but for the most part beyond the purview of the public. Even after the mid-1870s, when legislation recognized that the people deserved a larger role in the project, key decisions were made by corporations and politicians who paid only lip service to the public trust. And so it was altogether appropriate that the opening of the bridge involved bestowing the structure on the public—that is, granting it not to equals but to supposed inferiors. In this and other ways, as Alan Trachtenberg's story reveals, the bridge was a product of a transitional era in American history. It was an era in which large corporations and big factories were still the exception rather than the rule, millions of ordinary Americans worked in the skilled trades, and government played a limited role in encouraging and policing the economy.

But in other ways the bridge looked toward the future, and shunned the past. After generations of sectional conflict, culminating in a traumatic Civil War, many Americans longed for an end to division and discord. They built bridges across the Ohio and the Mississippi. In 1869, they celebrated the joining of the Union Pacific and the Central Pacific railroads at Provo, Utah, and with it the linking of the coasts. And in the aftermath of the disputed national election of 1876, the major parties laid aside the ideological politics and disagreements on questions of race that had helped bring on the Civil War and fostered the bitterness of Reconstruction, and agreed to an historic compromise—the Compromise of 1877—that gave the election to Republican Rutherford B. Hayes and signaled a final end to the involvement of the federal government in helping black people in the South secure their legal and political rights. (Among those who had a hand in this process was Abram S. Hewitt, the campaign

manager of the Democratic candidate, Samuel J. Tilden; a few years later, Hewitt
would be a featured speaker at the opening of the bridge). Uniting two land masses in
one giant span, the Brooklyn Bridge stood as a symbol of a desire for unity that went
well beyond the two cities that stood to gain the most from its construction. The unity
embodied in the bridge was not just geographical, but social and economic: the unity of
rich and poor, haves and have nots; and the unity of the unified and uniform national
market being created not just by bridges across the Ohio, Mississippi, and East rivers,
but by the proliferation of giant corporations.

The story of the bridge is also the story of corruption so far-reaching that even
the structure's enormous cables were braided with defective wire. Despite this sordid
reality, contemporaries did not succumb to the cynicism that marks the present.
Unlike the current generation of Americans, who believe themselves to be at the mercy
of dark forces beyond their control, the generation of Americans who built the
Brooklyn Bridge saw their creation as a wondrous sign that the world would yield—
surely and inevitably—to their knowledge, their expertise, and their desire.

Before the Brooklyn Bridge, which opened to the public on May 24, 1883, ferry boats provided the sole means of crossing the East River between the boroughs of Manhattan and Brooklyn. A leisurely ride, open to fresh breezes as it moved diagonally upstream from the foot of Fulton Street in Brooklyn to its landing near South Street in Manhattan, the ferry offered thrilling vistas of the two shorelines. By the 1850s lower New York had already become a crowded commercial and manufacturing center, its shorelines hemmed with tall-masted ships. While Manhattan had expanded rapidly into a world center of trade, a center of wealth with an increasingly visible population of wage-laborers without personal wealth or property, Brooklyn enlarged at a slower pace. Even at mid-century it retained the look of a village, its residential hills and open spaces tempting many middle-class New Yorkers to seek homes there. The ferry ride seemed to many people, such as the poet Walt Whitman, a native of Long Island and Brooklyn who loved the streets of Manhattan, a perfect way to make the transition from village to metropolis. Whitman's poem, "Crossing Brooklyn Ferry," written in 1856, sang of the beauty of the views, of the sun sparkling on the water, and the pleasure of mingling with the crowds of working people passing to and fro across the river.

But the ferry had its shortcomings. It did not always provide so pleasant and relaxing a ride. Really a tidal strait rather than a true river, the lower East River is often shrouded in fog and churns with treacherous currents, and in winter it can be gorged with jagged chunks of ice. The winter of 1851 to 1852 was notably severe, and voices of exasperation arose demanding relief. Why not throw a bridge over the river, a quicker, surer, more reliable method of getting from one shore to the other? The idea was not new; an East River bridge had been proposed as early as 1811. By the 1840s and 1850s, when the idea revived, Brooklyn businessmen became increasingly serious about the prospect of more reliable and efficient connections with the financial and commercial markets of Manhattan; the growing numbers of people commuting to jobs in New York concurred. But would such a bridge, spanning about a mile between the shores, be feasible? No bridge of such magnitude had yet been constructed anywhere in the world. Most commonly bridges in America and Europe still employed the time-honored materials of wood and stone carved into arches. Recently, engineers had applied iron in the making of trusses, a rigid framework formed of separate members such as bars or rods, to build trestles for railroads. Chain links were employed in America and Europe to suspend roadways from stone towers, as in the Clifton Bridge (1859) at Bristol, England, by I. K. Brunel. But metal had not yet been tested in structures of the magnitude necessary to span the East River.

During that frigid winter of 1852, a German-born engineer, who placed great value on promptness, sat fuming at the inconvenience of being stuck on an ice-bound ferry boat in midstream. John Augustus Roebling began at once to imagine how a bridge might be built to replace or supplement the inefficient ferry. He had been trained as a civil engineer at the Royal Polytechnic Institute of Berlin; blocked in his career by the Prussian bureaucracy, he emigrated to Western Pennsylvania in 1831 with a group who shared utopian ideals. They founded the agricultural community of Saxonburg. With the increase in commerce the construction of canals, railroads, aqueducts, and bridges soon became a necessity in the region. Roebling eventually found opportunities to put his training to practical use. By 1849 he had built a few aqueducts and small bridges in cities such as Pittsburgh. He added the manufacture of wire rope to the activities of Saxonburg, and then established a plant near Trenton, New Jersey, for the production of wire to be used in spinning cables for suspension bridges, the form to which he particularly applied himself.

From the beginning of his career Roebling pioneered in developing techniques for building suspension bridges. The form appealed to him for its simplicity and beauty. Combining several distinct elements, the suspension bridge embodied a philosophical principle especially attractive to Roebling. Along with engineering he had studied philosophy in Berlin with G. W. F. Hegel, who taught that opposition or contradiction lay at the base of nature, society, and mind. In a suspension bridge a cable is hung over two piers or towers and then anchored at each shore. The towers and anchorage represent force in compression, solid masses planted firmly on a solid base or ground; the cable, meanwhile, hangs in extension, approximating a catenary curve (the curve formed when you hold, say, a cord at each end and allow it to hang loosely). The entire structure represents, then, opposite forces, compression and extension, in harmonious balance. Using this form bridge builders are able to suspend upwardly curving central spans between the two towers, thus allowing for unhindered river traffic beneath the bridge. With the additional possibility of making such a bridge rigid enough to carry railroad trains, the suspension form seemed to Roebling an ideal solution to America's bridge-building needs.

At the time he was stranded in the ice-bound river, Roebling was at work on just such a railroad bridge over Niagara Falls, completed in 1855. In 1857 he wrote to Horace Greeley, editor of the New York *Tribune,* proposing "a wire suspension bridge crossing the East River by one single span at such an elevation as will not impede the navigation." Greeley responded enthusiastically and the engineer began to sketch his plans. But the time was not yet ripe. After the dramatic success of the Niagara bridge, Roebling was called on to build what would then be the world's longest suspension bridge, between Cincinnati and Covington over the Ohio River, a project that kept him occupied through the years of the Civil War. The bridge opened in 1867. Roebling then turned all his energy to the task of persuading people of wealth and influence in New York and Brooklyn that an East River bridge was both necessary and feasible.

In 1865, just after the Civil War in which his son Washington, also an engineer, served as a Union colonel, Roebling approached several Brooklyn businessmen to see if a private company might be established to recruit public support and money for such a bridge. Roebling preferred to deal directly with private capitalists rather than approach elected municipal officials. His experiences during the 1840s and 1850s taught him that public financing of construction projects often proved inefficient and expensive; politicians, he learned, tended to offer costly contracts in exchange for bribes. As early as 1860 Roebling anticipated similar problems in dealing with the city halls of New York and Brooklyn, and wrote that it was not "desirable to add to the complication

John Augustus Roebling (1806–1869). Roebling's piercing eyes were perhaps his most memorable physical feature.

and corruption of the governmental machinery of these cities" by seeking their official sponsorship for his proposed bridge.

In fact the problem of financing public projects had proved a complicated matter throughout the "internal improvements" period in the decades before the Civil War. One especially troubling issue concerned the respective roles of private capital and public funds raised by the sale of bonds. The issue centered on the question of ownership and control: Should private people or corporations, for example, be entitled to collect tolls on roads or bridges serving the public interest? The New York–Brooklyn situation was further complicated by the fact that the state government at Albany held final authority over the financing of public projects in both cities. The situation opened room for irregularities and corruption, exactly what Roebling feared.

In 1865 Roebling met with a dynamic Brooklyn contractor, William C. Kingsley, who in turn persuaded State Senator Henry C. Murphy to introduce a bill to charter the New York Bridge Company. The fact that the winter of 1866 to 1867 was one of the severest yet on record aroused popular support for the bill. Passed in April of 1867, the law fixed the capital of the Company at $5,000,000 and endowed it with the power to raise more funds. It also authorized the cities of New York and Brooklyn to subscribe to the capital stock of the Company to the extent of 60 percent. The arrangement thus resulted in a "mixed" enterprise, joining private and public funds in a project too large and costly to be undertaken alone by either the private or public spheres. Yet the Company was chartered as a *private* enterprise, with unlimited control over public funds. The charter allowed the cities to "guarantee the payment of the principal and interest" of Company bonds; yet only by an amendment in 1869 were city officials assured seats on the board of directors, and then only as a small minority. To be sure, the charter gave the cities the right to take full control of the project if they wished, for a price: the full value of "the said bridge and appurtenances," plus $33\frac{1}{3}$ percent of that value, to be paid directly to the Company.

No wonder suspicions arose. They appeared initially because the cities of New York and Brooklyn, and indeed the legislature in Albany, were then under the control of a group known as the Tweed Ring, after its leader, William Marcy "Boss" Tweed. Although not himself a holder of high office, Tweed, like other big city bosses in the post-Civil War era, exercised vast power through a system of graft and favoritism. Elected officials loyal to Tweed or indebted to him for their office, frequently through rigged elections, awarded contracts for public buildings and utilities to contractors willing to "kick back" a certain amount of cash. Tweed came to power in the late 1860s through the local New York Democratic Party club known as Tammany Hall. When the Ring was disbanded and Tweed indicted in 1871, it was estimated that his crew had stolen as much as $30 million. One of the Ring's typical devices for tapping the public purse was to arrange for delays in construction of public projects, resulting in higher expenses padded to include kick backs. The Chamber Street Courthouse was one of their most notorious schemes.

Was Brooklyn Bridge another? Doubts surfaced periodically throughout the lengthy 16-year interval between the approval of the charter in 1867 and the opening of the bridge in 1883. One newspaper listed the bridge among "the seven fraudulent wonders of the New World," and wrote: "Conceived in inequity and begun in fraud, it has been continued in corruption." And indeed, in 1878 Tweed confessed that in 1867 he took a bribe of $60,000 from Kingsley to help push the chartering bill through the legislature, and, further, that the deal allowed Tweed himself to buy shares at an 80 percent reduction, and gave Kingsley a 15 percent cut on all purchases of construction materials. Overpayment to Kingsley, the principal shareholder, had been publicly revealed as early as 1872, at which time the contractor promised to make repayment.

Was the problem merely the greed of evil people, or was the charter itself at fault for allowing a private corporation full control over a public enterprise? The legislative act set no controls over the decisions of the Company, no process of public review. It was an act "to incorporate the New York Bridge Company, for the purpose of constructing and maintaining a bridge over the East River, between the cities of New York and Brooklyn." The law empowered the Company "to purchase, acquire and hold as much real estate as may be necessary for the site of the said bridge," and to fix rates of toll. It also set a handsome limit of 15 percent per annum as allowable net profits for investors. Typical of such private corporations contrived to fund public projects in the antebellum era, the Bridge Company was free of accountability to the public whose funds it solicited. Only the federal government required obedience to any regulation; Congress in 1869 granted that the proposed bridge might receive status as a lawful post road, provided it met standards of height appropriate to river traffic as recommended by a commission of the Army Engineers.

In May of 1867, the Company appointed John A. Roebling as Chief Engineer. Given his role in initiating the project, his reputation as the world's master-builder of the modern suspension bridge, and his known doggedness in seeing his projects through to the finish, the choice was inevitable. The 61-year-old engineer, industrialist, inventor, and philosopher applied himself at once to surveying the site and drawing up plans. By September his report to the New York Bridge Company was ready.

Roebling wrote the report not only as a plan but an argument to meet any possible objection to his design. In the preface he set the tone of cold, irrefutable logic mixed with appeals to civic pride.

> The contemplated work, when constructed in accordance with my designs, will not only be the greatest Bridge in existence, but it all be the greatest engineering work of this continent, and of the age. Its most conspicuous features, the great towers, will serve as landmarks to the adjoining cities, and they will be entitled to be ranked as national monuments.

Roebling's report addressed an audience primarily of businessmen, shareholders in the New York Bridge Company who wanted to know if the bridge would pay in the short and long run. Most telling were his strategic comments about a change about to occur on completion of the Union Pacific Railroad (which occurred 2 years later, in 1869) in America's commercial relations with the world, a change of vast significance for business, especially for the commercial interests of New York:

> This change will at first be very slow, but the breadth and depth of the commercial channell will increase with every coming year, until at last the city of New York will have become the great commercial emporium, not of this continent only, but of the world.

The East River bridge, he argued, would be a major link within a national and eventually international system of transportation, communication, and trade, and would enhance the flow of wealth into the coffers of New York. One use of the spaces within the approaches to the bridge, he suggested, might be as vaults for accumulated gold and silver.

The public was more concerned with safety than profits, and justifiably so, given the unprecedented length of the bridge and its several novel features. Roebling's report envisioned a bridge almost 1,600 feet in length, one half again as long as the Cincinnati bridge. It would replace that bridge as the longest in the world. The roadway of the new bridge, to be held in place by four cables 16 inches in diameter, would bear 18,700 tons. A multipurpose roadway, it would allow for cable car traffic and horse-drawn traffic in side-by-side lanes in each direction, and an elevated promenade for pedestrians above the noise and dirt of the vehicular traffic; with benches and lamps and balconies around the base of each tower, the promenade was Roebling's particular pride. The granite towers, each pierced with two immense Gothic arches, would rise 276 feet and compete with the spire of Trinity Church on Wall Street as the tallest structures in New York at the time.

Roebling explained that theoretically "any span inside of three thousand feet is practicable." The only vital question was safety, and this was simply a question of cost. At this point Roebling estimated a cost of $7,000,000 exclusive of the amount necessary to acquire the land, about $3,800,000; the final cost (including the land) was closer to $15,500,00, largely a result of modifications such as raising the height of the bridge and increasing its width. Roebling explained the system of supports he had devised which, if followed according to his plan, would guarantee complete peace of mind about the stability of the structure:

> To guard against vertical and horizontal oscillations, and to insure that degree of stiffness in the flooring which is absolutely necessary to meet the effects of violent gales in such an exposed situation, I have provided six lines of iron trusses which run the whole length of the suspended floor from anchor wall to anchor wall. . . . I am not disposed to underrate the great force of a severe gale. . . . But my system of construction differs radically from that formerly practiced, and I have planned the East River Bridge with a special view to fully meet these destructive forces. It is for the same reason that, in my calculation of the requisite supporting strength, so large a proportion has been assigned to stays [diagonal wire supports, like the stays on sailing vessels] in place of cables. . . . The supporting power of the stays alone will be 15,000 tons; ample to hold up the floor. If the cables were removed, the Bridge would sink in the center but would not fall.

The confidence that speaks here, that the bridge would survive all imaginable traumas, persuaded the Company. But in order to obliterate all remaining doubts (absolute thoroughness being his style), Roebling convened a select board of eminent engineers to review his plans in meticulous detail, and to examine his other bridges on site. Their unanimous confirmation of his design and calculations in May, 1869, signalled that work could then commence.

Within 3 weeks there occurred a trauma Roebling's report did not anticipate: his own sudden death, the result of injuries when a boat crushed his right foot on the Brooklyn wharf as he surveyed the position of the main piers. He died horribly, of lockjaw, on July 22, 1869. The bridge had taken its first and most tragic toll.

Responsibility for the project now passed to Roebling's 32-year-old son, Colonel Washington A. Roebling, appointed in August to supervise construction of the bridge according to his father's design. A graduate of Rensselaer Polytechnic Institute and an engineer with the Union Army of the Potomac during the Civil War, Colonel Roebling's main experience had been as assistant to his father on the Cincinnati Bridge. In October, presumably to free his mind from all distractions but actual construction, the Executive Committee of the Company relieved Roebling of all responsibility for the awarding of contracts—and indeed of attending meetings unless specifically requested to—and appointed William Kingsley as General Superintendent precisely to perform that function. Colonel Roebling assembled his own youthful staff of assistants, whose age averaged 31 years in that year. E. F. Farrington, who had worked on the Cincinnati Bridge, was later named Master Mechanic. Among Colonel Roebling's responsibilities was the presentation in writing of exhaustive periodic reports on progress in construction to the Executive Committee of the Bridge Company.

Roebling's first dramatic step as Chief Engineer was the launching of the pneumatic caisson for the Brooklyn tower. While on a European tour after the Civil War, directed by his father to learn as much as he could about new building techniques, the younger Roebling studied closely the use of caissons for laying firm foundations for weight-carrying piers. Caissons are essentially large airtight boxes tapered into an open cutting edge on the bottom. For excavating the floor of the East River Roebling contrived a caisson with a timber roof 15 feet thick. Weighing 3,000 tons and measuring 168 feet long and 102 feet wide, his caissons would be the largest ever used. An enormous chamber using compressed air, the caisson was designed to provide breathing space for the workers known as "sand-hogs." They dug away at the mud and clay on the river bottom while masons laid the granite of the tower on the roof of the caisson. The weight of the stone combined with the digging sunk the caisson through the river bed to bedrock, where the finished tower would find absolutely solid support.

An intricate construction balancing a number of elements—an airlock into the work area, supply shafts, water shafts to make possible the removal of debris without loss of air pressure—the caisson was as hazardous as it was essential. If the water shafts were not kept tightly sealed, blowouts could shower stone and mud into the air. There was the constant threat of fire; explosives were often used to break up compacted materials on the river floor, and because electric lighting was not yet available, lighted candles served as illumination. One news-paper account described them as "submarine giants [which] delve and dig and ditch and drill and blast." They performed their work around the clock.

For the sand-hogs the work was often unbearable. "The work of the buried bridge-builder," wrote one newspaper, "is like the onward flow of eterni-ty; it does not cease for the sun at noonday or the silent stars at night. Gangs are relieved and replaced, and swart, perspiring companies of men follow each other up and down the iron locks, with a dim quiet purpose." The interior was hot, the air foul, and sickness quite common. Work shifts were reduced to 4 hours or less, at $2 a day for ordinary labor, increased to $2.25 a day as the caisson reached deeper below the river floor. The work crew for the Brooklyn caisson numbered 112 during each of the day shifts, and 40 at night; the New York caisson crew ranged from 50 to 125 during the day and 15 to 30 at night. Work crews for this relatively unskilled but extremely punishing labor were re-cruited mainly from Irish, German, and Italian immigrants, many undernour-ished and desperate for work. The turnover was enormous: 2,500 different workers for the Brooklyn caisson alone. In 1872, the entire New York caisson crew walked off the job, insisting on higher pay for such hazardous, fatiguing work: $3 for a 4-hour day. The strike lasted several days before the men settled for less of an increase than they demanded.

No serious accident occurred until December 2, 1870, when a burning candle ignited the oakum caulking lining the inside of the caisson; the fire was driven by air pressure deep into the caisson, but out of sight. Colonel Roebling rushed to the scene and helped fight the fire for 7 hours, until he lost conscious-ness. The caisson was finally flooded, and the water expelled some days later. The "Great Fire" caused no deaths but delayed work for 3 months. By March, 1871, excavation for the foundation was finally complete, the caisson filled with concrete, and the Brooklyn tower began to rise layer by layer, the first above-water sign that a monumental bridge was in the making. In October of 1871, the New York caisson was launched and reached bedrock in May of 1872.

Just at this time, in 1871, Tweed's empire began to unravel. Spearheaded by upper-class figures like Abram Hewitt, son-in-law of the revered Peter Coop-er, and partner in his iron business, and Samuel Tilden, who would be the Democratic candidate for president in the controversial election of 1876, a movement developed against the corruption and fraud that was draining the city's resources. Campaigns in the press and public meetings led to Tweed's downfall and arrest. Called "reformers," such upper-class figures sought to re-place corrupt party politicians with qualified political figures drawn from the class of "the best men," the rich, the cultivated, the socially respectable. Inves-tigative committees appeared in both cities, and in June of 1872, the old Tam-many representatives on the Bridge Company were replaced by figures with names like Vanderbilt, Aspinwall, Appleton, Hewitt, names of older wealthy and propertied families who viewed themselves as responsible for the civic health of the cities. Hewitt himself led an internal investigation on behalf of the Bridge Company, which resulted in exacting Kingsley's promise for repayment of funds, redefining his responsibilities, and essentially exonerating him and the Company of any fundamental wrong-doing. A report by Colonel Roebling assured the directors of the Company that all contract awards had resulted in the finest materials at the lowest costs; this proved decisive in dispelling the suspicion that the physical integrity of the bridge had been compromised.

The issue of accountability remained unresolved. Was the Company truly a *private* corporation, like a railroad company, free to do its business however it wished? Or, considering that the cities of New York and Brooklyn were both large stockholders, did the Company not have a special responsibility to the publicly elected bodies of those cities? These more critical views were advanced by Demas Barnes, chairman of the Committee of Investigation appointed by the board of the Company, who issued a separate report calling for board meetings open to the public. Hewitt and others agreed the charter should be amended to dispel ambiguities in the original document that made it seem an invitation to theft, but no changes were made at this time. After 3 years of construction, the jailing of Tweed, the chiding of Kingsley, the Bridge Company remained under a cloud of suspicion.

Then another sudden event profoundly affected the project. At the end of May, 1872, after spending long hours in the depths of the New York caisson, Colonel Roebling collapsed. Mysterious symptoms of paralysis had already attacked a number of the workers, and Roebling had asked a medical specialist to investigate. Little was then known about the sudden onset of caisson disease or "the bends," an affliction of the nervous system caused by living and working too long under atmospheric pressure much greater than normal. By 1883 the surgeon of the Bridge Company reported 110 cases of the disease, three of which were fatal, at that point. Roebling himself remained paralyzed the rest of his life, perhaps the result as much of a nervous disorder exacerbated by the strain of his position as of the bends. He never returned to the construction site, although he retained his position, making detailed drawings and writing out meticulous instructions that his wife Emily delivered to his staff, and following progress at the site through binoculars from his home nearby.

In June of 1874, the state legislature passed an amendment urged by Barnes requiring that the Bridge Company accept membership on its board of a significant number of representatives of the cities of New York and Brooklyn. The following year the legislature dissolved the original New York Bridge Company altogether; the bridge was now understood to be "a public work, to be constructed by the two cities for the accommodation, convenience and safe travel of the inhabitants." The change made a difference in the public's relation to the still ghostly structure slowly materializing into the shape of a bridge before their eyes—although the personnel of the actual day-by-day management remained the same.

What remained of the construction tasks were the completion of the towers and the two anchorages on each shore to which the four central cables would be attached. The Brooklyn tower reached its full height in May of 1875, and the New York tower in July of 1876. Then the real artistry of labor would commence—the spinning of the four main wire cables. By August of 1876, with the saddles designed to carry each cable over the top of each tower in place, the spinning itself began.

Apart from the drama of scandal and injury, the building of the bridge had provided another kind of daily spectacle: sheer physical work of the most demanding kind among new, odd-shaped pieces of machinery such as caissons, hoisting machines, cable saddles, the intricately arranged anchor plates. Through the press and firsthand observation, the public witnessed the skilled work of carpenters, machinists, masons, blacksmiths, sand-hogs, iron-workers, and seamen engaged to lash the diagonal stays to the vertical suspenders attach-

Washington Roebling became an increasingly remote and mysterious figure after his illness. He is depicted here, on the occasion of the opening of the bridge, as a somewhat grim but thoughtful Victorian gentleman, restraining his emotions of pride as his father's bridge nears completion. (*Frank Leslie's Illustrated Newspaper,* May 26, 1883)

ing the roadway to the main cables. At one time as many as 600 men worked together at the site, making this perhaps the largest outdoor concentration of a multiple-craft work force yet assembled in one site in the United States. It is impossible to say exactly how many workers lost their lives; estimates range from 20 to 40. Others suffered lasting effects from caisson disease.

None of the skilled tasks attracted as much attention as the spinning and wrapping of the four main cables. On August 14, 1876, a scow ran a rope across the river, which was then hoisted into position over and between the towers. Not until then could the structure be called a bridge. Now two cities were joined, or as a newspaper headline put it, "wedded." The next dramatic step would be for someone to cross the structure on the rope, and the Master Mechanic E. F. Farrington was selected to make the historic venture in a boatswain's chair. The date was Friday, August 25, 1876, and to the cheers of workers swarming on the towers, crowds on both shores and on boats in the river, Farrington made the first trip via bridge from Brooklyn to New York; it took 22 minutes. A footbridge of slatted wood was soon added for less adventuresome passage by workers and occasional visitors.

Just when the end of construction seemed in sight, further delays caused by charges of corruption and recrimination among the principals almost brought the entire project to a permanent standstill. By September of 1876, with the actual spinning of the cables ready to proceed, Roebling submitted his detailed specifications for cable wire to the Executive Committee, as required, for their approval. Abram Hewitt, vice president of the board and himself a dealer in wire, judged the specifications "eminently wise," but insisted that no bids for the wire contract be accepted from any person or firm with a direct interest in the bridge. He declared that he himself would refrain from bidding, and he insisted that Colonel Roebling, an owner along with his brothers of the cable wire manufactory his father had founded near Trenton, be especially forbidden from entering a bid.

Indignant, the incapacitated Chief Engineer instantly penned an angry letter of resignation. In his reply to the board's refusal of the resignation, Roebling wrote:

> I was publicly and specifically singled out by name by Mr. Hewitt, as if I had spent my whole life in concocting a specification which I alone could fill or as if I were a thief trying to rob the bridge in some underhanded manner and against whom every precaution should be taken.

Then he added:

> As you seem to be deeply impressed with Mr. Hewitt's action in declining to become a competitor for this wire, I desire to say that his magnanimity is all a show, as the firm of Cooper and Hewitt have no facilities for making the steel wire, and if you receive a bid from Mr. Haigh of South Brooklyn, it will be well for you to investigate a little.

And to be sure, the award was made to a Mr. Haigh of South Brooklyn.

Roebling's suspicion of venality on the part of Hewitt deepened as a result of another disastrous event. In July, 1877, spinning of the cables began by means of a huge mechanical device that travelled from anchorage to anchorage, taking about 10 minutes each way. In November a wire snapped, and on examining the broken pieces, Roebling judged the wire, supplied by Haigh, to be defective. The following June two men were killed when another wire rope snapped, raising even more public anxiety about the safety of the bridge into which some $9 million had already been poured. Among New York Democrats who wished to distance themselves as far as possible from the lingering taint of Boss Tweed, a number agitated to cut off all further money to the bridge. On July 22, 1878, Roebling presented board president Henry Murphy with physical proof that Haigh had been supplying the bridge with consistently defective wire, fraudulently returning rolls of wire that had been already rejected on regular inspection. Roebling informed Murphy that "the distressing point of this affair is that all the rejected wire which has come to the Bridge has been worked into the

The Brooklyn anchorage in the process of construction. Note the bundles of wire which comprise each of the four central cables, yet to be wrapped in this image, and the footbridge to the left. The picture conveys the awesome power of the cables and the security of their attachment to the anchor plates (not themselves visible in the print). Note, too the artist's rendering of the great height of the Brooklyn tower against the low skyline of the 1870s Manhattan. (*Harper's New Monthly Magazine*, May 1883).

cables, and cannot be removed." The Executive Committee chose to hush up a scandal potentially fatal to the completion of the bridge; It may be, though no certain evidence exists, that Haigh's friends, including Hewitt, insisted on the cover-up. The board was relieved to hear from Roebling, however, that because the cables had been designed with a sufficient margin of safety (six times beyond the tensile strength actually required), the damage was inconsequential—although the Chief Engineer did require that each cable be strengthened by 150 more strands of tested wire. On October 5, 1878, the spinning of the cables was completed—"this desirable event," remarked Master Mechanic E. F. Farrington, "was marked by no demonstrations, save the sounding of a steam whistle, and the raising of a United States flag on the Brooklyn tower." In later years Haigh was imprisoned in Sing Sing for passing bad checks.

The tasks that remained consisted chiefly of assembling the complex roadway, tieing it into place by the diagonal stays John A. Roebling had designed to guarantee the security of the span, and the construction of the terminals at either end of the bridge. But in the face of continuing threats from New York to close out its funding of the project and rapidly deteriorating relations between an increasingly impatient and snappish Roebling and the board of directors, almost 5 more years would elapse before these relatively undemanding objectives could be accomplished. As late as 1882 a move was launched to replace the Chief Engineer because of his physical disability; his position was saved partly by the eloquence of his wife in pleading with the board against such a move. When Abram Hewitt, now a congressman and future mayor of New York, wrote to Colonel Roebling requesting information he might use in his Opening Ceremonies oration, the blunt-speaking engineer replied: "It took Cheops twenty years to build his pyramid, but if he had had a lot of Trustees, contractors and newspaper reporters to worry him, he might not have finished by this time. The advantages of modern engineering are in many ways overbalanced by the disadvantages of modern civilization."

On May 24, 1883, the Hon. J. S. T. Stranhahan, a "leading citizen" of Brooklyn, and a trusted trustee of the New York and Brooklyn Bridge Company from the start, presided over the Opening Ceremonies of The Great Bridge—a public drama the central act of which would be performed by officials: the bestowing of the bridge directly to the people. As the souvenir publication of the Opening Ceremonies put it, "It was a holiday for high and low, rich and poor; it was, in fact, the People's Day."

It was a day of great local pride, in Brooklyn especially. One store window displayed a sign that became a kind of motto of the day: "Babylon had her hanging gardens, Egypt her pyramid, Athens her Acropolis, Rome her Athenaeum; so Brooklyn has her Bridge." Crowds in the tens of thousands—crowds of local citizens swelled by visitors from nearby towns, cities, and countryside, arriving by train, boat, and wagon—thronged along the thoroughfares in both cities leading to the bridge.

Local as the immediate meanings were for the participants, the day was also national in significance, as the red, white, and blue flags and banners everywhere, including at the summits of each of the bridge's two towers, indicated.

As Brooklyn Mayor Seth Low himself said, "it is distinctly an American triumph. American genius designed it, American skill built it, and American workshops made it." Thus the meaning of the presence of the chief of state himself, President Chester A. Arthur—a New Yorker, as it happened, the dapper former head of the New York Custom House and a great favorite among the crowds. The president played a role strictly symbolic—he had no speeches to make, no awards to present—only to be there in recognition of the national import of such a bridge. As the New York *Sun*'s reporter quipped: "the climax of fourteen years' suspense seemed to have been reached, since the President of the United States of America had walked dry shod to Brooklyn from New York."

Above all else it was a festive day—happy crowds scouting the celebrities, buying souvenirs, and awaiting with mounting excitement the evening's promised climaxes of the day's public drama. At midnight the bridge was to be thrown open to pedestrians, and many positioned themselves for that unique experience: their first walk "dry shod" across the East River. But first, as darkness fell, came the moment that thrilled the crowd beyond all description—the contours of the bridge suddenly illuminated by strings of electric lights! And as the lights just as suddenly went out there followed the most spectacular display of fireworks (as it was described) ever witnessed on the continent—bursts of color which cast an eerie, many-hued glow on the bridge that was destined, even from its start 14 years earlier, to hold a special place in the life and the imagination of the wedded cities, of the nation, and of the world. The age of steel and electricity had begun.

AN INTERPRETATION

A week later, on Memorial Day, the entire roadway was thrown open to pedestrians. Someone shouted, "The bridge is falling!" and twelve people were trampled or crushed to death in the ensuing panic.

That event provides another reminder, bloodier than others, of the entire ambiguous history of this bridge, in which the idealism of visionary engineers collided with the sordid realities of everyday political life in American cities of the Gilded Age. The meaning of the building of the Brooklyn Bridge in just these years, 1869 to 1883, must include recognition of such ambiguities, the complexities of motive, the many-dimensioned facets of behavior that comprise the larger truths of all historical "stories." It must also include the implicit threat to life and limb of modern construction projects based on new technologies.

In the case of the Brooklyn Bridge one is tempted to celebrate the creative acts of the Roeblings, their staffs, and the nameless corps of skilled and unskilled workers responsible for the actual building of the bridge, and to push aside the parallel story of Tweed and Kingsley and Haigh. Yet the two stories are not simply parallel; they are intertwined as tightly as the wire strands of each of the main cables. To interpret the building of the bridge in historical perspective, all aspects of the related stories must be taken into account.

One lesson of the bridge lies in the contradictions within the age's defini-
tions of private and public, between profit and the common good, which the
story of its construction brings to the surface. The scandals themselves, whether
substantiated or merely suspected, reveal a period of great uncertainty, of public
distrust of the hierarchy of political and social figures above them, a deep suspicion of wealth and power. Writing in 1883 in the month before the opening of
the bridge, the radical social critic and future opponent of Abram Hewitt in the
mayoralty election in 1886, Henry George, described the bridge as an emblem
of the underlying contradiction in modern America between wealth and poverty, private profit and public good:

> We have brought machinery to a pitch of perfection that, fifty years ago could not
> have been imagined; but in the presence of political corruption, we seem as help-
> less as idiots. The East River Bridge is a crowning triumph of mechanical skill; but

Someone shouted, "The bridge is falling," and a catastrophe followed. The
rendering here emphasizes the great crush of an urban crowd in panic, an image
calling to mind other mass scenes of the period, including those of soldiers firing at fleeing strikers during the 1877 Great Railroad Strike. Certainly such images helped plant the thought that city crowds held the menace of turning into
fearsome mobs. (*Frank Leslie's Illustrated Newspaper,* June 9, 1883)

to get it built a leading citizen of Brooklyn had to carry to New York sixty thousand dollars in a carpetbag to bribe a New York alderman. The human soul that thought out the great bridge is prisoned in a crazed and broken body that lies bedfast, and could only watch it grow by peering through a telescope. Nevertheless, the weight of the immense mass is estimated and adjusted for every inch. But the skill of the engineer could not prevent condemned wire from being smuggled into the cable.

The building of Brooklyn Bridge represented a historical transition, though what the future would hold was not at all clear at the time. John A. Roebling envisioned the bridge as a monument to the commercial and civic greatness of the cities. The story of corruption attending the making of the bridge certainly seems to sully that vision. But perhaps, in the face of the confused relations between private and public interest during this era, there was no other means of achieving Roebling's vision. The period of construction was dominated by the ruthless conviction on the part of the wealthy and powerful that they deserved whatever rewards they could achieve for themselves, whatever the social consequences. As it did for Henry George, the venality and mismanagement implied by the full story of the building of the Brooklyn Bridge would provide a useful lesson for progressive reformers in the following two decades, who proposed a more positive, direct, and responsible role by government in serving the collective interests of the public.

The Bridge in 1883 represented an initiation into a significantly different way of life. Consider its contrast with the old ferry boats. With their tempo keyed to currents and weather, the ferries belonged to a relatively simple era ending throughout the United States; their replacement by Brooklyn Bridge in the 1880s would dramatically signal the arrival of modern metropolitan and industrial life. By its size and scale, Brooklyn Bridge stood for something radically new in scale—and in danger, as the Memorial Day disaster vividly proclaims. Yet the bridge also represents a transitional moment, one that still retains a connection with the craft traditions of earlier, preindustrial modes and systems of labor. The abilities of the workers at the site of construction represented highly skilled crafts in working with stone, wood, and metal, and also collective coordination, willingness to take risks for the sake of performing a job, feats of personal courage. The mechanics, masons, sand-hogs, carpenters, surveyors, and the unskilled as well, all remind us that the built world was made by the refined and intricate manual efforts of human labor. The human features of the story of the bridge bring that great structure to life as a lesson in the coordination of mental and physical abilities.

Finally, we can interpret the building of the Brooklyn Bridge as manifestation of a conception, originally conceived by John A. Roebling and adapted by many others, of a harmonious metropolitan culture. Roebling thought of the bridge as a symbol of civic greatness, the towers standing as thresholds to the centers of each city. The elevated promenade was a special pride of the elder Roebling, signifying amenity; a respect for pauses in busy days, for the pleasures of open-air walks; and the unequalled visual excitement of the views of New York harbor. The least practical or profitable of the features of the bridge from

A panoramic view of the completed bridge, including its cable railroad trains, from the New York side. Note the variety of traffic: horse and wagon, electric-powered cable car, and pedestrian. (*Harper's Weekly*, June 2, 1883)

the point of commercial utility, the promenade remains one of the bridge's most eloquent gifts to the cities it joins. To the future it offered an ideal of urban experience tied into, shaped and formed by, and yet not overwhelmed by modern technology. Brooklyn Bridge emerges from an age steeped in corruption and greed, as a hope for the possibility of community. It for this that later generations have most valued Roebling's masterpiece. We can interpret the building of the bridge, then, as a story of a clash of values reshaping America as the nation entered the modern era.

Sources: The most convenient source of information about the building of the bridge, the personalities of the figures involved, the delays and scandals, is David McCullough, *The Great Bridge* (New York: Simon & Shuster, 1972). An interpretation of Brooklyn Bridge, including the art and literature it inspired, can be found in Alan Trachtenberg, *Brooklyn Bridge: Fact and Symbol* (New York: Oxford University Press, 1965). Most important among contemporary documents is John Roebling's initial plan, published as *Report of John A. Roebling, C. E., to the President and Directors of the New York Bridge Company, on the Proposed East River Bridge* (Brooklyn, N.Y.: Eagle Book and Job Printing Department, 1870). Other contemporary sources useful in reconstructing the story of Brooklyn Bridge include: William C. Conant, "The Brooklyn Bridge," *Harper's New Monthly Magazine* (May, 1883); E. F. Farrington, *Concise Description of the East River Bridge* (New York: C. D. Wynkoop, 1881), and Montgomery Schuyler, "The Bridge as a Monument," *Harper's Weekly* (24 May, 1883). The Roebling Collections at the Library of Rensselaer Polytechnic Institute include an indispensable collection of manuscripts and drawings by both John A. and Washington Roebling. The Special Collections of the Library at Rutgers University include a rich collection of personal manuscript materials and drawings by John A. Roebling, including his philosophical writings. Lewis Mumford sensitively places the Roeblings and the bridge in *The Brown Decades* (New York: Harcourt, Brace, & Company, 1931). Alan Trachtenberg's *The Incorporation of America: Culture and Society in the Gilded Age* (New York: Hill & Wang, 1982), provides an overview of the post-Civil War period.

3

THE HATFIELD–McCOY FEUD

ALTINA L. WALLER

Most Americans first heard about the Hatfields and the McCoys in early 1888, while reading newspaper accounts of the New Year's Day midnight raid of eight Hatfields on the home of Old Ranel McCoy, deep in the Appalachian hills of Pike County, Kentucky. Old Ranel had escaped, but 2 of his 16 children were dead. When big-city reporters discovered that this was only the latest in a series of incidents dating back at least a decade, an interpretation of the feud emerged: Two almost barbaric backwoods families, remote from the institutions, restraints, and refinements of civilization, were locked in a petty, senseless, and deadly vendetta.

Altina Waller's story of the Hatfield–McCoy feud has a very different message. The events she describes take place in a region already undergoing economic modernization and laced with legal institutions that the Hatfields and the McCoys often used to resolve their differences. Neither were the principals in the struggle— whether Old Ranel McCoy, Devil Anse Hatfield, or Perry Cline—the rustic hillbillies depicted in the popular press of the day. Even the families involved were not the monolithic blocs inscribed in the legend of the Hatfields and the McCoys.

The Hatfields and the McCoys were feuding, then, not because they were too isolated, but because they were not isolated enough. Rendered in these terms, the tale seems less like a rural curiosity and more like other stories that might be told of the same period: the story of the Sioux Indians on the Great Plains "reservations," fleeing before the new railroads, the mining companies, and the white man's unquenchable thirst for land; the story of the central Illinois farmer, selling his wheat in world markets and in competition with the newly opened granaries of the Dakotas; or the story of the proprietor of the general store in Kearney, Nebraska, who in 1890 is about to find out that his customers have direct access to the goods he sells through the Sears & Roebuck mail-order catalogue. These stories are all stories of penetration: the penetration of railroads onto the Plains, of the Sears company into rural homes; and— in the case of the Hatfields and the McCoys—of the penetration, first of timbering companies and then of railroads and coal-mining operations, into the Tug River Valley. The story of the Hatfields and the McCoys is very much a part of the central phenomenon of the age: the rise of big business.

But simply because we have a new way of understanding the feud does not mean that the old way has nothing to teach us. Indeed, the mythic perspective on the conflict, embodied in the photographs on p. 52, must have been especially compelling to have lasted so long and to have been fashioned in apparent defiance of the evidence. What, then, might account for the origin and persistence of the older view? One possibility is that the myth was fashioned by sophisticated eastern city-dwellers, for whom the primitives of rural Kentucky and West Virginia functioned as an "Other"—defining what they were not and did not want to be. But it is also possible that a nation engaged in a headlong rush toward the urban, industrialized, and bureaucratic world of the twentieth century relished the image of the gun-toting mountaineer as a sign that something still remained of the unfettered, intuitive freedom of the American frontiersman. Like Bonnie and Clyde in the 1930s, and Butch Cassidy and the Sundance Kid in the cinematic myth of the 1960s, the Hatfields and the McCoys were the objects of our collective desire.

In the 1870s Randolph and Sally McCoy lived on the Blackberry Fork of Pond Creek in Pike County, Kentucky. Randolph and Sally were in their 50s and presided over a family of 16 children. Their log home was typical of this mountainous region; called a "dog-trot" house, it consisted of two log houses connected by a kind of passageway or breezeway. In other external circumstances as well the McCoys were not very different from other families living in this remote region. Their log house was built on the side of a mountain with beautiful vistas on every side but little land that was level enough for cultivation. However, by supplementing farming with hunting and fishing, they managed to support themselves well enough.

Randolph and his wife Sally were the third generation of white settlers in this little community nestled along the tributaries of the Tug River. Despite the fact that the Tug River was the boundary between the states of West Virginia and Kentucky, Randolph and Sally, like most residents, considered *both* sides of the river their "neighborhood." Randolph—or "Old Ranel," as he was commonly known—had grown up just across the Tug in Logan County, Virginia (which became Logan County, West Virginia when the new state was created in 1863). Only after he married Sally did the two move to the Kentucky side, so many family members and friends still lived on the West Virginia side. The river was not an obstacle to this sense of community; it was shallow and could be forded easily on horseback and often on foot as well.

On a fall day in 1878, Old Ranel McCoy made his way down the steep mountain trail that traversed the ridge between the headwaters of Blackberry Creek and then followed the road down Pond Creek. Near the banks of the Tug River the road passed the home of Floyd Hatfield. Despite the Hatfield name, Floyd was also related to the McCoys—he was married to Old Ranel's niece. Passing by Hatfield's barnyard, McCoy noticed to his chagrin that the hog pen contained a sow and her pigs that Old Ranel was sure belonged to him—they had been missing for weeks. Enraged, Old Ranel hurried off to the nearest Justice of the Peace where he lodged an official complaint. Despite the fact that the Justice of the Peace was also a Hatfield—a common name (as com-

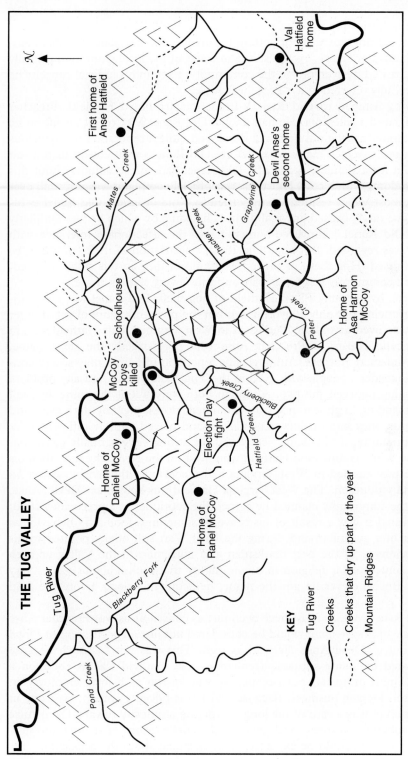

THE TUG VALLEY

N

Tug River

Pond Creek

Home of Daniel McCoy

Blackberry Fork

Home of Ranel McCoy

Schoolhouse

McCoy boys killed

Election Day fight

Hatfield Creek

Blackberry Creek

Mates Creek

First home of Anse Hatfield

Thacker Creek

Grapevine Creek

Devil Anse's second home

Val Hatfield home

Peter Creek

Home of Asa Harmon McCoy

KEY

Tug River

Creeks

Creeks that dry up part of the year

Mountain Ridges

The Tug Valley. (Reprinted, by permission of the publisher, from *Feud: Hatfields, McCoys, and Social Change in Appalachia*, by Altina L. Waller. Copyright © 1988 by The University of North Carolina Press.)

mon as Smith in other parts of the country) on both sides of the Tug River—
Old Ranel did not worry about getting fair treatment. The judge, William Anderson Hatfield or "Anse," was also the minister of the local church, universally
liked and trusted by everyone in the community; Even in his judicial capacity he
was respectfully referred to as "Preacher" Anse.

Having listened to Old Ranel's tirade against Floyd Hatfield, Preacher
Anse now faced a dilemma. He had known Old Ranel McCoy all his life so he
was well aware that the old man had developed quite a reputation for malicious
gossip. In one instance many years before, Old Ranel's own cousin filed a suit
against him for a slander; apparently Old Ranel had spread rumors about this
cousin's sodomy with a cow. However, this official complaint was unusual; over
the years, most Valley residents simply tried to avoid or ignore Old Ranel as his
loose tongue rarely caused any real harm. The name by which he was familiarly
known, "Old Ranel," conveyed something of the affectionate tolerance with
which he was regarded. But now, Old Ranel's accusation of theft could not be
easily dismissed. Hog theft, or indeed, any kind of theft in this small, isolated,
closely knit community was a very rare and thus a very serious crime.

Worse, by accusing Floyd Hatfield of hog theft, Old Ranel was also indirectly challenging not only Floyd himself but the powerful figure of yet another
Hatfield who lived across the Tug River in West Virginia. This Hatfield was, in
fact, a second cousin of Preacher Anse who bore exactly the same name,
William Anderson Hatfield. Although this repetition of names may sound confusing to outsiders, people who lived in the Tug Valley never had any problem
distinguishing between the two. Although both were about the same age, tall
and commanding in appearance with prominent noses, piercing dark eyes, and
black beards, they had distinct personalities and played entirely different roles
in the community. If "Preacher" conveyed the strong yet essentially gentle nature of the William Anderson Hatfield who lived on the Kentucky side, then his
namesake who resided in West Virginia had a sobriquet that encapsulated *his*
history and reputation. The West Virginia Hatfield was known as "Devil" Anse.
Some in the community claimed he earned the sobriquet as a precocious child;
others insisted it was a result of his brave, if sometimes foolhardy behavior as
the leader of a guerrilla band during the Civil War; still others pointed to his
accomplishments as the best marksman and horseman in the Valley or even
his open contempt for religion in a community that took religious values very
seriously. But wherever he got the name, he acquired it long before the feud
began.

Old Ranel McCoy must have been just as conscious as was Preacher Anse
that his tale of hog stealing would be considered not just an accusation of Floyd
Hatfield but of Devil Anse Hatfield as well. This was not so much because
Floyd shared the same surname (remember that Hatfield was as common a
name as Smith or Jones) but because he was known as a loyal employee in
Devil Anse's logging business. Because Old Ranel talked so much, everyone in
the community was aware of his long simmering animosity toward Devil Anse
and his timbering business. And, given Old Ranel's record of slander and gossip, local residents could be expected to be skeptical about the accusation. Yet

local judicial traditions were strong and could not be easily ignored; Preacher Anse would not, indeed could not, dismiss Old Ranel without a hearing.

True to his reputation for fairness, Preacher Anse came up with a diplomatic solution. Calling for an immediate trial, he chose an evenly balanced jury; six Hatfields and six McCoys. In a clever maneuver on his part, one of the McCoys he chose to serve on the jury—Selkirk McCoy—was a nephew of Old Ranel's but, like Floyd Hatfield, was a member of Devil Anse's timber crew. With such divided loyalties, Preacher Anse hoped, Selkirk would vote on the side of truth and who could complain? And Selkirk did, indeed, vote with the Hatfields; Old Ranel lost the case and Floyd kept the sow and pigs.

Although Preacher Anse's strategy was initially successful, in the long term it was this court case that began the escalation of a long simmering animosity between Devil Anse Hatfield and Old Ranel McCoy from the realm of neighborhood name calling into a bizarre series of murders, ambushes, and pitched battles. These events not only shocked the community but gripped the attention of a nationwide audience, contributing in no small way to stereotypes of mountaineer lawlessness and violence that persist even to the present. Yet there was more to it than petty family grievances. America's most famous feud

This photograph of Devil Anse Hatfield probably was taken about the time of the feud. The jacket, tie, and Confederate medals indicate Devil Anse's pride in his role in the Civil War and his respected status in the community. (Courtesy West Virginia and Regional History Collection, West Virginia University Library)

occurred at the very moment that economic modernization was about to destroy forever the rural isolation of the southern mountains. The history of the feud also reveals something of the capitalist transformation of Appalachia.

In the 1870s the Tug River community was still completely rural; it had no towns, no market center, no newspaper, not even a county seat. This meant that whenever a land transaction needed to be registered, a marriage license applied for, or taxes paid, a long and arduous journey was required. It was approximately a 30-mile trip by foot or horseback over rough mountain trails, either south to Pikeville, the county seat of Pike County, Kentucky, or north to Logan, the county seat of Logan County, West Virginia. The trip was physically exhausting and time-consuming and most people avoided it; they raised most of their own food—corn, potatoes, vegetables, cows, and pigs, voted in their own election districts within the valley, took their boundary disputes or other legal problems to the local Justice of the Peace and attended church only once a month when the circuit preacher made his rounds. For help in times of distress or sickness and for entertainment they depended on each other. It was a community more normally characterized by the stability of cooperation than by the divisiveness of conflict.

For the Tug Valley, even the Civil War—so divisive in many communities—reinforced community solidarity. During that conflict, despite its location straddling the boundary of two Union states, the people inhabitating the Tug Valley were almost unanimously loyal to the Confederacy. Ruled by state governments loyal to the Union and surrounded by Yankees (especially to the south in Kentucky where the county seat of Pikeville was Yankee dominated) the Tug River was not spared the violence of war. A Union force under James Garfield (later president of the United States) invaded the Valley and burned the county court house in Logan, not because of any hostile actions taken by the residents, but simply because they were known Confederate sympathizers. When Devil Anse Hatfield formed a guerrilla band known as the "Logan Wildcats" as a defense against the Union Army and Yankee guerrillas who raided the Valley from places like Pikeville, almost every young man in the community served. Randolph McCoy, later Hatfield's nemesis in the feud, collaborated with the Logan Wildcats. Even when Randolph's brother, Asa Harmon McCoy, one of the very few Union sympathizers in the Valley, was killed, presumably by the Logan Wildcats, there was no legal action taken nor is there any legendary evidence that Old Ranel attempted any retaliation. The absence of conflict over this incident suggests community solidarity against Yankee traitors. Devil Anse and all those who served in the Logan Wildcats, were universally regarded as heroes.

If the Tug River community weathered the Civil War without serious internal conflict, it was not so harmonious in the post-war era when a very different set of problems emerged. One was the land itself. The terrain was so rugged that only one-third could be cultivated. This fixed supply of land severely limited economic opportunity for the younger generation. Tug Valley families were large, six to eight children on average. Devil Anse Hatfield, for example, had 13 children while Old Ranel McCoy had 16. When these children grew to adulthood and required land, farms became smaller and located in more remote hollows. Indeed, the census schedules indicate that many young people could never hope to acquire farms. Between 1850 and 1880 the percentage of landless families rose dramatically from 35 to 50 percent. In a traditional culture in which land was essential not only for economic survival but for self-esteem and social status, this change had profound implications. But despite this declining economic opportunity, family ties remained strong, so much so that they constituted the second problem. Children expected to settle down near their families and were extremely reluctant to move out of the region. Changing economic circumstances had transformed a cultural asset—strong family bonds—into an economic liability.

In the 1870s and 1880s the hardship created by this demographic crisis had the potential of being partially offset by a new economic opportunity—one that did not require leaving home and family—the demand of industrialized America for timber. Although large-scale timbering was not feasible because of a lack of efficient transportation, the farmers of the Tug Valley, soon after the Civil War, had begun to supplement family farming by cutting small amounts of timber and floating it to market in the nearest urban centers of Cincinnati and Cattlettsburg.

Both Old Ranel McCoy and Devil Anse Hatfield engaged in the timbering business with very different consequences. McCoy's involvement in marketing timber was to cause such serious family conflict that his parents lost their farm and were eventually divorced. In a court deposition, Old Ranel's mother explained how this came about:

> . . . about eleven years ago [1867] as near as she recollects, said plaintiff [Daniel McCoy, Randolph's father] went into what is generally termed the timber business, that is cutting and hauling saw-logs for market, and . . . cut a huge quantity of timber upon lands . . . other than his own, and when remonstrated with by this respondent [Margaret McCoy, Randolph's mother] for doing so great a wrong and one that would involve him in a law-suit and eventually break him up, he became very angry with said respondent and has ever since acted towards her with a coolness and indifference that he never manifested before that time.

Unfortunately for Margaret McCoy's family, her prediction about the lawsuit and the "breakup" came true. Paying off the court ordered damages led to loss of the farm and the destruction of the family; Old Ranel's parents were divorced in 1871. Old Ranel himself escaped relatively unscathed economically because his wife had inherited a farm from her father. Yet he did not fare so well socially or psychologically. Old Ranel became notorious as a gossip and a complainer.

Devil Anse Hatfield, on the other hand, thrived on timbering. Undaunted by his lack of resources, Devil Anse, in a bold move, borrowed money and organized a company—a company rooted in family and neighborhood relationships. Of the approximately 30 men he hired, about half were kin, including his brothers Valentine, Ellison, and Elias, his brothers-in-law, John, Moses, and Tom

Chafin, his sons, William Anderson (or "Cap") and Johnson (or Johnse), and assorted nephews and cousins (like Floyd Hatfield). Not all Devil Anse's relatives approved of Devil Anse or the timbering business; his youngest brother, Pat, refused to become involved in timbering or the later feud. Needing more men than the family could or would provide, Devil Anse hired more than half of the timber crew from neighboring families, not necessarily related, men such as Selkirk McCoy and his two sons, Lorenzo and Albert, the Whitt brothers, Dan and Jeff, the Christian brothers, Dan and Moses, and the Staton brothers, Bill and John.

However, despite Hatfield's enterprising spirit, he still lacked the large amounts of forested land required for success. That obstacle was overcome when, as the result of a lawsuit against his nearest neighbor Perry Cline, Hatfield gained possession of a large tract of prime timber land. Although some aspects of the case remain puzzling because of incomplete court records, the broad outlines are clear. In 1872, Devil Anse sued Perry Cline, claiming that Cline and others had cut timber from Hatfield's land. Settling out of court 5 years later, Cline turned over to Devil Anse 5,000 acres of land—his sole inheritance from his father. In a startling reversal of social roles, Cline had been impoverished while Devil Anse became one of the wealthiest men in the Tug Val-

Before railroads and the mechanization of timbering, oxen, horses, or mules were used by family-based logging crews to cut timber in the mountains. (West Virginia State Archives, West Virginia Division of Culture and History, Charleston, West Virginia, 25305)

ley. Cline, now without farmland to sustain himself or his family, moved south across the mountain ridge to the town of Pikeville, Kentucky.

Devil Anse, entrenched with an unusually large parcel of land and a prosperous timber company, embraced the role of entrepreneur. He made contracts with local merchants, boldly sued them when disagreements arose, and instituted numerous lawsuits against his own neighbors when they dared trespass on his land. In an environment in which freedom to hunt, walk, or ride wherever one wished had been assumed, residents were shocked to discover that cutting one tree or trespassing on Hatfield land could land them in court where they stood to lose their own farms or animals. Although Hatfield certainly did not win most of these cases, the 5,000 acres of the "Cline tract" kept his timber crew busy. Hatfield had succeeded where Old Ranel McCoy had failed. But what Devil Anse won in profits and economic power he lost in friendship and good will. Worse, he angered his neighbors by demonstrating contempt for community values—values that associated such worldly pursuits as self-interest and profit with the Devil. "You can say," Devil Anse once declared, "that I belong to no church except the church of the world. You can say . . . I belong to the Devil's church."

Paradoxically, the opportunities provided by the timber market had accomplished what even the Civil War had not done: set neighbor against neighbor and seriously disrupted community and family harmony. In this newly competitive context, Devil Anse with his entrepreneurial manuevering and flaunting of his success, towered like a lightning rod, attracting the ill feelings of his neighbors. He seemed to be the most obvious example of just what happened when selfish competition replaced cooperation. Ironically, it was Old Ranel McCoy, whose family had been so severely scarred by greed and dishonesty in the timber business, who was the first to openly challenge the Hatfields. Old Ranel's accusation of Floyd Hatfield for theft was that challenge. The hog trial, then, was more than simply an argument over the possession of a sow and pigs. It threatened to expose community fault lines of such depth that most residents instinctively recoiled from the prospect.

At first, Preacher Anse's strategy worked; although Old Ranel vociferously complained and attempted to persuade some of his kinsmen (there were many who lived nearby) to take some action against Devil Anse and his family, none would. When even his wife urged acceptance of the verdict, Old Ranel, grumbling, agreed. But in the long term the matter was far from settled. The younger generation—a few of Old Ranel's nephews and sons and some of Devil Anse's timber employees—continued to insult and harass each other, sometimes engaging in out and out brawls. Finally, two of Old Ranel's nephews killed a Hatfield timber employee. Arrested and tried in a West Virginia court, where Devil Anse Hatfield's older brother was the Judge, the two McCoys were acquitted on grounds of self-defense. It was an unexpected verdict favorable to the McCoys but it did not cool the feud.

In the summer of 1880, McCoy hostility was refueled when Roseanna McCoy, the dark-eyed, 21-year-old daughter of Old Ranel McCoy, and Johnse

Hatfield, Devil Anse's son, fell in love. Disowned by her father, Roseanna moved in with the Hatfield family and was soon pregnant. However, Johnse was not a faithful lover; he spent most of his time away, flirting openly with other women. Hurt and angry, Roseanna fled to the household of her Aunt Betty. Although Old Ranel was furious and, despite tearful appeals from his wife, would not allow his daughter to return home, he did not instigate any violence against the Hatfields.

It was Old Ranel's son, 26-year-old Tolbert, who seized the leadership in pursuing a vendetta against the Hatfields. Tolbert had spent most of his life subjected to Old Ranel's repeated tirades on the subject of Hatfield knavery. He had watched as his cousin Perry Cline lost his land to Devil Anse. He harbored vivid memories of the family humiliation at the hog trial. Now his sister had been "stolen" and then abandoned by Johnse Hatfield. Yet the Hatfields' arrogance seemed to bring them prosperity, admiration, and respect, while Tolbert himself faced a bleak future. Although he was 26-years-old, a husband, and soon to be father, Tolbert McCoy was hired out as a farm laborer with negligible prospects of obtaining his own farm.

Tolbert formulated a plot to have himself deputized by the Pike County sheriff so that he could arrest Johnse for some trumped up charge like carrying a concealed weapon or violating the liquor tax law. He ambushed Johnse on the Kentucky side of the river and would have hauled him off to the Pikeville jail had not Roseanna, still in love with Johnse, discovered the plan and informed Devil Anse. Devil Anse surprised Tolbert escorting Johnse, at gunpoint, toward Pikeville and retrieved his son without violence. In the process, however, Devil Anse treated Tolbert like a bad boy who needed spanking—taking away his gun and administering a tongue lashing that was profoundly humiliating. Tolbert never forgot it.

On election day in August of 1882, Tolbert McCoy, according to his friends, was drunk and "looking for trouble." At first his hostility seemed unfocused. Badgering a neighbor for repayment of an old debt, he disregarded repeated warnings from the local constable and Preacher Anse to cease his belligerent behavior. Finally, Ellison Hatfield, a brother of Devil Anse and partner in the timber business, intervened. Ellison Hatfield was a big man, a Confederate war hero much admired by the young women of the Tug Valley and full of his own importance. Challenging Tolbert's drunken antics, he is reputed to have shouted, "I'm the best goddammed man on earth!" Electioneering festivities came to a sudden halt in stunned silence. Enraged, Tolbert seized a knife and lunged at Ellison even while screaming at his brothers for help. Two of them rushed to his side and the three McCoys attacked the powerful, massively built, but unarmed, Ellison Hatfield. Before the bystanders could untangle the feudists, the McCoys had stabbed Ellison Hatfield more than two dozen times as well as fired several shots into him. And although he was not dead, it was difficult to imagine that Ellison would survive for very long.

A strange drama followed. Devil Anse Hatfield had not been present that day so a shocked community seemed to hold its breath until Ellison's brothers were notified. What would they do—especially if Ellison died, as he was likely to do, of his severe wounds? Once again, as in the hog dispute, Preacher Anse Hatfield took charge of the situation. He began by urging Tolbert McCoy and his brothers to submit to arrest and go quietly to jail in Pikeville. When Tolbert protested, saying they would rather fight, Preacher Anse painted such a graphic picture of what was likely to happen when Devil Anse arrived on the scene that the three McCoys meekly submitted.

But it was not Devil Anse who came after the McCoys. It was his older brother, Valentine, who took the initiative. Valentine Hatfield was a justice of the peace in West Virginia and, like Preacher Anse, his counterpart in Kentucky, he was a respected elder statesman. The next morning it was the venerable Judge Valentine Hatfield who crossed the river into Kentucky in pursuit of the three McCoy sons and the constables. He finally caught up with the party only a few miles down the rugged trail to Pikeville. At the trial, one of the constables described the scene that ensued:

> I was one of the guards, guarding the McCoy boys when Wall [Valentine's nickname] came to us he said that all we wanted was that the boys should stand the civil law. That he had not slept any the night before and was tired and worn out and that he wanted them to go down to the mouth of the creek to have a trial. That he wanted to be near his brother [Devil Anse] and wanted to get the evidence of Dr. Rutherford and old Uncle Wall Hatfield. [Dr. Rutherford was the local physician and Uncle Wall was one of the oldest, most respected members of the community.]

Without apparent resistence the constables capitulated and agreed to return to the Tug Valley with their charges. Once there Preacher Anse made another effort to mediate the explosive situation. He invited Valentine and Devil Anse (who had finally appeared on the Kentucky side of the Tug river) along with the McCoys and the constables to have dinner with him. Apparently he tried to persuade the Hatfields to allow the McCoys to face trial in Pikeville, that justice would indeed be accomplished there. Needless to say, both Hatfield brothers were skeptical for Pikeville was not part of their world; they had long memories going back to Civil War days when Pikeville was the center of Union loyalty, a headquarters for the Union army and the place where Union guerrillas were outfitted to raid the Tug Valley. Moreover, Devil Anse's old enemy, Perry Cline, had become a powerful figure in Pikeville politics; he certainly could not be counted on to see that the McCoys faced justice for their crime. Still, Valentine seemed more inclined to consider this alternative than Devil Anse who, growing impatient, stomped out into the front yard and ordered "all Hatfields to line up." It was his way of announcing that the argument was over; he intended to take the McCoys back to West Virginia and find out whether his brother was still alive before any decisions would be made.

Once in West Virginia, Devil Anse converted an abandoned schoolhouse (near the present Matewan, West Virginia) into a makeshift jail. Here he stationed some of his followers as guards while sending others off to inquire about Ellison's condition. When he learned that Ellison was still alive Devil Anse informed Tolbert and his brothers that if Ellison died, so would they; if Ellison survived, they would be returned to the constables for trial in Pikeville. In the all-night vigil that followed, Devil Anse allowed Tolbert's wife and mother to visit the prisoners while Devil Anse and Valentine questioned witnesses about the fight and debated their next step.

Forty-eight hours after the fight, Ellison Hatfield died. Despite some disagreement in the family about killing the McCoys, Devil Anse could not be dissuaded from his ultimatum. He and about 20 of his followers (including Valentine) took the McCoys back to the Kentucky side of the Tug River, tied them to some pawpaw bushes on the banks of the river, blindfolded them and in an execution ritual, shot all three. It was the first time that Devil Anse Hatfield had engaged in feud violence. By the next day, a horrified community became aware of the gruesome retribution.

In spite of this unusual violence, however, most people in the community seemed unwilling to take any action against Devil Anse. Once again Old Ranel attempted but could not persuade any of his relatives or neighbors to take up arms against the Hatfields. Although Tug Valley residents may not have approved of Devil Anse, many of them had actually seen the three McCoys kill Ellison Hatfield in an unfair fight before dozens of witnesses. Thus, although indictments were issued in Pike County for the 20 Hatfields who had killed the McCoys, no attempt was made to serve the warrants or make arrests. The Sheriff of Pike County made a terse note on the back of the warrant issued for the arrest of Devil Anse and his supporters: "Not found," and no further action was taken for fully 5 years.

Indeed, it is likely that the feud would have ended in 1882, and the world would never have heard of the Hatfields and McCoys, had it not been for the actions, 5 years later, of Devil Anse Hatfield's old nemesis, Perry Cline. Cline's career in Pikeville, after the loss of his inheritance to Devil Anse and his flight from the Tug Valley, had been a successful one. By 1887 he was a lawyer and sheriff of the county and belonged to the small circle of businessmen and politicians who wielded power in Pikeville. Rumor had it that as a friend and political supporter of Kentucky's newly elected Governor, Simon Buckner, Cline's power extended beyond Pikeville to the state capital.

Not only was Cline now in a position of power, but in the intervening 14 years since he had left the Tug Valley, his resentment toward Devil Anse for the loss of his property had grown more acute. In 1886 and 1887 it was obvious that the value of his lost property was about to skyrocket. First, in 1886, the Norfolk and Western Railroad announced its intention to build the "Ohio Extension" from Virginia to the Ohio River. But the building of the railroad was only the beginning; the very next year, 1887, the Kentucky legislature published the results of a geological survey that confirmed discovery of extensive seams of high quality coal in the Tug Valley. The geological survey was more than a routine report; it was also a public relations document through which the legislature signaled its plans to actively recruit investment by eastern capitalists. Cline was only beginning to understand the extent of the economic boom about to engulf the entire region.

It was in this frame of mind, then, that Perry Cline listened to his old Uncle Ranel one cold winter day in the year 1886. Old Ranel had ridden over the mountain ridge to relate, once again, the tale of Hatfield crimes. In the 4 years since the election day fight and the killing of his three sons, Old Ranel had many times brought his complaints to Cline, who listened sympathetically but took no action. This time, however, Cline was more attentive. Although the most recent incident described by Old Ranel was not clearly part of the old feud, Cline perceived his opportunity to strike back at Devil Anse Hatfield. Yes, Perry Cline said to old Uncle Ranel, he would approach his friend the Governor about reinstating the arrest warrants against Devil Anse and the 20 men who had taken part in the execution of the McCoys. For the first time in 4 years Old Ranel rode back across the mountain ridge a happy man, while Cline began to marshal support from his influential friends.

By the following summer, Perry Cline had succeeded in persuading the Governor to revive the 5-year-old indictments against the Hatfields and actively prosecute the case. Just how he accomplished this, what arguments he used, it is impossible to know as no one involved kept any records or directly stated their reasons. All we can do is surmise from the circumstances surrounding the meetings. If the Governor did feel indebted to Cline, his inclination to go along with the request was probably strengthened by a desire to make Kentucky appear to be a law and order state, especially as recent national publicity about several other Kentucky feuds had created a violent image for the state. Newspapers in the state were already lamenting the inhibiting effect that feud violence might have on potential capitalist investment in the rich coal mining region and the Hatfield–McCoy feud, although not active at the moment, was located in the most highly visible region for attracting coal investors. Whatever his reasons, the Governor issued official rewards for the capture of the Hatfields and began legal proceedings to extradite them from West Virginia.

The Governor's action had the effect of reactivating the feud, this time pitting the power of the state of Kentucky against Devil Anse Hatfield and his supporters. Back in Pikeville, armed with the authority of the Governor, Cline recruited a posse to cross the state boundary into West Virginia and, ignoring the extradition process, captured his first Hatfield supporter. Ironically, this first "Hatfield" captive was none other than Selkirk McCoy, who had served on the hog trial jury and voted with the Hatfields. This intervention by the state government was a shocking departure from the local autonomy of county government. The first response of Devil Anse Hatfield, however, was not violence, but bribery. He tried to buy off Perry Cline by offering him $250 to stop the posse raids and rescind the rewards. Cline initially agreed and accepted the bribe but then continued to send his posse across the border.

Next Devil Anse attempted a political solution. He approached the Governor of West Virginia, E. Willis Wilson, through a friend and political crony, John B. Floyd. Floyd had grown up in the Tug Valley and knew Hatfield and his family well. Both Floyd and Wilson were sympathetic to the Hatfields' dilemma because of their politics. Both men belonged to a faction of the Democratic Party that defended the interests of farmers and working people against wealthy businessmen and capitalists. They perceived the mountain farmers of the Appalachian region as victims who were losing their land to railroad and coal companies and rapidly being reduced from independent yeomen to wage laborers. Wilson spent his entire political career fighting big corporations and trying to protect his constituents from such exploitation. He advocated state control of the railroads and reasonable levels of taxation for absentee corporations which controlled West Virginia's valuable mineral resources. An idealist, he was the last of a vanishing breed in late 19th century politics. In fact, he was the last Governor of West Virginia to actively oppose corporate domination of West Virginia's politics and economy. When Wilson heard from John Floyd of the Hatfields' history of legal and economic difficulties with Perry Cline, and Cline's influence with the Governor of Kentucky, he was willing to consider the possibility that the Hatfields, too, were victims. He delayed signing the extradition papers by requesting further information from Governor Buckner of Kentucky.

But for some of Devil Anse's supporters, including his sons Cap and Johnse, none of this was enough. Cap came up with a plan to get rid of the people who had caused their problems—the family of Old Ranel McCoy. He proposed burning down the McCoy home in a midnight raid that would destroy all potential witnesses against them. It was a desperate solution, so shocking to most Hatfield supporters that they refused to be involved.

But Cap Hatfield was so infuriated (and probably frightened) that he ignored all advice to the contrary, even his father's. Just past midnight on January 1st of 1888, accompanied by only eight of the Hatfield group (Devil Anse not among them), he led the attack on Old Ranel's home on the Blackberry Fork of Pond Creek. This was the infamous New Year's Day raid in which two of Old Ranel's children were killed—both shot as they attempted to run from the burning house—and his wife Aunt Sally McCoy beaten when she tried to reach her dying daughter in the snow. Old Ranel and the other children escaped and made their way to Pikeville where Perry Cline took them in. Meanwhile, the Hatfields realized with horror that the whole idea had been a tragic blunder, one that far from resolving anything, would only exacerbate the trouble.

It was this incident that catapulted the feud into national attention as Perry Cline and his friends seized the public relations offensive by circulating press releases to Kentucky newspapers, which were then picked up by papers all over the country. The first newspaper item that focused national attention on the feud was headlined, "A MURDEROUS GANG—A TERRIBLE TRAGEDY PERPETRATED BY DESPERADOES—MOTHER AND SON MURDERED WHILE FATHER AND DAUGHTER ESCAPE A FIERY GRAVE." During the next 6 months, the names Hatfield and McCoy became household words all over America, as newspapers from Maine to California sensationalized every detail and reported every rumor as though it were fact. Reporters from Pittsburgh and New York City arrived on the scene and attempted to interview anyone remotely connected with the two families but received most of their information from Perry Cline. *New York World* reporter T. C. Crawford rushed into print a book on the feud entitled *An American Vendetta: A Story of*

Barbarism in the United States. It was only the first of many sensationalized accounts.

Cline was not content with a journalistic war, however. He stepped up his raids into West Virginia during the month of January and managed to capture eight more Hatfield supporters, including Justice of the Peace Valentine Hatfield. In the process, two Hatfield supporters were shot and killed. The final violent confrontation came at the end of January when a Hatfield posse met a Cline posse and engaged in a quasi-military skirmish. It became legendary as the Battle of Grapevine Creek.

Now alarmed by violence in the Tug Valley, Governor E. Willis Wilson of West Virginia was willing to admit that he could have misjudged the situation. If so he was ready to take drastic action by sending in the militia to keep the peace. He even urged Governor Buckner to do the same. Before giving the order, however, Governor Wilson sent a personal emissary to the Tug Valley to investigate. The report returned by the special investigator assured the Governor that the violence was not as severe as had been rumored. It also, however, substantiated his earlier belief that the Hatfields were victims. "I visited all the Hatfields," stated the investigator, "and found them to be good, law-abiding citizens who have the respect and confidence of everyone in the neighborhood."

This information confirmed that of Wilson's trusted political ally, John Floyd, who argued that the trouble had only arisen because Perry Cline had decided "he would stir up the thing again and make some money out of it, knowing that the Hatfields owned some good property." Convinced of Cline's culpability in the affair and infuriated that the state of Kentucky was violating extradition procedures by kidnapping and jailing West Virginia citizens, Governor Wilson went on the offensive. Refusing to sign the extradition request, he issued formal rewards for the arrest and capture of members of Cline's posse who had killed the two Hatfield supporters.

But Governor Wilson was still not satisfied. There were important moral and legal principles involved, he thought, and he intended to pursue them at the highest possible level. Convinced that Governor Buckner and the state of Kentucky had illegally "invaded" West Virginia to capture its citizens, Wilson filed Writs of Habeas Corpus for the Hatfields in the federal district court in Louisville. This meant that the Sheriff of Pikeville had to produce the eight Hatfields in the Louisville court for a determination as to whether they were being illegally held in the Pikeville jail. When the appointed day arrived for the hearing, Governor Wilson himself, accompanied by John B. Floyd, appeared to argue West Virginia's case.

Although the district judges ruled against West Virginia and sent the Hatfields back to Pikeville to stand trial, the case was appealed to the United States Supreme Court where it was heard in May of 1888. However, the Supreme Court also decided in favor of Kentucky, arguing that states possessed only "limited sovereignty" and therefore could not seek redress with habeas corpus to reclaim citizens who had been kidnapped. In effect the Court ruled that it did not matter *how* the accused Hatfield supporters came to be in Kentucky— once there, the authorities could legally arrest them.

While these legal proceedings were in process, actual violence between the Hatfields, McCoys, and Cline had ended with the Battle of Grapevine Creek, but the rewards offered by both states brought into the Valley a number of bounty hunters, usually members of private detective agencies such as Eureka and Baldwin–Felts, intent on scouring the mountains for anyone remotely resembling a feudist. Fear and suspicion of strangers mounted as local residents, who were, after all, most of them related to the Hatfields and McCoys, could expect to be accosted, beaten, or even killed in the manhunt. Newspapers, employing sensational rhetoric, played up the violence and attributed every encounter between a Tug Valley resident and a detective as a feud incident directly caused, not by outside bounty hunters, but by the violent and lawless nature of mountain culture itself.

Ironically, Perry Cline had contributed to this growing national perception that *all* Appalachians were, as he said of the Hatfields in a letter to Governor Wilson, "outlaws" and desperadoes who had been "in arms" since the Civil War, the worst "merauders"[sic] ever who would not live "as citizens ought." Further reinforcing the stereotype, Cline spread the rumor that Valentine Hatfield, Devil Anse's older brother and long time respected county judge, had "five wives and thirty-three . . . children" and had "peculiar ideas of polygamy." Without any evidence other than Cline's word, the *New York Times*

Ellison Mounts was a Hatfield feudist and the only one to be executed by the state of Kentucky. His hanging on February 18, 1890 was the last such public spectacle in Pike County.

repeated this false story, reporting that the "fact" of Hatfield's five wives made it "evident that a strong course of common schools, churches, soap and water . . . is required before these simple children of nature will forbear to kill a man whenever they take a dislike to him." This latest "vendetta," declared the *Times*, ". . . shows the purely savage character of the population." In a strange twist of events, the hillbilly stereotype produced by the feud was to obscure to history the role played by Devil Anse as an ambitious, and typically American, entrepreneur.

As the Hatfields became the target for every private detective in the East, Devil Anse Hatfield decided that enough was enough and retreated. With nine of his supporters lodged in the Pikeville jail, and private detectives waiting to ambush him at every turn, Devil Anse concluded that life on the banks of the Tug had become too dangerous. He sold the hard won 5,000 acres for half of what it was worth to an agent for a group of Philadelphia capitalists. All through the 1880s this agent had been buying up the lands of local farmers in anticipation of the railroad and coal mines that would soon open up. Most farmers were completely unaware of the plans then being made that would soon make their forested slopes much more valuable. But he had not been able to persuade Devil Anse, who was far too independent and stubborn to sell. Now, however, with the threat of arrest by detectives, Devil Anse sold the land for half its value and moved his family back away from the Tug boundary to Main Island Creek near the town of Logan, where he built a virtual fortress on the side of a mountain.

Within a year of his move, at about the same time as Devil Anse's brother Valentine and other supporters were being tried in Pikeville, the railroad was built right through his former land and the town of Matewan sprang up where the three McCoys had been killed in 1882. Although the Pikeville trials led to the deaths of two (Valentine Hatfield died in prison while Ellison Mounts was hanged in February of 1890) and the life imprisonment of the others, Devil Anse was never captured or extradited. Safe on his mountain, Devil Anse outlived Old Ranel McCoy, who died in a fire in 1914 and Perry Cline, who had a heart attack in 1891 at the age of 42. In 1921 Devil Anse's death of old age was overshadowed in the press by the outbreak of a series of bloody wars between mine workers and private police employed by the coal companies. Progress, it seems, had not brought peace to Appalachia.

AN INTERPRETATION

The Hatfield–McCoy Feud traditionally has invoked images and stereotypes of ignorance, violence, and family loyalty gone berserk. Derogatory stories and jokes about Appalachian mountaineers continue to be acceptable today at a time in which there is sensitivity to insults directed towards blacks, women, Indians, and other minority groups. Even middle class Americans whose roots are in the southern mountains frequently accept these negative assumptions and feel ashamed of their background.

Yet in many ways the world of the Hatfields and McCoys was not at all unusual. The feuding families were part of a traditional farming community, like farming communities located in New England, upstate New York, Pennsylvania, and small farm areas of the South in the antebellum era. Extensive kin networks defined individual identity and status in the community as well as economic activity and local government. Community self-sufficiency and autonomy predominated, but there was never a complete absence of commerce with surrounding regions or isolation from larger political issues at the state and national level. The complex family relations manifested in the story of the feud could apply to almost any region before the Civil War. Appalachians, then, initially were not so different from most Americans; why then did the violence of the late nineteenth century erupt and why did it become so well-known?

The initial stage of the feud was brought about because of a demographic and economic crisis within the Tug Valley community itself. Not enough land and too many people with strong family bonds led to declining opportunity, which in turn produced anxiety, tension, and increased competition for scarce resources. To this increased competition for traditional farm occupations was added the "opportunity" to supply industrialized America with timber. Rising land values, competition for trees, and the cash that could be gotten from sell-

This photograph of the Hatfield family was taken in 1897 by an itinerant photographer well after the feud had made the Hatfields famous. Attempting to exploit that notoriety, the photographer posed the family with guns prominently displayed. This picture has become one of the most famous images associated with the feud. (West Virginia State Archives, West Virginia Division of Culture and History, Charleston, West Virginia, 25305)

ing them led to disruption of a traditional subsistence economy based on community cooperation and sharing. More significantly, it led to a breakdown in a spirit of cooperation in the community. The animosity that polarized around those committed to a market economy (timber) versus those still primarily engaged in semisubsistence farming became apparent in the initial stage of the feud when only members of the timber operation were singled out as enemies by the McCoys. Preacher Anse Hatfield as well as many of Devil Anse Hatfield's brothers, uncles, and cousins were not attacked by the McCoys, nor did they rush to the defense of Devil Anse. The feud story also reveals that many of Old Ranel McCoy's relatives refused to become involved or, like Selkirk McCoy, took the Hatfield side. Family bonds were strong in the Tug Valley but apparently not strong enough to overcome emerging economic conflict and the emotional response that went with it.

The story of the feud also reveals that mountain communities were neither chronically lawless nor violent. The local judicial system was strong and functioned effectively. Devil Anse, for example, apparently won his case against Perry Cline on solid legal grounds and when he did not win in court, Devil Anse did not use force or violence or ignore judicial authority. Violence emerged from the threat or the reality of outside infringement on the local system of authority. The first example apparent in the feud was the problems caused because the Tug Valley community was arbitrarily divided by the boundary between West Virginia and Kentucky. When Devil Anse's brother Ellison was killed on the Kentucky side of the river, the Hatfields, who had always before been willing to rely on the courts, could not allow Ellison Hatfield's killers to be taken to Pikeville for trial. Valentine and Devil Anse were reluctant to engage in vigilantism—to take the law into their own hands—but were convinced they had no choice. Significantly, they did not simply kill the three McCoys on the West Virginia side of the river; fearful that West Virginia authorities might take legal action against them, they took the McCoys back to the Kentucky side before executing them. It was a way of keeping themselves law abiding in West Virginia and, at the same time, administering justice. Still, it was not until Perry Cline took his case to the Governor of Kentucky that the local judicial system broke down entirely. When Cline and his Kentucky posse raided West Virginia and the Hatfields retaliated with the New Year's day raid on the McCoy home, it was obvious that state intervention had completely shattered the local system of authority.

At this point the feud took on much broader political and economic dimensions. Governor Buckner allied Kentucky with capitalists and modernizers both inside and outside the region; he perceived the mountaineers as obstructing the economic development of the region and hoped to make an example of the Hatfields. Governor Wilson of West Virginia represented that strain of late 19th century political thought identified as "agrarian" or "populist," which sought to resist the overweening political and economic power of the eastern industrialists. Wilson's earnestness in defending the Hatfields was part and parcel of his entire career as a defender of small farmers in his state. Thus, when the case went to the Supreme Court at Wilson's instigation, it could be interpreted as a national level dispute over the rights of weaker, powerless people in opposition to the economic and political power of the modernizers. Although this issue was not overt in the arguments before the Supreme Court, put in the larger context of the changes in the federal judiciary toward protecting corporations at the expense of individuals and ruling against minority groups such as blacks and Indians, this case can be interpreted as part of a larger pattern.

Finally, if the worst violence of the feud was brought about by the industrialization process, why was that process so much more violent than in the rest of the country? For the most part, antebellum communities in the North or even other parts of the South did not experience the level of violence during industrialization that Appalachia did. Part of the answer may be that the process was more gradual in other areas, allowing people time to adjust, but the key factor for Appalachians may have been that it was largely imposed on them from outside. Although local boosters collaborated with outside industrialists, local capital was not sufficient to make the process indigenous and thus most mountaineers were exploited in much the same way as the people of Latin America or the Philippines as the United States took on more and more foreign ventures. Thus, the relationship became adversarial and violent as many Appalachians, like the Hatfields after Kentucky's posse raids, realized that they would no longer be allowed to control their own future or benefit from the process of economic development.

Sources: This story is based on extensive research in the County Court Records of Logan County, West Virginia, and Pike County, Kentucky; the Kentucky State Archives in Frankfort, Kentucky, and the West Virginia State Archives in Charleston, West Virginia; newspapers such as the *Louisville Courier–Journal,* the *Logan Banner,* the *Wheeling Intelligencer,* the *New York World,* and the *New York Times;* and books written with first hand information such as T. C. Crawford's *An American Vendetta: A Story of Barbarism in the United States,* NY: Bedford, Clarke & Co. (1889), and Truda McCoy's *The McCoys: Their Story As Told to the Author by Eyewitnesses and Descendents.* Edited by Leonard Roberts. Pikeville, KY; Pikeville College Press. (1976) which is based on interviews with many women involved in the feud. The best short narrative treatment of the feud is Otis Rice, *The Hatfields and the McCoys,* Lexington: University Press of KY (1978). For the most detailed examination of the feud and its economic and social implications see Altina L. Waller, *Feud: Hatfields, McCoys, and Social Change in Appalachia 1860–1900,* Chapel Hill, University of North Carolina Press, 1988.

4

EMPIRE IN THE PHILIPPINES: AMERICA'S FORGOTTEN WAR OF COLONIAL CONQUEST

STUART CREIGHTON MILLER

The conquest of the Philippines was only one of a series of overseas actions that collectively forged a new American empire and redefined the United States as a formidable world power. Between 1898 and 1917, when the Congress approved Woodrow Wilson's call for a Declaration of War against Germany, the nation took Cuba, Puerto Rico, Guam, and the Philippines from Spain; promoted a rebellion in Panama that paved the way for the canal; dispatched troops to protect American commercial interests in Santo Domingo, Haiti, and Nicaragua; and—under the same General Frederick Funston who appears in the following account—occupied the city of Vera Cruz during the Mexican revolution.

In terms of square miles of territory taken, the American empire was hardly an empire at all—nothing at all like the vast African and Asian colonial empires of Great Britain, France, and Germany. Despite this difference, V. I. Lenin, the Communist leader of the Russian Revolution, lumped the American empire with the European ones, treating them all as an outgrowth of what he called in 1916 "the highest stage of capitalism"—that is, "monopoly" capitalism. The timing of America's imperial escapades roughly fits Lenin's model; a massive merger movement, beginning in 1897 and concluding in 1902, virtually completed the transformation of the economy into a system of oligopolies, with many industries dominated by a few massive corporations. According to this controversial theory, the new American empire reflected the needs of the new, giant corporations and the desires of the men who ran them. American "New Left" historians of the 1960s and 1970s also emphasized the economic origins of empire.

In contrast, not a single businessman appears in Stuart Creighton Miller's account of the American intervention in the Philippine archipelago. Instead, Miller's analysis relies on the behavior and rhetoric of ordinary soldiers and their commanding officers to give us some sense of what Americans were doing in the jungles of the Pacific. It will take some courage to see ourselves in this story, for Miller's portrait is unflaggingly critical, with each character establishing an impressive—and depressing—new standard for racism, bigotry, and truculent nationalism.

Nonetheless, this story of how Americans fought the Filipinos and talked about their exploits can help reveal the lines of influence that came together to yield an American empire. One of them, surely, was the frontier—officially declared "closed" in the 1890 census when the supply of unsettled land seemed to have been exhausted—yet remarkably alive in the American mind. Another was the exuberant self-confidence of the United States, refracted in the words of thousands of soldiers who went overseas absolutely convinced that they had only to show up to win great victories (Americans would export their products with the same assurance). Racism was another line of influence, running from the Philippines back and forth through turn-of-the-century laws that segregated blacks from whites and disfranchised black voters in the Southern states. American empire was the product, too, of just the sort of confusion over ideals and purposes that made it difficult for even Filipino leader Emilio Aguinaldo to be certain what American troops were doing in his homeland. Was the United States the standard-bearer of civilization and democracy? Or an elitist nation with unfulfilled imperial ambitions? As Americans and Filipinos eyed each other warily in the wake of the siege of Manila, no one—least of all the Americans— knew for sure.

The evening of February 4, 1899, was an ideal moment to begin the war with the fledgling Republic of the Philippines, as most of its leaders were off at a celebration in Malolos, some 30 miles north of Manila. The United States Army had taken Manila the preceding August during the war with Spain, only to be bottled up in the city when the Filipino army, America's erstwhile, de facto ally against the Spanish, re-formed its line of siege around the land side of the city on August 11, 1898. The nationalist leader, General Emilio Aguinaldo y Famy, justified this aggressive action, reasoning that the city could be returned to Spain in the peace negotiations underway in Paris from which his government was excluded. Once the Treaty of Paris was made public in December, converting the Spanish colony into an American one, Aguinaldo continued his siege, insisting that two thirds of the Senate would never consent to a treaty that so violated cherished American principles. That august body heatedly debated an imperial future for America, and finally scheduled a vote on the treaty for February 6, 1899, one that was predicted to be extremely close.

Meanwhile, the two armies facing each other on the outskirts of Manila were ostensibly at peace, but tensions between them escalated daily. Finally, just 2 days before the Senate's scheduled vote, around 8 o'clock that evening, some unarmed, probably drunk, Filipino soldiers refused to heed commands by a sentry of the Nebraska volunteer regiment, and mocked him with their own shouts of "halto! halto!" They were quickly gunned down, and a crescendo of gunfire erupted from both the American and Filipino lines facing each other on the outskirts of Manila. Heavy firing continued until 2 o'clock the next morning, most of it pretty wild in the ensuing darkness, and largely coming from the state volunteer regiments manning the northern sector of Manila's defense

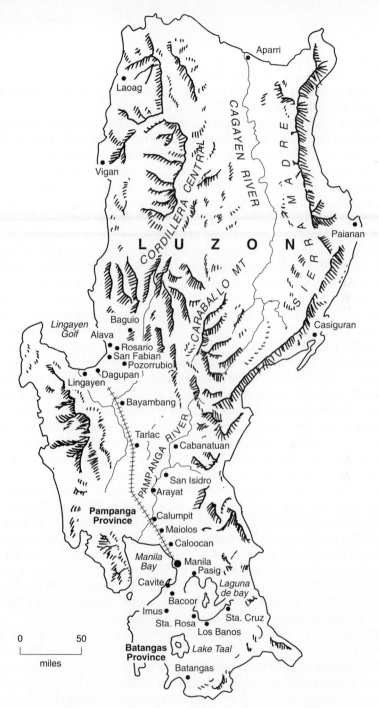

The island of Luzon is the largest and most populous within the Philippine archipelago. Much of the fighting between Americans and Filipinos occurred in the immediate vicinity of Manila and in the provinces of Pampanga (just north) and Batangas (to the south). The hideout of Filipino leader Emilio Aguinaldo was in the town of Palanan, on the northeast coast.

perimeter. One regular officer assumed that they must be repulsing a Filipino attack and sent his aide to see if they needed help. He returned to report with disgust that there was no attack, just "green Dakotans wasting ammunition firing away at no discernible targets."

Neither side made a serious effort to advance on the other, and no significant casualties had occurred by the time the firing ceased at 2 A.M. So the skirmish could have easily been dismissed in the sobering light of the next morning as an unfortunate incident caused by the growing tension between the two armies. Instead, land batteries, along with the heavy guns of Admiral George Dewey's warships, began to hammer Filipino positions once the first rays of light had put them in silhouette. At 8 A.M., after several hours of this devastating barrage, the bugles sounded, and the "boys in blue" charged out of Manila with "Montana screams, Tennessee howls, Jayhawk cheers" and fixed bayonets. As Private William Christner described it to his parents: "With a good old Pennsylvania yell we charged up the hill through a hail of bullets," reassuring them that "I hardly think I was born to be killed by a nigger." Actually, the "Pennsy vols" were among the few regiments that received significant fire that day. Most found only dead or wounded in the opposing trenches and continued on for miles past their assigned objectives. Colonel Frederick Funston led his Kansas regiment up the coast so fast that it came under fire from the *U.S.S. Charleston*. Officers of the California regiment even threatened to shoot their own men if they did not halt, but only fatigue ended that charge miles later. Once the Washington and Idaho regiments trapped some retreating Filipinos at midstream in the Pasig River, the slaughter began with a murderous cross fire. "From then on the fun was fast and furious," as the dead "piled up thicker than buffalo chips," one soldier wrote home. Another informed his father that "picking off niggers in the water is more fun than a turkey shoot."

The wild scramble for glory left Filipino stragglers behind American lines to snipe from the rear. The American Commander, General Elwell Otis, ordered a scorched earth tactic to deny cover for them, although he later attributed all the burning to the retreating enemy. The incident also created the widespread belief among American soldiers that wounded Filipinos left on the field were shooting at them. "Because a Filipino is so treacherous even when badly wounded, he has to be killed. When we find one that is not dead, we have our bayonets," one soldier explained to his parents. About 3,000 Filipino soldiers—but only 60 Americans—died that first day.

The American presence in Manila had begun with Admiral George Dewey's stunning victory on May 1, 1898, over Spain's Pacific Squadron anchored in Manila Bay, only days after Congress had declared war. Many Americans were surprised by the action, because the propaganda against Spain leading up to the war had focused on Spanish cruelty in suppressing a rebellion in Cuba, ignoring other Spanish colonies. Indeed, most Americans had never heard of the Philippines. As the character "Mr. Dooley" confessed, in a humorous newspaper column, he "didn't know if they were islands or canned goods." According to legend, the news of Dewey's victory even sent President William McKinley scurrying to a globe to discover the location of "these darned islands."

A small group of dedicated imperialists in government, led by Theodore Roosevelt and Massachusetts Senator Henry Cabot Lodge, knew their precise location, as they had their eyes on the Philippines for potential coaling stations and a naval base to protect America's trade routes to China. As assistant secretary of the navy, Roosevelt was instrumental in stationing a fleet under Dewey's command in Hong Kong to lie in wait for the war to begin. While waiting, the admiral and two American diplomats stationed in Hong Kong and Singapore began negotiations with exiled Filipino leaders of an earlier failed rebellion against Spanish rule in 1896. They would be potential allies against Spain should a war begin. Rebellion in the Philippines had flared anew, and Dewey urged this junta to join him when he sailed for Manila. The Filipinos were in Singapore, however, when America declared war, so Dewey left without them. Following his victory, he dispatched a ship to bring them to Manila. Before departing, Aguinaldo left money with an American diplomat to purchase arms for his cause.

Filipino dead in their trenches on the first day of combat, victims of deadly American naval and land bombardment that began without warning at dawn of February 5, 1899, after a 3 hour lull in the extensive, but ineffective, exchange of rifle fire that had erupted between the two lines the preceding evening. (National Archives)

Once back on Luzon, the largest, most populated island in the archipelago, Aguinaldo took charge of the rebellion and began to attack Spanish garrisons throughout the Philippines. He laid siege to Manila on its land side, bottling up the Spanish commanders. He also wrote a formal Declaration of Independence modeled after that of his "ally, the Great North American Nation, the cradle of liberty, and therefore friend to our people." The Declaration was "witnessed by the Supreme Judge of the Universe," and was "under the protection of the Mighty and Humane North American Nation." Lieutenant Colonel L. M. Johnson, commanding a small American advance party, signed this document for Aguinaldo as a witness. The nationalist leader then created a government at Malolos, designed a national flag, and ordered his legislative branch to write a constitution, again using the American one as a model. Most of this was accomplished before the American army arrived in significant force, and through it all, Aguinaldo received encouragement from his "good friend," Admiral Dewey.

By mid-June, the steady flow of American soldiers arriving aroused Aguinaldo's suspicions, but he reasoned with his own subordinates that the war

Filipino officers posing for a photographer before the Philippine-American War began. Most of these soldiers were shoeless and poorly equipped and trained, however proud and courageous. (Library of Congress)

in common against Spain, the apparent alliance, plus America's anti-colonial tradition and the fact that the U.S. Constitution made no provision for colonies, would ensure that America would not replace Spain as a new colonial master. Dewey was even able to persuade Aguinaldo to make room for the newly arrived American troops on his line of siege around Manila.

Aguinaldo discovered the extent of America's duplicity on August 11, 1898, when American troops took Manila after a prearranged sham battle with the Spanish that excluded the Filipinos. Aguinaldo's immediate resumption of his line of siege, bottling up the Americans in Manila, enraged American commanders, but Washington refused to give them a green light to attack him.

By December, when the Treaty of Paris officially confirmed Aguinaldo's worst suspicions, the relations between the two armies had already deteriorated to the breaking point. Insults, hostile gestures, and occasional bullets flew in both directions. American soldiers addressed Filipinos of whatever rank as "nigger," and, as one officer warned, "the natives are beginning to understand what 'nigger' means." American sentries took their frustrations out on unarmed Filipino soldiers passing through their lines to visit Manila. Some were knocked down with the butt of a Springfield rifle merely for "looking surly" or "seeming disrespectful." A few were shot for "looking suspicious." Such acts were generally committed by volunteers in the state regiments, already notorious among the regulars for their lack of discipline.

General Otis launched his own diplomatic offensive designed to humiliate the nationalists, ranging from petty refusals to return salutes from an "armed mob," lest it constitute recognition of Aguinaldo's "so-called government," to extraordinarily worded threats if Aguinaldo did not relinquish positions that Otis had quite arbitrarily decreed to be within Manila's municipal boundaries. Otis appears to have undertaken this entirely on his own. Indeed, on September 5th Otis informed Washington that "relations friendly, but require delicate manipulation." Three days later, he ordered Aguinaldo out of one position by September 15th, or he would be "obliged to resort to forcible action." So outrageous was the language of this ultimatum that Aguinaldo asked Otis to withdraw it in favor of a simple request with which he would comply. Otis refused even this face-saving plea. Aguinaldo withdrew, which evoked disgust from Otis's aide that the Filipinos would not fight in the face of such "humiliation." Otis also started a provocative surveillance of Filipino positions under the guise of "recreational activities," and he expressed outraged innocence when Aguinaldo banished back to Manila Americans caught photographing and measuring Filipino fortifications.

When the Spanish garrison at Iloilo on the island of Panay, some 300 miles south of Manila, offered to surrender to the Americans in December, Otis readied a task force under General Marcus Miller to occupy that city, but Dewey refused to transport it without specific orders from Washington. The orders came, but stipulated that the transfer of power must be peaceful. By the time Miller arrived at Iloilo at the end of December, the Spanish had already departed, and he was greeted by the mayor, who informed him that he may "not land foreign troops without express orders from the central government" at Malolos. In spite of Washington's orders, both Miller and Otis wanted to take the city by force, but Dewey vetoed this. Otis ordered Miller to hang on at anchor "until something happened."

Over the next few weeks, Otis made sure that "something" did. In the meantime, he carefully prepared himself for that event, ordering his officers out of dress whites and into "fighting khaki." He moved the Utah Battery up to a more favorable offensive position and coaxed Dewey into maneuvering his warships closer to shore on the flanks of Aguinaldo's semicircular line. On February 2, 1899, he discharged all Filipino civilians in his employ, placed his army on full alert, and tested the waters by ordering sentries posted at a hotly disputed position from which he had earlier forced the Filipinos to retreat. The colonel commanding the Nebraska regiment was personally on hand to post them, and a Filipino lieutenant called him a son of a bitch, whereupon the colonel ordered him arrested. The next day, Otis posted no sentries there, but on February 4th, he did so again, this time with instructions to shoot intruders. It paid off, creating the incident that justified Otis's full scale offensive the following dawn.

America had experienced only easy victories in the war against Spain. It lasted 100 days, leading Roosevelt to complain that "there wasn't war enough to go around." Dewey needed less than 6 hours to destroy the Spanish fleet caught napping at anchor, and the phony Battle of Manila lasted 3 hours. It was easy to assume that Aguinaldo's army had now been shattered in less than 12 hours. As evening approached on February 5th, Otis refused to meet with Aguinaldo's emissary carrying a peace proposal, who was curtly informed by an aide that he "lacked proper credentials," and that an audience with Otis might be construed as "recognition of [his] so-called political organization." Headlines proclaimed a total victory over a thoroughly demoralized enemy:

Aguinaldo Weeps for His Blunder
Sits Crying in His Quarters
Afraid to Surrender to the Americans

In reality, the war had just begun, and it would last another 41 months, claiming the lives of 4,200 American soldiers, while up to 20,000 Filipino troops would perish, along with about 200,000 civilians, most of whom would die of war-related starvation and disease. Nevertheless, to this day Washington maintains the official fiction that it was not a war, but merely an "insurrection."

General Arthur MacArthur, the father of Douglas (then a plebe at West Point), commanded the northern division that continued in pursuit of Aguinaldo. The Filipino commander was much too wise to risk battle with the Americans, who had superior firepower and marksmanship. He settled for delaying actions as he continued his steady retreat northward to a mountain refuge. He abandoned Malolos in flames, and narrowly missed entrapment several times by an American amphibious landing to his rear and "flying columns" of hard riding U.S. cavalry. Meanwhile, Otis, back in Manila, fired off salvos of press releases describing "smashing victories," or "crushing blows" and "final moments," which were dutifully parroted in the nation's press. Editors favored an analogy with former Indian wars, labeling the enemy "Filipino Braves," or even "Apaches" in their headlines.

Actually, the more heavily equipped Americans, prepared for more conventional battle, rarely caught up with their lightly clad adversaries, who moved swiftly on bare feet over familiar terrain. As one soldier complained to his parents, "you have niggers you can't see shoot at you until you get close enough to shoot at them and then Mr. Nigger tears off to another good place and shoots again." One wife in Kansas City sent hometown clippings to her husband, Lieutenant Samuel Lyon, a regular officer, who had fought in the "battles" ballyhooed in the local press. He wrote back: "I hope the idiotic newspapers haven't had you worried to death about those heavy engagements. 'Battles' out here are greatly exaggerated. This rebel is like a flea you can't see."

The war was fought as much in the headlines as it was on the field. It was not just a question of Otis's misleading dispatches, but also of some senior officers engaging in histrionics that had little military value in order to impress correspondents on hand and garner some personal media attention. Colonel Funston, one of the most feted heroes of this war, led a company-size charge into an already abandoned Malolos in flames. He joined three men to swim across a river to take an abandoned fortification when MacArthur had already forded that river elsewhere much closer to the retreating foe. Another publicity hound, General J. Franklin Bell, leapt from a rowboat to reconnoiter enemy defenses while swimming. Lyon pointed out to his wife that "the newspapers featured this, ignoring the fact that from the level of the water his view wasn't nearly as good as it would have been with a good glass on one of the ships or even in the rowboat."

Funston's heroism at Calumpit, however, was quite genuine in carrying out a very daring maneuver to outflank General Antonio Luna's well fortified position on the Rio Grande de Pampanga. Funston had two Kansans swim a line across the river and secure it to the opposite bank. He joined eight men on the first raft propelled across by that line. More trips augmented his force to 41, with which he surprised the enemy, who quickly retreated before discovering how small Funston's contingent was, and before dismantling the railroad bridge so coveted by MacArthur to haul supplies and artillery across the river. Funston was awarded the Congressional Medal of Honor and promoted to brigadier general of volunteers for this brilliant feat.

By May, the rainy season arrived, with the U.S. Army controlling little territory outside of Manila. When towns were taken, they were soon abandoned rather than permanently garrisoned, allowing the nationalists to return and murder any inhabitants suspected of cooperating with Americans during their brief occupation. Otis protected his ludicrously optimistic view of the war by imposing a rigid censorship on the correspondents. It became clear that the censorship was designed less to keep information from the enemy than to cover up Otis's ineptness as a commander. Reporters could bypass the censor by mailing dispatches to Hong Kong for transmission on its cable terminal, but that took time and also risked the general's wrath and possible deportation for "sedition." Finally, these correspondents, including those who were Otis's "favorites," rebelled, mailing a collective protest to their editors. Headlines in response blared that "Situation in the Philippines Is Not 'Well In Hand'," reversing one of Otis's pet phrases. The entire nation had been "snookered" by the "foolish pollyanna" of General Otis, lamented many editors. Oblivious to this reaction, Otis denied that there was any censorship, then announced the appointment of a new censor. He continued to release reports of "final blows" and "crushing victories," until one editor declared that Otis did not "even have enough sense to come in out of the rain."

Under the terms of their enlistment, the state volunteer regiments returned in the summer of 1899 and disbanded. As civilians, these veterans were free to impugn the official view of the war with no reprisal from Otis. They also corroborated the rumors of American atrocities that originated in private letters from soldiers, which were not subjected to censorship. As long as these letters were confined to small, local audiences, they were of little concern to Otis or the government. But sometimes one would fall into the hands of an editor opposed to the war, who would promptly publish it, and it would soon make the rounds of the anti-imperialist press. Then citizens would open their morning paper over coffee to discover a private "report on this nigger fighting business" in the Philippines:

> Last night one of our boys was found shot and his stomach cut open. Immediately orders were received from General [Lloyd] Wheaton to burn the town and kill every native in sight which was done to a finish. About 1,000 men, women and children were reported killed. I am probably growing hard-hearted, for I am in my glory when I can sight my gun on some dark skin and pull the trigger.

Other letters described widespread looting and senseless destruction of property. Captain Albert Otis (no relation to the general) boasted that he "had enough plunder for a family of six. The house I had in Santa Ana had five pianos. I couldn't take them, so I put a big grand piano out of a second story window. You can guess its finish." An Iowa volunteer expressed amazement over such conduct: "You have no idea what a mania for destruction the average man has when the fear of the law is removed. I have seen them . . . knock chandeliers and plate glass mirrors to pieces just because they could not carry them. It is such a pity."

Captain Matthew Batson wisely warned his wife not to let "outsiders" see his complaints to her about the conduct of American soldiers, "as it reflects on the discipline of our Army, and if published would cause me trouble." Batson described barbaric destruction, looting, and the slaughter of innocents. Americans "ransacked churches, private homes, and wantonly destroyed furniture, and not satisfied with this they enter cemeteries, break open the vaults and search the corpses for jewelry." He worried that "these people seem to be devout Catholics, and it will do no good to take their images of Christ and their saints and dress them up in ridiculous garb and generally insult their religion." Some soldiers, he added, "make no distinction between property belonging to insurgents, or the innocent, they simply loot everything they come to." Batson described the total destruction of a pretty village in Pampanga and the slaughter of its inhabitants for no apparent reason, before writing in anguish: "We come here as a Christian people to relieve them from the Spanish yoke and bear ourselves like barbarians."

Once such a letter found its way into print, it could not be ignored, and the War Department would order Otis to investigate. His idea of an investigation was to send a copy of the offending letter to the writer's commanding officer, who had little trouble wringing a retraction from him. It was just "a tall tale to thrill some maiden aunt in Wichita," or some such explanation was proffered. The imperialist press dutifully crowed that "the truth is now made clear," and "another atrocity fable failed the test of time."

On one occasion, however, Private Charles Benner refused to recant his report that Colonel Funston had ordered the Kansas regiment to take no prisoners. This forced Otis to order MacArthur to investigate. Benner confronted that general's advocate general with Private William Putnam, who confessed to shooting two prisoners under orders. Major John Mallory collected a number of corroborative affidavits, including two from officers, suggesting that Benner's original charge was accurate. Private Harris Huskey swore under oath that he had witnessed Major Wilder Metcalf shoot a prisoner on his knees begging for mercy. MacArthur forwarded Mallory's report to Otis, who, amazingly, ordered Benner court-martialed "for writing and conniving at the publication of the article which brought about this investigation," and also Putnam "for assisting by shooting, in the execution of two prisoners." When the judge advocate wisely warned Otis that "if put on trial, it is probable that facts would develop implicating many others," the matter was dropped.

As a civilian, however, Funston was not so easily protected. Charges that he had "commanded, condoned, and rewarded rapine and murder" came from his former officers and seeped into the press. One editor published a letter from a former civilian teamster with the Kansas regiment describing Funston leading a mock mass in a church while wearing stolen ecclesiastical garb to amuse his soldiers from the "Bible belt." A nurse accused him of looting two silver chalices and a lavishly embroidered robe he had removed from a statue of the Madonna to give to his wife.

Under clouds of suspicion, Funston accepted an offer to command a brigade of three new national volunteer regiments. He arrived in Luzon at the end of 1899, when the Filipino nationalists began guerrilla tactics, a mode of warfare not entirely suited to Funston's impetuous personality. He was not back long when he called a press conference to announce that he had just summarily executed two prisoners in retaliation for a successful ambush of his Macabebe Scouts. This confirmed the worst rumors that he had left behind, and a headline in the San Francisco *Call* announced that he would be court-martialed. Funston then claimed that he had been misquoted: The prisoners had been killed "while attempting to escape."

A year later, having survived yet another Army inquiry into his past conduct that was more of a cover-up, Funston again became the hero of the hour in the spring of 1901 when he masterminded and led a daring maneuver to capture Aguinaldo in his remote hideaway in Palanan, just off the rugged northeastern coast of Luzon. Soldiers in Funston's command captured a courier from Aguinaldo to his cousin, Baldomero, with a coded message requesting more troops. Once Funston deciphered it and persuaded the courier to reveal Aguinaldo's location, he assembled 80 Tagalog-speaking Macabebe volunteers to pose as the requested reinforcements. Four renegade "insurgent" officers and a former Spanish officer were recruited to play the roles of officers. Naturally, Funston had to get in on the act, so he and four American officers went along as "prisoners" captured en route to Palanan. The Navy dropped them off on the coast far enough away to avoid any detection, and the group trekked over 100 miles to grab Aguinaldo in the midst of a birthday celebration for him. The ruse was carried off so cleverly that the astonished Aguinaldo first thought it was a joke. Funston brought his prize back to the coast for a prearranged rendezvous with the U.S.S. Vicksburg on March 25, 1901.

Once again, Funston dominated the headlines. Editors compared his latest feat to Roosevelt's charge up San Juan Hill in Cuba, and even to Dewey's victory on Manila Bay. A year earlier, Republican leaders had thought his heroism at Calumpit would take Funston to Topeka as Governor of Kansas, but now they began to think in terms of a Roosevelt–Funston ticket in 1904. Vice

General Frederick Funston, aboard the U.S.S. Vicksburg. (National Archives)

President Roosevelt, long an admirer of Funston, whom he classified as "a perfect corker," pushed the president to reward him with a regular commission at his present rank, the youngest in the Army at age 41. Only weeks earlier McKinley had declared that Funston was "not a man of proper temperament for any rank higher than that of a lieutenant in the regulars." But now that Funston had become a national idol, McKinley, once dubbed "The Emperor of Expediency," capitulated.

As he often did following one of his escapades, Funston rushed into print his own version of this spectacular coup for a popular magazine in order to milk more publicity from it. By entitling the article "The Exploit Which Ended the War," he reinforced the popular view that he had singlehandedly ended this vexatious conflict. In reality, Aguinaldo was little more than figurehead for the nationalist forces during the guerrilla phase of the war. Indeed, the complete autonomy afforded local commanders by Aguinaldo's isolation made the guerrillas much more effective, as quick decisions could be made in response to immediate conditions. Thus the war continued for another 15 months officially, and on September 27, 1901, the Army suffered its worst setback in the war when bolomen, disguised as mourning women, charged out of a church in Balangiga on the island of Samar to massacre the American garrison there.

General Adna Chaffee, a celebrated Indian fighter with hard-line views on how to deal with "savages," had recently relieved MacArthur in command. He was encouraged "to take the most stern measures to pacify Samar" by his new commander-in-chief, Roosevelt, who had succeeded the assassinated McKinley shortly before the Balangiga disaster. Roosevelt made it clear that he did not intend "to repeat [in the Philippines] the folly of which our people were sometimes guilty when they petted hostile Indians." For the "pacification" effort, Chaffee handpicked another famous Indian fighter, General "Hell Roaring" Jacob Smith, already infamous in the anti-imperialist press for violating flags of truce and for having proudly posed for photographs in front of his "tiger cages," in which he crammed Filipino suspects for months with no toilet facilities. Smith's orders to Marine Major Littleton Waller, commanding a brigade on loan to the Army for the Samar campaign, were not subtle: "Kill and Burn! The more you kill and burn the more you will please me." He ordered Waller to make the island "a howling wilderness," and to kill all males 10 years and older found outside of the coastal towns. Actually, Waller had more respect than Smith for the rules of civilized warfare, and informed his men that under no circumstances were they to make war on women and children.

Chaffee had already unleashed General J. Franklin Bell in the province of Batangas in Southern Luzon. Bell, too, was a well known veteran of Indian wars, and like Chaffee, a cavalry hero. While his orders were not as bizarre as Smith's, they were in some ways more sinister. In writing, he gave his officers the "right of retaliation," and directed them "to execute a prisoner of war" for each guerrilla assassination, "one selected by lot from among officers and prominent citizens held [prisoner] . . . chosen when practicable from those who belong to the town where the murder or assassination occurred." Bell also created concentration camps. The Army euphemistically labeled these facilities "models of sanitation" and worried that their inhabitants might not want to leave them following pacification, but an estimated 11,000 Filipinos perished in them, although Bell's tactics merely exacerbated smallpox and cholera epidemics that had preceded him to Batangas.

The year 1902 opened with an investigation into the conduct of the war by Senator Henry Cabot Lodge's Committee on the Philippines, largely due to pressure from the senior senator from Massachusetts, George Frisbee Hoar, a rare anti-imperialist Republican. The first 2 months were spent listening to "safe" witnesses, such as Generals Otis, MacArthur, and Robert Hughes, Admiral Dewey, and Governor of the Philippines William Howard Taft. Even they made some damaging concessions. Hughes, for example, conceded that civilized warfare was not being waged by America, and then tried to justify this by insisting that it was impossible to do otherwise because the enemy was not "civilized." Taft admitted that the "water cure" had been used "on some occasions to extract information." He was referring to a rather mild form of torture in which the victim on his back was forced to swallow huge quantities of water, sometimes salted, until he talked. None died, or was rendered permanently disabled from it, but anti-imperialist propaganda had made it much more draconian in the public mind. As though sensing the enormity of his error, Taft tried

The *Evening Journal* in New York infuriated apologists for this war of conquest with this cartoon, inspired by General Smith's infamous orders to Marine Major Waller. "Of all the sins of 'yellow journalism,' this is by far the worst," The *New York Times* declared of it. There is some truth to this charge as Waller was much too professional to follow Smith's orders literally. (Newspaper Collection, The New York Public Library, Astor, Lenox and Tilden Foundations)

to make light of it, recounting that some Filipino suspects actually demanded that they be first subjected to this torture to have an excuse for divulging information. But the damage was done.

Critics on Lodge's committee soon forced the chairman to subpoena more critical witnesses, and by March, the public was being exposed to daily litanies of American atrocities. Ex-Corporal Richard O'Brien, for example, described the senseless destruction of a peaceful village ordered by ex-Captain Fred Mac-Donald, who spared only the life of a beautiful mestizo mother, whom he and the other officers repeatedly raped before turning her over to the men for their pleasure. Lodge desperately sought more "reliable" veterans, subpoenaing Mac-Donald to deny O'Brien's charges, which the chair then decreed to be "hearsay." Sometimes this backfired when a carefully selected witness, such as ex-Sergeant Mark Evans, testified that extermination of the natives was the only solution to the problem in the Philippines, and had to be quickly hustled off the stand. To end his investigation on a better note for the administration, Lodge recalled Dewey, Otis, MacArthur, and Taft before abruptly terminating the hearings in June, over anti-imperialist protests.

By then, however, new developments embarrassed the administration. Secretary of War Elihu Root rushed into print a document designed to demonstrate to the public that in those allegedly "rare instances" in which an American atrocity was committed, the perpetrators were swiftly and severely punished. Forty-four specific crimes committed by Americans were listed along with the punishments meted out. Despite Root's good intentions, the punishments were so ludicrously light that they quickly evoked editorial chortles in the opposition press. Six officers drew nothing more than reprimands for such crimes as rape, murder, and torture. But it was the case of Lieutenant Preston Brown that became the cause célèbre among anti-imperialists. Brown had been appropriately dismissed from the service and sentenced to 5 years at hard labor for murdering a prisoner, only to have President Roosevelt commute that sentence to forfeiture of half his pay for 9 months and a loss of 35 places on the promotion list!

Added to this was a series of devastating leaks to the press of very damaging documents thought to have been safely closeted under lock and key in the War Department. Investigations of Funston and of the rapine of Macabebe scouts against the hated Tagalogs, along with whistle blowing reports on Bell's Batangas campaign suddenly appeared in print. General Wheaton even agreed that "all native troops when they can escape the immediate control of their officers, are liable to commit murders, and they will rob and ravish whenever they have the opportunity." However, the private letters of their commanding officer, Major Batson, the same officer who once complained about similar conduct by American soldiers, reveal that he had encouraged such tactics:

> I am king of the Macabebes and they are terrors. . . . Word reaches a place that the Macabebes are coming and every Tagalo hunts his hole. . . . The time has come when it is necessary to conduct this warfare with the utmost rigor. "With fire and sword" as it were. But the numerous, so styled humane societies, and the poisonous press makes it difficult to follow this policy if reported to the world. . . .

> At present we are destroying, in this district, everything before us. I have three columns out, and their course is easily traced from the church tower by the smoke of burning houses. . . . Of course no official report will be made of everything.

The individual responsible for these leaks was unquestionably the Army's top commander, General Nelson Miles, who had presidential aspirations. To this end, he had pestered Roosevelt to place him in personal command of the army in the Philippines. When this was denied, Miles went on an inspection tour of the islands, and returned in complete agreement with the anti-imperialists that his Army had routinely committed atrocities, hoping that this issue might open a path for him to the Democratic nomination later that year. The *New York Times* called Miles "one of those birds which fouls its own nest," but Roosevelt refused to make him a martyr for the anti-imperialists, and he served until he reached mandatory retirement age in 1903.

In March, Root got word that Waller had executed eleven prisoners on Samar without benefit of trial. He must have seemed an ideal scapegoat to Root, coming from the rival Navy Department. To Root's chagrin, however, Waller was acquitted by a court-martial in Manila when he revealed the bizarre orders that he had received from Smith. Editors committed entire front-pages to bits and pieces of these orders in extraordinarily large type such as, "KILL ALL!" and "MAKE SAMAR A HOWLING WILDERNESS." One political cartoon depicted little Filipino boys lined up before a firing squad over the caption: "Criminals Because They Were Born Ten Years Before We Took the Philippines." In it, the American eagle was portrayed as a vulture in the national shield. Root simply had no choice but to court-martial Smith. He insisted, however, that Smith's orders were never meant to be taken literally, whereupon Smith declared to reporters that they were, and that this was the only way to fight "savages." Smith was found guilty in May and forced to retire.

As though the administration needed any more embarrassments, the war's greatest hero, "Fighting Fred" Funston, returned to the states early in 1902 to recover from a botched appendectomy. Over the next few months, Root might have wished that Army doctors had sewn up the general's mouth by mistake. Funston soon embarked on a cross country speaking marathon at various banquets in his honor. He was idolized by adoring crowds that blocked his train at whistle-stops until he emerged to say a few words. Headlines greeted "Aguinaldo's Brave Captor" in each city while hordes of reporters dogged him everywhere he went. He rarely disappointed them. Funston scorned the veterans testifying before the Lodge committee as "prattlers" feeding "tall tales" to a few "scoundrelly politicians"—that is, Democratic war critics. Such veterans had "ornamented the inside of a grog house longer than they distinguished themselves in the field," he declared. Funston also mocked Governor Taft's "misguided attempt to establish democracy" in pacified areas: "We believe everything and everybody should have a vote, down to cattle and horses." Instead, "bayonet rule" was needed, as "the only thing a Filipino respects is force." His greatest contempt was aimed at war critics, who "prolonged the war by giving the Filipinos false hopes." The "blood of fallen American boys was on their hands." Such speeches won congratulatory headlines and fawning editorials in the imperialist press: One front-page declared:

Bravo! General Funston
Great Speech By Little Kansan
Silence While Bullets Fly
Ignorant Talk At Home Has Slain Our Soldiers
Got Tremendous Applause and Prolonged Applause
And Cries of "That's Right!"

Either such headlines went to the general's head, or gin rickeys affected his judgment, as he would later claim, but Funston also bragged about an escalating number of prisoners that he had summarily executed to deter guerrilla activity. At the posh Lotus Club in New York City, this braggadocio took an even more ominous turn when Funston told of hanging two black American deserters, and suggested that it would have been better to string up war critics at home. For starters, he even suggested hanging those who had recently signed a peace petition to Congress. While imperialist editors remained silent, their anti-imperialist counterparts first expressed shock and then rage. "Funston Advises Hanging. Gallows Would Suit Some Americans," announced the *Call*'s front page, while its editor explained how prominent were Funston's proposed victims: "the presidents of nearly all American universities and the leading clergymen of all denominations in the union." The paper advised Funston "to repair his inflated condition and sheath his unruly mouth."

In the middle of his "gallows speech," Funston periodically shouted: "Bully for Waller!" All the way back to San Francisco, he would emerge from his train to shout this and "Hooray for Smith!" at adoring crowds. When he arrived, he insisted to the waiting reporters that he "stood by everything" he had said, although he did claim that his suggestion of hanging Americans was "merely an abstract comparison." He also informed astonished reporters that the president was in complete agreement with his views. That was too much for Roosevelt, who sent a private warning to Funston via their mutual friend, William Allen White, the eminent Kansas journalist, confidant of presidents and Republican leaders, and Funston's fraternity brother at the University of Kansas. Apparently Funston was unable to control self-destructive impulses. At his next duty station in Denver after his long "recuperation" furlough, he mocked "the overheated conscience" of Senator Hoar at a local banquet. This was the proverbial straw that broke the camel's back, and Root ordered him to give no more speeches or press interviews. An official presidential reprimand followed.

Not everybody was satisfied with front-page headlines announcing that "Roosevelt Muzzles Funston." Over the next few weeks, Hoar and fellow war critics denounced Funston for hours on the floor of the Senate. Senator Edward Carmack of Tennessee called him "the mightiest Sampson who ever wielded the jawbone of an ass as a weapon of war." Congressman Samuel McCall informed the Harvard Republican Club that he would push for an indictment, and would not be intimidated "by the threats of some microscopic general [Funston was about 5 feet, 4 inches tall] who knows as much about the rules of civil government as he does about the rules of civilized warfare." But Funston led a charmed life, and he managed to escape relatively unscathed.

In the midst of all this political *sturm and drang,* Roosevelt pulled the rug from under his critics by simply declaring that the war was over in his Fourth of July speech in 1902. Describing it as the most glorious war in the nation's history, he commended "the bravery of American soldiers" fighting "for the triumph of civilization over the black chaos of savagery and barbarism." He did express regret over "the few acts of cruelty in retaliation [for] the hundreds committed by Filipinos against American soldiers."

AN INTERPRETATION

Roosevelt would have been on firmer ground arguing that atrocities on both sides are endemic to guerrilla warfare, enhanced in this case on the American side by the rapid expansion of the Army that spread experienced junior and noncommissioned officers too thin. Senior officers, such as Wheaton, Bell, and Smith, along with the commanders who protected them, Otis, MacArthur, and Chaffee, had spent most of their military careers fighting Indians, which probably hardened them to a certain amount of brutality. Funston did not have the luxury of this excuse. While most soldiers were too young to have fought in Indian wars, they were predominantly Western and Southern descendants of Indian fighters, often alluding to this in letters home. Add to this recipe, the intense nationalism of the era along with the vicious racism that permeated American society at the turn of the century, and one comes up with a formula that made it that much easier for many American soldiers to dehumanize the Filipinos, often ignoring the rules of civilized warfare. Even those who initially criticized such brutality, such as Batson and Lyon, soon capitulated to the view of the majority.

There has been considerable scholarly debate over the causes of an American empire. Some argue that empire was the product of monopoly capitalism. Yet most businessmen opposed the war with Spain; the country had just emerged from a serious depression, and they simply did not want to risk the recovery with new, unpredictable adventures. Other scholars have emphasized the roles of a few well-placed imperialists, including Roosevelt, Lodge, and Dewey. But their imperialistic appetites were severely limited. They wanted strategically located pin-point colonies rather than large, heavily populated ones. Their interest was in coaling stations and naval bases to protect American interests in Asia. They specifically wanted to avoid "England's folly in India," and were initially interested in keeping Manila alone. Aggressive German naval maneuvers in the Philippines plus Japan's colonial interests enhanced the military's argument that Manila alone was indefensible.

Ultimately, the popular appeal of an empire was too strong to resist. The jingoistic fury of the people pushed McKinley into escalating his demands beyond Manila to Luzon and, by summer's end, to the entire archipelago. Having been patriotically aroused to fight Spain, emotional inertia alone made it easier for Americans to conquer the Philippines in the name of "civilization."

There is a related lesson to be learned in the attitudes toward the war that are revealed in the letters that servicemen sent home to family and friends. In our own day, the official ideology of war requires that war at least be talked about as if it were at best an unfortunate event, to be completed as quickly as possible and with as little blood and gore—hopefully, as in the Gulf War of 1990, in a series of "surgical" strikes.

The turn-of-the-century youth who fought in the jungles of the Phillipines did not feel that way. They were full of passion for the action and excitement, the shooting and killing, that were part of the conflict. Youth enthusiastically embraced imperialism at the turn of the century, perceiving an empire as a new "frontier" that would both challenge them and provide new opportunities. Above all, the empire offered adventure. As a result, there were no problems getting young men to volunteer to serve in the war, and the morale of the soldiers was extraordinarily high, in spite of the inept and uninspiring leadership of General Otis. Young, swashbuckling, and bumptious leaders, such as Frederick Funston and Theodore Roosevelt, became national idols and spokesmen for the nation's warrior tradition.

American rule was also characterized by ambivalence and limits. As the story reveals, not all Americans approved of the nation's overseas adventures, and criticism in the press and congress did not end with the war. While the United States was the last of the major powers to acquire an empire, it was also the first to become disillusioned with a formal empire, turning internal control over to Filipino *independistas* by 1907 and pledging future independence in the Jones Act of 1916, when Britain was still jailing Indians calling for independence. At bottom, neo-imperialism—those indirect informal controls over legally independent states—has always been more attractive to Americans. Not only is it more cost effective, but it also protects American innocence with the illusion that the nation can at once have an informal empire, and yet be true to its sacred principle of self-determination.

Sources: Most of the sources for this essay were primary ones, particularly the manuscript collection at the United States Army Military History Research Center at Carlisle Barracks in Pennsylvania. Letters, diaries, unpublished manuscripts and unofficial army newspapers written by hundreds of soldiers from private to general are here. More such records are in the Library of Congress and the National Archives, particularly papers of important leaders, civilian and military, during the war. Other archives, at Harvard, the Boston Atheneum, and the Historical Societies of Massachusetts, Pennsylvania, and California were valuable for the papers of anti-imperialists. Senate and House documents, reports of commanding generals and the War Department were also used along with a carefully balanced, geographically and politically, sample of newspapers and periodicals. Such contemporary publications as *Public Opinion* and *Literary Digest* were valuable in tapping editorial opinion across the nation.

Related secondary works were also examined such as the books written by Teodoro Agoncillo, Bonifacio Salamanca, Reynaldo Ileto, Theodore Friend, Glenn May, Peter Stanley, David Joel Steinberg, E. Berkeley Tomkins, and Richard Welch, among others.

5

ARTIFICIAL INSEMINATION: THE FIRST DEBATE

ELAINE TYLER MAY

The story that follows is really two stories, each with its own context, but curiously inseparable. The first story is from 1884, when, if one can believe a report that later appeared in a medical journal, a prominent physician artificially inseminated a woman—in front of a class of medical students, and without the woman's permission. So extraordinary are the details that the author, Elaine Tyler May, is not entirely sure if all the events described really happened. While disturbing in one sense, this uncertainty is helpful and interesting in another: the story can be useful in evaluating how historians—indeed, all of us—sift and weigh evidence and determine what is true. Among the methods May uses to examine the veracity of the "facts," historical context is especially important. That is, stories are more likely to be true if the details and facts appear to exist comfortably within a larger, identifiable, historical context.

The second story May tells is from 1909—in the midst of the period of social reformism known as the Progressive Era—when the earlier event was first revealed and then vigorously debated within the medical community. Even if the first story never happened, the second can yield important insights into the society and culture of the early twentieth century. As May's story reveals, the 1909 discussion posed the necessity of scientific and technological "progress" (represented by the insemination) against the requirements of religion and morality. The debate also swirled around questions of genetic breeding that were very much a part of an era when even respectable people—among them Theodore Roosevelt—were concerned that the "racial purity" of the American population was being compromised by high levels of immigration from the "wrong" nations.

The physicians who debated the case also shared a perspective very common among Progressive-Era reformers: They believed that all problems could be solved, and that only experts—experts like themselves—could solve them. This attitude could lead to dramatic social progress. But all too many experts also believed that ordinary people were too stupid or ignorant to have anything important to say, even about their own lives. Thus the physician who impregnated the woman in this story did so with a lack of respect for her wishes. And of those who years later exchanged opinions in the medical journals, few were much concerned with discussing the case from her point of view. Although women actively campaigned for the suffrage throughout the

Progressive Era, their claim to equality in the political sphere had not—at least not yet, or for the male physicians who held forth in the pages of the medical journals— spilled over into the area of reproductive rights. Decades later, when birth control, abortion, and surrogate motherhood are regularly discussed in the most public forums, a curious and even bizarre turn-of-the-century case of artificial insemination presents a rare opportunity to look back—back to the future.

In 1909, a brief article in the *Medical World* unleashed a storm of controversy. A physician by the name of Addison Davis Hard wrote that he had witnessed the first human conception by a procedure he called "artificial impregnation." The event he reported had occurred 25 years earlier, in 1884, when he was a student at the Jefferson Medical College in Philadelphia. He claimed that the event he witnessed was performed by his professor, the noted physician Dr. William Pancoast. According to Dr. Hard, a prominent couple living in Philadelphia in the 1880s were distraught over their inability to have children.

Dr. William Henry Pancoast, 1835–1897, is reported to have performed the first artificial insemination by donor on an unconscious female patient in 1884, using the sperm of a medical student. (National Library of Medicine, History of Medicine Division, Prints and Photographs Collection)

The 41-year-old husband was a successful merchant; his wife was a wealthy Quaker woman 10 years his junior. They had the means to pursue their goal of parenthood by seeking the best medical assistance available.

The couple sought out the assistance of one of Philadelphia's most prominent physicians, Dr. William Pancoast, who was affiliated with the prestigious Philadelphia Hospital. Dr. Pancoast found their case to be puzzling, as he found no apparent cause for the couple's difficulty. In spite of the knowledge of the function of sperm, it was still widely believed that if a man was not sexually impotent, he was presumed to be fertile. Because the husband did not suffer from impotence, Dr. Pancoast suspected that the problem resided with his wife. He therefore decided to examine her first. Victorian delicacy did not prevent the doctor and his six students from conducting a thorough investigation. Dr. Hard described the exam as "very complete, almost as perfect as an army examination." The doctor concluded that there were no physiological impediments to impregnation. He went so far as to claim that the examination provided evidence to prove a widely held theory about reproduction: that female orgasm facilitated conception. While it is not clear precisely how the examination proved this theory, Dr. Hard noted that "during this examination was discovered for the first time, as far as I know, the suction function of the uterus, which takes place during orgasm." Whether or not the evidence was valid, it does suggest that the exam went beyond the merely superficial. It also indicates that medical theories at the time were profoundly influenced by ancient folk beliefs, such as the myth of the suction of the uterus during orgasm.

The examination revealed no physiological abnormality. The woman was therefore spared the common treatments used to correct female sterility, such as bleeding of the cervix with leeches, the application of electricity, and the use of various surgeries and mechanical appliances to rearrange the reproductive organs. She was also spared the typical behavioral prescriptions, such as the regime recommended by one contemporary physician: infrequent coitus, pure air, quietude of mind, temperance in food, drink, and sleep, and the "cultivation of correct habits of mind and body." Having determined that the woman had no impediment to fertilization, Dr. Pancoast surmised that the problem might reside with her husband. Although the husband was not impotent, there was the chance that something might be wrong with his semen. The doctor examined him and found no physical defect. But when he studied the semen under the microscope, he found that it contained absolutely no sperm. Dr. Pancoast informed the man of his findings, and suggested that the problem probably resulted from an early bout of gonorrhea, contracted in his youth. Dr. Pancoast then began a course of treatment that he assumed would remedy the problem.

After 2 months of treatment, however, the patient showed no sign of improvement. At this point, one of the students in the class allegedly made a joking remark, suggesting that "the only solution of this problem is to call in the hired man." Although made in jest, the remark gave Dr. Pancoast an idea, which led to an unusual plan of action. In the presence of his six students, he anesthetized the woman with chloroform. While she was unconscious, Dr. Pancoast selected the "best looking member of the class" to provide semen for the experiment. Using a rubber syringe, he inserted the semen of the student into the uterus of the patient. As it turned out, conception occurred, and she became pregnant.

At this point, according to Dr. Hard, Dr. Pancoast became a bit nervous. He had neither asked permission nor even informed the woman or her husband of the procedure before doing it, and now the woman was expecting a child. Reluctantly, Dr. Pancoast decided he must inform the husband (although not the wife) of what he had done. Fortunately for the doctor, the man was pleased. His only request was for absolute secrecy, so that nobody should ever know what happened, not even his wife. He preferred that she remain ignorant of his early bout of gonorrhea, as well as the method of her impregnation. It was a request Dr. Pancoast was more than happy to grant. Because the procedure was ethically questionable, Dr. Pancoast pledged the six students who witnessed the event to absolute secrecy.

Nine months later, the patient allegedly gave birth to a healthy son, whom she raised according to appropriate middle-class standards. He grew up to follow in his father's footsteps, and by the time he reached the age of 25 years he had moved to New York and become a successful businessman. Nobody ever knew about the peculiar means of his conception. His mother assumed he was the biological child of her husband—indeed, it was said that he resembled his father. But the medical students present at the insemination did not forget, and one in particular—most likely the sperm donor himself—maintained a lifelong interest in the case.

Twenty-five years after the child's birth, when Dr. Pancoast was no longer alive, the most interested of the former medical students finally decided to go public with his story. Dr. Addison Davis Hard, 25 years earlier undoubtedly the "best looking" student in Dr. Pancoast's class, was now a general practitioner in Marshall, Minnesota. To satisfy his curiosity, he traveled to New York in 1909 to see the young man (who in all likelihood he had sired), and there "shook his hand."

The above account, written in 1909 by Dr. Addison Davis Hard, is all that we know about the event that he described. Dr. Pancoast had died 11 years prior to the publication of the article, and therefore could neither verify nor deny the account. No other witness stepped forward to confirm the report, and no other medical journal at the time made reference to the event. Yet we do know that Dr. Pancoast was a well-known physician at the time, and it is also true that Dr. Addison Davis Hard was indeed a physician in Marshall, Minnesota, in 1909, because his name appears in the professional roster. As the couple who allegedly parented this child are not named, there is no way to locate them or their offspring. How do we know that the event really happened? In fact, we do not know. Perhaps Dr. Hard made it up. But there are reasons to believe that it might have happened. It was certainly consistent with medical knowledge, procedures, and ideas in late-nineteenth century America.

At the time of the alleged experiment, faith in science to bring about progress was increasing. A few decades earlier, Charles Darwin had proclaimed his famous theory of evolution, affirming the "survival of the fittest." At the same time, the crusade for scientific human breeding, known as eugenics, was gaining popularity. Throughout the nineteenth century, several experimental utopian communities developed novel ways to manage sex, reproduction, and family life. One of the most controversial was the Oneida community, which in the 1840s put into place a program of eugenic reproduction that lasted 2 decades, and gained a great deal of attention—mostly negative. The Oneida reproductive experiment was known as stirpiculture, a system in which the founder of this perfectionist religious community, John Humphrey Noyes, determined which individuals could procreate, in order to create a generation of people who were better (that is, more free of sin) than the previous generation. The system prohibited marriage or any exclusive attachments, but established a "free love" environment in which any two individuals could have intercourse, according to certain rules. The man was to make the request through a third party, the woman was expected to consent, and the couple were to avoid pregnancy by "male continence"—a sexual practice based on prolonged intercourse without ejaculation.

Needless to say, contemporaries criticized the community as "promiscuous" and evil, even though it was based on Noyes' notions of the best way to achieve perfect holiness. It attracted the attention of the scientific community, however, because of its experiment in human breeding. As the nineteenth century advanced and the national population became more diverse, the notion of human breeding as a means of social reform became increasingly popular. Eugenicists believed that the "best" human stock (generally defined as white Anglo-Saxon Protestant) should be encouraged to reproduce, while those they defined as inferior (including poor southern European immigrants, people of color, and the "mentally defective") should be discouraged or prevented from procreating. These ideas gained adherents among the American-born white middle class, whose numbers had been declining, relative to the rest of the population, for nearly a century. In this context, childlessness among the "better classes" became a matter of national concern.

By the time the affluent Philadelphia couple turned to the medical profession for help, physicians had been attempting to cure childlessness for decades. Medical knowledge in the area of reproduction was advancing rapidly. Although a full understanding of the female cycle was still decades away, enough was known about female physiology to diagnose the malfunction of certain organs. Medical practitioners also recognized the function of sperm in the process of conception, and by the 1880s the more knowledgeable physicians routinely investigated husbands as well as wives in their efforts to discover the causes of childlessness.

The physician drew on earlier experiments in treating infertility and came up with a novel innovation. Dr. Pancoast was undoubtedly familiar with the work of a physician by the name of J. Marion Sims, who wrote up his notes in 1869 after decades of clinical practice. In his book, *Notes on Uterine Surgery with Specific Reference to the Management of the Sterile Condition*, he recounted several cases of sterility in women treated by surgical and non-surgical means. He was apparently among the first to use an "impregnator" tool, a syringe device, to facilitate conception. In cases where sperm did not travel adequately to fertilize the egg, Dr. Sims used the tool to deposit the semen of the husband directly into the uterus of the wife. The procedure was used when the man's sperm appeared to be viable but some physiological impediment seemed to hinder conception. It was not a very successful form of treatment. Dr. Sims used the syringe 55 times, with only one pregnancy resulting, and ultimately gave up the practice.

Dr. Sims also used anesthesia to render his female patients unconscious in order to perform procedures without their discomfort. He related some infertility cases in which anesthesia was used to facilitate conception without the aid of the syringe. He termed the procedure "ethereal copulation." One patient in par-

What Kind of Children?

By courtesy of Edison Lamp Works

Children get their basic qualities by inheritance. If they are to be strong, keen, efficient, and great, there must be good blood back of them

If you want your children to be well-born, choose your husband because of fine qualities in his family as well as in himself. Then add the best training

These make a square deal for the children

This poster, part of the Youth and Life exhibit of the American Social Hygiene Association in 1922, illustrates popular eugenic values about properly bred progeny. Ideas such as these influenced the discussion of artificial insemination as a means to "improve the race." (American Social Health Association Records, Social Welfare History Archives, University of Minnesota)

ticular suffered extreme pain with sexual intercourse, rendering conception impossible. Dr. Sims described the case as it developed under the care of another physician, before the couple came to him for assistance. "Suffice it to say that it became the business of the physician to repair regularly to the residence of this couple two or three times a week to etherize the poor wife. . . . They persevered, hoping that she would become pregnant. . . . This etherization was continued for a year, when conception occurred. . . . At the end of another year of ethereal copulation, there was another conception, which resulted in [a miscarriage] at the third month. After this she was etherized constantly for nearly another year, when at last they saw no hope of a cure, and becoming alarmed at the frequent repetition of the anaesthesia, they concluded to give it up altogether. And when they consulted me there had been no effort at copulation for three or four years." The woman's two conceptions "took place while she was in a state of complete anaesthesia," which was apparently the only way she could tolerate intercourse. Eventually, Dr. Sims performed surgery. Dr. Pancoast must have been aware of this use of anaesthesia, as well as the experiments with the syringe. But he utilized these tools in a new way. His novel innovation was the use of a sperm donor.

It was the introduction of the sperm donor into the process of reproduction that was most intriguing to eugenicists and most appalling to moralists. To understand the impact of the story, it is critical to keep in mind the historical setting in which the story unfolded. Although the actual event presumably took place in 1884, it was not reported until 1909, when Dr. Hard described it in the *Medical World*. By this time, the Progressive Era was in full swing, and social reforms backed by scientific theories gained the support of much of the middle class. While many reformist impulses of the era were humanitarian and forward-looking, such as concerns over working conditions in factories and regulation of big business, others were backward-looking efforts to preserve the status quo in the face of social change, such as immigration restriction. One of the features of the new century that most worried some of the more conservative reformers was the declining birthrate of the white American-born population. Although the downward trend had prevailed for over a century, it caused increasing alarm in the early years of the 20th century because of what appeared to be the relatively high birthrate of the immigrants, ethnic minorities and nonwhite peoples. Many feared the rapid population growth of what they believed to be inferior people. Some even argued that medical advances extending the lives of the poor were disrupting the natural processes of evolution. President Roosevelt was one of the first Progressive leaders to warn of "race suicide," and urged the "best stock" of Americans to attend to their reproductive duties so that the nation would not be overrun by the "inferior races." Other reformers, including the radical birth-control advocate Margaret Sanger, were also drawn to the concept of scientific breeding known as eugenics, because of its utopian possibilities. The different strains of Progressive reform came together in complicated ways over the issue of reproduction.

Among those who believed in the principles of planned breeding as a means to improve society was Dr. Hard. In his article in the *Medical World* in which he described the artificial impregnation of 1884, he extolled the virtues of the procedure as a way to improve the racial stock of the nation. "[A]rtificial impregnation offers valuable advantages," he wrote. "The mating of human beings must, from the nature of things, be a matter of sentiment alone. Persons of the worst possible promise of good and healthy offspring are being lawfully united in marriage every day. Marriage is a proposition which is not submitted to good judgement or even common sense, as a rule. . . . Artificial impregnation by carefully selected seed, alone will solve the problem." The problem, according to Dr. Hard, was that the wrong people would mate and create inferior offspring.

Hard argued that the seed carries the essential human qualities. But he immediately reversed himself by claiming instead that the "true father" is not he who contributes the sperm, but rather the husband of the mother who gives the child birth. "It may at first shock the delicate sensibilities of the sentimental who consider that the source of the seed indicates the true father, but when the scientific fact becomes known that the origin of the spermatozoa which generates the ovum is of no more importance than the personality of the finger which pulls the trigger of a gun, then objections will lose their forcefulness, and artificial impregnation become recognized as a race-uplifting procedure."

Dr. Hard chose a particularly vivid and violent metaphor to describe the process. A gun is a symbol of masculine prowess and force. By using the metaphor of the "personality of the finger," he downplayed the role of the father in raising the child, while underscoring the power of the man's "gun." It was an effective means of reconciling the apparent contradiction in his argument. He then extolled one of the most time-honored of all American values: motherhood. Ultimately, he argued, it matters little who contributes the sperm because "[i]t is gradually becoming well establisht [sic] that the mother is the complete builder of the child. It is her blood that gives it material for its body, and her nerve energy which is divided to supply its vital force. It is her mental ideals which go to influence, to some extent at least, the features, the tendencies, and the mental caliber of the child. 'Many a man rocks another man's child and thinks he is rocking his own,' for it looks like him. And often two children by the same parents have features entirely dissimilar. It is the predominating mental ideals prevailing with the mother that shapes [sic] the destiny of the child." In other words, the "gun" creates the child, but the mother molds it.

Hard's final comments represent the sentiment of turn-of-the-century eugenicists who believed that scientific breeding held the key to the nation's future. He exhorted his readers to heed his advice: "A scientific study of sex selection without regard to marriage conditions might result in giving some men children of wonderful mental endowments, in place of half-witted, evil-inclined, disease-disposed offspring which they are ashamed to call their own. The mechanical method of impregnation, whether it be the orthodox way, or the aseptic surgeon's skillful fingers, counts but little, except sentiment, and sentiment is fast becoming a servant instead of a master in the affairs of the human race. Few are the children who are brought intentionally into this world. As a rule they are but the incidental result of a journey in search of selfish pleasure. They are seldom sought, and often unwelcome when they put in their first appearance. The subsequent mother's love is largely a matter of growth, for affection is but an attribute of selfishness."

Recognizing that these ideas might offend his readers, Hard defended his proposition by attacking the virtue of his critics, while also articulating the widespread alarm over epidemic venereal disease prevailing at the time. "The man who may think this idea shocking, probably has millions of gonococci swarming in his seminal ducts, and probably his wife has had a laparotome which nearly cost her life itself, as a result of his infecting her with the crop reaped from his last planting of 'wild oats.' One man in every five in New York City was found to be free from the contamination of venereal disease to an extent that rendered him safe around the house in which a woman lived.

"Go ask the blind children whose eyes were saturated with gonorrheal pus as they struggled thru the birth canal to emerge into this world of darkness to endure a living death; ask them what is the most shocking thing in this whole world. Ask Helen Keller what is the most shocking thing in this sin-soaked ball of selfish pursuits. They will tell you it is the idea that man, wonderful man, is infecting 80 percent of all womankind with the satanic germs collected by him as his youthful steps wandered in the 'bad lands.'"

Dr. Hard must have been familiar with a report of a committee of New York physicians that estimated that as many as 80 percent of the men in the city had been infected with gonorrhea. Whatever the actual incidence, such reports fueled concerns over an epidemic of venereal disease. There is no doubt that venereal disease was a serious problem. A Boston doctor at the time found over one-third of a sample of male hospital patients infected with gonorrhea. But it was not Dr. Hard's discussion of venereal disease that provoked his readers. It was the procedure he described.

When Dr. Hard published his account in 1909, the reaction ranged from outrage to applause. The controversy centered around the role of the medical profession in reproduction. It is important to recognize that although the procedure was identified as a medical phenomenon, it required no complicated medical technology nor specialized expertise. Artificial insemination required nothing more than a rubber syringe and a willing donor. Virtually anyone could do it. Yet, the process was claimed as a medical innovation, and the offspring born by this method were the first to acquire the misnomer of "test-tube babies." For nearly a century after Dr. Pancoast allegedly performed his experiment, artificial insemination, as it came to be called, remained under the control of the medical profession.

Because the notice of this event appeared in a medical journal, the controversy remained confined to the medical community. Most of the readers who responded in the Letters to the Editor section of the journal were horrified by Dr. Hard's account. Two questioned whether the event actually took place. Dr. C. H. Newth, for example, found the entire account unthinkable. "I wondered what [Dr. Hard] had eaten for supper, or what is his brand of drinking water. Dr. Pancoast was a gentleman, and would not countenance the raping of a patient under anesthetic. I must say that it should not have been told as a fact, but as a dream, which it probably was." Dr. Newth went on to question the very idea of a couple subjecting themselves to such indignities. "In the first place it is an impossible story that a wealthy merchant should present himself and wife for a 'private and confidential examination,' with a 'section of the class' of medical students to 'assist.' The story of taking the gentleman's seminal fluid to be examined by the students to see if it contained any 'spermatozooans' is a flight of fancy. . . . Accusing the professor of raping his patient with the semen of 'the best looking member of the class,' a preposterous crime, is certainly going a little." Dr. Newth also refuted Dr. Hard's theory of the relative insignificance of the sperm in terms of the resulting offspring. He argued that if Dr. Hard were correct that the sperm is merely the agent that triggers conception, like the "finger which pulls the trigger of a gun," then the child should resemble not the father but rather "the hard rubber syringe used after the masturbation of the best looking member of the class." He closed by railing one last time against "this chimera of a disordered brain."

Dr. N. J. Hamilton agreed with Dr. Newth that the event couldn't have really happened. In the June issue of *Medical World*, Dr. Hamilton explained that initially he was reluctant to respond because "it was so ridiculously criminal I hesitated to say anything on the subject." But then he went on to note that he actually performed a similar procedure frequently in his own practice. He noted that since his graduation in 1886, he had been in general practice and had "given the study and treatment of sterile married ladies much thought and attention." He claimed that "All cases coming under my treatment have been relieved in one of two ways: medicinally or by using the impregnator (of course, I mean all cases where the fault was the woman's). Have used the impregnator frequently. Have used these treatments for fifteen years without failure." His success record is, of course, a dubious claim, but he went on to describe using "an instrument which has a long, flexible point" to insert semen directly into a woman's uterus. The critical difference here, of course, was that the "impregnator" facilitated conception with the sperm of the woman's husband in cases where some physiological impediment existed in the woman. The purpose of Dr. Pancoast's procedure as described by Dr. Hard was exactly the opposite: to enable a woman to bear a child when her husband was sterile. Dr. Hamilton concluded by claiming that there was nothing new about the procedure itself; indeed, it had been used for decades. But as for Pancoast's use of the sperm of a donor, "I could hardly give it credence." His point, of course, was that although it was certainly possible—even simple—to perform such a procedure, it was entirely unthinkable to believe that any self-respecting physician would do such a thing.

The June issue of the *Medical World* contained additional responses. C. L. Egbert apparently believed the story, but was outraged by it. Dr. Egbert moved the debate from the realm of science to the realm of religion. He claimed that insemination was worse than rape, for it violated the laws of God, which are "good and sufficient on the subject of false intercourse. . . .[Y]ou have no right by any process of reasoning developt [sic] in your own mind or otherwise to break down the marriage laws of God. The deed of your professor was nei-

ther honest nor moral. It would have been a thousand fold better and more
honorable had your professor seduced that woman while conscious; or, if you
please, just as honorable had he had intercourse with her while unconscious."

The same writer also took issue with Dr. Hard's claims about the mother
as the one who shapes the child. He was offended that the role of the father was
considered so unimportant. He called Dr. Hard's argument "a ridiculous jum-
ble of facts. As to his scientific (?) part, he tells us that it is the mother who is
the complete builder of the child." He then pointed out Dr. Hard's contradictory arguments: "Now he has just told us that the male seed didn't amount to
anything. That all the tendencies . . . were from the mother." If so, then how
could inferior sperm lead to "half-witted, evil-inclined, disease disposed" offspring? Finally, Egbert defended himself against Hard's accusation that "the
man who thinks this idea shocking probably has millions of gonococci swarming
in his seminal ducts." He asserted that he did find the article shocking, "not

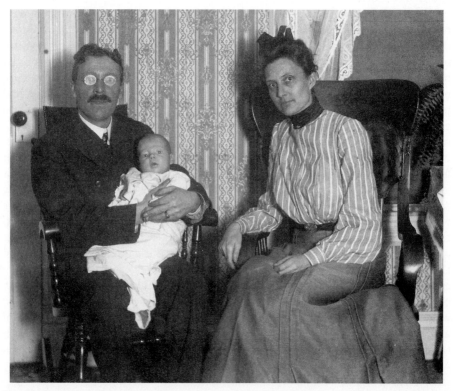

By the turn of the twentieth century, fathers became more fully identified as
participants in the nurturing of children. A formal family portrait such as this,
with a father holding an infant, would have been highly unusual in the nineteenth century. The controversy surrounding artificial insemination included
questions about the importance of fathers in the act of conception as well as
childrearing. At a time when motherhood was considered the epitome of womanhood, what was the role of men in parenting? (Minnesota Historical Society)

only to me but to any male or female who has a proper understanding of marital relations or the laws of God. But I wish to assure [Dr. Hard] that there are no gonococci in my seminal ducts, even if this answer would imply such to his mind. And furthermore, I have as healthy and bright a child as one could wish for, and she was not begotten with a hard rubber syringe, either." James W. Graham echoed this sentiment, and wrote, "As regards the finding of the gonococci: If I were anxious to make a microscopical examination of this micro-organism, I should select the semen of the fellow with the hard rubber syringe, or the one who advocates the abolishing of the marriage bond; and would be disappointed if I couldn't find them."

Others were more enthusiastic about the reproductive experiment Dr. Hard described. J. Morse Griffin endorsed the procedure on eugenic grounds. Griffin himself had "personally used the impregnator with success on mares that were apparently steril [sic]" with good results, and claimed that if "from a commercial standpoint, it be a paying process in the animal kingdom, why would not its influence be many times greater in the human family?" Griffin went beyond the impregnation process, however, in his advocacy of efforts to eradicate the scourge of venereal disease: "Male colts that are not promising individuals are promptly castrated, and yet they are not diseased, and in this way the quality of horse flesh is looking forward; but we are standing idly by and witnessing thousands of infected young men of fine families select a pure, innocent young girl, perhaps your own, to deposit the deadly seed of his 'prodigal' reaping, resulting in the train of symptoms in women so common to the surgeon today. And further than this, the effect is carried down to posterity . . . if the unlikely colt is denied the privilege of sending down the line of his descent an inferior progeny, why tolerate the same, combined with disease, to go on unmolested in the human family. . . . Why not adopt the castration plan in the human family and save the state and Nation the responsibility of having the charge in the state institutions of these deaf, blind, insane, and criminals?"

While not going so far as to advocate castration, Dr. Ernest Barton wrote in the July issue of the *Medical World* that "it was bad taste to tell this story on a dead confrere." Still, he endorsed the procedure: "If Dr. Pancoast had permission from the woman in the first place and the husband in the second place, then whose biznes [sic] is it to find fault?" Of course, no such permission was requested or granted. Dr. Barton nevertheless denounced those who criticized Dr. Pancoast's experiment in the name of the "laws of God." He affirmed the principles of eugenic breeding in terms of science over superstition. To make his point, he noted, "Just think how Luther Burbank has violated 'God's Ways' and committed rape and promiscuousness thousands of times with his flowers, by putting pollen where it would otherwise not have fallen. . . . The result is a thornless rose, thornless cactus, new variety of fruits and berries. . . . Would to God we could, by proper selection and still other means, breed off the thorns from *our* nature, the dunghill tendencies of our habits. . . . What matters it, if the children are fine, whether the instrument is a hard rubber syringe. . . . ?" He called for scientific progress to free humankind from the shackles of the past: "How long, oh, how long shall we allow the shades of the dead, the notions of the dead, the edicts of the dead and follies of the dead to rule us, to blind us, to tyrannize over us, and to cramp us in our struggle for knowledge?" In a strong attack on the religious opposition, he asserted, "Truly the living belongs to us—the dead past belongs to God."

After months of controversy, Dr. Hard finally responded to the many letters his article had sparked. He described his delight at the debate he had provoked: "I cannot convey to you an idea of the amount of pleasure that the varied answers to my article on 'Artificial Impregnation' have given me." But then he backed away from his original claims. "In answer to all my critics and reviewers, I wish to say that while the article was based upon true facts, it was embellisht [sic] purposely with radical personal assertions calculated to set men to thinking on the subject of generativ influences and generativ evils. Bless my critics. I would not wish to own a child that was bred with a hard-rubber syringe. And I do not care to think that my child bears toward the millenium no traces of his father's personality, humble tho it be. I am a firm disciple of impregnation in the good old orthodox manner, with all its esthetic features and risks of evil." Returning to his favorite metaphor, he concluded, "Let us now pull the trigger of some other gun, and set free another explosion of cerebral action. Yours for all there is in it for good, A.D. Hard, M.D." The editor quipped in reply, "And the editorial department will hereafter realize that you are not to be taken seriously, and act accordingly."

AN INTERPRETATION

The reactions in 1909 to the news of the first alleged donor insemination reveal a great deal about the social tensions in American society at the time. Twenty-five years had passed since the event supposedly took place, yet the debate raged largely around issues of "science" versus "nature." In spite of the widespread affirmation of science in the first decade of the 20th century (indeed, it is appropriately known as the Progressive Era because of the optimistic faith in progress that prevailed at the time), readers of Dr. Hard's article reacted vehemently to the description of such a drastic manipulation of the reproductive process. The use of the syringe, and the use of the sperm of a donor, pleased those who believed that science could and should further the goal of Progressive reformers who advocated increasing the propagation of the "best" class of people. Hard's article offended others who objected to interfering with the "natural" means of reproduction. These critics were, above all, horrified by the challenge to traditional beliefs about marriage, the family, sex, and reproduction. They found the idea of artificial insemination socially repugnant, religiously unacceptable, and morally outrageous. The debate foreshadowed many that would surround later discussions of birth control, abortion, and various other forms of artificial reproduction.

Most striking about the controversy that ensued, however, is what was not discussed. With the exception of the writer who mistakenly assumed that the couple had granted permission for the procedure, and the other who likened the event to a rape, no other respondent made reference to the enormous deception perpetrated on the woman. After the fact, the physician, the husband, and the students who witnessed the insemination all conspired to keep the woman ignorant of what happened. In the 1909 controversy, respondents paid a great deal of attention to the rubber syringe, but virtually none to the woman involved.

Several decades would pass after the publication of this article before artificial insemination by donor would become a standard treatment for infertility. It is not certain that the event reported was actually the first donor insemination; no doubt throughout history countless women have become pregnant by sperm provided by men other than those to whom they were married, with or without a rubber syringe. Nor is it certain that this particular event took place. Dr. Pancoast was no longer alive to verify or dispute the claim, and no other publication on the subject made reference to the experiment until 1965, when it was cited in an article in the medical journal, *Fertility and Sterility*. Still, the story is no less interesting if it was simply a fantasy dreamed up by Dr. Hard. It was plausible enough to have happened; indeed, within a few short years donor insemination would be a routine procedure in cases of infertility. What the article and the debate do reveal are the powerful assumptions about gender, which made the woman in this story nothing more than a vessel of procreation; and the attitudes about procreation, which indicate how medical science adopted the principles of eugenics in their earliest efforts to cure infertility.

Whether or not Dr. Hard's account was a factual representation of a real event, surely it could not happen now. The rigorous standards of informed consent would prevent the deception perpetrated in this story. Yet some of the practices of today resemble those described by Dr. Hard. Sperm donors are still selected on the basis of eugenic criteria, such as grade point average. The medical establishment still controls most of the means of artificial reproduction, even those that require no particular medical expertise or techniques. Witness the recent controversy over surrogate motherhood, which raised many of the same issues. Infertility treatment remains a privilege of the affluent, who have the time and resources to devote to its cure. And in most cases, even if a woman is perfectly fertile and her male partner is not, she is the one likely to become the infertility patient and suffer all the indignities such treatment involves, as was the case in the alleged "first" artificial impregnation a century ago.

Sources: Sources for this story are drawn from the medical literature, the popular press, and eugenic tracts written during the late-nineteenth and early-twentieth centuries. The original article reporting the insemination is from the April issue of the *Medical World* in 1909; the controversy that erupted is documented in letters and comments written to the journal in the following several months. I have also drawn extensively on the secondary literature written by historians, particularly the work on family history, sexuality, and Progressive reform.

6

MARCHING TOWARD POWER: WOMAN SUFFRAGE PARADES, 1910–1915

ELLEN CAROL DUBOIS

On August 26, 1920, the ratification of the 19th amendment to the Constitution of the United States granted American women the right to vote. The amendment had a dramatic impact in Pennsylvania, Maryland, West Virginia, and five southern states in which women had no voting rights at all. But by and large it only extended a movement in the states that had by 1915 produced full women's suffrage in 11 states and partial suffrage in 23 others. Like most other Progressive-Era social reforms— including legislation providing for compensation to injured workers, for safety inspection in the factories, and for limiting the working hours of women and children —suffrage was won in the states.

To gain the suffrage, women had to do more than convince men to give it to them. As Ellen Carol DuBois explains in this story, women also had to organize, unify, invigorate, and broaden their own movement; they had to transform themselves. At the center of these efforts was the suffrage parade, a great public spectacle with its roots in the militant nineteenth-century labor movement. The suffrage parade functioned on several levels. The movement of women into the streets stood for their claim to a role in the public sphere, including politics. The conviction and determination of the marchers communicated to men how much women wanted the vote—and to what lengths they would go to achieve it—while encouraging reluctant women to join the cause. Even more remarkable, the parade was a visible sign of what women would do with the vote when they got it.

There was much in this that was threatening, both to men in general and, especially, to the middle-class, upper-middle-class, and wealthy men who owned the factories and the banks, were mayors and legislators, and otherwise had most of the power and influence in early twentieth-century America. For these men, the parades were unsettling, to be sure. But they also reassured. The organization and discipline of the parades made it easy to believe that the marchers were not a dangerous bunch of radical agitators out to disrupt the society, but rather women prepared to join with men in pursuit of efficiency, order, professionalism, militarism, and other typical Progressive-Era goals and values. Watching the military precision of the 1913 parade

*in New York City, it would not have been difficult to imagine women using the vote to
reorganize the public schools and municipal governments, to create a government
commission on economy and efficiency or a Federal Trade Commission to rationalize
and regulate business, to take the nation into a world war—or to carry out any
number of other "male" projects of the Progressive Era.*

*In addition, the changing structure of the suffrage parade contained an arguably
conservative message. While the occupational organization of the early marches
reminded observers of the economic and class divisions that threatened the progressive
vision of a society based on social unity and consensus, the election-district
organization of later parades hinted at a more "responsible" and traditional politics of
geography.*

*A half century before the passage of the 19th amendment, Elizabeth Cady
Stanton had downplayed the vote; it was, she said, "not even half a loaf . . . only a
crust, a crumb." Caught up in the drama of a burgeoning movement, twentieth-
century suffragists grew less cautious, predicting that women would use their votes to
fashion a more moral and just society. However, by the mid-1920s it was becoming
clear that many women did not vote and, when they did, they generally voted like their
husbands, rather than as part of a women's bloc. Although many observers were
surprised at these developments, they need not have been. In the parades that had won
the vote, there was evidence enough.*

"I could never forget this day if I were to live for a thousand years," exclaimed
Emily Howland, 94 years old and a woman suffragist for well over a half century. "As we rode through the streets to-day and saw the friendly faces, the re-
spectful attitude of all classes, it was an inspiration." What thrilled her on that
sunny May Saturday in 1913 was the sight of tens of thousands of New York
women marching up Fifth Avenue on behalf of votes for women, in what the
New York Evening Mail called "the greatest suffrage parade of history." It would
be another $4\frac{1}{2}$ years before Howland and the rest of the women of New York
State would actually have the opportunity to vote, and 3 years longer for the
U.S. Constitution to be amended to enfranchise women in all the states. But
the numbers of woman suffragists on the streets of New York City, the impressive political demonstration they staged, and their impact on public opinion
made the May, 1913, New York parade one of the turning points of the United
States woman suffrage movement.

The U.S. woman suffrage movement was more than a half century old as
of 1913. New York was the state of its birth: The first public call for equal suffrage came at the women's rights convention in Seneca Falls, New York in July
of 1848. In its early years, the woman suffrage movement was small but vociferous and the object of considerable opposition. Opponents were not yet concerned with what women would actually do with their votes once they had
them: women in politics was still too unimaginable—too far in the future—for
such concerns. Instead, anti-suffragists were preoccupied with the destruction
that they imagined woman suffrage would wreak on cherished values such as
femininity and masculinity, romantic love, and family harmony. On the infre-

quent occasions that legislators discussed woman suffrage, most of them either railed at or ridiculed the domestic disorder that they were sure would follow on its heels. In defense of the 1867 New York Constitutional Convention's refusal to enfranchise women, its chairman wrote, "We are satisfied that public sentiment does not demand and would not sustain an innovation so revolutionary and sweeping, so openly at war with a distribution of duties and functions between the sexes as venerable and pervading as government itself, and involving transformations so radical in social and domestic life."

Because the demand for equal rights to the franchise brought with it such notoriety, the numbers of women who were willing to advocate it remained very limited for many years. Throughout the late 19th century, organized pro-suffrage sentiment was weak. Existing suffrage societies were small, local, and fearful of being too strident. Members were overwhelmingly white, aging, middle class and from small towns. As one second-generation New York suffragist wrote, "The suffrage movement was completely in a rut. . . . It bored its adherents and repelled its opponents. Most of its ammunition was being wasted on supporters in private drawing rooms and in public halls where friends . . . heard the same old arguments."

But change for the woman suffrage movement was bubbling up from changes in women's lives, especially from women's growing involvement in the world outside the home. By the end of the nineteenth century, women were becoming engaged in public life in a variety of ways. National organizations like the Woman's Christian Temperance Union and the General Federation of Women's Clubs brought together tens of thousands of middle-class women to improve community life and create charitable institutions. After the Civil War, colleges were established for women, and by 1900 85,000 women a year were enrolled as students, eager to apply their new knowledge and skills to a larger purpose. By far the most important development was the growing numbers of women working for wages. By 1890, the census listed over four million women workers. More and more, these women were working in factories and offices, less and less in other women's kitchens. The domestic logic that had once made the notion of women's involvement in politics seem so outrageous was beginning to give way.

By the turn of the century, women were becoming interested and active politically. This took many forms. Middle-class women aided in reform campaigns to "clean up" city politics. In New York City, for instance, the Women's Municipal League helped to elect a reform mayor in 1901. In Chicago, San Francisco, Cleveland, and elsewhere, women began to be appointed to municipal social welfare positions. In New York, the first woman appointed to a city position was Bryn Mawr graduate (and Yale Ph.D.) Kate Claghorne, who served as a Tenement Department Commissioner from 1906 through 1910. Nor were these forays into the male territory of politics limited to middle-class women with college educations. Trade unions, into which women workers began to flock early in the twentieth century, provided a political training school for the working class. Not particularly welcomed into men's unions, women began to form their own and to rise to positions of leadership in them. The Women's Trade Union League, formed in 1902 by a coalition of working-class women activists and middle-class women reformers, encouraged these new women's unions. In New York City in 1909, it helped 20,000 to 30,000 women in the ladies' garment industry conduct a remarkably successful general strike, one of the most memorable events of the era. Even without the vote, women could be found, active and involved in all aspects of the reform upsurge of the period.

Eventually, these changes in women's public lives and in their political engagement began to infuse and transform the woman suffrage movement. The modern revival within suffragism took many forms—new organizations, newspaper attention, and ultimately the formal, constitutional enfranchisement of American women. But for many women of the 1910s, the most memorable expression of the size, passion, and power of the twentieth-century woman suffrage movement was the mass suffrage parade. "The parades offered a striking barometer of the rising of the woman suffrage host," observed Gertrude Foster Brown, a wealthy New York City matron. "There is no question that the parades did much to convert the city to woman suffrage." "I wish you could have seen the suffrage parade this year. It was simply great! I marched the whole length," a New York marcher wrote to a friend in California. "The crowd to see it was beyond anything. Before very long there is going to be a woman suffrage landslide all over the country."

The underlying inspiration for suffrage parades came from the woman suffrage movement of England, which adapted parades, outdoor speaking, and other tactics that had been used by less genteel protest movements, such as labor and Irish nationalism, to woman suffrage. The English newspapers derisively dubbed these women "suffragettes" while giving their publicity-starved cause unprecedented coverage. U.S. women, eager to duplicate the British movement's success, began to imitate the British women's militant approach. In San Francisco, Boston, and Chicago, small groups of suffrage supporters organized their own "processions." Even in Boone, Iowa, a handful of women, with "great trepidation and many misgivings" organized what the local newspaper called "a monster parade" in imitation of the British suffragettes.

The first attempt at organizing a woman suffrage parade in New York City, and perhaps in the United States, occurred on February 16, 1908. A small group calling itself the American Suffragettes announced that it would march from Union Square, the traditional site of labor rallies, to Central Park, where it would conduct an open-air suffrage meeting. The American Suffragettes wanted to attract working women and so they held their parade on Sunday, the only day that wage-earning women could attend. Many of the American Suffragettes themselves were working women, albeit of a more middle-class variety. Their leader, Maude Malone, was a librarian. To recruit other "self-supporting women" they brought their plans to the Women's Trade Union League. As a woman reporter observed, the parade "was heralded for weeks in advance by the accommodating papers," which found the notion of women marching in the streets on behalf of their rights extremely amusing.

The American Suffragettes were refused a parade permit by the police, who were responding to pressure from local merchants fearful that a political demonstration would be bad for business. However, the denial of a police permit backfired. The American Suffragettes liked the idea of being unconventional, and in the words of a sympathetic journalist, were eager to "defy the authorities by parading in the street without a permit." The newspapers predicted a procession of 500 to 1000 women, but parades of women were still too new and on the appointed day, only about 30 showed up. Photos show them swamped by the large, mostly male crowd that came to gawk. Instead of the full route, the Suffragettes managed to march just ten blocks to a schoolhouse on 23rd street, where they held a rousing suffrage meeting. "We are trying to work up public sentiment in favor of our demands," declared Malone. "When we get that we can force the politicians at Albany to allow a vote on a constitutional amendment giving women their American birthright, the right to vote. (Violent applause.)" The crowd made up in fervor what it lacked in numbers. The newspapers reported that socialist sentiments were strong in the audience.

The next effort at a parade, 2 years later, was somewhat more successful. By that time, a concerted lobbying effort was underway to get the New York state legislature to authorize a voters' referendum on woman suffrage, which gave public demonstrations a strategic focus. Harriot Stanton Blatch, daughter of nineteenth-century suffrage leader Elizabeth Cady Stanton, announced that a

The first woman suffrage parade in New York City in February 1908. The handful of suffragettes, their large picture hats just visible through the crowd of men and boys, are rushing up Fifth Avenue to an indoor hall to give their speeches. (Library of Congress).

suffrage parade, directed at influencing politicians in Albany, would be held on Saturday, May 21, 1910. "Convinced as I was that mankind is moved to action by emotion, not by argument and reason, I saw the possibility in a suffrage parade," she wrote. "Emotion," she hoped, would bring women into the streets on behalf of political equality, and lead men to support their demand enough to impress party politicians. "What could be more stirring than hundreds of women, carrying banners, marching, marching—marching!"

However, parading openly down a city street still seemed a very radical act for women of the middle and upper classes. City streets were regarded as men's territory, and going out in public without a male escort was something that "respectable women" did not do. (Recall that prostitutes were known as "street walkers.") As one suffrage parader, initially quite reluctant, described it, "Parades . . . did violence to ideals of female gentility." One wealthy woman dropped out of the suffrage movement because, as she declared to the press, "my opinion of the parade is that it is most undignified and women will gain nothing by it. It certainly lowers the dignity of the cause. Men I believe, do not have respect for women who will walk through the public streets in such a manner." Other wealthy suffragists were willing to participate, but only from the safety of their (often chauffeur-driven) autos. Organizer Blatch did not approve. "Riding in a car did not demonstrate courage," Blatch insisted, "it did not show discipline; it did not give any idea of numbers of 'marchers'."

Nonetheless, on Saturday, May 21, 1910, under threatening skies, dozens of suffrage supporters "climbed into automobiles" at 59th and Fifth "and rushing down the avenue, gave the on-lookers one flash of yellow [the suffrage color] and were gone." Following the autos were 400 to 500 paraders on foot. The first group of women willing to march were college graduates, all smartly dressed in cap and gown. They were joined by the "trade union" contingent, wage-earning women led by the well-known working-class feminist, Leonora O'Reilly. Paraders carried large banners that declared "New York denies the vote to lunatics, idiots, criminals—and women" and "600,000 industrial women need the protection of the vote." The procession ended at Union Square where several hours of speeches began, even though, by this time, the rain had started in earnest. Suffrage leaders stood on soap boxes around the park, and the large crowd, simultaneously curious and hostile, gathered around them. Among the speakers was tiny Rose Schneiderman, a young but determined garment worker, who spoke in Yiddish. Hecklers abounded, determined to test the suffragists. "One young man pompously announced that suffragettes would neglect family life and bring forth a race of weaklings," Blatch recalled. "I got a laugh from the crowd by my quick retort, 'My dear young man, I am a grandmother. All my progeny, although I was graduated from college, are bouncing and lusty.'"

A year later, on May 6, 1911, the New York City suffrage forces paraded down Fifth Avenue again, but this time everyone was on foot. Despite continuing objections to such radical methods, parade organizer Harriot Blatch decided it was time "to venture out into the great unknown alone" and lay down the law that everyone who wanted to participate must march. For some middle-class women, this was an extremely emotional step to take. "I screwed my courage up to the sticking point," explained one suffrage supporter who found marching uncomfortable "by thinking that from the times of the first crusades, my family . . . had never failed to respond to the first bugle call in the cause of humanity." "I was afraid . . . something might happen," another women confessed. "But now I see how easy and nice it was; I feel ashamed of my cowardice."

The day of the parade was sunny and warm. The New York marathon was also being held that day, and suffragists had to wait for the runners (all male, of course) to clear the streets. At 4 P.M., the parade down Fifth Avenue began. With the exception of the college graduates, who wore cap and gown, most marchers wore white. Leading off the parade were three young suffragists carrying a banner that read:

Forward out of error
Leave behind the night;
Forward through the darkness,
Forward into light

Then came a group of floats that depicted "the change in the position of women during the past hundred years." *The little lady of olden days,* an idle woman in a sedan chair, was followed by the *home industry of our grandmothers' time,* honoring the unrecognized, unpaid work women did before the rise of modern industry. Most of the marchers were grouped by occupation and carried symbols and banners designating their trades and professions. Actresses, artists, musicians, writers, physicians, lawyers, engineers, architects, teachers, social workers, businesswomen, and mothers marched. The most numerous of all were the industrial workers, "shirtwaistmakers, tailors, dressmakers and other factory girls."

The prominence of wage-earning women was politically strategic because Democrats, the traditional party of workers, now controlled the state government at Albany. Some of the younger figures in the New York Democratic party—men like Robert Wagner, Al Smith, and Franklin Roosevelt—were trying to lure reform-minded voters away from the Republican party with a progressive program of social welfare and labor legislation. In March of 1911, a spectacular industrial fire took the lives of 146 Manhattan women garment workers. The fire, which came to be known as the Triangle Shirtwaist Fire, roused the trade union movement of New York City and reformers in general to the exploitation of women in industry. In response, Democratic Governor Dix formed a New York State Factory Inspection Commission, with which women reformers cooperated. Rigorous factory safety laws, thorough inspection and genuine enforcement were exactly the kind of self-protection women would be able to establish with the ballot. The Triangle Fire was on people's minds in May of 1911. "The shirtwaist makers had the one tragic note of the parade," the *New York Times* reported. "Their crimson banner was draped with black for their companions lost in the Triangle factory fire."

Between 3000 and 4000 women participated in the 1911 parade. Crowds lined the streets for the whole length of the march and for the first time, the

New York Times gave the suffragists front page coverage. Also, for the first time, men participated. Even though their numbers were small—less than 100—their impact was large. "They were accompanied every step of the two mile walk with hoots and jeers and catcalls," Gertrude Brown recalled. "The mildest of these was 'Go home and wash the dishes,' or 'rock the baby'." Brown recalled the story of newspaperman Wallace Irwin, later to become the husband of a suffragist, who had planned to join the parade. "Hurrying up Fifth Avenue to 50th Street . . . he saw the head of the procession, already coming down the avenue. All white and gold in the brilliant sunshine, with fluttering flags and banners, and rank after rank of women marching in rhythmic step to the beat of drums, it was a thrilling pagent . . . but when he saw that forlorn little group of men, facing a solid wall of hostility, of jeers, catcalls and profanity, instead of joining them, . . . he vowed a seven foot candle to the Virgin, because she had so mercifully spared him."

Later that year, in a campaign very much inspired by the methods and militance of the New York women, the suffragists of California undertook a campaign among male voters to support their cause and amend the state constitution to include votes for women. A progressive state administration had put a referendum on the ballot. There were no special suffrage parades in the California campaign, which took place over a very rushed 8 months. But suffragists did participate in the San Francisco Labor Day parade a month before the election, and toured the outlying areas in "automobile caravans" to bring their message to voters outside the large cities. The California suffragists worked hard to craft their image in the public mind, to create a pro-suffrage emotional atmosphere among women and men alike. "Although the proposition that women should vote is seriously and profoundly true," one explained, "it will at first be established . . . much as the virtues of a breakfast cereal are established . . . ", that is, by advertising. On election day, the California referendum passed. Although the margin was heart-stoppingly narrow (4000 votes), California joined the small list of states in which women were full-fledged voters.

Inspired by the California victory, New York suffragists prepared for the 1912 parade with added determination. They had learned from the California victory, in the words of one of its leaders, that "all the cause needs is advertising." Recruitment for marchers started early. In February, a "Votes for Women" ball was held, and both working women and society ladies attended, danced, and signed pledges to participate in the parade in May. Suffrage leaders were particularly effective in getting the newspapers, some of which had traditionally been very hostile, to cover their activities in a way that helped them to recruit and educate women to their cause. In the weeks before the parade, they conducted a series of what they called "stunts," to draw reporters' attention. For instance, they announced the formation of the "Suffragette Ladies of the Barnum & Bailey Circus," and invited reporters to tea with some of the members, including acrobats, the bareback rider, and "the strong woman, who lifts three men as if they were kittens."

The parade was set for Saturday, May 4. The starting time was moved up from 3:30 to 5:00 P.M., in order to make it possible for more wage-earning women (most of whom worked on Saturday) and, especially, for Jews to attend.

Leading off the parade was a corps of expert equestrian suffragists on horse-back. The first division of the parade was organized politically. Inasmuch as women believed themselves to be on the verge of voting, the organizers thought it appropriate to march by election district. They took precedence over the oc-cupational groups—physicians and lawyers, teachers and nurses, milliners and dressmakers—who marched second. The third division, a new feature of the 1912 parade, was a special section for representatives of the growing number of women who were already enfranchised, such as the women of California. Marching bands provided tunes that ranged from "Tramp, Tramp, Tramp the Boys [sic] are Marching" to "La Marseilleise" (for the Socialists.) The bands constituted one of the major expenses of the parade, which cost several thou-sand dollars to organize.

The 1912 parade was very diverse. Much attention was paid to the hand-ful of Chinese and Chinese-American women who participated. Mabel Lee, a visiting student at Barnard, was part of the equestrian corps; others marched. As a result of the 1911 Chinese revolution, propertied women in Nanking Province were about to be enfranchised. Anna Howard Shaw, president of the National American Woman Suffrage Association, marched under a banner that read, "Catching Up With China." Although racism was on the rise, especially against Black men's right to vote, some Black women marched as well. Overall, the parade made a very democratic impression as women of all sorts marched "shoulder to shoulder" for a cause that seemed to span the vast social differ-ences that otherwise separated them. "It is the most remarkable thing that a movement like the suffrage agitation can cause thousands of us women in New York to know one another well," one marcher wrote of her experience.

In particular, the great gap between rich and poor seemed to be bridged by the common demand for the vote. "Woman's Suffrage is indeed a great river into which a vast number of small streams flow," one journalist wrote. "There are not many points of contact between the Socialist and the society woman, but when it comes to suffrage they meet on common ground." While working women had been marching for suffrage since 1908, women of the leisured class-es, who had once objected to such tactics as "unwomanly," were beginning to be quite enthusiastic about marching in parades. As Harriot Stanton Blatch observed, "Suffrage Parades were becoming respectable. Many who at first hes-itated to march, now marched as a matter of course." In 1912, Alva Belmont, one of the most famous "society queens" of the era and an immensely wealthy woman, marched for suffrage. Virtually every newspaper featured a picture of her, proudly marching up the Avenue at the head of her own suffrage or-ganization.

Estimates of the number of marchers began at 10,000, and the *New York Tribune* judged the crowd, which was so large that it spilled off the pavements and into the streets, at half a million. One police officer, struggling to keep the crowds in line, was quoted as saying that "it's about time to give them the vote." As a reporter put it, "There is probably no one in New York who does not now know the meaning of the word 'suffragette'." After the parade, suffrage leaders protested to the Police Department that the number of officers assigned to the parade had been grossly inadequate for its size, and that the marchers had been in real danger. "Rowdies" in the crowd, sharing in the widespread notion that it was amusing to harass and make fun of suffragists, threatened marchers and suffragists charged that their own female marshals provided the only order on the streets. "A New Jersey woman said that the marshals of her division beat with a flagpole men who were ill-treating a little colored girl, belonging to her ranks". Another marcher thought that inadequate police protection was a deliberate effort on the part of "Tammany" (the Democratic machine that ran New York City politics) to undermine the women. At police headquarters the week after the parade, a suffrage delegation arrived complete with affidavits and photos to sustain their complaints.

While securing the City's promise of adequate police protection for the next parade, the episode also served to extend the "newsworthiness" of the parade for several weeks after the event. Newspaper coverage of the 1912 parade was generally lavish. Even the *New York Times,* notorious for its hostility to woman suffrage, published a "special suffrage pictorial section" on the Sunday after the event. While the *Times* was willing enough to use popular curiosity about suffrage to sell papers, it continued to argue against the wisdom of enfranchising women. The bemused and condescending tone of earlier articles and editorials was replaced by a note of genuine alarm. One editorial called for a full-fledged male counteroffensive to defeat the imminent danger of votes for women. "[Men] must make it plain to the women that they intend to retain possession of the Government and the forces which maintain the Government."

Arguments against woman suffrage had developed over the years. From the beginning, woman suffrage had been opposed as an unnatural violation of the widespread notion that women and men belonged in separate "spheres" of life. Even in 1912, the *New York Times* was still arguing that suffragists were "a very small minority [with] a natural inclination to usurp the social and civic functions of men." However, as the suffrage movement began to grow, especially among wage-earning women, anti-suffrage arguments became more pointed. "Unfit" women, it was argued, would take advantage of the vote while women of the best sort would remain at home, unwilling to venture out to cast their ballots once a year. A more sophisticated version of the same argument identified votes for women with socialism, a spectre that drew strength from the decidedly progressive thrust of so many women's reform efforts. Special arguments were aimed at women. Political equality, they were told, would mean the end of the protected dependence their sex enjoyed. "The struggle women are making for suffrage is a renunciation of faith in the willingness and the ability of men to protect them," wrote one anti-suffrage woman in a letter to the editor. "In the cry of suffrage triumph I hear the moan of a generation yet unborn." Such arguments, if they convinced anyone, spoke only to the leisured classes. Most women, certainly the wage earners and the college graduates who were ready to march for power, felt the sting of discrimination more than the balm of privilege.

What the 1912 New York parade symbolized was true: The suffrage movement was genuinely on the march. For years, the state legislature had been burying woman suffrage bills in committee. Finally, late in the summer of 1912, all the state's major parties—Republican, Progressive, and Democratic—placed planks in favor of a woman suffrage referendum in their platforms. While the politicians still refused to go on record on the issue itself, they yielded to the democratic logic of suffragists' arguments that the voters had the right to have their say on this crucial issue. In January of 1913, both houses of the Democratic-dominated legislature passed a bill authorizing a voters' referendum on woman suffrage to be held in November of 1915. Suffragists took special pleasure in the fact that the bill was introduced by Senate Majority Leader Robert Wagner, once one of their staunchest opponents. With only 2½ years and an entire state to organize, the New York suffrage movement plunged into the enormous task of convincing enough men to vote for woman suffrage to win the referendum.

Meanwhile, a second front was opened up in the campaign to win women's votes, this one in the national capital. Years before, suffragists had abandoned their effort to amend the federal Constitution to concentrate instead on winning votes for women in various state constitutions. By 1913, seven states (Colorado, Idaho, Washington, California, Kansas, Oregon, Arizona) had enfranchised women, who could vote in federal as well as state and local elections. In other words, congressmen from these "suffrage states" were now answerable to female as well as male voters. Women now had another tool in their struggle for enfranchisement—their own votes! Seeing new possibilities for federal action in this development (and aware of the futility of amending each and every one of the 48 state constitutions) suffrage leaders sought to revive the campaign for an amendment to the United States Constitution.

In addition, the wave of reform politics had finally reached the national level. The presidential election of 1912 was one of the most exciting in years. Four candidates ran (Progressive and Socialist as well as Republican and Democratic), three of them openly "progressive" in tendency. The splintering of the Republican party between its liberal and conservative factions swept Woodrow Wilson, a new style Democrat of the same sort that had come to power in New York State, into office, along with a Democratic House and Senate. Suffrage leaders decided to waste no time in making their demands known to the new administration. They decided to hold the first national mass suffrage parade on the eve of Wilson's inaugural.

The mark of the New York parades was all over the 1913 Washington, D. C. demonstration. New York leaders provided advice about organizing the parade, sent their elegant banners to Washington, came to march in large numbers and served as officers of the event. On March 3, 1913, 5,000 marchers (about half the size of the 1912 New York parade) marched down Pennsylvania Avenue, led by New Yorker Inez Milholland. As with the New York parade, police were few, crowds were large and unruly, and marchers were swamped all along the route. The New York parade had demonstrated the publicity value of protesting the lack of police protection, and after the parade, formal complaints were brought to the proper authority, which in this case was the United States Congress. Congressional hearings on the suffrage parade

"riot" generated tremendous publicity and, as Harriot Stanton Blatch observed, actually benefited the cause by producing a strong reaction among "men
the country over who . . . have been won over through the appeal to their
sense of fair play, caused by the anti-demonstration." As one veteran marcher
wrote, "A parade which seemed to end in disaster brought amazing results in
publicity."

Three months later, on May 3, 1913, New York suffragists organized another "monster parade" of their own. The 1913 New York City parade signaled
the end of one phase and the beginning of another in the "march" towards
woman suffrage in that state. Women in large numbers and with great emotion
had come to identify with the demand for woman suffrage, a process in which
the parade experience had been very important. Now that this grand women's
movement had organized itself, the tasks that it faced were primarily political
and largely directed at men: lobbying legislators and educating voters. Thus,
even though the vote had not yet been won, the 1913 parade was a celebration
of sorts, of the size and dedication of the woman suffrage forces, and their determination to see the political process through to enfranchisement. It was its
own triumph, declared the *New York Post,* as well as a "prophecy of another
great suffrage victory in 1915," when voters hopefully would pass the measure
to enfranchise New York women.

The May, 1913, New York parade was very large. Some papers estimated
20,000, others 30,000. Anti-suffragists, so disturbed by the rapid growth of the
suffrage movement, actually stood outside their headquarters on Fifth Avenue
and counted the marchers, to be sure that the numbers were not inflated. To
prevent a repeat of the previous year, police were present in large numbers, and
all agreed that the result was an overwhelmingly friendly and polite crowd. Suffragists returned the favor by designating a special "white wings" squad to clean
the streets, both before and after the parade. Indeed, so decorous was the whole
affair, that the *New York Times* observed, "There were never so many people
out to view a suffrage parade . . . and never was there less excitement." A suffrage newspaper said virtually the same thing: "there is one danger in our suffrage parades today, and that is that the strangeness has worn off and our
women march as naturally and joyfully as they would walk along Fifth Avenue
in a shopping tour."

The day of the parade was very hot, but so many suffragists were veteran
marchers by this time that they were unfazed. The parade was led off by the
same Inez Milholland who had served as herald for the Washington, D.C., parade in March, but this time she was on horseback. A Vassar graduate, trained
lawyer, and great "suffrage beauty," Milholland made a tremendous impression
at the head of the procession. Tall astride her "splendid chestnut," her image
became for many *the* memory of what it meant to parade for woman suffrage.
Some suffragists still marched by occupation, but the great bulk of participants
were organized by the election districts in which they would eventually vote.
After all, the ballot was "the thing which actually counts," observed Alice Stone
Blackwell, well-known suffrage journalist, "and that is what will win if victory
perches upon our banners in 1915."

Although this was a generation that believed that women were naturally pacifistic, there was an almost military air to the parade that year. "The precision with which the women kept step and the uniformity of their alignment aroused the admiration of the spectators" observed the *Times,* which had long argued that so long as women weren't soldiers, they shouldn't vote. The organizers of the parade emphasized discipline. Marchers were encouraged to dress uniformly and wear the same "suffrage hat." Marching orders were issued ahead of time: "eyes to the front; heads erect; shoulders back; dignity and silence." "The enemy must be converted through his eyes," Harriot Blatch, chief parade organizer, declared. "He must see uniformity of dress. He must realize without actually noting item by item, the discipline of the individual, of the group, of the whole from start to finish. He must hear music, as must each marcher too, music all the time, as if the beat, beat of the feet were to be kept in time and tune with the beat of the heart." To the marchers themselves, it was as if they were members of a great women's army. "No woman who marched in a suffrage parade will ever forget the thrill of hearing her own band strike up, the command of her leader, of swinging out into the Avenue in step with the music, passing the multitudes of spectators, head up, eyes straight ahead, in perfect formation, with the conviction that she was marching for a great cause."

Inez Milholland, on horseback and looking triumphant, leads the May 1913 New York City woman suffrage parade up Fifth Avenue. Behind her, disciplined marchers carry banners from major suffrage organizations. (Library of Congress)

In keeping with its other "military" dimensions, the 1913 New York parade introduced a suffrage reviewing stand, which "proved one of the greatest attractions of the parade." Only men were permitted on the stand. All women must march, for "if you do not march with us . . ., you will be counted against us." The Manhattan borough president and New York City police chief were among those present. The extraordinary effort of parade leaders to demonstrate women's discipline to the cause was intended largely to impress this handful of "prominent men." "'We are approaching the Union League Club, the Grand Stand, march your best',", marshals called out to paraders. Then, as she passed the reviewing stand, "Each woman drew herself up to her full height, was poised straight as an arrow, every banner was carried at one height, at a uniform angle. Left, right, left, right, each soldier marched for a principle." The parade concluded with a giant indoor rally at Carnegie Hall, at which suffragists commended themselves for their spectacular showing, pledged to press on to victory, and reaffirmed what they had learned from the parades—that "meekness" would never win the vote.

There was no New York City parade in 1914, although local marches were held in Buffalo, Syracuse, and Albany. New York suffragists were deeply involved in organizing for the 1915 referendum, and much of their energy went to upstate counties, which lagged far behind New York City in terms of suffrage

One of the many professions into which women flocked was trained nurses. The 1913 woman suffrage parade was organized by occupation as well as by organization and election district. Banners to the rear name figures in the history of nursing. (Library of Congress)

awareness. In addition, the kind of enthusiasm that had enlivened previous parades was directed elsewhere, for instance at constant outdoor speaking to workers in front of factory gates. Of a series of local "Suffrage Day" rallies held around the state in May, 1914, the *New York Tribune* observed "The electric spark, which fired the throngs that watched the thousands of women march up Fifth Avenue on May 3, 1913, was nowhere evident." A grand final parade was held on October 23, 1915, 10 days before the election. Using a scientific "comptometer," the *New York Times* announced that exactly 20,789 women and 2539 men had marched. Called "the banner parade" because of thousands of especially prepared flags, the 1915 parade signaled the move towards more expensive, more commercial ways to spread the suffrage message.

Had suffrage leaders, who had committed so many years and so much energy to their cause, been able to see more clearly, they might have realized that this declining enthusiasm for suffrage rallies did not bode well for the fate of the woman suffrage referendum at the polls. External factors complicated the situation, as they always do in politics. A simultaneous referendum over whether to hold a general Constitutional Convention for the state confused voters and cost woman suffrage votes. Above all, the coming of world war altered the political

A long shot of the 1913 woman suffrage parade, highlighting the reviewing stand for local (male) political figures set up on the steps of the New York Public Library. Notice how large the crowds were. (Library of Congress)

and emotional environment for woman suffrage. Men's political attention was directed to who and what would take America into war, and like men, women divided between pro- and anti-war camps. On November 2, 1915, the male voters of New York rejected woman suffrage by almost 200,000 votes. New York City went against the referendum, but the upstate counties were even more strongly opposed. Within the city, "the only assembly districts . . . that carried were . . . purely laboring class districts."

New York suffragists eventually got their victory, but only after running a second, 2-year long campaign. Immediately in the wake of their 1915 defeat, they convinced the legislature to authorize another voters' referendum, scheduled for 1917, and began to remobilize their forces. This time, wealthy women, the very ones who had initially refrained from marching because of its radical implications, led the referendum campaign. The campaign they ran relied not so much on giant demonstrations of women's power as on door to door canvassing and on extensive commercial advertising to influence male voters. In the last 12 months, the campaign spent over $400,000, more than half of it on press and publicity work. New York City hosted parades in these years, in which women were active participants, but they focused on preparedness for war. One last suffrage parade was held immediately before the referendum, on November, 1917, but, according to one participant, "it was not half as long as the mammoth parade of 1915; it did not have to be. Women had taken on a value which nothing but war seems to confer on human beings in the eyes of men." Whether it was the war, the money, or the seeds planted in the years from 1911 to 1915, the second New York referendum was successful, and with this state victory, the tide towards a federal Constitutional amendment turned decisively.

AN INTERPRETATION

This account of the woman suffrage movement focuses on the giant mass demonstrations of the early 20th century that women organized to demand political equality. It suggests a different kind of story about the enfranchisement of women than is commonly told. Instead of focusing on national politics, the story of suffrage parades looks to the localities in which women massed on behalf of their political rights, especially to the great industrial cities, where their roles were changing fastest. The chronology is different too: From the perspective of the suffrage parades—that is, of the mass organization of women—the fight for the vote was "won" by the mid-1910s, once masses of women had already made it quite clear that they intended to have their political rights. Men—both as legislators and as voters—ultimately "gave" women the vote, but it was women's actions that forced them to do so. If politics is about power, we have here the irony that women's power may have been greater in securing for themselves the vote than in virtually anything they have done collectively since and with their enfranchisement. Questions about the relationship between voting and the ability to effect serious change in society are by no means limited to women: They haunt American politics as a whole. This version of the story of women's "march into power" directs attention, not to the end point of having the vote (or any other reform goal, for that matter), but to the process of winning it.

From this viewpoint, it is important to ask why street parades of women were considered so radical, why the decision to participate in them and the spectacle they constituted had such an impact, both on the tens of thousands of women who marched and on the hundreds of thousands of men who witnessed them. The early suffrage paraders felt they were challenging common standards of feminine propriety by marching openly down city streets. (Not only women, but men who marched for woman suffrage invited harassment for their transgression of traditional sex roles.) The emotional decision to demonstrate publicly bound women to the cause for the duration of the campaign. Through their parades, women answered in spectacular fashion the charge that they did not want the vote. By marching, they also declared their desire for access to the "public" sphere, for equal rights to move freely through the world outside the home. By the time the parades reached their peak, their discipline, organization, seriousness, and size had become crucial in convincing voters and legislators alike to concede women's claim to political power and to accept (as a virtual *fait accompli*) their status as equal citizens.

The woman suffrage movement was a movement of women on behalf of women. Disfranchisement was the common fate of the entire sex and the parades were the dramatic representation of organized womanhood, marching "shoulder to shoulder" on behalf of equal political rights for "woman." Parade organizers took great pride in the diversity and unity of their demonstrations. But the historian has to go on to ask: "woman" from whose perspective? A close examination of the changing class character of the New York suffrage parades helps to answer that question. While middle- and upper-class women chafed at the outdated restrictions on their sex, it was women wage earners who were initially willing to brave disapprobation and march in public. Their presence, perspective, and leaders characterized the early parades in New York, and through their actions, the restraints around "womanly behavior" began to give way. Within a few years, however, middle- and upper-class women were willing to follow suit, to march (not ride) on public thoroughfares. As wealthier women overcame their fear of public demonstrations, their cultural power, political connections, and above all their money changed the character of the movement. Parades no longer went down Fifth Avenue, culminating at the traditional site of trade union rallies, Union Square; now they went uptown, and ended in elegant Carnegie Hall. Hall rents, banners, bands—these all cost money. By the time of the second New York campaign (1915–1917), reliance on public demonstrations had been replaced by ways of reaching male voters that involved more money and less mobilization of women. Control over the conduct of the suffrage movement led into control over the women's movement once the vote had been won.

In this and other ways, the woman suffrage movement gives many clues to the character of the larger progressive epoch of which it was such an important part. There are many approaches to the diverse and sometimes contradictory manifestations that the spirit of reform took in the Progressive Era. Certainly one definition, which applies very well to the woman suffrage movement, is that Progressives were engaged in a fundamental reconsideration of government, both its purposes and those who had the political power to shape it. The woman suffrage movement was first and foremost a democratizing movement. It insisted that women be equal actors in government along with men, and that politicians address their concerns as a sex, ranging from the conditions under which women worked to the needs of mothers and children. But the class relations within the suffrage movement, the complex relation between and subtle shift from mass mobilization to elite control, also suggest the ways that politics came under greater elite control in these years. Historians have frequently observed that although an important impulse of progressivism was to make politics more democratic, its end result, in many ways, was to distance voters from crucial issues of governance. The woman suffrage movement provides a case study in these contradictory tendencies in politics.

In this regard, "the politics of image" at which suffragists were so adept, tells a larger tale of what was happening to modern politics in these pre-war years. The very form that suffragists chose to express themselves—the mass parade—drew on forms of popular politics common in the nineteenth century (from which, of course, women had been excluded). Yet if the suffrage parades looked back to the torchlight processions by which men expressed their partisan affiliations and campaigned for their candidates in the prior century, they also looked forward, to the publicity oriented, "advertised" character that politics was to take on in the future. Organizers recognized that what the newspapers published about the parades was important—perhaps more so—than what the women in the streets or even the men on the sidewalks thought or said. The richness of visual evidence available from the parades—some of which is here reproduced—reminds us how consciously the marches for suffrage were a matter of image. Suffragists insisted on the role of emotion in reaching—one might say manipulating—voters, and in this way contributed to emptying politics of serious substance at the very moment when they won women's access to it.

Finally, the story of the woman suffrage parades may offer clues to one of Progressivism's greatest ironies: A generation deeply committed to values of social justice and modern reform welcomed the coming of the first great world war. The way that marches were organized, the emphasis on precision and discipline, the introduction of a reviewing stand, all indicated that suffrage leaders took the notion of a "women's army" quite seriously. What do these military associations among the allegedly more peaceful sex signify? By forging themselves, literally, into a women's "army," suffragists sought to demonstrate that women had the discipline, the ability to subordinate individual concerns to that of the larger group, to deserve a share of political power with men. Their emphasis was not really on destroying the enemy (in this case, men), but on selfless service to the state, on collective organization on behalf of the larger good. Suffragists shared this naive, romantic kind of militarism with men of their generation, which helps us to understand how such an optimistic, humanistic group as the reformers of the Progressive Era could soon slip, with so many illusions, into the death and destruction of world war.

Sources: Eleanor Flexner's *Century of Struggle: The Women's Movement in the United States,* published in 1959, is still the best history of American feminism and has much interesting information on the suffragettes, mass demonstrations, and the final winning of woman suffrage.

　　　Primary sources are plentiful. For the New York parades, newspaper coverage was extensive. This essay has relied on the *New York Times,* which is thoroughly indexed and easily accessible. Contemporary magazines also covered the rise of "the suffragette," and these can be located through *The Readers Guide* for the period. Many suffrage leaders of this period, eager to communicate their sense of having changed history, wrote autobiographies. *Challenging Years,* by Harriot Stanton Blatch, chief organizer of the New York parades, is particularly useful. Finally, *The History of Woman Suffrage,* a unique six-volume compendium of materials covering the entire seventy-year history of the movement, offers a rich and inexhaustible source of names, places, organizations and other details for exploring the campaign for women's enfranchisement.

7

THE BLACK SOX SCANDAL

RONALD STORY

In the fall of 1919, key members of the pennant-winning Chicago White Sox conspired with gamblers to throw the World Series to the Cincinnati Reds. Two years later, following a trial in which the players were found innocent, a stunned nation learned from baseball czar Kenesaw Mountain Landis that eight members of the team, including Shoeless Joe Jackson, one of the greatest natural hitters ever to play the game, were banned from organized baseball for life.

As harsh as the Commissioner's decision seemed, there were many who found it justified. After all, most of the eight were clearly guilty—in fact, several had signed confessions—and many Americans no doubt believed that the national pastime could be maintained in its pastoral purity only by expunging the offending players. That interpretation of the "Black Sox" scandal seems logical enough, and it certainly accords with professional baseball's current image as an impeccably "clean" game, played on artificial turf rather than grass, and under domes that shelter fans and players from the weather itself.

But, as Ronald Story's vivid narrative suggests, baseball wasn't like that at all—not in 1919, anyway. The sport had a pastoral quality, to be sure; but the men who played it—and the men who watched it—were an unruly bunch that drank, swore, and, fatefully, gambled. Against this background, Landis's ruling takes on a different meaning. Far from being an attempt to reclaim for baseball its own lost virtue, the ruling was part of a larger process through which the game was "modernized" and made compatible with the developing consumer society. While Landis presented his decision as if it were a neutral and moral one, the ruling was, in fact, highly political. It could not touch the gamblers who paid the athletes, nor did it acknowledge the responsibilities of White Sox owner Charles Comiskey, whose policies had alienated many of his best players. In retrospect, Landis might be understood as sport's version of Woodrow Wilson, whose two-term presidency was ending just as the scandal was breaking: puritanical, moralistic, and convinced of his own rectitude, yet pursuing policies that were very much those of a particular economic class.

Conflicts between classes and ethnic groups are central to the American historical experience, and never more so than they were in the extraordinary year of 1919. A militant labor movement, emboldened by the Russian Revolution of 1917, launched dramatic strikes in the Seattle shipyards, among Boston policemen, and—

only days before the World Series opened—in the steel mills. Apparently convinced that the nation was about to be overrun by Bolsheviks, Wilson's Attorney General arrested thousands of immigrant aliens and Communists in a series of dramatic raids undertaken in total disregard of elemental civil liberties. In late October, Congress passed the Volstead Act, providing the enforcement apparatus for the 18th amendment on prohibition—a measure that came down especially hard on the urban working class. When the baseball season opened the following April, fans had to go without their usual beer.

The Black Sox scandal took place in a climate broadly shaped by these events. Like the nation, the White Sox players were polarized by class and ethnicity. In the intensely political atmosphere of 1919, some of them decided that they had been victimized by an unfair employer, just like other workers. Landis would have none of this. His decision not only ignored the baseball player's claim to the status of worker. It also accelerated baseball's evolution from a rowdy representation of male, working-class culture to the respectable, middle-class, family game that modern Americans know so well. By the fall of 1921, Landis had put baseball back on the straight-and-narrow and Congress had passed an important law severely restricting immigration. Baseball, and the nation, were headed full speed into the homogenized world of the mid-twentieth century.

Cincinnati was astir on October 1st, 1919, as seldom before. The Cincinnati Reds, champions of the National League, winners of their first pennant since joining the fledgling league back in 1876, were getting ready to play game one of the World Series. It would be their first Series ever, and therefore their first Series game at home, so that even though it was Wednesday and a workday, people began streaming toward Redland Park long before noon to cheer the boys on to victory that afternoon.

The Reds faced a formidable foe: the Chicago White Sox, winners of the American League flag 2 of the last 3 years. The White Sox sported a fearsome attack—leftfielder Joe Jackson batted .351, Happy Felsch in center field slammed 52 extra-base hits, second baseman Eddie Collins hit .319 with 33 stolen bases; and a balanced attack—seven of the eight regulars hit .275 or better, seven stole 10 or more bases, five scored or drove in at least 80 runs. In the field the Sox featured the flashy Collins at second base, a strong-armed Felsch in the outfield, fiery catcher Ray Schalk, tough third baseman Buck Weaver, and the remarkable Chick Gandil, who led American League (AL) first baseman by making just three errors all season! As for pitching, future Hall-of-Famer Red Faber had a sore arm. But that still left Eddie Cicotte at 29 wins and 7 losses, Lefty Williams at 23-11, and rookie Dickie Kerr, 13-7 in two-thirds of a season, and a manager in feisty Kid Gleason who knew (or thought he knew) how to use them.

But the Reds were plenty good. They had won the pennant by nine full games over John McGraw's tough New York Giants, and they considered themselves the probable winners of this Series. And so did the 31,000 tick-etholders for game one and the tens of thousands of others who crammed every

Cincinnati hotel lobby, cigar store, barbershop, and saloon to talk baseball and bet on the hometown favorites.

Cincinnati's backers, to be sure, were not getting the odds they might have expected, given Chicago's reputation. As of the morning of October 1, in fact, the odds were downright bad, only 5-6 on the Reds to take the nine-game Series, down from 2-1 a few days earlier and even money only yesterday. Lots of Reds backers bet anyway, despite the odds. More should have. Because what they did not know, and what underlay the shifting odds, was that eight Chicago players had agreed to "throw" the 1919 World Series.

It began in early September when Chick Gandil, the fancy-fielding White Sox first baseman, telephoned Joseph "Sport" Sullivan, a Boston bookie and gambler, to set up a meeting at the Hotel Buckminster, where the Chicago players were staying during their series with the Red Sox. A flashy operator with good connections, Sullivan earned a fair living making book on sports events, especially ball games. Gandil had fed him tips on how various games might go since Chick's Washington Senators days before 1916. He knew Chick was a rough customer who lived on the edge of honesty. But that hardly prepared him for Gandil's current proposition—that for $80,000, the White Sox would "bag" the upcoming World Series. Initially incredulous, then excited, Sullivan hastily closed the deal with Gandil in principle and started to scout around for the money.

Betting on baseball had been common enough since baseball became the most popular American spectator sport after the Civil War. One reason for the standardization of playing rules was to make games easier to handicap. With gambling, however, often went corruption. Gamblers sometimes paid players to lose particular games; sometimes promoters or saloonkeepers paid players to divide a series of games in order to keep interest, and therefore attendance, high. In 1877 four major league players were expelled for throwing games, but gambling accusations and investigations remained commonplace throughout the nineteenth century. Because baseball retained more than a few traces of the brawling, sensual, hard-drinking nineteenth-century male subculture from which it originally grew, there was undoubtedly much fire behind the smoke.

The actual fixing of games supposedly declined after 1900, but baseball betting pools thrived, particularly after the closing of the nation's racetracks during World War I, and players were still suspected of "lying down" in exchange for money, whiskey, or women, or under the threat of violence. "Prince" Hal Chase, a graceful first baseman with five big-league teams, was supposedly behind countless thrown games. But league investigations of Chase and others were little more than perfunctory whitewashes. After all, accusations against one player might lead to accusations—and penalties—against many others and to the wreckage of valuable big-league franchises. So reporters, players, and owners, whatever they might think, kept quiet in public.

Nevertheless, Gandil's proposition was startling. First, it involved the World Series. There would be big money around but also much publicity; and therefore, much risk of detection. And because sports fans, and Americans generally, were so passionate about the Series, if things went awry the penalties might involve more than whitewash. Also, here the players, not the gamblers, seemed to be taking the initiative—and not just players, but members of the best and most famous team in baseball.

There were reasons, to be sure. For one thing, the owner of the White Sox, Charles Comiskey—"Commy" himself, the famous "Old Roman"—paid his ballplayers poorly. A son of Irish Chicago, an outstanding player–manager with the fabled St. Louis Browns of the 1880s, the only ex-player to become sole owner of a big-league team, a popular hero of South Chicago where Comiskey Park was located, Comiskey's substantial fortune came entirely from his ownership of the White Sox club, which he had established in 1900 at the

Charles Comiskey, owner and president of the Chicago White Sox, with his crosstown counterpart, William Veeck of the Chicago Cubs, 1920. A wealthy man who affected, like Veeck, the expensive hats and three-piece suits favored by tycoons of the day, Comiskey was never comfortable among Chicago's established families, preferring the rougher company of journalists, politicians, and baseball magnates such as Veeck, an ex-sportswriter as well as Cubs president. At one time the most powerful owner in the American League, Comiskey seemed to be on the verge of founding a baseball dynasty until the Black Sox scandal destroyed his team. (Chicago Historical Society)

time he was helping found the American League. In the process of becoming rich Comiskey had gained two reputations: one for generosity with fans and reporters, many of whom touted him for mayor, and one for tight-fistedness with his players. After a war-shortened 1918 season, Comiskey had capped salaries unusually tightly, except for players like Eddie Collins who were on multiyear contracts. He then added insult to injury by distributing only $3 per day in meal money when the team was on the road, the lowest stipend in the league, and deducting the cost of laundering the players' uniforms from the players' paychecks. When attendance unexpectedly boomed in 1919, the White Sox players nearly struck in July to protest continued low pay in the midst of sky-high revenues.

There was also a festering factionalism on this ball club. One clique centered around Eddie Collins, a college graduate whose $14,500 salary was twice that of any other player, creating much resentment. Near Collins could usually be found catcher Ray Schalk, an intense competitor, pitchers Red Faber, a college man like Collins, and Dickie Kerr, the rookie, and a part-time outfielder and leadoff batter, Shano Collins. The chief antagonists of this Collins faction were Gandil, a rough ex-copper miner and boxer from California; Swede Risberg, the shortstop, another Californian and even tougher, reputedly, than Gandil; and Risberg's buddy, utility infielder Fred McMullin. Around this trio were ranged at various times the club's two Southerners, Jackson and Williams; plus Felsch and Weaver, good-time Charlies who enjoyed an occasional drink and roll of the dice; plus the team elder, Cicotte.

There may have been a class factor in this factionalism. The Collins group and others on the club came mostly from small-town America and had a secondary education or better. Jackson, by contrast, was an illiterate Carolina millhand, Felsch a Milwaukee carpenter, Weaver a mechanic from the Pennsylvania coal country, Cicotte a copper miner like Gandil. There may also have been an ethnic and regional factor. The Collins group included no one who was not of English, German, or Irish extraction or from the Northeast or Midwest; their adversaries included two French-Canadians and a Scandinavian as well as two Southerners. Perhaps reflecting this divergent background, several members of the Gandil clique had supported an unsuccessful effort in the early 1910s to organize a players union.

This gang of eight was probably less a tight clique than a coalition of "hard livers" shaped by grudges against Comiskey off the field and Eddie Collins on it. To be sure, the faction's hard living—drinking, gambling, fighting, flashy clothes—would have been less distinctive a generation earlier when baseball was closer to its roughhouse roots than it was in 1919, or at least less than the Collins group was. At any rate the factions existed—for one 2-week period Risberg actually refused to throw the ball to Collins even to start a double play! And Gandil knew it.

Chick Gandil's first recruit was Eddie Cicotte. Gandil had to have Cicotte, who would pitch game one and start at least two additional games in a long Series. Cicotte listened. He'd just had a great season, but at 35 years of age he was nearing the end of his career, and he faced stiff mortgage payments on a new Michigan farm with no financial cushion beneath him. Cicotte agreed, for $10,000 in advance. Next came Lefty Williams, certain to start game two and another likely three-game pitcher if the Series dragged on. Lefty hesitated, then agreed because Cicotte was in, again for the going rate of $10,000. There was also Swede Risberg, whose glove at short would be a Series key; Comiskey paid Risberg under $4,000, one of the lowest salaries of any starting American Leaguer. The Swede not only came in but insisted that his pal McMullin be included, too. Gandil agreed. Finally, with pitching and defense in tow, Gandil went after Buck Weaver, Joe Jackson, and Hap Felsch, the three-four-five hitters in the lineup. Jackson, nicknamed "Shoeless" from an incident early in his career when he removed his spikes during a game because they were new and hurt his feet, came in for the money and because his friend and fellow Southerner, Williams, was in. When Felsch and Weaver finally agreed, the scheme was complete. Chick had worked not only the grudges against Comiskey but the team factionalism—and in doing so had the players he needed to work the fix.

Because the players never discussed just who would do what to lose which Series games, this crucial part of the scheme remained murky to the last. Things

The most famous practitioner of the slash-and-run "inside baseball" favored by the White Sox of 1919 was the great Ty Cobb, seen here hook-sliding into third base. It was a game well-suited for old-fashioned rough-cut men such as Buck Weaver and Chick Gandil (who fought Cobb twice on the field) and for old-fashioned ballparks where fans sat close enough to the action to respond to its nuances and intensity. (National Baseball Library, Cooperstown, NY)

were equally murky, for now, on the gamblers' end. Not only had Sport Sullivan failed as yet to line up the $80,000, another "operator"—a former big-league pitcher named Sleepy Bill Burns—had rolled into New York fresh from a successful speculation in Texas oil leases. When Burns heard rumors of a Series fix, he contacted Eddie Cicotte, an old baseball friend, who confirmed the rumor but said no money had changed hands. Burns now determined, with the help of a couple of cronies, to raise the money himself, only to discover that Gandil was now demanding $100,000 rather than $80,000.

In 1919, $100,000 was a considerable sum, especially for a small-time plunger like Sleepy Bill Burns. So for help Burns turned to the one man sure to have that kind of money on hand: Arnold Rothstein—known as "AR," the "Big Bankroll"—a New York sports gambler and hoodlum with initimate ties to New York City politicians and police and a luxurious gambling establishment in Saratoga, New York. AR discussed the fix with Burns, then, on reflection, informed Burns that he would not underwrite so risky a scheme. In actual fact, he had decided to do precisely that—except that he would work through Sport Sullivan, whom he knew and respected, rather than through Burns, whom he did not. Rothstein gave Sullivan $40,000 to give to the players prior to the Series opener, and had another $40,000 placed in a safe in Chicago for distribution when the Series was over. Sport found the $40,000 advance money (which was all he had access to) a grievous temptation—so much so that, thinking he had the players on a string anyway, he bet $30,000 of it, on the Reds to win, for himself. He then gave the remaining $10,000 to Chick Gandil, with a promise of "more later."

This was far less than Gandil expected or than he had promised the players, who were getting jittery. With the Series mere hours away, Cicotte still refused to throw game one without cash in hand; so Sullivan's $10,000 had to go to him. But Williams now told Gandil he wanted out, and so did Weaver. Jackson told him he wanted $20,000 instead of $10,000, then told Kid Gleason, the Sox manager, that he didn't feel like playing at all. Obviously no one was happy. Fortunately for Gandil (or so it seemed) Bill Burns had decided, even without Rothstein's participation, that he, too, would try to play the fix by promising to pay the players money after each game they lost from the profits he would make by betting on that game. With money coming from two directions, from Sullivan and from Burns, Gandil and the others believed they would still get something significant. In any case, several of them had placed bets of their own on the Cincinnati Reds. By now Cincinnati was alive with rumors of a Series fix, and a swarm of gamblers was now in evidence, including a St. Louis syndicate and a gaggle of Chicagoans that numbered the likes of Nick "The Greek" Dandalos, songster George M. Cohan, and Big Tim O'Leary, owner of the biggest speakeasy in the stockyards district. The odds had swung so far toward the Reds that gamblers were trying to "fix" the Reds, too! The Black Sox were in deep, maybe over their heads—maybe too deep to get out.

As for the Series, it was an insiders' game all the way. In the bottom of the first inning, Eddie Cicotte hit the Cincinnati leadoff man squarely in the back with his second pitch—a prearranged sign to Arnold Rothstein, who was watching the game's progress on an electric scoreboard in a New York hotel lobby, that the fix was on. Rothstein promptly added another $100,000 to the $200,000 he already had down on the Reds to win the Series. In the fourth inning, with the score tied 1-1, Cicotte booted a double play ball and started grooving his pitches, and by the time the inning was over the Reds had a 6-1 lead that would lengthen to 9-1 by game's end. Game two was tighter. Lefty Williams allowed just four hits while Chicago got ten. But the Reds combined two of their hits with three Williams bases on balls for a three-run fourth inning. Final score: 4-2. Arnold Rothstein by now had another $85,000 on the Reds.

The teams headed for Chicago and games three through five under thick clouds of suspicion, not only from the press corps—Ring Lardner of the *Chicago Tribune* strolled through the train singing "I'm Forever Blowing Ballgames"— but from Ray Schalk, who jumped Lefty Williams under the stands after game two; from Kid Gleason, who publicly tongue-lashed Cicotte and Risberg and swung at Chick Gandil; and from Charles Comiskey himself, who was tipped by a Chicago gambling acquaintance about what might be happening. Not that much money had materialized. Sleepy Bill Burns managed to come up with a measly $10,000, which he passed on to an enraged Gandil (who stuffed it in the lining of his suitcase) along with the brazen suggestion that maybe the Sox should win game three to improve the odds! Gandil, incensed, told Burns the fix was still in all the way. That afternoon he handled 15 chances without an error and drove in two runs while Swede Risberg made 10 flawless plays, stroked a long triple, and scored. Little Dickie Kerr tossed a three-hit shutout. Chicago won 3-0. Sleepy Bill lost his shirt betting on the Reds and bowed out of the Series doings.

This Chicago victory and the roles that Chick Gandil and Swede Risberg had played in it disturbed Sport Sullivan enough to prompt a call to Gandil, who told him that the group of eight was no longer bought. Sullivan panicked, quickly scraped together $20,000, which he wired to Gandil. Chick split it evenly among Risberg, Felsch, Williams, and Jackson. Gandil and Cicotte had their $10,000 already. McMullin would have to wait. Weaver, who in Chick's view was playing to win, was asking for, and would get, nothing.

Game four was a near-repeat of game two. Cicotte allowed only five hits, but two came in the fifth inning along with two errors by Cicotte to allow two runs. The White Sox collected a meager three hits. Final score: Cincinnati 2, Chicago 0. And so with game five, the third straight before standing-room-only Comiskey Park crowds. Lefty Williams gave up four hits, but three came in the sixth inning along with errors by Felsch and Risberg, enabling the Reds to score four times. The Sox again had just three hits. Final score: Cincinnati 5, Chicago 0.

Gandil expected another $20,000 from Sport Sullivan to be waiting when the clubs arrived back in Cincinnati on October 7 for game six. When it wasn't, there was more rage and yet another change of heart. Dickie Kerr did not sparkle the way he had in game three, but Weaver, Jackson, and Felsch went 7-for-14 with three doubles, and Gandil drove in a run in the ninth for a 5-4 victory. The next day Jackson and Felsch drove in two runs each, and Cicotte held the Reds to a lone tally. Chicago pulled within a game of Cincinnati in the Series with two possible games remaining, both in Chicago where the White Sox, apparently back on track and with Lefty Williams up, would have a home field advantage.

Arnold Rothstein had seen enough. With nearly $400,000 riding on this Series, he was in no mood to take chances. AR summoned Sport Sullivan to New York and told him to make absolutely certain that Chicago lost game eight, preferably in the early innings. There could be no mistake; matters were critical. Sullivan, duly frightened, put a call into one "Harry F." of Chicago, a hired gunman. Sport told Harry F. to make sure Lefty Williams threw tomorrow's game in the first inning, even if it meant threatening to murder his wife, and sent him $500 advance money.

Harry F. did what he was paid to do. Kid Gleason sent Williams to the mound after delivering a clubhouse harangue in which he threatened all sellouts with "iron"—meaning a gun. But the Kid's words were just words; the gunman's iron was real. Buck Weaver singled and doubled, Shoeless Joe Jackson homered and doubled, Chick Gandil tripled, and Ray Schalk made the only error, all before another big Comiskey Park crowd. But Lefty had made his decision. Disregarding Schalk's signals, he threw batting-practice fastballs down the heart of the plate to the Reds batters, who feasted on them, then feasted some more on Gleason's parade of journeyman relievers. Final score: Cincinnati 10, Chicago 5. Arnold Rothstein's money was safe. So was Sport Sullivan's—along with Lefty Williams and his wife.

One bit of unfinished business remained. Sullivan went out to Chicago to give Chick Gandil the $40,000 that Rothstein had had sequestered in the safe. Of this amount, Gandil gave $10,000 to Risberg and $5,000 to McMullin. The remainder he kept, unbeknownst to his accomplices, for himself.

For Charles Comiskey, the Series had been a dismal affair. He strongly suspected seven players of throwing games; he even named them (omitting only Buck Weaver) to a friend. Understandably, Commy felt betrayed by his players and desperately wanted to punish the guilty parties. But there was much to consider, as talks with his lawyer, the urbane Alfred Austrian, made clear. If Comiskey acknowledged that there had been a fix and released the guilty players, he would weaken his team and damage his franchise, while the very players he released might sign with other clubs and play against him. On the other hand, if he did nothing, he ran the risk of exposure at some later date, with possibly the same consequences, except that he would look guilty along with the players. Austrian advised him to do nothing because there seemed to be more hearsay than hard evidence in the case. Comiskey could cover himself by announcing a "private" investigation with a reward for information on Series corruption.

Comiskey took Austrian's advice. Informants seeking reward money did emerge. One said Risberg bet on the Reds; another mentioned the St. Louis syndicate. Austrian considered both leads flimsy because neither described money changing hands. Joe Jackson wrote offering to discuss "crooked" plays; he received no answer. Comiskey hired a private detective to investigate the players, then not only shelved the report but urged the Illinois State's Attorney, a friend of his, not to inquire into Series corruption in view of the "insubstantial" nature of the evidence. Comiskey had initially withheld the World Series checks (losers' shares amounting to $3,254) of his seven suspects. Now, with talk of a fix smothered, he mailed them.

The 1920 season began on a sour note. Chick Gandil did not report for spring training. Swede Risberg reported just 2 days before the opening game. Jackson and Buck Weaver held out before signing 3-year contracts. Once set, however, the team played excellent baseball, settling into a summer-long three-way pennant race with the Cleveland Indians and the New York Yankees. With Jackson and Collins leading the way, the Sox topped the league in batting average, stolen bases, and runs scored, while Cicotte and Williams won 20 games again. So did Red Faber, back from arm trouble, and Dickie Kerr, who proved that 1919 was no fluke. Attendance at Comiskey Park—and revenues into Charles Comiskey's pocket—rose by 50 percent.

If the White Sox were so good, why didn't they run away with the pennant in 1920? Partly because the Indians and Yankees were also good. Tris Speaker hit .388 at Cleveland; Babe Ruth walloped an incredible 54 home runs for New York. But there was another, less visible reason: Midwestern gamblers were threatening the Series fixers with exposure if they did not throw additional games from time to time. And throw games they did, all through the summer—not many, but enough. Eddie Collins went to Comiskey about suspicious play in August, to no avail.

Ban Johnson, president of the American League, now quietly began an investigation of his own that turned up not only enticing, if circumstantial, evidence about suspicious activity during the 1920 season but leads to possible Series corruption the previous fall. Johnson, a respected baseball man, had co-founded the American League with Charles Comiskey, then his close friend. For obscure personal reasons, by 1920 Johnson had become Comiskey's mortal foe, eager to see the White Sox shattered. He therefore pressed his investigation hard. By mid-summer, stories about possible crooked play were peppering the nation's sports pages.

The result was exactly what Charles Comiskey had feared and Ban Johnson had hoped for: the empanelling in early September of an Illinois Grand Jury to probe reports of corruption in major-league baseball. Comiskey loudly proclaimed his loyalty to the national pastime and his willingness to suspend any Chicago player proven to have thrown games and accused Ban Johnson of pursuing a personal vendetta against him. The Grand Jury, undeterred, began its work.

Initial testimony was more tantalizing than conclusive. Gamblers and baseball officials reported various, sometimes contradictory, rumors of payoffs to various players, including White Sox players. Rube Benton, a pitcher for the New York Giants, said he heard about a Series fix from none other than Hal Chase, recently retired as a player but long reputed to be on the take. Chase (said Benton) had heard from Sleepy Bill Burns that gamblers gave Chick Gandil, Happy Felsch, Lefty Williams, and Eddie Cicotte $100,000 to throw

Series games, and that they had done it. Much of this testimony leaked out to the newspapers, producing sensational headlines concerning baseball—and World Series—corruption and the need, as the Chicago Tribune put it, to "SAVE BASEBALL FROM GAMBLERS."

Then on September 27 a Philadelphia newspaper published a story, based on interviews with anonymous gamblers, entitled "THE MOST GIGANTIC SPORTING SWINDLE IN THE HISTORY OF AMERICA." The story described how a group of White Sox players headed by Eddie Cicotte had thrown games one, two, and eight of the Series for a promise of $100,000. The players, said the paper, saw only $10,000 of the promised payoff money because the gamblers who started the whole thing lost everything when Chicago won game three. The story was only partially accurate in its account of the Bill Burns initiative and mostly inaccurate in its omission, save for the game eight loss, of the far more significant Rothstein–Sullivan initiative. But it rang true enough to panic Eddie Cicotte, who went that morning to see Alfred Austrian, Comiskey's lawyer, who got him to sign a confession, together with a waiver of immunity that would show the confession to have been uncoerced. Austrian then took Cicotte to the Grand Jury. "Yeah," said Eddie, "we were crooked. Gandil was the mastermind. I did it for the wife and kids and a farm. I'm through with baseball."

The floodgates were open. Joe Jackson, hearing that Cicotte had talked, went to see Felsch and Risberg. Swede, recounted Jackson, threatened "to kill you if you squawk." Jackson went to the Grand Jury judge's chambers anyway. There he met Alfred Austrian, who had Jackson, like Cicotte, sign an immunity waiver and a confession and advised him that the authorities were after the gamblers, not the players, and that he should tell everything. What he told the Grand Jury that afternoon was that although he had gotten his $5,000 from Williams, the ring leaders were Gandil and Risberg. He then asked for bailiff protection because "the Swede is a hard guy." Lefty Williams also met with Austrian, to whom he gave a signed statement confirming the Series fix and his part in it and fingering Gandil as the organizer. Later that day Felsch said much the same thing to a Chicago reporter. Weaver spoke briefly to Austrian and the State's Attorney but refused to confess. When Charles Comiskey informed the suspected players of their "indefinite" suspension by cable that evening, he sent eight cables. One went to Weaver.

The White Sox lost their last season series, and therefore the pennant, to Cleveland. According to Chicago novelist James T. Farrell, when Shoeless Joe Jackson and Happy Felsch emerged from the locker room after the final Cleveland loss, a fan shouted "It ain't true, Joe!" The surrounding crowd (which included the young Jimmy Farrell) took up the call, "It ain't true, Joe!" Both men walked silently away through the crowd. In late October the Grand Jury, its work completed, announced 13 indictments. Five were from the gambling fraternity: Bill Burns, Hal Chase, Sport Sullivan, and two other minions of Arnold Rothstein. From the baseball fraternity came Gandil, Risberg, Jackson, Felsch, Williams, Cicotte, McMullin, and Weaver—thereafter to be known as "the Black Sox."

Arnold Rothstein did not like the looks of the indictment list because it included men whose testimony could drag him deeply into the proceedings. This he proposed to avoid, even if it cost him a significant amount of money to do so. First, he would ensure that Sullivan and his other gambling contacts could not be extradicted to Chicago for trial. He would—and did—pay Sullivan to go to Mexico until the trial ended; he would—and did—pay to ensure "errors" in the extradition proceedings against Hal Chase and the rest. Secondly, Rothstein himself went to Chicago in early October, where he testified that he was entirely innocent, that the Series tampering had all been the doing of Sport Sullivan (now safely in Canada) and the rest, and (most outrageously of all) that he personally had bet "not a cent" on the World Series. While in Chicago, AR also met with Alfred Austrian about the Grand Jury testimony and the players' confessions and immunity waivers. Was there a way to obtain these documents and thus avoid the possible incrimination of Rothstein and also, if Charles Comiskey was interested, the conviction and likely disbarment of these valuable ballplayers? Apparently there was. The documents turned up missing shortly thereafter. Austrian meanwhile declared, for the record, that he believed Arnold Rothstein to be "entirely innocent"—just as he claimed.

Amidst the storm of corruption charges sweeping the nation and the prospect of widespread public disaffection and anger with the "grand old game," organized baseball, too, was moving to shore up its interests. The high tribunal of baseball at this time was a three-man National Commission comprised of the presidents of the National and American Leagues plus a third member selected by the other two. But many people had no faith in this Commission, including its most influential member, Ban Johnson himself. The Commission had already proven ineffectual in dealing with baseball corruption, and given current circumstances this ineffectualness simply could not continue if the game were to remain financially and also morally healthy. Albert Lasker, an advertising executive and Chicago Cubs stockholder, proposed a simple solution: Abolish the National Commission and replace it with a single Commissioner of uncompromising rectitude from outside professional baseball, who would be paid enough to place him above temptation and have enough power to make decisions stick. All eight National League owners liked the Lasker Plan because it would undercut the influence of American Leaguer Ban Johnson; three American League clubs—the White Sox together with the New York Yankees and Boston Red Sox, both under new ownership—also supported it. Two meetings of the 16 major league clubs failed to reach consensus because five American League clubs remained loyal to Johnson, who naturally opposed the new plan. Only after the "reformers" threatened to establish a new 12-team major league did the Johnsonites relent. And so in November, 1920, not long after the Grand Jury handed down its indictments, organized baseball got its new Commissioner, a flamboyant federal judge named Kenesaw Mountain Landis. His salary: $50,000 a year—$42,500 more than he had made as a mere judge. No one knew quite what Landis would do. But everyone, Charles Comiskey included, hoped for the best.

Comiskey, after all, had big interests at stake, bigger perhaps than anyone (save possibly the ballplayers), and he was maneuvering hard to protect them. The Lasker Plan, which undercut Johnson, Comiskey's nemesis in this as in every other affair, was a part of that maneuvering. So was the pilfering from the State's Attorney's office of the ballplayers' signed confessions and immunity waivers. Copies existed, but the copies were unsigned and therefore might not be admitted as evidence, and without them neither guilty verdicts nor disbarment were likely. In addition, as the July 1921 trial date approached, the indicted players were approached by prosperous-looking lawyers offering to help with the players' defense. These lawyers were prominent in the Chicago bar—"fancy operators" and "lawyerin' birds," in the players' parlance, including one who started the case working for the prosecution only to switch, for no apparent reason, to the defense. Not only that, they were offering their services for little or no money. Charles Comiskey's telegram suspending the Black Sox had said that they would be reinstated if they were "innocent of any wrong-doing." Clearly, he was pulling out all stops to ensure that at least in the eyes of the law, innocent they would be.

As the long-awaited trial began in the summer of 1921, the prosecution sought to prove five charges of conspiracy against the defendants: conspiracy to

The Black Sox seated in court, summer 1921 (L to R beginning second from left): Joe Jackson, Buck Weaver, Eddie Cicotte, Swede Risberg, Lefty Williams, Chick Gandil. Standing behind them (and seated to far left) are their attorneys. Normally gaudily attired with spats and diamond stickpins, the players are wearing subdued suits for their court appearances. Their relaxed good humor suggests that they knew the trial was going their way. Weaver and Jackson later sued Comiskey for the salary from the years remaining on their three-year contracts. Comiskey eventually settled both cases out of court—although not before the missing confessions showed up in his lawyer's briefcase. (Chicago Historical Society)

defraud the public, to defraud Ray Schalk, to commit a confidence game, to injure the American League, and to injure Charles Comiskey. Because no gamblers ever materialized, thanks to Rothstein's machinations, the only defendants were the Black Sox. Bill Burns, whom Ban Johnson's agents had found hiding in the backcountry of Mexico, was the State's chief witness because Burns could testify that he attended meetings at which the defendants discussed throwing the Series and, more important, that he himself gave money to some of them. Burns also testified that, according to Cicotte, it was the players, not the gamblers, who instigated the scheme. The prosecution persuaded the judge to admit copies of the confessions and immunity waivers of Cicotte, Jackson, and Williams as evidence, even though they bore no signatures. The ballplayers themselves were never called to the witness stand, presumably because they would have denied having thrown any games. The prosecution concluded, in what was probably a tactical mistake, by demanding 5 years imprisonment and a $2,000 fine for each defendant.

The defense lawyers attempted to undermine Burns as a witness by showing that Ban Johnson had paid him to come to Chicago and that his testimony could not be corroborated. Because only the players could have corroborated it, the defense, too, avoided calling them to the stand. The defense also labored to prevent testimony as to whether the Black Sox had played beneath their abilities. When the prosecution questioned Kid Gleason and Ray Schalk on this point, the defense successfully objected on the grounds that the witnesses could not answer the question reliably.

The main defense strategy, however, was to portray the players not as perpetrators but as victims. The players had agreed to throw ballgames, argued the defense, not to defraud anybody but for the money, which they needed because Charles Comiskey (who was hopping mad at this line of reasoning by lawyers that he was paying) paid them such miserable salaries. The real culprits, claimed the defense, were not these poor ballplayers but big-time gamblers who were not even on trial, especially the "Big Bankroll" himself, Arnold Rothstein. It was an argument designed to appeal to the jury, which consisted of blue-collar and clerical workers who might identify with players depicted in this light. It was also an argument designed to appeal to the judge, who might construe the charges literally by requiring the jury to find premeditated malice on the part of the players rather than simply injurious effect.

The defense strategy worked. On August 2, after a trial of almost 6 weeks, the judge instructed the jury that the State's charges required a finding of malicious intent to injure particular parties, not simply the throwing of games. Two hours later the jury returned a verdict of "not guilty," and the courtroom erupted in cheers and congratulations. The players retired to a nearby Italian restaurant to celebrate. When they found the jury doing likewise, the two groups celebrated together. Charles Comiskey's gambit appeared to have succeeded. The players had been found "innocent," if not of "any wrongdoing," at least of any legal crime, and would presumably not only avoid the penitentiary but be reinstated—and in the nick of time, too, as the decimated White Sox were mired deep in the second division.

The celebration was premature. Legal innocence was not the same as moral innocence, at least to Kenesaw Mountain Landis, the new commissioner of baseball. The following morning Landis issued this statement: "Regardless of the verdict of juries, no player who throws a ball game, no player that undertakes or promises to throw a ballgame, no player that sits in conference with a bunch of crooked players and gamblers where the ways and means of throwing a game are discussed and does not promptly tell his club about it, will ever play professional baseball!" The Black Sox might be free from prison, but they were not reinstated, whatever Comiskey might think. On the contrary, they were barred from all professional baseball everywhere—for life.

Not everyone accepted this decision. A group of Chicago citizens circulated a petition urging reinstatement; Kid Gleason signed it. Some American League owners expressed outrage, as did a few editorial writers. Landis, however, was unyielding, and for the most part he was hailed in the national press as a hero whose "reassuring dictum" earned him "the nation's confidence and respect" for returning sports to "decent sporting circles." The Illinois State's Attorney meanwhile declared the case closed—meaning that there would be no inquiry into either the stolen Grand Jury documents or the role in the affair of one Arnold Rothstein.

The Black Sox scandal ended the careers of the eight indicted players, who tried to play semipro ball, then drifted into other work unconnected with baseball. It also shattered Charles Comiskey, who increasingly withdrew from active club management or league participation and lived more and more at his summer retreat in upstate Wisconsin. He did spend freely in an effort to rebuild his shattered franchise and, like other owners of the 1920s, to expand Comiskey Park's seating capacity. But few of the gaudy purchases worked out, and in any case the Old Roman reverted to form. After Dickie Kerr won 19 games in 1921, Comiskey cut his pay because his earned run average was too high. When Kerr returned the contract unsigned, Comiskey refused to tender him another, and Kerr sat out the 1922 season in protest. Then because he played for pocket money in a semipro game against expelled players, Landis suspended him for 1923 as well. So Comiskey's stinginess cost him a good pitcher for 2 years instead of one. The White Sox finished in the second division every year from 1921 until Comiskey's death in 1931 and in 16 of the next 20 years. The franchise was still valuable—Comiskey left his son $3,000,000—but nothing like what it might have been with no scandal.

Arnold Rothstein, the only big winner to emerge from the Black Sox scandal, was shot dead a few years later in a high-stakes New York poker game. Sometimes you win, sometimes you don't.

The Black Sox episode had both less and more influence on the history of baseball than people expected. The public revulsion against money-grubbing and corruption that many feared never really materialized. Attendance was as strong in early 1921, months after the fix had hit the newspapers, as in early 1920, and the fans, reassured perhaps by Commissioner Landis's hard line against the Black Sox, remained enthusiastic throughout the decade.

There was smaller, less obvious influence, however. When the story of the fix hit the papers in September of 1920, the Chicago White Sox were about to win their third pennant in 4 years, and as only Eddie Cicotte was close to retiring they looked good for more years of American League dominance during baseball's most lucrative decade to date. Kenesaw Mountain Landis's accession to power changed that. Landis not only ruined the White Sox franchise by barring its best players, he permitted practices that led to striking long-term imbalances within major-league baseball. He showed extraordinary leniency toward the New York ballclubs in particular, refusing, for example, to press inquiries into the widely known gambling affairs of John McGraw, manager of the Giants and, more important, failing to prevent the establishment, following the purchase of Babe Ruth, of a long-term sweetheart relationship whereby the New York Yankees acquired outstanding players from the Boston Red Sox for modest remuneration, including five 20-game winners who went a collective 541-346 while wearing a New York uniform. Baseball supremacy passed from the White Sox to the Yankees for the next 40 years in part because Landis tolerated this dubious relationship. By supporting the new commissioner system, Comiskey may have gotten rid of Ban Johnson, but it cost him and the rest of the league dearly. In this respect, they were perhaps the final victims of the Black Sox scandal of 1919.

AN INTERPRETATION

American baseball and American culture crossed a great divide with the advent of Babe Ruth and Kenesaw Mountain Landis. Baseball was, most notably, both effect and cause of the consumerism that was so defining a force in the culture of the 1920s. Even casual fans, after all—even men who had never played baseball or women and small children—could appreciate Babe Ruth's exploits and Yankee prowess and would buy tickets to see them. Seeing the money to be made, other clubs, too, cultivated powerful offenses; batting averages and power hitting jumped sharply everywhere. Baseball's potential audience, already large, thus became larger. And because a significant part of this new audience consisted of girlfriends and wives and families, management labored to make the game and the parks more decorous and respectable. Grandstands became better policed. There was less open gambling, rowdiness, swearing, and bottle-throwing. Spittoons vanished, as did hard liquor. Umpires, backed by Commissioner Landis, reduced fighting among players and arguing among managers. Spitballs were banned because they were distasteful not only to power hitters but to fans. Landis and the great owners with their big, cleaned-up stadiums thus wrenched baseball farther from the drinking, brawling, gambling, ramshackle nineteenth-century subculture of sensuality where it was born, and planted it solidly at the center of twentieth-century consumer society, a fit companion to the great department stores on the one hand and the giant movie palaces on the other.

The comparison with the motion picture industry is instructive in another way, too. When the movie studios faced criticism of Hollywood immorality in the 1920s, they drew on the example of baseball to appoint an "outside commissioner," Will Hays, to review film content. Progressives had long urged the use of central administrators—city managers, a federal trade commissioner—to control unruly areas of life. The appointment of baseball and movie "czars" merely extended this control mechanism to the world of leisure and entertainment. Moreover, the illusion of control, of "somebody in charge," was nearly as important as the control itself. Image mattered. Albert Lasker, whose plan made Landis commissioner of baseball, had made his money in advertising. His most memorable slogan was for Ivory Soap: "99 and 44/100 percent pure—and it floats!" Banishing the Black Sox was a step toward a pure image for baseball.

The most famous practitioner of the new "power game" favored by the New York Yankees, who dominated the American League after 1921, was Babe Ruth, pictured here during batting practice at Yankee Stadium in the mid-1920s. There was nothing subtle about Ruth, who held his bat at the end and swung for the fences. When he connected, the ball flew—much to the delight of fans everywhere in the giant park. Comiskey expanded his own park in the 1920s not so that Chicagoans could see the White Sox, who by now were no good, but so they could see the Yankees and Babe Ruth. (National Baseball Library, Cooperstown, NY)

Not surprisingly, when other professional sports came looking for ways to deal with instability and image, they imitated baseball, too.

Landis's expulsion of the Black Sox also corresponded to major efforts—prohibition in 1919, the arrest and deportation of radicals in 1919 and 1920, restrictive immigration laws in 1921 and 1924—to impose greater homogeneity and conformity on American society. Until the Black Sox scandal, professional ballplayers had conducted themselves pretty much as they pleased while they were not playing. Many of them drank, fought, ran pool halls, played dominoes, chased fire engines, hung out at vaudeville houses, and patronized prostitutes the same way most young urban males did when they had the chance, and club owners paid little attention as long as they showed up to play ball the next day. Landis's ruling against the crooked players began to change that. The ruling sent a signal to professional ballplayers that from now on their behavior off the field and out of season would be subject to unprecedented scrutiny from the Commissioner's Office.

And this level of control involved more than homogenization. It also involved hard-nosed economics. The 1920s witnessed sweeping triumphs not only by consumer culture and commission politics but by industrial corporations over their labor adversaries, who lost three big strikes—by police in Boston, steelworkers in Illinois, and workers generally in Seattle—in 1919 alone, then virtually every big conflict for the next 15 years. As the defense attorneys claimed, the Black Sox scandal was in part a quarrel between a profit-maximizing capitalist, Charles Comiskey, and his underpaid workers, the players. Chick Gandil and the others threw ballgames, it is clear, in order to increase their income. In banishing them, Commissioner Landis announced, in effect, that the subversion of the integrity of the game by the players in this way was an unfair labor practice that would not be tolerated. What's more, Landis ruled repeatedly over the next decade that because players were bound by contract to play ball exclusively for their owners, they could not participate, except by permission, in unauthorized barnstorming or semiprofessional games during the off-season. Landis defended this ruling on the grounds that appearances in the off-season might dilute the value to the owners of regular-season play, which may have been true in some cases. What he did not say, although it was equally true, was that off-season income from playing ball might strengthen the negotiating leverage of the players at contract time, thereby raising salaries and reducing profits.

In other words, not only would the ballparks be well policed in the 1920s, so would the players, and not in the interests of public image and homogeneity alone. Indeed, one implication of Landis's stance was that if players wanted to improve their lot, they would have to do so not through gambling or organizing their own teams but through forming a real labor union. In the 1930s industrial workers finally stopped losing. A generation later, ballplayers did, too.

Sources: The standard account of the 1919 World Series and the grand jury investigation and trial that followed is Eliot Asinof's novelistic *Eight Men Out* (1963). Asinof should be supplemented by the summer 1920–1921 issues of the *Chicago Tribune* and *New York Times,* and by "Harry's Diary" in Bill Veeck and Ed Linn, *The Hustler's Handbook* (1965). Useful for leading personalities are G. W. Axelson, *"Commy": The Life Story of Charles A. Comiskey* (1919); Donald Gropman, *Say It Ain't So, Joe!: The Story of Shoeless Joe Jackson* (1979); Leo Katcher, *The Big Bankroll: The Life and Times of Arnold Rothstein* (1959); Marshall Smelser, *The Life That Ruth Built* (1975); and J. G. Taylor Spink, *Judge Landis and 25 Years of Baseball* (1947). The most helpful interpretative study of the American sporting scene is Benjamin G. Rader, *American Sports from the Age of Folk Games to the Age of Spectators* (1983).

8

DEADLY FUEL: AUTOS, LEADED GAS, AND THE POLITICS OF SCIENCE

DAVID ROSNER
GERALD MARKOWITZ

When workers began dying at a Standard Oil of New Jersey plant in late October of 1924, the newspaper headlines were vague and frightening: "Another Man Dies from Insanity Gas"/"Gas Madness Stalks Plant." It was soon clear that the killer was tetraethyl lead, a recently discovered compound that was being manufactured as a gasoline additive. For the next 2 years, scientists, public health officials, government agencies, social reformers, the press, representatives of organized labor, and the nation's largest and most powerful corporations studied the potentially lethal substance, debated its merits and liabilities, and determined a course of action—one that allowed the unfettered use of tetraethyl lead for more than a half century.

The almost hysterical response to the deaths at the Elizabeth, New Jersey facility was unprecedented. Disasters of much greater magnitude had occurred during the Progressive Era—in December, 1907, a single explosion killed 361 West Virginia coal miners—but aroused nothing like the level of public anxiety and even paranoia that followed the Standard Oil tragedy.

Two factors were responsible for the heightened response to tetraethyl lead. One was the nature of the hazard. Death in a coal mine was horrible, to be sure, but it was also understandable and, statistically, at least, predictable; to work underground in the presence of methane gas was to take a certain obvious risk. In contrast, tetraethyl lead did its damage gradually and virtually imperceptibly, attacking the nervous system in ways that ordinary people found almost incomprehensible.

The second factor was even more important. While an earlier generation of reformers had been almost entirely concerned with occupational hazards, tetraethyl lead posed a potential environmental problem, as the substance in question was to be used in automobiles, and automobiles were everywhere. In general, occupational hazards affected only workers. Environmental hazards affected members of every economic and social class.

Had the crisis over tetraethyl lead occurred in the Progressive Era, it no doubt would have been resolved differently—probably with federal or state legislation. But it occurred in the 1920s, only a few days before the voters would enthusiastically elect a conservative Republican, Calvin Coolidge, to the presidency. Of course, Progressive-Era reformers like Alice Hamilton were still around. But the imperatives of the 1920s were far removed from the moral concerns that had helped humanize the industrial and business system only a few years before.

Instead, the world described by David Rosner and Gerald Markowitz was driven by the imperatives of technology, consumerism, profit, and what was labeled "progress." At the Washington conference that determined the fate of tetraethyl lead—and that of millions of Americans who were condemned to inhale its fumes—the most powerful voice was not Hamilton's but that of the Ethyl Corporation's Frank Howard, trumpeting the virtues of growth and progress while glorifying tetraethyl lead as an "apparent 'gift of God.'" In a society given over to such values, science was inevitably corrupted and "regulatory" agencies proved incapable of regulating. Worst of all, the decision was made to sacrifice the future to the god of the present.

Ernest Oelgert of Elizabeth, New Jersey, a laboratory worker in the Standard Oil Company's plant in Elizabeth, New Jersey, died strangely on Sunday, October 26, 1924. Witnesses declared that he had been hallucinating on Thursday, had become severely paranoid and, by Friday, was running around the plant "in terror, shouting that there were 'three coming at me at once.'" On Saturday, he was forcibly restrained and taken to Reconstruction Hospital in New York City, where he died the next day. Although company officials at first denied any responsibility, claiming that Ernie "probably worked too hard," the workers at the plant were not surprised. They all knew that Ernie worked in what was called "the looney gas building," an experimental station secretly established the previous year. Only 45 workers were employed in the laboratory and their fellow laborers had already made them the object of "undertaker jokes and farewell greetings." Standard Oil spokesmen suggested that "nothing ought to be said about this matter in the public interest."

By Monday, another worker had died and 12 others were hospitalized from what everyone at the plant called "insanity gas." Terror-stricken workers were being carted away to New York City in straight jackets, hallucinating, convulsing, and screaming about the visions that were coming before their eyes. Yandell Henderson, professor of applied physiology at Yale University, said that the victims had been poisoned by a gasoline additive called tetraethyl lead, which he regarded as one of the "greatest menaces to life and health." At first, Standard Oil said that Henderson's charge was itself a paranoid fantasy, and, in fact, "bunk." But, as the workers continued to be hospitalized and as the New York newspapers began to pick up the story, it became more and more difficult to deny its significance. Without naming the gas, Standard Oil issued a statement that claimed that the company had done everything possible to "make the work safe." They maintained that every new product carried with it certain inherent risks, but that these risks were necessary for the nation's progress: "This newly invented gasoline combination made it possible for automobile engineers to produce a more powerful engine than any yet in use . . . plans for putting this new engine on the market have advanced simultaneously with the experiment on lead gasoline."

By Friday, as the fifth victim of "looney gas" died—and as three-quarters of the laboratory's workers lay sick—the New York City Board of Health, the City of Philadelphia, and various municipalities in New Jersey banned the sale of leaded gasoline. The *New York Times,* the *New York World,* and all the regional newspapers were by this time blaring out front-page headlines like, "'Mania Gas' May Kill Through a Dual Poison," "Odd Gas Kills One," "Tetraethyl Lead in Victim's Brain," and "Gas Madness Stalks Plant."

The story really begins with the emergence of the American auto industry in the early 1900s. Throughout the country, scores of local bicycle and buggy companies began to attach to their vehicles motors powered by steam, electricity, and gasoline. One producer, Henry Ford, broke away from the pack by revolutionizing the production system through the development of the assembly line to produce an affordable automobile. Suddenly the car was not a luxury and thousands upon thousands of Americans could think for the first time of owning their own cars. By 1919, there was one automobile for every 16 Americans.

This enormous expansion of the market for cars whetted the appetite of other industrialists eager to cash in on a potential bonanza. E. I. DuPont, for example, patriarch of the famous chemical conglomerate, invested heavily in the General Motors Corporation (GM). In contrast to Ford's famous Model T that looked the same year after year, GM offered powerful cars whose appearance and engineering changed constantly. No longer would a 6-month-old car look the same as one that was 4 years old. It was now possible to tell who had the latest, the most powerful, and most fashionable automobile. Built-in obsolescence and the consumer society were born. GM's fortunes took off and, by the end of the 1920s, it replaced Ford as the nation's leading car manufacturer, producing 40 percent of all the cars in the country. By 1929, there was one car for every six Americans and President Herbert Hoover predicted that there would soon be a "car in every garage."

But to provide the power required by the new generation of automobiles, the manufacturers needed a more efficient fuel than plain gasoline, which burned far too quickly and unevenly in larger engines. In 1922, Thomas Midgley and his co-workers at the General Motors Research Laboratory in Dayton, Ohio, discovered an answer. Gasoline mixed with tetraethyl lead—a viscous, dark-brown, foul smelling liquid composed of lead molecules embedded in a compound of hydrogen and carbon—would burn evenly in a car engine. That would eliminate engine "knock," enabling the car to get more power from every gallon of gas. GM, which had an interlocking directorship* with the DuPont Chemical Company, quickly contracted with DuPont and Standard Oil of New Jersey to produce leaded gasoline. It was placed on sale in several markets on

---

*DuPont owned more than 20 percent of General Motors' stock and had several members of its board of directors on GM's board.

February 1, 1923. The "no-knock" product was popular, and the following year DuPont and General Motors created the Ethyl Corporation to market the substance. A few years later, the new company took over the manufacture of tetraethyl lead, which it still makes today. (In 1985, its plant near New Orleans produced millions of barrels of the additive.)

In the very year that Midgley and his team made their find, however, several scientists warned that the use of tetraethyl lead could expose large numbers of people to the dangers already associated with simple lead—neurological problems, kidney damage, even madness—or to other hazards that could not be predicted. DuPont and GM recognized that they would have to respond to scientists' apprehension. They also knew that such fear would not be assuaged in a study conducted by a corporation with an interest in tetraethyl lead. So the companies struck an agreement, in September, 1923, with the U.S. Bureau of Mines. The agreement called for the General Motors Research Corporation to provide funding for an investigation of the dangers of tetraethyl lead. The Bureau of Mines would provide the facilities and do the work. And the U.S. Government would certify the results. The Bureau, which had authority to regulate and stockpile fuels and other resources that would be needed in wartime, was considered to have the greatest familiarity with the occupational hazards posed by gasoline.

The contract was the first in a series of agreements that would develop between the Bureau of Mines and the corporations. It allowed the government agency considerable freedom to report its conclusions. But the contracts also indicated the subservience of government to the commercial interests of the corporations. S. C. Lind, the chief chemist of the Bureau of Mines, wrote to the superintendent of the Bureau's Pittsburgh field station where the investigation was being carried out, objecting to the government's use of the trade name "ethyl" when referring to tetraethyl lead: "of course, their [GM's] object in doing so [is] fairly clear, and among other things they are not particularly desirous of having the name 'lead' appear in this case. That is alright from the standpoint of the General Motors Company but it is quite a question in my mind as to whether the Bureau of Mines would be justified in adopting this name so early in the game before it has the support of popular usage." The superintendent replied that the avoidance of "the use of 'lead' in the interbureau correspondence" was intentional because of fears of leaks to the newspapers. As the Bureau had agreed to a blackout of information, he asserted that "if it should happen to get some publicity accidentally, it would not be so bad if the word 'lead' were omitted as this term is apt to prejudice somewhat against its use." The willingness of the Bureau of Mines to avoid publicity and even the use of accurate scientific terminology reflected the Bureau's weak position vis-à-vis the giant corporations, GM and DuPont.

By June, 1924, GM wanted much more control over the results of the research. It rewrote the contract to require that the popular press not be informed of the research results and added a new stipulation that "all manuscripts, before publication, will be submitted to the Company for comment and criticism."

Two months after the Bureau acquiesced to this new stipulation, the newly created Ethyl Corporation took over the contract from GM and asked for an important change. A new clause providing for corporate review of findings, read, ". . . before publication of any papers or articles by your Bureau, they should be submitted to [Ethyl] for comment, criticism, and approval."

The Bureau of Mines, which had always been sympathetic to the industries it regulated, agreed. Not surprisingly, its decision was widely interpreted as a sign of apparent collusion with GM, DuPont, Standard Oil, and Ethyl to certify the safety of tetraethyl lead. On September 27, 1924, Yale Professor Henderson, who was to become an important opponent of tetraethyl lead's manufacture, wrote an angry letter to R. R. Sayers, the Public Health Service researcher who was conducting the studies for the Bureau of Mines. "It seems to me," Henderson wrote, "extremely unfortunate that the experts of the United States government should be carrying out this investigation on a grant from General Motors." He called for "an absolutely unbiased investigation." C. W. Deppe, the owner of a competing motor car company, was much blunter in his criticism of the government's relationship to GM: "May I be pardoned if I ask you frankly now, does the Bureau of Mines exist for the benefit of Ford and the GM Corporation and the Standard Oil Company of New Jersey, and other oil companies parties to the distribution of Ethyl Lead Dopes, or is the Bureau supposed to be for the public benefit and in protection of life and health?"

Soon, however, tetraethyl lead's opponents found that they had much of the public on their side—thanks to the disaster in late October, in Elizabeth, New Jersey, (the site of Standard Oil's Bayway chemical plant) and to the growing skepticism of government and industry fostered by the exposure of massive corruption during the administration of President Warren G. Harding. After Harding died in August, 1923, the public gradually learned that major industries had bribed high government officials. It became apparent that there was a pattern of officials being manipulated by private industries in violation of the law and the public's trust. Significantly, the most famous scandal—called "Teapot Dome"—involved the oil industry and the Department of Interior, home of the Bureau of Mines. In 1924, a Congressional investigation revealed that Secretary of Interior Albert Fall had leased vast oil reserves owned by the government to a private oil company in exchange for hundreds of thousands of dollars delivered to him as cash in "little black bags." Fall was the first member of any presidential cabinet to go to jail.

In the midst of these revelations, and on the day after the fifth victim from Standard Oil's Elizabeth plant disaster died, the Bureau of Mines released its preliminary findings. Not surprisingly, its report exonerated tetraethyl lead. Also, not surprisingly, public officials did not trust the integrity of its conclusions. New York City banned the sale of leaded gasoline and New Jersey quickly followed suit.

While public health officials largely ignored the report, many labor activists and scientists agreed with Dr. Alice Hamilton, the Harvard professor and reformer who was a noted expert on the hazards of lead poisoning, when she called for "an investigation by a public body which will be beyond suspicion."

Perhaps the strongest criticism of the Bureau of Mines' report came from the Workers' Health Bureau, an organization of labor activists who investigated hazards to workers' safety and health. The group's advisor, Professor Henderson, voiced the concern of the public health profession—a loose fellowship of sanitarians, toxicologists, health educators, and bench scientists—over the fact that "the investigators in the Bureau of Mines have used experimental conditions which are fundamentally unsuited to afford information on the real issues." The Bureau's researchers had examined gas-station attendants and truck drivers. But they looked neither for the subtle motor problems that signal organic lead poisoning nor even for gross coordination trouble; the only sign of poisoning that their studies were designed to detect was raving lunacy or death. Further, the research on humans focused on workers in plants and gas stations—there was no inquiry into the effects of exposure on those who did not work with the substance, but simply lived in a city where it was used. Henderson was the most persistent critic of the Bureau's report and his critique went farther than mere criticism of their technique. Charging that the introduction of tetraethyl lead into the environment was "probably the greatest single question in the field of public health that has ever faced the American public," Henderson warned that the use of lead in gasoline "would cause vast numbers of the population to suffer from slow lead poisoning with hardening of the arteries, rapidly decaying teeth, weakening of certain muscles and other symptoms."

Not all public health professionals sided with the opponents of lead, however. In the months after the Bureau of Mines report, as the corporations involved sought to win back a skeptical public, a leading figure in their efforts was Emery Hayhurst, a respected and ostensibly independent industrial hygienist who worked for the Ohio Department of Health. Even before the Bureau of Mines issued its report, Hayhurst had decided that tetraethyl lead was not an environmental toxin. He had advised the Bureau of Mines to include a statement that "the finished product, Ethyl Gasoline, as marketed and used both pure or diluted in gasoline retains none of the poisonous characteristics of the ingredients concerned in its manufacture and blending." No one knew that throughout the months of public controversy over tetraethyl lead, while Hayhurst was advising the Workers' Health Bureau and other labor groups about industrial hygiene, he was also working for the Ethyl corporation as a consultant. In fact, Hayhurst was supplying advocates of tetraethyl lead with information regarding the tactics to be used by their opponents. After the Bureau of Mines report had been released, Hayhurst secretly sent to the Public Health Service a copy of the criticisms developed by the Workers' Health Bureau (which that group had decided not to send to the Government) so that the Public Health Service and Bureau of Mines could frame a detailed reply.

Hayhurst and Sayers also worked together to build public and professional support for the Bureau of Mines' and the Ethyl Corporation's position that tetraethyl lead was not a public health danger. After the Bureau of Mines' report had been criticized, Sayers urged Hayhurst to use his position as an editor of the prestigious and ostensibly neutral *American Journal of Public Health* to lend "scientific" credence to industry's position. Hayhurst obliged, and his statement ran as an unsigned editorial that proclaimed, "Observational evidence and reports to various health officials over the country . . . so far as we have been able to find out, corroborated the statement of 'complete safety' so far as the public has been concerned."

While Hayhurst and the public health officials sought to quell professional doubts about the safety of tetraethyl lead, Midgley, now vice-president of General Motors and known as "the father of ethyl gas," called a press conference to quiet popular fears. In an effort to show the harmlessness of tetraethyl lead, he asserted that workers could have it spilled on them without ill effect. To prove his point, Midgley called for an attendant to bring a container of tetraethyl lead to him and he "washed his hands thoroughly in the fluid and dried them on his handkerchief." He told the reporters, "I'm not taking any chance whatever. Nor would I take any chance doing that every day." What he did not reveal was that only a year before he had taken a prolonged vacation in Florida to cure himself of lead poisoning.

This public relations effort was incapable of quashing the doubts about the safety of leaded gasoline or the integrity of the Bureau of Mines report. After the incident at Standard Oil's Elizabeth facility, newspapers around the country began printing accounts of death, illnesses, and cover-ups occurring at other tetraethyl plants, including the DuPont facility in Deepwater, New Jersey, and the General Motors Research Division site in Dayton, Ohio. The *New York Times* revealed that there were over 300 cases of lead poisoning among workers at the Deepwater plant during the past 2 years. Workers at the DuPont facility dubbed the plant "the house of the butterflies" because so many of their colleagues had hallucinations of insects hovering around their heads during bouts of lead poisoning: "The victim pauses, perhaps while at work or in a rational conversation, gazes intently at space, and snatches at something not there." The *Times* reported that "about 80 percent of all who worked in 'the house of the butterflies' or who went into it to make repairs, were poisoned, some repeatedly."

The local papers, on the other hand, printed very little news about what was happening at the plants. They said nothing about the death of Frank W. (Happy) Durr, who had worked in Deepwater for DuPont for 25 years. Durr had literally given his life to the company. He had begun working for DuPont as a 12-year-old child and died from exposure to tetraethyl lead at the age of 37 years. The editor of the local paper told the *Times*, "I guess the reason we didn't print anything about Durr's death was because we couldn't get it. They [DuPont] suppress things about the lead plant at Deepwater. Whatever we print, we pick up from the workers." DuPont's control even extended to the local hospital, where it was almost impossible to get information about the source of workers' illnesses.

Throughout April and May of 1925, *The New York World* ran nearly daily front-page headlines. The *World* proclaimed leaded gasoline a "Menace." Elsewhere, it warned that even "Columbia [University] Experts Assert[ed] Ethyl Gas is Public Menace." The *Times* tried to get in on the action by asserting that leaded gasoline was a "Deadly Peril In The Streets." The *World*, known nationally as a leading muckraking paper, sought to use the Bureau of Mines' Report against the industry by asserting that "Tetraethyl Peril To All Motorists Indicated in Tests by Mines Bureau." These and other three-column front-page headlines dwarfed other stories on the fall of the German economy and "red scares" throughout the world. As a result of this publicity and the continuing public disquiet over the Bureau of Mines Report, the head of the Public Health Service, the Surgeon General, called a national conference to assess the tetraethyl lead situation.

On May 20, 1925, the conference convened in Washington, D.C., with every major party to the controversy in attendance. Each corporation and organization had prepared a statement, which its representative read to the assembly and then defended during a question and answer session. In the words of one participant, the conference gathered together in one room "two diametrically opposed conceptions. The men engaged in industry, chemists, and engineers, take it as a matter of course that a little thing like industrial poisoning should not be allowed to stand in the way of a great industrial advance. On the other hand, the sanitary experts take it as a matter of course that the first consideration is the health of the people."

The companies—General Motors, DuPont, Standard Oil, and the Ethyl Corporation—went first. Their speakers outlined the history of leaded gasoline and the reasons its continued production was essential to the nation. The Chairman of GM, Charles F. Kettering, and a lead researcher from GM's Kettering Laboratories, Robert Kehoe, both invoked one of the industry's most common arguments—that oil supplies were limited, and that tetraethyl lead would help stretch them out. (Industry spokesmen claimed that the world's petroleum supplies would run out in the 1940s if lead was not added to gasoline. With leaded gas, studies said, supplies might last until the 1950s.) Frank Howard, the Ethyl Corporation representative, stressed the broader point that, whatever the health risks, the entire controversy had to be seen from the economic and political perspective, as well as the environmental one. "You have but one problem," he remarked rhetorically, "Is this a public health hazard?" He answered that "unfortunately, our problem is not that simple." Rather he posited that automobiles and oil were central to the industrial progress of the nation, if not the world. "Our continued development of motor fuels is essential in our civilization," he proclaimed. Noting that at least a decade of research had preceded the discovery of tetraethyl lead, he called it an "apparent 'gift of God.' . . . Because some animals died and some do not die in some experiments, shall we give this thing up entirely?"

These remarks proved to be the recurrent themes for the industry: The nations's progress depended on gasoline, and the risks involved were worth it. Dr. H. C. Parmelee, editor of the industry trade magazine *Chemical and Metallurgical Engineering* stated, "The research and development that produced tetraethyl lead were conceived in a fine spirit of industrial progress looking toward the conservation of gasoline and increased efficiency of internal combustion motors." Parmelee believed that the companies did their best to safeguard the workers. In the end, he said, "its casualties were negligible compared to

human sacrifice in the development of many other industrial enterprises." The
company representatives blamed workers' carelessness for the deaths and illnesses in tetraethyl lead plants.

For their part, the labor activists and public health specialists who were
fighting leaded gas pointed out that lead compounds were already known to be

By 1929, Sunoco was appealing to the public rather than to the experts,
who had by then deemed tetraethyl lead "safe." Here, Sunoco asked consumers
to "be the judge and jury" and "render your own verdict." In another advertisement that same year, Sunoco claimed that "the verdict of the jury" was in and
that unleaded Sunoco had triumphed. (Courtesy of Hagley Museum and Library)

slow, cumulative poisons. They believed that the federal government had to assume responsibility for protecting the health of the nation, and they rejected the notion that the workers were the ones responsible for their own poisoning. Finally, they asked the conferees to consider not just lead's potential for causing occupational diseases, but also its effects on the environment as a whole. As the country's foremost authority on lead, Alice Hamilton, put it, "You may control conditions within a factory, but how are you going to control the whole country?"

Henderson, the Yale physiologist, compared tetraethyl lead to a serious infectious disease like the influenza and diphtheria that periodically swept the country. He was horrified at the thought that hundreds of thousands of pounds of lead were going to be deposited in the streets of every major city of America. The problem was not that more people would die like those in the laboratory in New Jersey, but that "the conditions would grow worse so gradually and the development of lead poisoning will come on so insidiously . . . that leaded gasoline will be in nearly universal use and large numbers of cars will have been sold . . . before the public and the government awaken to the situation." In a private letter to R. R. Sayers of the Bureau of Mines, Henderson wrote: "In the past, the position taken by the authorities has been that nothing could be prohibited until it was proved to have killed a number of people. I trust that in the future, especially in a matter of this sort, the position will be that substances like tetraethyl lead can not be introduced for general use until it is proved harmless."

Opponents were most concerned, however, about the industry propaganda that equated the use of lead with industrial progress and the survival of civilization itself. Reacting to the Ethyl Corporation representative's statement that tetraethyl lead was a "gift of God," Grace Burnham of the Workers' Health Bureau said it "was not a gift of God when those eleven men were killed or those 149 were poisoned." She denounced the priorities of "this age of speed and rush and efficiency and mechanics" and said, "the thing we are interested in [in] the long run is not mechanics or machinery, but men." A. L. Berres, secretary of the metal trades department of the American Federation of Labor, also rejected the prevalent conception of the 1920s that "the business of America is business." He told the conference that the American Federation of Labor opposed the use of tetraethyl lead, saying, "We feel that where the health and general welfare of humanity is concerned, we ought to step slowly."

Of course, the public health experts listening to the two camps hoped that scientific research would prove one position correct and the other wrong. Yet a final, scientific answer was impossible for two reasons. In the first place, scientists at that time did not adequately understand what they were studying. All previous experience with lead poisoning had involved inorganic molecules, which do not create symptoms until large amounts have been absorbed in the bones. Tetraethyl lead is what we would now call an organic compound, which creates symptoms very soon after entering the body. So while inorganic lead in the body tends to appear in blood or excretions before symptoms appear, traces of organic lead compounds may not be found until after severe symptoms have occurred. Naturally, the first cases of poisoning by organic lead compounds did not fit well into models created to explain the action of inorganic lead com-pounds, and so evidence of poisonings by tetraethyl lead was regarded as per-plexing and ambiguous. Even the medical director of Reconstruction Hospital in New York, probably the only facility devoted exclusively to the study and treatment of occupational disease and accidents, could not explain the strange manifestations of chronic tetraethyl lead poisoning. Of the 39 patients he treat-ed after the Elizabeth disaster, he said, "some . . . gave no physical evidence and no symptoms or any evidence that could be found by a physical examina-tion that would indicate that they were ill, but at the same time showed lead in the stools."

The second reason that public health officials could not look to science was political. Pressured by industry's desire to market ethyl gasoline and the public's desire for speedy, definitive answers, scientists were designing studies that could be finished in a few months—simple research on worker health records, or a few tests on humans or animals with no follow-up after the initial work was done. These were not sufficient to provide the definitive proof of harm that the public wanted and the companies said did not exist. Many public health officials agreed with the industry that it would be unfair to ban the new gasoline additive until there was proof it was dangerous. Suggestive studies and possible problems were not enough to keep the product off the market, because of vigorous industry opposition. Pure science would not provide the answer. In the face of industry arguments that oil supplies were limited, and that there was an extraordinary need to conserve fuel by making combustion more efficient, most public health workers believed that there should be overwhelming evi-dence that leaded gasoline actually harmed people before it was banned.

In private, even the advocates of tetraethyl lead were ambivalent about the scientific issues. Hayhurst, for example, wrote Sayers that he accepted the argu-ment that "lead has no business in the human body . . . everyone agrees lead is an undesirable hazard and the only way to control it is to stop its use by the general public." But, he went on, "I am afraid human progress cannot go on under such restrictions. Where things can be handled safely by proper supervi-sion and regulation they must be allowed to proceed if we are to survive among the nations." Another investigator, Frederick Flinn of Columbia University, voiced similar reservations in private: "The more I work with the material [TEL], the more I am confused as to whether it is a real public health hazard." In the end, however, he was "convinced that there is some hazard—the extent of which must be studied around garages and filling stations over a period of time and by unprejudiced persons." As Flinn was a consultant for the Ethyl Corporation, it is not surprising that he ended his letter by saying, "Of course, you must understand that my remarks are confidential."

The public was not so philosophical. People were still alarmed by the pre-vious year's accident and continuing reports of other deaths caused by tetraethyl lead. The *New York Times*, for example, continued reports of poison-ings and deaths from tetraethyl lead: "Tetraethyl Lead Fatal to Makers," one headline announced in an article that claimed that 8 had died and 300 were poisoned in one DuPont plant in Deepwater, New Jersey.

At the end of the Surgeon General's conference, the Ethyl Corporation announced that it was suspending the production and distribution of leaded gasoline until the scientific and public health issues involved in its manufacture could be resolved. Furthermore, the conference called on the Surgeon General to organize a Blue Ribbon Committee of the nation's foremost public health scientists to conduct the unbiased study of leaded gas that the Bureau of Mines had failed to produce.

But this apparent triumph for scientific inquiry over economic interests was ephemeral. The conference decided that the new committee had to report definitive findings by the end of the year—only 7 months away. To meet the deadline, the committee members designed a short-term, and in retrospect, very limited, study of garagemen, filling station attendants, and chauffeurs in two cities in which lab equipment was available, Dayton and Cincinnati. The brief inquiry naturally missed the most significant aspects of possible lead poisoning from car fumes—the slow accumulation of the compound in the body over many years of exposure.

After its 7 months were up, the committee duly found that "in its opinion there are at present no good grounds for prohibiting the use of ethyl gasoline . . . provided that its distribution and use are controlled by proper regulations." The report suggested the Surgeon General formulate specific regulations for the product's use, to be enforced by the states. Although it appears that the committee rushed to judgment, it must be pointed out that this group saw their study as only interim, to be followed by longer range follow-up studies in the coming years. Indeed, the Committee had warned that

The Organic Chemicals Department, DuPont Deepwater Chambers Work, Deepwater Point, New Jersey, 1951: the site of the Deepwater disaster, where tetraethyl lead production workers were poisoned in 1924. (Courtesy of Hagley Museum and Library)

Longer experience may show that even such slight storage of lead as was observed in these studies may lead eventually in susceptible individuals to recognizable or to chronic degenerative diseases of a less obvious character.

Recognizing that their short-term retrospective investigation was incapable of detecting such danger, the Committee concluded that further study by the government was essential. Noting a "vast increase in the number of automobiles throughout the country," the Committee remarked that this was "a matter of real importance from the standpoint of public health." It strongly suggested that studies be continued and that Congress appropriate funds for long-term investigations to be carried out by the Surgeon General.

These suggestions were never carried out. Instead, the Public Health Service dropped the issue and allowed all following studies on tetraethyl lead to be conducted by the Ethyl Corporation and scientists employed by it. The man

An advertisement from the British journal _Punch_, October 19, 1932, shows one way in which producers of leaded fuel overcame doubts about the safety of the tetraethyl lead additive. (Courtesy of Hagley Museum and Library)

who conducted those studies was Kehoe, who, in direct contradiction of the committee, interpreted its report to mean that there was no need to waste public money studying tetraethyl lead: "as it appeared from their investigation that there was no evidence of immediate danger to the public health, it was thought that these necessarily extensive studies should not be repeated at present, at public expense, but that they should be continued at the expense of the industry most concerned, subject, however, to the supervision of the Public Health Service." It should not be surprising that Kehoe concluded that his research "fails to show any evidence for the existence of such hazards." Over the next 40 years, other studies came to the same conclusion. That too is not surprising, because between 1927 and 1967, there was no research conducted on tetraethyl lead that was not funded by either the Kettering Laboratories or by General Motors.

AN INTERPRETATION

The history of public policy regarding leaded gasoline must be understood as part of the history of the American chemical and auto industries. During the 1920s these industries emerged as the corporate backbone of the United States. Because leaded gasoline was critical to the development of these industries, a heated controversy arose regarding its possibly unhealthful effects. Public health professionals found themselves under intense pressure to sanction and minimize the hazards associated with the manufacture and use of this new potentially toxic substance.

Yet this controversy arose at a very particular moment in American history. The 1920s were marked by the almost unrestrained growth of corporate power and an ideology in government that, in Coolidge's words, the "Business of America is business." In the 1920s the federal government was small and weak in comparison with such giant corporations as General Motors and DuPont. Unlike the first two decades of the 1900s, when many groups were pressuring the federal government to expand it powers and assume responsibility for regulating big business, the 1920s saw unrestrained corporate aggrandizement as a part of the "Age of Normalcy." Hence, the protests that led to the initial ban of tetraethyl lead represented, in part, the older Progressive Era vision of government's role as regulator of business. During the 1920s, however, the country abandoned its older faith in public regulation and allowed voluntary agreements to replace legislative action.

The questions and issues raised in the 1920s continue to haunt us in the 1990s. How should society regulate private interests that threaten the public health and safety? Should public officials or private organizations have responsibility for establishing standards? How does one study potentially toxic substances while protecting the right to health of human subjects? Does industry have to prove a new substance safe or do public health experts have to prove it dangerous? In the face of scientific uncertainty concerning the safety or dangers posed by leaded gasoline, and the perceived need for this substance by the auto industry, the broader question became what was the level of acceptable risk that society should be willing to assume for industrial progress? At every stage of the debate, the political, economic, and scientific issues were inextricably intertwined.

Every year thousands of new chemical agents are developed by industry and introduced into the work place and environment. All too often, the threat these agents pose to the health and well-being of the community is only discovered after an environmental or occupational disaster. Bhopal, Three Mile Island, and Love Canal* have all come to symbolize the hazards of our modern industrial and chemical society. Although most people assume that toxic chemicals are introduced into the environment through ignorance or error, the actual history is usually more complicated. Lead's presence in our air, lungs, and bones was a product of political, economic, and public policy decisions, not simply a scientific mistake.

Forty years after the Surgeon General's conference, in the late 1960s, doctors in inner city hospitals began reporting instances of lead poisoning among children living in tenements—coats of leaded paint, which had been applied to buildings before it was banned in the 1940s, and sometimes after, were peeling and being eaten by the children. By the early 1970s, studies of children's exposure were turning up the fact that people on lower floors had more of the metal in their systems than their upstairs neighbors. This led a new generation of researchers to look into automobile emissions. They found what their predecessors could not: evidence of lead's insidious and pervasive effects on the development of children. Thanks to the research, and the burgeoning environmental movement of the era, the federal government ordered the phasing out of leaded gasoline. The amount of lead permitted in gasoline is steadily shrinking. In the meantime, the political and scientific battles focus on how much lead can be put into "unleaded" gas. The issue of tetraethyl lead is still with us but no one thinks of it as "a gift of God."

As we look back on the controversy today from the era of nitrites, PCBs, and asbestos, we may be tempted to disapprove of a public health profession that failed to stop the introduction of ethyl gasoline. After all, prominent experts such as Alice Hamilton and Yandell Henderson warned about the dangers and strongly advocated an impartial government-sponsored scientific study, and opponents did manage to win a temporary moratorium on the manufacture of the substance until the scientists' results became available. What went wrong? Why is tetraethyl lead still a prime source of lead in the environment? Of course, there were those who had such an ideological commitment to industrial progress that they were willing to put their science aside to meet the demands of corporate greed. But more important, we should look at those who considered themselves honorable scientific investigators for, ultimately, they could not distinguish their "science" from the demands of an economy and society that was

---

*Bhopal, India was the site of a massive disaster in which thousands of people were poisoned by the release of highly toxic gas from a Union Carbide Chemical plant. Three Mile Island was the site of the nation's worst nuclear reactor accident and Love Canal is a community in upper New York State that was found to be contaminated by chemicals dumped by the Hooker Chemical Company.

being built around the automobile. Any boundaries between science and society, if they ever really exist, broke down as they agreed to conduct a short-term study that would provide quick answers—answers guaranteed, in retrospect, not to disrupt this vital industry. The symptoms of lead accumulation due to exhaust emissions would be unlike anything they had previously encountered in industrial populations. But because of compromises in their experimental design they could not possibly understand what we now know today: that those most affected would not be adults, but children, slowly accumulating lead. Their suffering is all the more tragic because of the amorphous and still poorly understood effects of lead on the nervous system of children. The best of the public health scientists of the 1920s were working from an inadequate model of disease causation. But their inability to draw conclusions valid from modern standards speaks more to the interlocking relationships between science and society than to the absence of a link between lead and disease.

Sources: A wide variety of different types of material was used to unravel the complex history of leaded gasoline. We began by looking at the newspapers and magazines of the period. This material gave us a good sense of the controversies that accompanied the introduction of lead into gasoline in the 1920s. The *New York World*, the *New York Times*, the *American Journal of Public Health*, *The Survey*, and various industry journals provided a sense of how the public, professionals and industry viewed the issue. But this public literature provided only part of the story. Private correspondence and memos between industry spokesmen, government officials in the U.S. Bureau of Mines, and the Public Health Service were invaluable for understanding the interlocking relationships between government and industry during the period. The National Archives in Washington preserved this material, but other material in the hands of the industry is unavailable to scholars.

9

THE TOWNSEND MOVEMENT AND SOCIAL SECURITY

WILLIAM GRAEBNER

He was an old man and not much of a public speaker. He held no political office and, like millions of older Americans, he had no money. Despite these handicaps, in the midst of the Great Depression of the 1930s Francis Townsend became one of the most popular and influential men in America. The source of his strength was a plan— indeed, a very simple plan—for providing federal pensions to all retired people over the age of 60 years. In less than 2 years, Townsend parlayed his idea for old age pensions into hundreds of Townsend Clubs and millions of devoted followers—the Townsend Movement—with the strength to bully Franklin D. Roosevelt's New Deal into the landmark Social Security Act of 1935.

When Townsend first made his proposal in the fall of 1933, a small number of Americans already had some kind of claim to an old-age pension. Federal civil service employees were minimally covered under a law passed in 1920. Some military veterans and state and municipal employees could look forward to future benefits. And about 10 percent of employees in the private sector had some kind of coverage. But otherwise, most people had to depend on personal savings in their old age or count on their children to take care of them. If these sources of security proved inadequate, older people had only two options: In some states, the indigent aged could apply for public assistance; or they could seek room and board in the county almshouse. Although Germany, Great Britain, and most of the other industrialized nations of the world had had comprehensive national programs of old-age pensions and assistance in place for many years, the United States had nothing of the kind.

Even in ordinary times, the worsening condition of the nation's elderly would probably have brought forth an advocate such as Townsend. But these were no ordinary times. Across the country, young and old struggled to make ends meet, even to survive, in the most severe depression in the nation's history. The trauma was symbolized by Detroit, a city whose automobile assembly lines had represented the boom of the 1920s and that now found itself devastated by the Great Depression: By 1933, more than half of the city's workers were unemployed, and once-proud citizens dug homes in the ground, rummaged for food in alley garbage cans, or stole dog biscuits from the city pound. Conditions in other American cities, and in the small towns and countryside, were only marginally better.

142

Into this chaos stepped Townsend, full of hopes and high expectations, tempting the nation's aged with the promise of a better life. To Roosevelt, Townsend's spectacular promises made him a dangerous radical, a demagogue whose politics threatened the comfortable two-party system and whose economics endangered the fragile and partial recovery from the trough of the Great Depression that the New Deal had begun to piece together in 1934 and 1935.

There was, to be sure, a core of truth in this assessment of Townsend and his movement. But if Townsend was a radical, his was an odd sort of radicalism that came packaged as the American dream. To proud older people who valued their independence, Townsend stood for the prospect of a dignified retirement. To younger people, he offered the jobs that had been vacated by the recently retired. To young and old, he proposed a new kind of national economy, driven not by production but by consumer purchases. This mixture of security and social engineering was hardly revolutionary. In its own, more oblique way, Roosevelt's New Deal was moving in similar directions. And a half century later, Townsend's ideas—if not his plan—were national policy.

It was 1936. For 6 years, all of them years of the Great Depression that had begun with the crash of the stock market in the fall of 1929, Charles Lewis had struggled to make ends meet while working a 260-acre, rented dairy farm in the foothills of Chautauqua County, New York, not far from Lake Erie and only a few miles from the Pennsylvania line. Since 1898, Lewis had kept a day book— a brief daily record—of weather and work. For the most part, the entries chronicle the year-around drudgery of cutting "poles" for fencing and drawing manure. But they also reveal Lewis's interest in the major spectacles of the day. During the year 1936, Lewis noted the death of the King of England; the electrocution of Bruno Richard Hauptmann, kidnapper and murderer of Charles Lindbergh's infant son; and Joe Louis's victory in a prize fight ("nigger Lewis & dakota farmer only 1 blow/struck and the nigger did it"). For June 28, Lewis wrote:

> Cold wind clowdy [sic] I picked some berries P.M.
> We all went over to Lily Dale to a big
> Townsen [sic] meeting awful crowd

Lily Dale was an established spiritualist community—the sort of place where one could find help in contacting the soul of a dead relative. But on this particular Sunday, the grounds had been given over to an all-day political rally. According to the *Jamestown Evening Journal,* an estimated 8000 people, most of them representing Townsend clubs in Buffalo, Niagara Falls, Lockport, and other Western New York communities, showed up for the day's events, which included a morning concert by the Falconer Townsend Club band, a noon "picnic basket," and an evening softball game.

Although Franklin D. Roosevelt had only the day before accepted the nomination of the Democratic Party for a second term as president, most of those who attended the Lily Dale rally had little interest in Roosevelt or, for

that matter, in the more conservative Republican candidate, Kansas governor
Alfred M. Landon. Many were considering voting for William Lemke, a North
Dakota republican who was running for president on the new Union Party ticket. But even Lemke's candidacy was suspect. As the day wore on, the Lily Dale
delegates passed a resolution urging fellow Townsend followers to withhold
support from the Union Party until Lemke had pledged his unequivocal support for the single-issue platform of the Townsend movement: the old-age revolving pension (OARP), otherwise known as the Townsend Plan.

At its core, the Townsend Plan was simple: Give every retired person over
60 years of age a "pension" of $200 per month, provided only that the pension-
er agree to retire from the work place and spend the money before the next
check arrived. With the presidential election only months away, it seemed possible that millions of Americans would forsake the major parties to cast their ballots for nothing more than an old-age pension plan.

The cause of this bizarre situation was Francis E. Townsend, a gaunt, energetic, white-haired man 69 years of age. Born in a log cabin near Fairbury,
Illinois, in 1867, Townsend was one of seven children reared in a poor, religious, and hard-working farm family. "We knew poverty in those days," he recalled in *New Horizons,* his 1943 autobiography,

> but it seems to have been a different sort of poverty. There were many years
> of my childhood when I am sure my father handled less than $100 a year in
> actual cash, but I have no recollection of ever being hungry after I was
> grown up. . . . As neighborhoods and as families, we were self-sufficient.
> We made our things or did without.

Participating in the same sort of unending round of labor that would characterize Charles Lewis's life in the 1930s, Townsend acquired a "distaste" for

The Townsend Plan logo. The letters OARP stand for Old Age Revolving
Pension, the plan's formal name, while LTD (for limited liability) was perhaps
intended to emphasize that the plan was as solidly grounded as any other business organization. The slogan highlighted the plan's goal of redistributing by
age a finite amount of work.

what he described as "this toilsome existence in which men were conscripted by life into an endless battle with nature and in which women grew old before their time." In contrast, Townsend fondly recalled the entrepreneurial energy of his brother-in-law, who in the serious depression of the 1890s had bought up Kansas lands that had been seeded and then, under conditions of drought, abandoned:

> The snows melted and soaked the good ground and the volunteer wheat came on from the dormant seed. . . . Crops grew and matured amazingly and these far-seeing men were ready with their great machinery [the enormous harvesting "combines" of the day] when the harvest time came on. They reaped and they reaped until all bins and granaries and barns that could be rented were full and overflowing. Such a harvest! At such an insignificant cost!

Following the family's move to Nebraska in the mid-1880s, Townsend spent more than a decade as a virtual transient. In 1887, he tried—and failed—to make his fortune during an early California land boom. A series of odd jobs in Spokane and Seattle were no more productive. Returning to Nebraska, Townsend taught school, worked a tract of land in northwestern Kansas, and completed a college preparatory course at Franklin (Nebraska) Academy. In 1899, having lost his farm, he enrolled at Omaha Medical College. Graduating in 1903, he practiced medicine among the miners and cowhands of Belle Fourche, South Dakota, and, in 1906, married "Minnie" Brogue.

After the Great War (World War I), when health problems made life in the Black Hills intolerable, Townsend took his family to Long Beach, California. Despite the city's rapidly growing population of older people, Townsend's medical practice remained a marginal one. Perhaps for this reason, in 1927 he put his ever scarcer resources in Midway City, a Southern California real estate venture—again without success. Most of his remaining savings were lost in the first year or two of the Great Depression.

Townsend's luck seemed to have turned in 1930, when a former medical school classmate hired him for the staff of the county hospital to provide in-home care for the "needy ill" of Long Beach. "We were besieged incessantly with calls for help," Townsend wrote. But in the summer of 1933, in the depths of the Great Depression, the county program under which Townsend was employed was discontinued, and the job was gone. The stage was set for the Townsend Plan.

Just how Townsend emerged from the despondency of unemployment to advocate a celebrated "plan" is a matter of some dispute. One analysis, written in 1936, emphasized that Townsend's rise to "the position of national political dictator" was undeserved, the product of a "series of fortuitous incidents"—the last one a Long Beach election that had resulted in a political decision to discontinue the county's health programs. In *New Horizons,* Townsend preferred to represent his personal experience—indeed, the plan itself—as a typical product of twentieth-century life. "Here were mother and I," he wrote referring to his wife, both past 60, both intelligent and experienced but not active enough to compete in the world of commerce and economics. Or was that true? Economics in America is something controlled by politics—and politics is votes. We might be too old to work, but we were not too old to vote. And there were millions of others like us. . . . An idea came to me which might alleviate the hopelessness of the aged people of our community.

According to the most frequently repeated explanation of Townsend's politicization—and, curiously, one that is not repeated in his autobiography— Townsend conceived of the plan one day in 1933, when he happened to observe three old women rummaging in garbage cans for something to eat. As Townsend later told the story: "A torrent of invectives tore out of me, the big blast of all the bitterness that had been building in me for years." Minnie's efforts to calm her husband were to no avail. "I want all the neighbors to hear me!" Townsend purportedly said. "I want God Almighty to hear me! I'm going to shout until the whole country hears!"

On September 30, 1933, the first version of the Townsend Plan appeared in the Long Beach *Press-Telegram* as a letter to the editor:

> Because of man's inventiveness less and less productive effort is going to be required to supply the needs of the race. This being the case, it is just as necessary to make some disposal of our surplus workers, as it is to dispose of our surplus wheat or corn or cotton.

Referring to an infamous New Deal program that had resulted in the slaughtering of six million little pigs to head off a glut in the hog market, Townsend wrote:

> But we cannot kill off the surplus workers as we are doing with our hogs. . . . We must retire them from business activities and eliminate them from the field of competitive effort.

Estimating the population of Americans over 60 years of age at between 9 and 12 million, Townsend proceeded to the heart of his plan:

> I suggest that the national government retire all who reach that age on a monthly pension of $150 a month or more, on condition that they spend the money as they get it. This will insure an even distribution throughout the nation of two or three billions of fresh money each month. Thereby insuring a healthy and brisk state of business, comparable to that we enjoyed during war times.

Townsend was just as frank about financing the plan. New taxes—substantial taxes—would be necessary. The proper tax, he argued, was a sales tax—"sufficiently high to insure the pensions at a figure adequate to maintain the business of the country in a healthy condition." Finally, Townsend called on readers to understand the growing role that the national government must take in stimulating economic activity when private businesses were too cautious. "This function of the Government," he concluded, "could be easily established and maintained through the pension system for the aged."

In the years that followed, there were changes in certain details and emphases of the Townsend Plan. The $150 would soon become $200—a lot of money at a time when only about 10 percent of all American families earned more than $2500 in a year—and in legislation introduced in congress in April 1935, the $200 would become a maximum rather than a guaranteed sum. It was not long, either, before Townsend dumped the sales tax for a "transaction" tax of 2 percent on all commercial and business transactions. "A sales tax would hit the little man," he told a Senate committee. "A transactions tax will make the rich fellow pay. The Townsend tax is in no way a sales tax." In addition, the movement's most widely used slogan—"Youth for Work/Age for Leisure"—reflected Townsend's growing inclination to present his pension movement as a boon to workers in their 20s and 30s, who in the absence of his pensions might have trouble finding employment. Referring to the Civilian Conservation Corps, a New Deal program that employed some 500,000 young men in forestry projects, a Townsend Plan ready-reference book said, "[Youth] do not want a mountain camp, segregated from society, under military dictatorship and martial law. THEY WANT A HOME and a place in the civil life of the na-

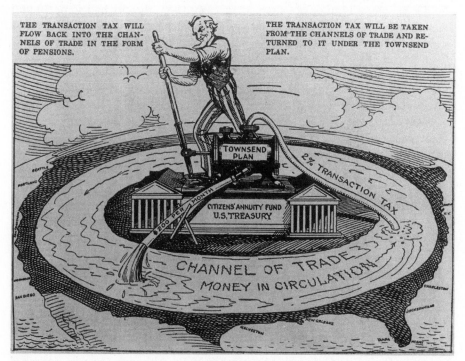

How the Townsend Plan was supposed to work: a closed system, with the government at its center, helping things along. The cartoon also reflects the Plan's reliance on theories of the circulation of money as well as the confidence that American economic recovery could be achieved independent of the rest of the world. This illustration appeared in a Townsend publication in 1936.

tion." By and large, the Townsend Plan that soon became familiar to Americans closely resembled Townsend's first letter to the editor.

Within months, Townsend's simple idea was transformed into a social movement. By the end of October, the *Press-Telegram* carried a regular page of reader reactions to Townsend's proposal. By early November, in response to a 1-inch newspaper ad, a platoon of Long Beach elderly were accumulating thousands of signatures on the first of many Townsend petitions. From an 8- by 10-foot room in the rear of a real estate office, the Townsend organization moved to larger quarters. On New Year's Day, 1934, Townsend and his new partner, 40-year-old real estate promoter Robert "Earl" Clements, hung a large sign: "Old-Age Revolving Pension Headquarters." A few days later, the organization was incorporated as a non-profit corporation; Clements, Townsend, and Townsend's brother, a Los Angeles hotel porter, were the organization's only directors.

Using direct-mail techniques, voluntary and paid organizers, and a newspaper, *The Modern Crusader* (later renamed *The Townsend National Weekly*), Townsend and Clements rapidly expanded the organization beyond Long Beach. San Diego, a city of 180,000 people with the nation's largest percentage of older people, was an obvious target. By early 1935, the city had some 30,000 dues-paying members and was able to produce 105,000 signatures on a petition

A sign in Saw Pit, Colorado, September 1940. Although the sign describes what it means to be a "Townsendite," the heading—"Townsend"—reflects the continued importance of Townsend's personal leadership within the movement. Russell Lee, who took the photograph for the Farm Security Administration, probably also intended to emphasize that Townsend was no less a "product" of advertising than Bubble Up and Chesterfields. (Library of Congress)

endorsing the Townsend Plan. Stimulated by "Townsend budgets" that showed precisely how $200 per month might be spent (monthly payments on a refrigerator, an electric washer, a radio, and a vacuum cleaner totaled $30), many residents of San Diego and other cities acted as if payment of the pension were imminent. One San Diego couple, convinced that the November, 1934, congressional elections would lead immediately to passage of a Townsend measure in congress, insisted that a furniture dealer allow payments to be deferred until January, when the first Townsend Plan checks would arrive.

The movement registered similar successes in cities and towns throughout the Far West and the Midwest; among other communities, Los Angeles, Seattle, Portland, Chicago, Toledo, and Cleveland were bastions of Townsendism. By 1936, Townsend was claiming 3,500,000 supporters and a circulation for *The Townsend National Weekly* of some 2,000,000. The Northeast, and especially the South, where employers feared that the movement would threaten the supply of black labor, proved more resistant to the Townsend message.

Real estate and insurance salesman and Townsend club member John W. Dillard, reading the *Townsend National Weekly* in his Washington, Indiana office, June 1941. Like Dillard, many Townsendites were thoughtful, respected— and elderly—members of their communities. Photo by John Vachon for the Farm Security Administration. (Library of Congress)

As the movement grew, it was sustained by a network of locally organized but nationally administered Townsend Clubs. The first club was chartered in Huntington Park, California, in August, 1934; by January of 1935, there were 3,000 clubs, each with from 100 to 1,000 dues-paying members. Reporting on the Townsend movement in the election year of 1936 for the *Twentieth-Century Fund,* a committee a prominent citizens expressed concern over the growth and power of the clubs. "If there are 7,000 Townsend Clubs with a membership of 3,500,000 organized by congressional districts, as Dr. Townsend claims, the organizations give him the balance of power between the two parties. That is, if one candidate of either party endorses the Plan and his opponent does not, the Townsend sentiment may decide the election."

The typical Townsend Club gathering of the mid-1930s drew a middle-class membership of farmers, clerks, clergymen, skilled workers, insurance agents, and small businessmen, many of them already retired and others thinking about retirement, to a small-town church or public school building. On the walls of the auditorium are the slogan "The Townsend Plan is religion in action" and cardboard pictures of the founder. Following the salute to the flag, a patriotic song or two, and a prayer led by a minister (amens echo through the hall), the local president reads a message "direct from Dr. Townsend and Mr. Clements in Washington" and exhorts the faithful to pay their dues—no doubt emphasizing, as a Townsend pamphlet did, that the plan was "an organization of the masses, the common people, supported by their nickels, dimes, and quarters." Addressing the throng as "You dear old folks," the evening's speaker—perhaps a candidate for Congress in the district—lavishes praise on the plan, lauds Townsend as a David slaying the Goliaths of "Wall Street" and "Moscow," and enjoins those assembled to "take up the cross of this crusade." The speech over, plans are made for selling official literature, collecting signatures on petitions, and securing new members—all with the goal of electing congressmen and senators pledged to vote for the Townsend Plan. The meeting closes with the audience on its feet, repeating after its leader: "The Townsend Plan must succeed. I therefore pledge my allegiance to its principles, its founders, its leaders, and to all loyal co-workers; and re-dedicate myself to maintain the democratic spirit and form of government in America."

In the first 6 months of 1934, as Townsend was building the strength of his organization in southern California, the President of the United States was laying the groundwork for his own program of old-age insurance (i.e., pensions), putting his administration on a collision course with the Townsend movement. In early March, Roosevelt discussed the problem over lunch with General Electric president Gerard Swope, a reform-minded businessman whose company had a "contributory" pension plan to which employees contributed a portion of their earnings. Like many executives of the nation's largest corporations, Swope believed that only contributory plans would allow employees the freedom to leave one job, and one geographical location, for another. He also favored a pension system run by the federal government rather than individual states, as only then would the costs of doing business be equalized across state lines and industries.

On June 8, Roosevelt outlined for Congress a comprehensive program of federal–state cooperation "to provide at once security against several of the great disturbing factors in life—especially those which relate to unemployment and old age." And he made clear that unlike Townsend, he favored a system funded by contributions, not by "an increase in general taxation." To produce the administration's package of legislation, Roosevelt appointed a special cabinet-level committee—the Committee on Economic Security (CES). The CES was headed by executive director Edwin Witte, a University of Wisconsin professor of economics. At Roosevelt's urging, Witte left Washington to consult with Swope, Walter Teagle of Standard Oil, and John Raskob of General Motors. Witte also met with Henry Harriman, president of the United States Chamber of Commerce, whose "general attitude," Witte reported, "was that some legislation on social security was inevitable and that business should not put itself in the position of attempting to block this legislation, but should concentrate its efforts upon getting it into acceptable form."

Although the Raskobs and Harrimans had their say, the administration's old-age legislation was actually conceptualized and written by four people who were not exactly household names: Barbara Armstrong, professor of law at the University of California at Berkeley and author of a book, *Insuring the Essentials*, that advocated contributory old age pensions; Murray Latimer, for years an employee of Industrial Relations Counselors, a private firm involved in pension consulting for Standard Oil of New Jersey and other large corporations; J. Douglas Brown, a young economist from the Industrial Relations Section at Princeton University; and Otto Richter, a pension actuary employed by American Telephone and Telegraph.

Armstrong and her colleagues in the old-age section of the CES did their important work—and wrote one of the most important bills in American history—under a variety of constraints and pressures. Although Roosevelt had given them a great task to do, his instructions—the June 8 address—were remarkably vague. Indeed, for a time even his commitment to old-age security legislation was in doubt. In her 1946 memoir, Secretary of Labor Frances Perkins presents the president as an early and firm advocate of a "cradle to the grave" system of social insurance. "There is no reason why just the industrial workers should get the benefit of this," Roosevelt told his cabinet. "Everybody ought to be in on it—the farmer and his wife and his family." But Roosevelt was giving the CES other, more negative signals. In fact, in a November 14 public statement, Roosevelt appeared to set aside a good portion of the CES agenda: "I do not know whether this is the time for any federal legislation on old age security." According to Douglas Brown, a deeply distressed CES staff now took "desperate measures." Armstrong used her contacts at the Scripps–Howard chain of newspapers to generate an editorial questioning Roosevelt's commitment to old-age legislation. Upset and exasperated, the President got on the phone to Perkins, who in turn sounded out Witte. As Brown tells the story, a "much excited" Witte rushed to the office that he and Armstrong shared. "He asked us if we knew how and why the speech had received such a bad press. From then on, the President seemed to take a greater interest in old age insurance."

Throughout the fall of 1934, the CES functioned under the shadow of the growing Townsend movement. As Perkins recalled, "The pressure from its [the Townsend Plan's] advocates was intense. The President began telling people he was in favor of adding old-age insurance clauses to the bill and putting it through as one package." Within weeks of his arrival in Washington, D.C., in late July, Witte had asked the Postmaster General to investigate the Townsend movement to determine if funds sent through the U.S. mails were being used for illegitimate purposes. (By late September he had his answer: the Townsend Plan was clean). The heat was turned up a notch in November, when the election of a number of pro-Townsend representatives, including the eloquent and personable poet laureate of California, John S. McGroarty, made the introduction of a Townsend measure imminent. By December, when Townsend opened an office in the nation's capital to begin the lobbying process and sought a meeting with the president, Roosevelt refused to grant him an audience—an act described by the *Townsend Weekly* as "an insult that the masses of the people should resent."

At the Committee on Economic Security, an anxious Witte wrote a colleague of the growing danger:

> In the last three months I have become more concerned than ever with the
> Townsend Plan. There is no doubt that this movement has made tremen-
> dous headway. The battle against the Townsend movement has been lost, I
> think, in pretty nearly every state west of the Mississippi, and the entire
> Middle Western area is likewise badly infected. At this time the Republican
> party organization is at least flirting with the Townsendites. . . . The
> Townsend movement has become a terrific menace which is likely to engulf
> our entire economic system.

When the 74th Congress convened in January, the two sides were prepared for combat. The comprehensive administration package included a plan for unemployment insurance and two old-age measures. One of the old-age bills was a welfare measure, designed to provide joint state and federal relief for the elderly poor and for those who were too old to make sufficient contributions to an insurance plan. The other—in its essentials the future program of Social Security—provided for a national system of old-age insurance, to be funded by contributions from employers and employees. The Townsend bill, introduced by Rep. McGroarty, sought to do everything the administration measure did, but through the mechanism of the Old Age Revolving Pension Plan.

The issue was joined in the House Committee on Ways and Means, where the administration bill was the only one being formally considered, and where advocates of the administration measure—Democrats, all—were in control. Labor Secretary Perkins offered lengthy testimony. In language that sounded very much like Townsend's, she emphasized that "new and labor-saving machinery" and "new methods of work" on the one hand raised the standard of living "of the whole community" and, on the other hand, produced "transition periods" that were "extremely difficult for the individuals put out of work."

When asked about the Townsend Plan, however, Perkins was brutally critical. It was not "insurance," but a "dole," and an expensive dole at that. According to her estimates, payments under the plan would amount to "something considerably more than half of the total national income of the U.S.A. . . ." Perkins also challenged the claim that appropriations under the Townsend Plan would immediately and dramatically increase purchasing power and create a market for consumer goods. The plan, she concluded, was "in the realm of fancy rather than in the realm of practical statesmanship."

The next to testify was Murray Latimer. As head of the agency charged with administering the recently passed Railroad Retirement Act, Latimer could explain to the committee how that law had been openly designed to relieve crowded labor markets and increase efficiency by forcing the retirement of railroad workers over age 65. Latimer believed that the administration's proposal for old-age insurance could provide a similar service for the larger economy. If payments were large enough, they would induce considerable numbers of people to "withdraw from the labor market." "Nor," he added, "should the advantages of the maintenance of a large and continuing stream of purchasing power directed almost entirely to consumers' goods be overlooked."

Still another administration spokesperson, J. Douglas Brown, offered a rationale for the joint worker–employer contributions called for under the old-age insurance proposal. He emphasized that by contributing, workers would establish an "earned contractual right" to their annuities. And because employee contributions would result in larger payments in old age, they would "encourage the displacement of superannuated workers and of minor children and women supporting dependent old persons from the labor market."

Although the Committee on Ways and Means was not officially considering the McGroarty bill, it agreed to allow Townsend to testify; to have done otherwise would been politically unwise. Townsend appeared on a Friday morning, February 1, 1935, as the Committee was concluding its second week of testimony. In a prepared statement, he set the stage for the presentation of his plan. "For the past 5 years," Townsend said,

> the people of the United States . . . have been starving in the midst of plenty. They have seen experiment after experiment tried out; experiments which bore the recommendation and hearty approval of men we call "economists." Experiment after experiment has failed. . . . The rich are growing richer and the poor are growing poorer.

Townsend called for a "new experiment," one that had not had "the blessing of the so-called 'economists.'" Describing his plan as "only incidentally a pension plan," he claimed it would solve the unemployment problem and, by restoring purchasing power to the people, bring back prosperity. "The old people," he added, "are simply to be used as a means by which prosperity will be restored to all of us."

As much as Townsend disliked economists, he knew the politicians would want evidence of how his plan would work economically. He told the committee that because he was "simply a country practitioner of medicine," he had arranged for Glen Hudson, an actuary, to appear before the committee. On the following Monday, Townsend and Hudson testified together.

Almost immediately, the committee's inquiries became pointed and aggressive. Representative Samuel Hill, a Washington state democrat, questioned Townsend about who was eligible under his plan:

DR. TOWNSEND: We agree that the plan shall be nondiscriminatory and applied to all citizens equally.

MR. HILL: In other words, it would apply to John D. Rockefeller, Sr., to Henry Ford, to J. P. Morgan, as well as to a man who has no means or income at all?

DR. TOWNSEND: If they wish to acquire the pension under the provisions of the act.

When Hill inquired about the "revolving" concept claimed for the plan, Townsend appeared unsure and even confused. He could not clearly explain just how his plan "revolved," or how its revolving feature differed from any other dispersement of tax monies by the government. Townsend also had trouble fielding simple questions about the inner workings of the Townsend move-

Francis Townsend, addressing a newly organized club in Washington, D.C., March 6, 1937. The original caption for this photo noted that Townsend had been recently found guilty of contempt of the House of Representatives yet was "not the least apprehensive" that he might be sent to jail. (Library of Congress)

ment. Concerned about the size and strength of the Townsend organization, committee Chairman Robert Doughton (D-N.C.) asked Townsend to describe the plan's salaried sales force and explain the commission system used to compensate other employees.

DR. TOWNSEND: Mr. R. E. Clements is vice president and secretary, and he has all of that data.

THE CHAIRMAN: You ought to know. You are the head of the organization, and you should have such data before you.

Fortunately for Townsend, Hudson held forth through most of Monday afternoon, defending the plan with intelligence and enthusiasm. One congressman charged that the transaction tax would dramatically inflate the economy by adding 9 percent to consumer prices; another attacked the McGroarty bill for its failure to meet the needs of workers between ages 45 and 60, many of whom had trouble getting or holding jobs; and another claimed that at best, the Townsend Plan would retire only 3 million persons, far less than the 10 million retirements needed to eliminate unemployment altogether. Time and again, Hudson answered the critics by emphasizing that the plan depended for its success on the velocity of money. Because, he claimed, the average dollar turned over 34 times in 1 year, the economic stimulus provided by the Townsend pensions would be many times that of the money taken in through the transaction tax. Yet even Hudson was not thoroughly committed to every aspect of the McGroarty bill. Sensing Hudson's distance from the very measure he was there to support, Rep. Jere Cooper, a Tennessee Democrat, asked a revealing question:

MR. COOPER: Suppose you sat in the seats that we occupy at this table. As the [Townsend] bill now stands in its present form, do you think you would be safe in voting to report it and support it, as a representative of the people?

MR. HUDSON: No; I do not.

Not long after the hearings concluded, an amended version of the administration bill passed the House on April 19 by a vote of 371 to 33. Most of the opposition came from republicans. An earlier effort to substitute the McGroarty bill—the Townsend measure—received only about 50 votes. Nonetheless, the Senate Finance Committee seemed ready to reject compulsory old age insurance—that is, until Witte told committee members in closed session that "the probable alternative was a modified Townsend plan." In mid-June, the Senate passed the bill, 77 to 6. When Roosevelt signed the measure on August 14, 1935, the Social Security Act became law.

Even then, the Townsend movement would not go away. Indeed, it gained strength as the provisions of the Social Security Act became known. Over nine million Americans—domestic servants, government employees, farm workers like Charles Lewis, and everyone over age 65—were not eligible for old-age insurance benefits—what Americans today refer to as "social security." In contrast, even the very rich were entitled to benefits. Those who qualified were to begin paying into the system immediately, but they would not see their first check until 1942. Until then, those over age 65 could apply to their respective states for old-age assistance payments that averaged $19.21 per month ($3.92 in Mississippi). Eleanor Roosevelt, who continued to speak out against the Townsend Plan even when her husband would not, received thousands of letters from irate Townsendites, many of them women. "Security Bill is a joke so far as assisting the old people is concerned," wrote one woman. Another described the "so-called 'social security' act" as "niggardly and inadequate."

In October 1935, less than 3 months after the passage of the Social Security Act, some 7000 inspired Townsendites assembled in Chicago for the organization's first annual convention. They seemed ready to launch a movement rather than end it. A delegate from Texas took the floor to explain his hope

> to see erected in Washington, D.C. a statue with arms and legs made of strongest steel . . . adorned with a crown and priceless pearl . . . on his brow the word "Liberator," and under it all the name *TOWNSEND*. [applause, amens]

Although not a powerful speaker, Townsend rose to the occasion. To thunderous applause he described his movement as "an avalanche of political power that no derision, no ridicule, no conspiracy of silence can stem." Reaching for an analogy, he found one:

> Where Christianity numbered in hundreds in its beginning years, our cause numbers its millions. And without sacrilege we can say that we believe that the effects of our movement will make as deep and mighty changes in civilization as Christianity itself.

Later, when some delegates asked for clarification during the reading of the financial report, the convention burst into song:

> Onward Townsend soldiers
> Marching as to war,
> With the Townsend banner
> Going on before.

Flushed with the triumphal meeting at Chicago, Townsend increasingly attacked the major parties. Looking ahead to the fall, 1936, Congressional elections, he predicted that politicians of both parties would have to renounce their Republican and Democratic affiliations and support the Townsend Plan in order to get elected. Against Clements's advice, he pressed for a third party. In doing so, he may have attracted some additional followers—among them, perhaps, Charles Lewis—but he had also threatened the existing distribution of political power. In mid-February, 1936, the House of Representatives voted to initiate a bipartisan investigation of the Townsend movement. In late May, after 3 days of grueling testimony before a hostile committee, Townsend denounced the inquiry and walked out. A contempt citation was not issued until late in the year. In the meantime, Roosevelt had been elected to a second term in office with 27,751,612 votes; the Republican Landon, who had denounced the Social

Security Act, received 16,681,913; running on the Union Party ticket and carrying the banner of the Townsend Plan, Lemke received only 891,858.

AN INTERPRETATION

The story of Francis Townsend and the Townsend movement is in part the story of how a significant and organized minority was kept on the margins of American political life. Roosevelt played a major role in this process of marginalization by refusing to meet with Townsend or to comment publicly on the Townsend Plan. At the Committee on Economic Security, Witte tried to use the U.S. Post Office to sabotage the movement. The Congress did its part, denying to the Townsend bill the primary status that was granted to the administration measure. The major parties, fearful that an attack launched by either the Republicans or the Democrats would injure the party taking the initiative, joined forces to investigate the Townsend movement, then, when Townsend walked away from what he rightly called an "inquisition," made sure that the 1936 elections were over before issuing a citation for contempt of Congress.

One could argue that this effort to purge Townsend and his movement from American political life was justifiable, in that Townsend was a demagogue—that is, he made irrational and irresponsible appeals to a mass audience incapable of separating truth from falsehood. As events at the 1935 national convention reveal, there is no doubt that he had a devoted and even fanatical following; that he was enamoured of his own movement and perhaps, even, eventually attracted to his movement as a sort of modern-day Christianity. In addition, the movement utilized a variety of up-to-date promotional techniques that contributed to Townsend's personal success and to the movement's rapid growth. Charles Lewis, whose diary reveals an attraction to spectacle, might be interpreted as a typical Townsend victim. On the other hand, Townsend makes an unlikely demagogue: an old man, a boring speaker, incapable of controlling critical information. Hardly a man driven by the desire for adulation, Townsend emerged as a prominent political figure almost by accident. The most disturbing aspect of the Townsend movement's appeal was its reliance on religion, probably because this gave the cause a foundation exterior to traditional politics.

What makes Townsend's marginalization so remarkable is that many aspects of the man and his movement seem quite conservative. Although Townsend often couched his appeals in a familiar populist rhetoric of rich and poor, the Townsend Plan itself promised no significant distribution of income from one social class to another. As opponents pointed out, the sales tax, and the transaction tax that replaced it, were both harshly regressive. Furthermore, Townsend's desire to make his plan "nondiscriminatory" meant that even extremely rich people would be receiving checks for $200 per month that they did not need and probably would not spend. As Townsend's account of his life experiences reveals, the founder embraced and applied many aspects of capital-

ism, including speculation, promotion, entrepreneurship, and mechanical efficiency. His sharp criticism of the Civilian Conservation Corps confirms that
Townsend did not wish to ameliorate suffering by creating agencies and bu-
reaucracies; on the contrary, the Townsend Plan was essentially decentralist, a
way of distributing money in order to reinforce home and family. If anything,
Townsend valued individual independence too highly. Overall, Townsend's
conservatism explains his appeal to the rural middle class. But it may also account for the movement's failure—and it was a critical one—to attract significant support from industrial workers.

His radical-sounding rhetoric aside, perhaps Townsend was just another
of those "economists" he regularly denounced. Indeed, Townsend's ideas about
the economy and economic recovery resembled those of his New Deal adversaries. During the hearings before the House Committee on Ways and Means,
Perkins expressed Townsend-like anxieties about the long-term impact of technology. She and Latimer echoed the Townsend Plan's position on the importance of stimulating consumer spending; Latimer and Brown shared
Townsend's enthusiasm for reducing unemployment by using old-age insurance
to encourage the retirement of older workers from the labor force. While
Perkins lambasted the Townsend Plan as a "dole," the Social Security Act was
not strictly an insurance plan, as payments to the elderly were funded largely by
the current contributions of those still working. The Townsend Plan probably
was more than the nation could afford in 1935; its scope may even have been
fanciful, as Perkins claimed. But its assumptions and mechanisms were in many
respects part of the mainstream. In fact, Townsend's idea of turning the elderly
into what historian Abraham Holtzman has called "distributor custodians" fore-
shadows the prominent role of consumerism in the post-World War II economy
of affluence, and Townsend's emphasis on retirement anticipates the rising social security rates and private pension plans that would fuel the postwar retirement boom. Although the plan might well have damaged the economy had the
McGroarty bill become law, Townsend's point—that the economy had been severely harmed while being managed by the same economic establishment that
now attacked his plan as unworthy—was not unreasonable.

One could argue, in fact, that Townsend was anathema to politics not because his ideas were unfamiliar, but because he so blatantly articulated and presented the assumptions on which mainstream policy was based. When Roosevelt spoke about social insurance, he used the language of altruism, talking
about a "cradle-to-the-grave" system of "security." Townsend, in contrast,
spoke the language of the hard-nosed realists at the Committee on Economic
Security. Although he was not without an altruistic side, he could also be very
frank in explaining his goal of using the elderly to redistribute available work
and to revive the economy.

By being so open, Townsend succeeded for a time in revealing the sources
of the welfare state. One view of the origins of the welfare state, suggested by
Roosevelt's rhetoric, locates the origins of measures like the Social Security Act
in a benign response to the long-term insecurities produced by industrialization
and urbanization. Even Townsend's life—a mobile life that began in the securi-

ty of a large farm family and ended in the isolation of a city on the edge of the continent—supports this interpretation. Townsend's claim that the idea for the Townsend Plan came to him as he observed elderly women searching the garbage for food also sustains this view, although the fact that the story is not repeated in Townsend's autobiography suggests that the event may never have happened, and that Townsend concocted the incident only because he knew it coincided with what people expected to hear. Another interpretation of the emergence of the national welfare state emphasizes the growing power of organized labor. But as the story implies, organized labor did not play much of a role in the events leading to the passage of the Social Security Act.

The Townsend movement came under attack in part because it put in bold relief two other important explanations of the welfare state. Roosevelt's flacid leadership and lack of commitment to old-age insurance, as well as the Senate Finance Committee's rapid turnaround on the issue, are evidence that the New Deal was moved to create a national welfare state partly by the ongoing challenge of a movement that lay beyond the regular party system. Once goaded into action by Townsend, Roosevelt, Perkins, Witte, and other New Deal liberals turned to the big business community—to Swope and Teagle, and to Latimer, Richter, and other experts who had advised the nation's largest corporations. Townsend's forthrightness in describing the operations of the welfare state stripped the welfare state of its ideological protections, revealing the prominent role played by big business in its evolution. In the process, Townsend became a marked man.

Sources: Francis E. Townsend's autobiographical *New Horizons* (Chicago: J.L. Stewart, 1943), remains an important source on the pension advocate's personal background. On the Townsend movement, see Richard L. Neuberger and Kelley Loe, *An Army of the Aged: A History and Analysis of the Townsend Old Age Pension Plan* (1936; New York: Da Capo Press, 1973); Abraham Holtzman, *The Townsend Movement: A Political Study* (New York: Bookman Associates, 1963); and David H. Bennetts, *Demagogues in the Depression: American Radicals and the Union Party, 1932-1936* (New Brunswick, NJ: Rutgers University Press, 1969), and the Twentieth Century Fund's indictment, *The Townsend Crusade* (New York: Twentieth Century Fund, 1936). Differing perspectives on the Social Security Act of 1935 can be found in W. Andrew Achenbaum, *Social Security* (Cambridge, MA: Cambridge University Press, 1986); Edwin E. Witte, *The Development of the Social Security Act* (Madison: University of Wisconsin Press, 1963); William Graebner, *A History of Retirement* (New Haven: Yale University Press, 1980); and Jill Quadagno, *The Transformation of Old Age Security: Class and Politics in the American Welfare State* (Chicago: University of Chicago Press, 1988). Frances Perkins's memoir, *The Roosevelt I Knew* (New York: Viking, 1946), is an important source, and there is much to be learned from Congressional hearings on old age measures (see U.S. Congress, House, Committee on Ways and Means, *Economic Security Act: Hearings on H.R. 4120. . . . 1935* (Washington, DC: GPO, 1935).

10

THE POSTWAR SEX
CRIME PANIC

GEORGE CHAUNCEY, JR.

*From time to time Americans have found themselves caught up in moments of
collective fear and anxiety—what is labeled a "panic" in the story that follows. In
1919, in the wake of the first world war and the Russian Revolution of 1917, the object
of that fear and anxiety was the ideology of Communism. In the 1970s, the obsessive
concern with cults had some of the earmarks of a panic. And so did the child-
kidnapping scare of the early 1980s.*

*The late 1940s proved to be a particularly fertile ground for such events. The
UFO scare of mid-1947 began in late June, when the pilot of a private plane claimed to
have seen nine "saucerlike" objects; by mid-July, "flying saucers" had been reported in
35 states. The "sex crime panic" began that same year and held the nation's attention
through the early 1950s. For more than 5 years, newspapers and magazines were full
of stories and articles on brutal sex murders and assaults; state commissions studied
the problem of the sexual "deviant"; and parents agonized over whether it was safe to
send their children outdoors to play.*

*While some panics are just what they appear to be—that is, real expressions of
concern over genuine social problems—others need to be read and interpreted like any
other "text." When this is done, the flying saucer scare can be understood in part as a
reaction to anxiety-producing events in Europe, including the failure of the United
Nations to resolve a serious crisis in the Balkans and the Soviet decision not to
participate in the Marshall Plan, a program for European reconstruction. The UFO
sightings were one expression of Cold War anxieties.*

*The sex crime panic, too, was a more complicated event than it seemed at the
time. Like the UFO scare, it was partly a product of the Cold War, reaching a peak of
intensity in the winter of 1949 to 1950, just as the Soviet Union exploded its first
atomic bomb, China fell to the Communists, and Wisconsin Senator Joseph McCarthy
began charging that Communists had infiltrated the State Department.*

*In the following narrative, George Chauncey, Jr. probes a very different side of
the sex crime panic. For Chauncey, the panic was no mere reflection of postwar
anxiety over world events, although his account gives the Cold War its due. More
important, he argues, the panic reflected the deep tensions in family life and sexual
culture that had resulted from the upheavals of the war. The conflict had divided*

160

families, put women into men's jobs, and brought men into intimate—and sometimes sexual—contact with other men. Many Americans wanted to put an end to these and other threatening developments, and to enforce conformity to orthodox ideas of gender, sexuality, and family.

The sex crime panic evoked genuine fears about sexual violence. But it was seized on by a variety of groups that sought to mold it and use it to advance their own social programs and organizational interests. As a result of their efforts, the panic— for all the lurid tales of ice pick murders and rape mutilations of women and children—ultimately had as much to do with keeping women in the home as with keeping sex criminals off the street.

On November 14, 1949, Linda Joyce Glucoft, aged 6 years, was sexually assaulted by an elderly relative of the friend she had gone to visit in her Los Angeles neighborhood. When she cried out, her assailant, a retired baker whom the police had already charged in another child molestation case, choked her with a necktie, stabbed her with an ice-pick, and bludgeoned her with an axe, then buried her body in a nearby rubbish heap. Only a few days later, a drunken farm laborer assaulted and murdered a 17-month-old baby girl outside a dance-hall in a small town near Fresno. That same week, the Idaho police found the body of 7-year-old Glenda Brisbois, who had last been seen entering a dark blue sedan near her home; she had been murdered by a powerful assailant who had heaved her body 15 feet into an irrigation canal.

The gruesome details of these murders and of the hunt for their perpetrators were telegraphed to homes throughout the country by the nation's press. According to police statistics, such assaults were proportionately no more common than in previous years, but in late 1949 these three murders epitomized to many Americans the heightened dangers that seemed to face women and children in postwar America. Many regarded them not as isolated tragedies but as horrifying confirmation that a plague of "sex crime" threatened their families.

They had reason to fear such a plague. Ever since the war's end, a growing number of newspaper and magazine articles had focused the nation's attention on the murder of women and children; even more chillingly, they had argued that the motive for such assaults was sexual and that their perpetrators were men who had lost control of deviant sexual impulses. Stories with titles such as "Murder as A Sex Practice," "The Psychopathic Sex Menace," and "What Can We Do About Sex Crimes?" appeared with growing frequency in magazines as varied as the *Saturday Evening Post, Sir!,* and *Parade.* Between July of 1949 and March of 1951, *Collier's,* a weekly magazine with a large, middle-class family readership, ran a particularly explosive series of 13 articles by Howard Whitman which identified the growing "Terror in Our Cities," particularly the terror caused by the threat of sexual violence, as a national phenomenon. Newspapers throughout the country picked up on the issue and spotlighted local incidents involving children and women. "How Safe is Your Daughter?" J. Edgar Hoover had asked America's parents in a famous article published by *The American Magazine* in 1947; a barrage of articles on sex crime seemed to confirm his claim that she wasn't very safe at all.

Some of the reporters and editors responsible for such stories published them because they thought they would help sell papers. Other editors, genuinely convinced that the "sex criminal" posed a major new threat to American families, hoped the articles would alert the public to the danger such criminals posed and generate popular support for the drastic new measures they thought were needed to curtail them. "Let's get cracking before it's too late," *Collier's* challenged its readers in one editorial. "Who knows where or when the next psychopath or hoodlum will strike? In your town? In your street?"

The press campaigns worked: They did not just report on the fear of sex crimes gripping many cities, but helped create it. When Michigan's newspapers

Illustrating J. Edgar Hoover's famous article, "How Safe is Your Daughter?" (1947), this photograph evoked every parent's greatest fear—that some harm might come to his or her child—to urge support for the policing of a wide range of sexual nonconformists. The picture's giant hand also evoked the period's sci-fi horror films, which depicted the threats posed to America by alien ways of life; it suggested that every "sex deviate" was equally alien to traditional American values.

spotlighted the murders of three children in the state in 1949 and 1950, for instance, many parents became so alarmed that they wrote the governor to demand action. As one father wired the governor in September 1950: "Who is going to protect my Joey when he is out playing tomorrow[?] The death of eight year old Joey Hausey only speaks to millions of how wicked sex deviates are." After hearing a radio report about sex crimes in February, 1950, a woman wrote to remind the governor that "Every mother of a daughter—and I am one—can not rest with sex perverts at large."

In many cities, parents did more than write letters. In one community after another, they organized to demand governmental protection for their children. The pattern in most cities was the same: a single violent, sometimes murderous assault on a girl, boy, or woman galvanized a public already made deeply anxious about sex crime. Local newspapers and church, women's, and parents' organizations mobilized popular support for increased police protection and more effective legislation to control sex offenders. In Philadelphia, where a newspaper poll reported that 90 percent of the city's women and 50 percent of its men were afraid to walk the streets at night, a series of incidents in 1949 resulted in neighborhood demands for increased police surveillance. On Palm Sunday in 1950, Chicago's "Fighting Priest," Father Jerome Dehnert, asked his parishioners to attend a mass protest meeting at a parochial school where two children had been attacked—and 600 people showed up.

As a result of the press's preoccupation with the issue, the problem of sex crimes and "sex deviation" became, to an astonishing extent, a staple of public discourse in the late 1940s and early 1950s. A popular topic for young orators (one Michigan girl won her high school district's first prize in oration for a talk on sex deviates in 1950 and was later asked to repeat the speech at a Lions Club luncheon), it was also a regular subject of PTA discussions ("PTA Plans Panel on Deviate," announced one banner headline; "Experts Asked to Serve"). Some high school boys heard so much discussion of "deviates" that they even began referring to certain boys they disliked as "Dee-Vees" instead of "sissies."

The local press campaigns and panics set the stage for the eruption of a genuinely national hysteria in the winter of 1949 to 1950, when newspapers riveted the nation's attention on the November murders of the three little girls in California and Idaho. Papers throughout the nation followed the story of each murder in the grim detail normally reserved for local murders. Many also exacerbated local fears by providing additional coverage of local attacks on children, which, while less severe, took on greater significance because of their association with the national stories.

The *Detroit News,* for instance, generally the least sensationalist of Detroit's three daily newspapers, devoted extensive coverage to sex crimes during the week of the girls' murders. Every day that week, the *News* carried stories, several under front-page banner headlines, about the California and Idaho murders, the attempted abduction of a 7-year-old girl in Detroit, and FBI statistics about sex crime. Three editorials in as many days demanded stronger laws to control sex criminals; one in Saturday's paper warned of the "large, potentially murderous population [of sex deviates], floating about in the larger community, [which] constitutes the problem which in the last week has reasserted itself with appalling force." The front page of Sunday's paper carried the first installment in an 18-part series of articles on "Controlling the Sex Criminal," and another page was devoted to "Michigan's Most Revolting Sex Crimes—In Words and Photos." Monday's paper inaugurated a week-long series of articles, "Somebody Knows!," which reminded readers of the circumstances of eight recent "sex murders" in the Detroit area and offered rewards for information leading to the murderers' apprehension. Not surprisingly, 9 of the 14 letters to the editor published on Tuesday focused on sex crime. The press had created the image of a country whose streets and alleyways were overrun with murderous sex psychopaths.

The sensationalist accounts of the children's murders led church and women's groups throughout the country, as well as the local and national press, to demand state action, and state governments responded in ways that focused even more attention on the issue. The two sex murders in California in mid-November prompted 1000 people to meet in Los Angeles on November 21 to

---

Sex Crimes Growing Problem In State

FBI Drives on Perverts

| Some Of Toughest Laws In Years OK'd By Session | Legislation Curbs Reds, Sex Deviates And Dope Peddlers |

Wave Of Sordid Sex Incidents Stirs Police To Tighten Curfew

107 State Dept. Workers Fired, 74 Homosexuals

Mother Blamed for Neurotic Child

Plan to Overhaul Laws on Deviates

Large Audience Attends Meeting On Sex Deviates

PTA Urges Action on Sex Deviate Bills

Deviate Bills Pass Senate
Year-to-Life Clause One of 4 Approved

Life Terms OK'd For Sex Deviates

Governor's Study Panel Airs Community Problem In Three-Hour Session

Move To Treat Sex Offenders As Mental Patients Shows Gain

Headlines like these filled the nation's papers in the late 1940s and early 1950s, helping to construct the image of a nation whose streets were overrun by murderous "sex deviates."

demand state action. California's legislators established a Subcommittee on Sex Crimes the following week, and in December Governor Earl Warren convened both a special session of the state legislature and a conference of law enforcement agencies on "Sex Crimes Against Children" to respond to the crisis. The New Jersey Commission on the Habitual Sex Offender, established the previous spring, kept the issue alive in its state that fall by inviting some 750 judicial, medical, police, church, and civic authorities to testify at well-publicized hearings in Atlantic City and Newark. In February, 1950, it issued its report, and in March a New York study commission reported the results of its 2-year study of sex offenders confined at Sing Sing Prison and recommended legislation that was heartily endorsed by Governor Dewey. Both states' reports received nationwide press attention.

Fifteen state governments responded to the public's concern about sex crimes by establishing such study commissions, and while press reports had generated the initial panic, the commissions played the major role in its subsequent development. In Michigan, for instance, Governor G. Mennen Williams appointed a study commission on the "Deviated Criminal Sex Offender" in November of 1949 in response to the demands of civic and parents' organizations, scores of letters and petitions, and a vociferous press campaign. But a review of subsequent developments in Michigan shows that, once the commission was established, it quickly took charge of the panic, managing it and giving it direction.

The commission was well aware that the public's outrage over sex crimes might decline when the memory of particular crimes had faded, so for 2 years it worked to sustain that outrage and to channel it into support for the long-term programs it thought would effectively prevent such crimes. The commission cultivated the press in a successful effort to have itself portrayed as the major authority on the problem and to gain extensive, favorable coverage of its work (two of Detroit's three dailies, for instance, ran long series of articles explaining its proposals). In order to keep the public's attention focused on the sex crime issue the commissioners addressed public meetings sponsored by women's, farmers', and police organizations, local health councils, and PTAs. They also established official liaisons with the state's bar and medical associations and informal ties with other important civic, professional, and women's groups in order to mobilize their support for the legislation they recommended to the state assembly. In August of 1951 they mailed copies of their 245-page final report to some 2300 individuals and organizations. During the most important stages of the legislative battles that winter the commissioners sent "Legislative Bulletins" to more than 70 organizations, keeping them posted on legislative developments and urging them to orchestrate letter-writing campaigns and meetings with legislators in support of the bills they had proposed, and arranged for supportive women's and professional associations to send speakers to the public hearings on them.

The commission that so skillfully marshalled this support from the press and the public was dominated, like those in most states, by the psychiatrists and psychologists who served on it. The several clergymen, police, and court officials who served on the commission with them were accustomed to thinking of sexual behavior in terms of its morality or legality. But the psychiatrists persuaded them that unconventional sexual behavior should be considered not just immoral or illegal, but—more significantly—as a deviation from the psychological norm and the symptom of a deeper pathology or mental illness, which could be treated more effectively by medical men than by clergymen or the police. In Michigan, the one commissioner who dissented from this consensus—an attorney who denounced his colleagues' recommendations for threatening due process and individual liberty—soon stopped attending meetings because, he said, "no one listened to [his] objections."

Psychiatrists might not have had so much influence on the commissions earlier in the century, but their prestige had grown enormously during World War II because of the crucial role they had played in screening and managing the millions of people mobilized for military service. Their role in the Michigan commission both reflected their new prestige and helped them enhance it. As psychiatrists, the men who dominated the work of the commission genuinely believed that psychiatry had the most important contribution to make to the explanation of sexual "deviation" and to the solution of sex crime. As strategists, they heeded Governor Williams' advice in his address at their first meeting that they should "take advantage of the widespread public concern about this problem for the establishment of [mental health] facilities and programs dealing constructively with this situation."

Thus in the name of protecting women and children from sex deviates, the commission's psychiatrists urged the public to support the expansion of existing psychiatric institutions and the development of new ones, even if they were only peripherally related to the problem of sex crime. Before a special session of the Michigan legislature in March, the commission argued that the governor's proposal to expand psychiatric treatment programs and programs to educate clergymen, physicians, police, and school children about mental health issues should be supported because sex deviates were likely to remain undetected, untreated, and possibly dangerous without them. Eight months later, the commission urged voters to support a state bond referendum for the construction of mental hospitals; such programs, as the *Detroit Times* put it, would provide the "means of detecting the deviate before he becomes a killer."

The most innovative recommendation made by most state commissions—and the one most specifically geared to the problem of sex crime—was that the role of psychiatrists in the disposition of criminal "sex cases" be expanded. The Michigan commission's original proposal would have required the courts and prisons to cede authority to psychiatrists at every stage in such proceedings: Psychiatrists were to examine all sex offenders; those they diagnosed as dangerously psychopathic were, at their recommendation, to be sentenced to psychiatric hospitals for indeterminate terms, which would last from 1 day to life; and they were to be released only when a psychiatrist decided that they no longer posed a threat to the community. Some state commissions recommended that such commitment procedures apply to people convicted of specified offenses; others wanted anyone even suspected of psychopathic tendencies to be subject to them. Such indeterminant sentencing to psychiatric treatment, the Michigan commission argued, promised to cure and change psychopathic sex deviates, rather than just punish them; it was not only more humane but more effective than putting offenders in jail.

Several commissioners in Michigan and other states criticized such procedures for violating defendants' constitutional rights to counsel, cross-examination of witnesses, trial by jury, and other due process safeguards. They expressed particular concern about indeterminate sentencing, which allowed people labeled sex deviates to be confined indefinitely, no matter how serious their alleged offense. But the police, many judges, and the majority of commissioners in most states argued that the gravity of the danger posed by "sex deviates" justified the abrogation of traditional constitutional safeguards. As a sociologist and Nebraska municipal court judge argued in 1949:

> Such factors as the presumption of innocence, proof beyond a reasonable doubt and all of the other valuable and ancient safeguards by which the person accused of crime has been surrounded are perfectly proper in their correct application. Still they have no more logical place in the investigation of a known or suspected corrupter of the minds and bodies of little children than in the case of the insane person before the insanity board . . . for such proceedings are based upon theories utterly different from those of the criminal law.

But who was to be subject to such laws? Commissioners and other interested parties disagreed about this as well, although they agreed in general about who should be labeled a sexual deviate. Most of them put "sex murderers" at the top of the list, but they also included sadomasochists, pedophiles (adults sexually interested in children), rapists, homosexuals, exhibitionists, and voyeurs. Some extended the list to include anyone who was too "immature" to "adjust" to the "norms" of society and accept his or her gender-defined social responsibilities as a parent, husband, or wife, including people who engaged in premarital or extramarital sex. Benjamin Karpman, chief psychotherapist at the prestigious St. Elizabeth's Hospital and one of the decade's most important medical writers on sex offenses, argued that the sexual deviate displayed "patterns of sexual behavior" that

> are not desirable biologically or culturally and are therefore prohibited. . . . [Such patterns] are not directed ultimately toward procreation, the goal of all normal sexual life. . . . [The deviate] has not matured sexually, having failed to integrate his sexual needs and activities in such a way as to accord with socially accepted modes of sexual expression.

The postwar consensus thus maintained that to be sexually "normal" was to behave in a way the dominant culture considered not only socially acceptable and moral, but also statistically average and "mature;" the term "normality" thus embodied a moral judgment, a statistical presumption, and a psychological goal all at once. Failure to adhere to the sexual conventions, moral standards, and (supposed) majority practices of one's culture made one a deviate.

What contemporary authorities thought distinguished a sex criminal from a mere deviate—and made him both especially frightening and difficult to control—was that he was *psychopathic,* not only unconventional (or "abnormal") in his sexual impulses but unable to *control* his impulses. He was not technically insane, as a noted psychiatrist, Edward Strecker, pointed out in his testimony at the 1949 Philadelphia murder trial of Seymour Levin, a teenager who had raped and killed a neighborhood boy, as he was "able to distinguish between right and wrong behavior." But he was "still not willing or able to exert inhibitions against anti-social behavior as strong and effective as those which can be excited by the average person." The purpose of special sex psychopath laws was to place people capable of making such moral distinctions (and thus legally "sane") but unwilling or incapable of acting in accordance with them (and thus "psychopathic") under the jurisdiction of psychiatrists.

The dominant public image of the psychopath—based on press accounts of people like the Philadelphia murderer Levin—was that of a murderer out of control. But psychiatrists and jurists regarded murder as only the most extreme manifestation of a mental disease that more commonly resulted in less severe forms of nonconformist behavior. The judges who convicted Levin hastened to note that while psychopaths "commit a tremendous number of anti-social behavior acts, the [acts] are usually not in the major category. They are misdemeanors and slight offenses against the law." Indeed, many jurists and psychiatrists defined almost any failure to conform to social expectations as psychopathic. The chief medical officer of the Supreme Bench of Baltimore, Manfred Guttmacher, defined psychopaths as people "unable to conform to the standards of their social group, . . . tragic failures in establishing lasting and satisfying interpersonal relationships." In effect, then, some authorities regarded almost any "deviate" as psychopathic and almost any failure to conform to social norms as a sign of mental illness.

Although most authorities shared this broad definition of sexual deviance and psychopathy, they sharply disagreed about how wide a range of nonconformist (or "deviant") sexual behavior should render one subject to the new laws. One group of sociologists, psychiatrists, and civil libertarians agreed that a wide range of unconventional sexual behavior resulted from mental disorder, but argued that deviates should nonetheless be divided into two groups. Most deviates, they maintained, were harmless: They violated social norms but posed no direct danger to the lives or freedom of others. The state, they argued, should focus its limited resources on the apprehension, confinement, and treatment of the relatively small number of deviates whose sexual behavior posed a genuine danger, in their estimation, because it involved force or children. It should ignore relatively harmless nonconformists, such as people who engaged in premarital sex or homosexual relations, so long as they kept their behavior hidden (although most of them did still advocate the prosecution of gay people for doing some of the same things heterosexuals regularly did, such as trying to pick up a date at a bar, because they considered *any open* expression of homosexuality to be a public nuisance). They also argued that even if some currently harmless deviates might ultimately become dangerous, there was no way to determine which ones would; in particular, psychiatrists had not proven their claim that they could make such distinctions. In any case, imposing an indeterminate sentence on a man who had not even been charged with a crime—or, at most, had been convicted of a minor sex offense—simply because a psychiatrist had judged that he *might* become dangerous, would violate his constitutional rights.

A second group of psychiatrists, who received more support from police and court officials and were generally more influential in the debates of the 1940s and 1950s, regarded it as much more likely that a "minor deviate" would "degenerate" to more dangerous forms of deviance. Any nonconformist behavior, including window-peeping and consensual adult homosexual activity, they warned, might be only a symptom of a deeper pathology that would ultimately lead them to harm others. And while such officials disagreed about how likely

Psycho, **Alfred Hitchcock's 1960 thriller,** confronted its audiences with the same sort of bizarre, seemingly inexplicable murders that had terrorized urban communities in the postwar decade, and it rehearsed much of the postwar discourse concerning "sex murderers." The film's depiction of Norman Bates matched the prevailing clinical definition of a psychopath: the typical guy-next-door, a mild-mannered Mama's boy who had trouble developing mature relationships with adults. (Copyright © by Universal City Studios, Inc. Courtesy of MCA Publishing Rights, a Division of MCA, Inc., and the Academy of Motion Picture Arts and Sciences)

such degeneration was, they shared the conviction that psychiatrists could be trusted to determine which sexual nonconformists posed a long-term social danger.

Accordingly, this group argued that if the state wished to prevent sex crimes, rather than simply punish or treat their perpetrators after it was too late, it should seek to identify and examine all sexual nonconformists in order to determine which ones might become dangerous—and to confine those who might, even if they had not yet committed a crime. As a policewoman on the Michigan commission argued: "The police know that although many known sex deviates cannot be charged with a crime, . . . unless these individuals receive help they will probably continue to deteriorate and many of them will be dangerous in the community." The medical director of a state hospital in California put the case even more strongly: "Whenever a doubt arises in the judge's mind . . . that [an offender] might be a sexual deviate, maybe by his mannerisms or his dress, something to attract the attention, I think he should immediately call for a psychiatric examination." Detroit's Prosecuting Attorney demanded the authority to arrest, examine, and possibly confine indefinitely *"anyone* who exhibited abnormal sexual behavior, whether or not dangerous."

The press reports that shaped public perceptions of the problem usually blurred the lines between different forms of sexual nonconformity. They did this in part simply by using a single term, sex deviate, to refer to *anyone* whose sexual behavior was different from the norm. Like the term abnormal, the term deviate made any variation from the supposed norm sound ominous and threatening, and it served to conflate the most benign and the most dangerous forms of sexual nonconformity. People who had sex outside of marriage, murdered little boys and girls, had sex with persons of the same sex, raped women, looked in other people's windows, masturbated in public, or cast "lewd glances" were all called sex deviates by the press. The term sex deviate could refer to an adult engaging in consensual homosexual relations with another adult, an adult involved in consensual sadomasochistic relations—or a sadistic murderer of children. The very ambiguity of the term served to reinforce the press's message that any "sex deviate" might engage in any such activity. As the distraught mother of a 4-year-old boy wrote Michigan's governor after the papers were filled with such stories in late 1949, "Please get some laws in Michigan that protect even a pre-school child, and that also protect boys—not just girls. These deviates do not care."

The conflation of all forms of sexual nonconformity in press accounts of sex crime had particularly significant consequences for the public image of gay men. While the officials and reporters concerned about degeneration believed in principle that almost any sexual nonconformist might become a psychopathic sex murderer, the deep-seated anti-gay prejudices of the era led them to be particularly concerned about male homosexuals. Not only did they consider homosexual behavior reprehensible and a sign of mental illness (an opinion psychiatrists later repudiated), but they rejected the contention that gay men were harmless and should be left alone so long as they kept to themselves, because they believed gay men were *incapable* of keeping to themselves. "The sex pervert, in his more innocuous form, is too frequently regarded as merely a 'queer' individual who never hurts anyone but himself," warned the Special Assistant Attorney General of California in 1949. "All too often we lose sight of the fact that the homosexual is an inveterate seducer of the young *of both sexes,*" he insisted, "and is ever seeking for younger victims."

Moreover, they asserted, men who engaged in homosexual behavior had demonstrated the refusal to accommodate to social conventions that was the hallmark of the psychopath—and they could easily degenerate further. "Once a man assumes the role of homosexual, he often throws off all moral restraints," claimed *Coronet* magazine in the fall of 1950. "Some male sex deviants do not stop with infecting their often-innocent partners: they descend through perversions to other forms of depravity, such as drug addiction, burglary, sadism, and even murder."

The stereotype of the homosexual as an "inveterate" child molester had prestigious official advocates, but its most powerful proponents were the local and national press, the reports of which transformed the dominant public image of the homosexual into that of a dangerous psychopath during the postwar decade. The vast majority of cases of child sex murders reported by the press involved men attacking girls. But the press paid special attention to the murders of little boys and used them to try to persuade the public that all gay men were dangerous (attacks on little girls, it almost goes without saying, did not lead the press to make the same argument about heterosexual men). The brutal rape and murder of 6-year-old George Counter in a Detroit basement in the spring of 1949 was graphically described in the national press. Seven months later a description of the murder and the basement furnace behind which Counter's body had been hidden began Howard Whitman's *Collier's* article on crime in Detroit, and the image of it shadowed his description of his tour with a vice squad detective of a Detroit neighborhood where gay men gathered. For half an hour, according to Whitman, they followed one man whom he described as "a hefty six-footer dressed in a flowered shirt"—at once menacingly large and distinctively gay.

> Other deviates met and paired off, but this fellow stalked and hunted without success. He grew a little panicky. [. . . He moved to another block, where] he took up the hunt again—the same sordid cycle of exhibitionism, search and enticement. We saw him disappear down the steps of the latrine. . . . 'That fellow is at large on the town. Who knows what he might do?' said [the detective] resignedly. Suppose he got more panicky as the evening wore on? Suppose he finally snapped up a child? In an alley somewhere. Or a basement. And if the child screamed or threatened to tell. . . . I remembered the hissing furnace against which Georgie Counter's body was crammed.

Whitman's article appeared in *Collier's* in November 1949, just as the nation's attention was riveted on the murders of the three little girls in Idaho and California. Along with other articles, it led many people to fear that tolerating homosexuals resulted in just such crimes against boys and girls. Local press campaigns against sex criminals frequently turned into campaigns against homosexuals, and thus helped turn their readers' understandable fear about the safety of women and children into an irrational fear of gay men.

At a time when few heterosexuals knew openly gay men or women who might counter such stereotypes, the public representation of gay men in the press assumed special cultural authority. If homosexuals had been relatively invisible before the war, they had also been considered fairly harmless. But press reports in the postwar period created a new, more ominous stereotype of the homosexual as a child molester, a dangerous psychopath likely to commit the most unspeakable offenses against children. Magazine reports that homosexuals were almost impossible to detect—that even your next-door neighbor could be one—heightened public fears, provided additional evidence that psychiatrists' special diagnostic skills were needed, and helped justify police surveillance of gay bars. The growing intolerance and fear of gay people forced many of them to become even more careful to hide their sexual identities from their heterosexual associates, which only increased their invisibility and vulnerability. As one gay man lamented in 1956, "To the average parent I am a menace to warn their children against."

The study commissions and press focused on men's behavior when discussing the dangers of sexual deviation, but they had much to say about women's gender roles and responsibilities as well. For although most state commissions requested sweeping new authority for the police to apprehend and investigate sexual nonconformists and for psychiatrists to supervise their treatment, they insisted with equal vigor that such emergency programs alone could not solve the problem of sex crime. Most psychiatrists had little confidence that they could do more than train particularly receptive adult sex offenders to control their impulses. "It is seldom possible," one psychiatrist emphasized at a public forum in Michigan, "to cure completely a chronic sex offender of mature years." But if sexual deviation could not be eradicated in the present generation, it might be prevented in the next. "Abnormal sex behavior, be it in the adult or child," Benjamin Karpman asserted, "derives from the unwholesome family and social atmosphere in which the child develops. The fault lies with the parents."

Many psychiatrists therefore devoted considerable effort to advising parents about the proper way to rear their children. They had done this before, but fears about sex crime made many people more receptive to their counsel, and newspapers frequently reported on their speeches at forums on sex crime sponsored by the PTA and other civic groups.

Mothers took most of the blame. "Psychopath's Start Traced: Lack of 'Mothering' in Youth Blamed" ran one headline in the *Detroit News;* "Mother Blamed for Neurotic Child" ran another. Such warnings implied that the women who failed to follow psychiatrists' advice had only themselves to blame for the men who attacked them and their children.

Much of the advice psychiatrists gave women, however, concerned their roles as wives as much as their roles as mothers. It emphasized the importance of parents making clear to their children the differences between their gender roles as husband and wife and their genuine contentment with those roles. It warned that failure to do so could confuse the child about his or her own role, undermining his or her development as a mature, gendered human being. Thus, women were encouraged to stay at home while their husbands went to work, to invest their self-worth in their "homemaking" and childrearing, and to affirm their husband's authority in the marriage.

Postwar advice also contended that "domineering mothers" were the single most important cause of homosexuality. This effectively warned women that a family structure in which women held power or refused to be subservient to their husbands (that is, were "domineering mothers" married to "passive fathers") bred pathology. The culture's simultaneous denunciation of homosexuality and glorification of women who invested their self-worth wholly in their children made the idea that domineering mothers could turn their children into homosexuals an exceptionally powerful warning to women.

Many psychiatrists and government officials were unwilling to depend on parents following their advice, however; they also recommended new government programs that would supervise the rearing of children to ensure their socialization into acceptable gender roles and sexual identities. They called for the establishment of programs to train school personnel, clergymen, and police to recognize children who displayed nonconformist sexual tendencies and to refer them to psychiatric programs for treatment. "Obviously the teaching population should be alerted to the urgency of 'typing' emotionally maladjusted children as incipient sex deviates," one Michigan consultant pointed out to a gubernatorial assistant; "all teachers should be given training to recognize the symptoms of sexual deviation," concluded the Utah study commission.

Once identified as sissies, bullies, tomboys, or some other problem type, the children were to be referred to an expanded program of child guidance clinics for treatment by psychiatrists. Many teachers took such advice seriously, although inadequate state funding meant that few clinics were established to which they could refer "deviant" children. In a Philadelphia suburb in 1950, for instance, a teacher sent the parents of a 9-year-old fourth grader a note warning them that because their son was uninterested in sports the other boys considered him a sissy and there was a danger he might grow up to be a homosexual; she recommended that they get him counseling and force him to play sports. (His parents ignored the advice about counseling, but did set up a basketball hoop in the backyard.) The panic over sex deviates gave new urgency to adults' efforts to ensure that boys turned into rugged young men and girls into proper young women; the engendering of children (their socialization into conventional gender roles), which was supposed to be so natural, had never seemed so difficult.

Police and school officials also instituted security programs to prevent children from having any contact with sexual nonconformists: They began investigating teachers and other school personnel to ensure that none were homosexual and requiring that men convicted of sex crimes register with the local police department whenever they moved. They also taught children to avoid strangers: At the height of the sex crime panic in the winter of 1949 to 1950, schools and police departments across the country began to distribute pamphlets on a massive scale to parents and children warning about the dangers of unknown adults. One photo-illustrated booklet issued to thousands of school-children in Detroit warned girls to "NEVER go with strangers when they ask for directions" and boys to "NEVER wait around toilets."

Strangers certainly could be dangerous to unsuspecting children, but according to studies conducted in the 1950s, whose methodology tended to underrepresent intrafamilial sexual activity, the majority of children who had sexual experiences with adults knew the adult involved. More recent studies have argued even more strongly that incest is more common than attacks by strangers. The postwar pamphlets nonetheless focused exclusively on "strangers" as the source of sexual danger to children, and identified the family as a sanctuary for children from the violence of the external world. Thus they misrepresented some of the real dangers facing children, but in a manner consistent with the ideology of the Cold War nuclear family. The pamphlets intended for children, like the lectures intended for their parents, embodied and defined the dominant postwar vision of the proper family.

NEVER play alone in alleys, or in deserted buildings. Keep together.

NEVER wait around toilets. Always leave immediately.

The sex crime panic both reflected and heightened many people's fears that suburban and urban life had become more transient, anonymous, and dangerous in the wake of World War II, and prompted local police departments to distribute thousands of brochures like this one to school children, warning them of the dangers posed by strangers in the postwar urban landscape.

AN INTERPRETATION

The postwar outcry over "sex crimes" and "sex deviates" exhibited many of the characteristics of what social theorists have termed a moral panic. Moral panics usually occur in periods of social stress when large numbers of people, already apprehensive about the stability of the social order, focus those anxieties on a social phenomenon, incident, person, or social group, which comes to symbolize (even as it obscures) the forces that seem to threaten their way of life. The mass media often exacerbate or even create such panics, by focusing public attention on the phenomenon and portraying it in stereotypical and threatening ways; public officials and professional "experts" of various sorts usually also play important roles in defining (or even creating) the "problem." The explosion of concern in the 1980s about the problem of child abuse in day care centers, for instance, could be considered such a panic. In retrospect, the problem seems to have existed not so much in the centers as in the minds of the media and the police, but the media "exposés" of abuse both evoked and focused widespread anxieties about the family, working mothers, and the problems of sexual violence and incest.

Why did a moral panic about sex crimes engulf postwar America? Although a number of horrifying murders of children did occur in the late 1940s, they alone cannot account for the panic for the simple reason that such murders were not new. Police statistics showed no disproportionate increase in the number of crimes of sexual violence; statistically speaking, there was no crime wave.

What distinguished the murders of those years was neither their number nor their intrinsic horror but the magnitude of the coverage they received and the manner in which they were interpreted. Press crusades frightened the public (and not incidentally sold papers) by using the murders to create the image of a country whose streets and alleyways were overrun with murderous sex psychopaths. The deliberations of the state study commissions then perpetuated those fears by keeping the public's attention focused on the issue even when the memory of particular crimes had faded; they expanded the panic's ideological significance by becoming an important vehicle for postwar discussions about the boundaries of acceptable sexual and gender behavior and about the extent to which the state ought to enforce such boundaries. State governments acted as forcefully as they did because of the interest several constituencies had in using the panic, once it developed, to advance their own (sometimes conflicting) interests: elected officials keen to demonstrate their ability to manage a problem that had aroused their constituents; police forces anxious to secure new mechanisms for controlling homosexuals and other people they considered "sex criminals"; psychiatrists hoping to enhance their cultural authority and institutional power.

Yet the panic could not have become so widespread and powerful had it not tapped into deep anxieties already existing within the culture about the disruptive effects of World War II on family life, sexual mores, and gender norms. The war had removed millions of men from their families, forced hundreds of thousands of those families to migrate to overcrowded military and industrial centers, and allowed unprecedented numbers of married women to enter the paid labor force and take over industrial jobs previously considered suitable only for men. Although women's industrial employment was always described as a temporary expedient, it nonetheless had demonstrated that women could do so-called "men's work" and allowed many women to live independently and earn unprecedentedly high wages, gains that many were loath to give up when the war ended.

At the war's end discriminatory management and union policies ensured that most women workers lost their new industrial jobs to returning veterans, and government policies (especially the GI Bill of Rights) allowed many of those veterans to buy suburban homes and establish families. Such efforts to reconstruct the gender order were accompanied by a postwar media campaign that championed the virtues of suburban domesticity, glorified women's roles as homemakers, and warned of the dangers posed by married women's employment. After the hardships of the depression and war, many women welcomed the postwar social order; others discovered there were risks involved in questioning it. The sex crime panic served to increase the pressure on women reluctant to leave their jobs by stigmatizing those who did not devote themselves full-time to mothering. Repeated accounts of rape and child molestation reminded women of the very real dangers they and their children faced outside the home (even as the accounts ignored the dangers they faced inside it), and the commissions provided a platform to experts (rather than to women themselves) who blamed sexual deviation and violence on women's bad mothering.

The panic also reflected and contributed to a more general effort to reimpose the social controls on sexual behavior that had been weakened by the war. The war's disruption of family life led to an increase in nonmarital sexual activity of all sorts, but its most striking effect was to facilitate the growth of urban gay and lesbian communities. By removing men from the supervision of their families and small town neighborhoods and placing them in a single-sex military environment, military mobilization increased the chances that they would meet gay men and be able to explore their homosexual interests. Many recruits met other gay people for the first time, saw the sort of gay life they could lead in large cities, and chose to stay in those cities after the war, rather than return home where they would almost surely have had to hide their sexual preferences. Some of the women who joined the military, as well as those on the homefront who shared housing and worked in defense industries with other women, had similar experiences. The number of bars and restaurants serving gay and lesbian customers grew enormously during and after the war, and in larger cities gay enclaves became noticeable in certain neighborhoods. The Kinsey Report on male sexual behavior, published in 1948, highlighted these changes—and shocked the nation—by showing how widespread homosexual behavior was.

The sudden growth in the visibility of gay people led to an upsurge in anti-gay prejudice, as many Americans sought a return to prewar "normality." Even before the war most homosexual behavior—from actual sex to one man trying to pick up another man for a date or two women dancing together at a bar—was illegal, and in many states the law prohibited bars, restaurants, and other public establishments from serving lesbians and gay men or even letting them gather on their premises. After the war the police in many cities intensified their enforcement of such laws. By 1950 Philadelphia's six-member "morals squad" was arresting more gay men than the courts knew how to handle, some 200 each month.

Local panics over sex crimes, even when they originally had nothing to do with homosexuality, often resulted in even harsher anti-gay crackdowns, as such crackdowns were often the only concrete steps (or at least the most visible ones) the police could take in response to public demands for action. One man who moved to Detroit shortly after George Counter's murder recalled how worried the gay people he met there were about the "campaign against gays" being waged by the city's newspapers and police. He met several men who had been arrested by the police while socializing in gay bars, and he knew others who would not even visit a gay bar for fear of being caught in a police raid. After only 2 months in the city he was himself arrested in such a raid and forced to spend a night in jail. The native Detroiters arrested with him, he later recalled, were terrified they would be sent to a psychiatric prison. "They hold you there," one cellmate warned, in an apparent reference to the state's new indeterminate sentencing law, "until the unlikely event that you turn straight."

Gay people were particularly hard hit by the new climate of intolerance, but the widely publicized deliberations of the state study commissions increased the cultural sanctions against unconventional sexual behavior of any sort. Even when the press reported that authorities disagreed about how dangerous gay men and other "deviates" were, the very terms in which it described those disagreements reinforced the public's anxiety that *any* form of gender or sexual nonconformity was pathologically abnormal and merited analysis and treatment, whether on a voluntary or forced basis. The wide publicity given such ideas served to establish boundaries for the gender and sexual behavior of all. The spectre of the sex psychopath led to the unfair stigmatization of all homosexuals as potential child molesters or murderers, and the spectre of the hidden homosexual contributed to the stigmatization of anyone who violated certain gender norms as "immature" and potentially (or "latently") homosexual. Boys who didn't play sports—and girls who did—were sometimes stigmatized this way, and the public's increased awareness of (and anxiety about) the extent of homosexuality in postwar society quietly contributed to the pressure put on men and women who were reluctant to marry to do so and to assume other culturally defined gender roles, lest they be considered abnormal. The spectre of the hidden homosexual haunted the cult of suburban domesticity.

That spectre haunted the Cold War as well. In February, 1950, when Senator Joseph McCarthy seized the nation's attention by charging that hundreds of Communists had infiltrated the State Department, the sex crime panic was at its height. McCarthy shrewdly played on and exacerbated Americans' apprehensions about communist subversion, and he played on their fears about sex criminals as well. From the beginning he charged that sex deviates had infiltrated the government along with communists, and the State Department fired hundreds of employees whom it discovered to be gay.

The sex crime panic was also linked to—and reinforced—the postwar hysteria about communism in other ways. Both the anti-communist and anti-sex deviate campaigns claimed that minimal deviations signaled greater dangers: Just as homosexuals were branded as child molesters or murderers, so were liberal dissenters, civil rights activists, and union organizers attacked as communists or communist dupes. Both campaigns sought to develop programs that would identify, investigate, and limit social or political nonconformity. Both argued that the dangers posed by such nonconformity justified the abrogation of traditional constitutional safeguards. And both encouraged the conformity that became a hallmark of postwar American society—and against which the social movements organized by African-Americans, students, women, and lesbians and gay men would rebel in the 1960s.

In a moral panic, diffuse public apprehensions and concerns are symbolically embodied in a single object on which public attention is focused. The national panic over sex crimes constituted such a panic, for it became one means of expressing the deep postwar apprehensions about the sexual and gender order and of weighing religious, medical, judicial, and police claims to the authority to arbitrate them. A series of murders came to symbolize, for many people, the dangers of gender and sexual nonconformity. Denounced by the press, explained by the state commissions, and burned into public consciousness by both, the "sex deviate" became a means of defining, by his transgressions, the boundaries of acceptable behavior for anyone who would be "normal."

Sources: This story is an abbreviated version of a paper I originally presented at the University of Toronto in 1985 and at the annual meeting of the Organization of American Historians in 1986. The story's most important sources include the papers of Governor G. Mennon Williams of Michigan, the manuscript records of the Michigan Commission on the Deviated Criminal Sex Offender (including the minutes of their meetings, copies of correspondence, and internal memoranda), the reports published by a dozen other state commissions, several oral histories I have collected, articles from contemporary medical and legal journals, and scores of articles published in national magazines and local newspapers during the postwar decade. For a discussion of the intellectual background to the work of the study commissions (as well as a somewhat different interpretation of their politics), see Estelle Freedman, "'Uncontrolled Desires': The Response to the Sexual Psychopath, 1920–1960," *Journal of American History* 74 (June 1987): 83–106. On women and politics in the postwar decade, see Susan M. Hartmann, *The Home Front and Beyond* (1982) and Elaine Tyler May, *Homeward Bound* (1988). For more on the federal government's attacks on homosexuals, see John D'Emilio, "The Homosexual Menace: The Politics of Sexuality in Cold War America," in *Passion and Power,* ed. K. Peiss and C. Simmons (1989). Stanley Cohen's *Folk Devils and Moral Panics* (1972) is the classic study of moral panics.

11

THE MAKING OF DISNEYLAND

GEORGE LIPSITZ

The decade of the 1950s has a special place in Americans' collective memory. It is fondly recalled as the last "good" decade: an innocent, affluent, peaceful, and secure time, before the riots and protests of the 1960s set Americans against one another, and before the defeat in Vietnam, the Arab oil boycott, Watergate, and other events of the 1970s forced the American people to begin the painful process of reevaluating the nation's position and role in the world. God's country. Hula Hoops and Pat Boone. A two-bedroom ranch house in the suburbs. Television. Disneyland.

Many Americans actually lived this idealized version of the fifties—enough so that it could be fashioned into a believable myth. After the Korean War ended in early 1953, the nation was at peace. Beginning in 1946, an unanticipated baby boom helped sustain high rates of economic growth while fostering a new family-based domesticity in the rapidly expanding suburbs. By mid-decade, living standards were at an all time high, and Americans were buying consumer goods in unprecedented quantities. In a story entitled "Everybody Rich in the U.S.?" U.S. News and World Report *claimed that poverty had virtually disappeared, and that it was an "unusual family that does not own a home, a car, a TV, many luxuries. Nothing like it has ever been seen before." Holding this "new economic order" together was the intrepid consumer, whose purchases would presumably prevent the economy from reverting to the depression conditions of the 1930s. There were, to be sure, anxieties about the "affluent society," even in the 1950s: Consumers were heavily in debt; automation was threatening to eliminate skilled work; and to some social critics the homogeneity of the suburbs seemed boring and even threatening. But by and large, Americans wanted to believe that their worries were over—and they did.*

When it opened in 1955, Disneyland represented this collective dream. As George Lipsitz' account reveals, all of Disneyland was fantasyland, an imaginary world of universal experience where poverty didn't exist, where slavery had never happened, and where no real work was ever done. Like the postwar suburbs, which generally excluded blacks and other minorities, Disneyland was designed not for all families, but for those—mostly white and middle-class—that could afford the admission charge and desired the isolating experience that the park provided. And in

*the shops on Main Street, park patrons lined Walt Disney's pockets and did what in
the fifties seemed very much an act of social benevolence: They consumed.*

*If at times Disney's perspective seems narrow and provincial, it is well to
consider that Disneyland was the success it was in part because the founder's fantasy
so closely resembled the shared desires of millions of Americans. To what extent, then,
does the Disneyland experience merely reflect American values? Were the white,
middle-class Americans who patronized Disneyland in search of uniformity,
homogeneity, and passivity? Were Americans responsible for Disney's pioneering
multimedia promotions, or for the ugly heritage they have yielded: hour-long
commercials that masquerade as entertainment; news "documentaries" that
dramatically recreate past events; and feature films that relentlessly promote
particular products? Did Americans seek to be constituted as consumers rather than
producers? When youngsters bought Davy Crockett coonskin caps and spent their
weekly allowances on Mickey Mouse ears, were they exercising free choice, or were
they being prepared—like millions of visitors to Disneyland—for advanced consumer
capitalism?*

On July 17, 1955 a nationwide television audience watched the opening of the
Disneyland amusement park on that evening's broadcast of the Disneyland television program. Before what was then the largest concentration of television
equipment and personnel assembled for any one event (63 engineers and 24
live cameras) hosts Bob Cummings, Art Linkletter, and Ronald Reagan
presided over ceremonies that one critic likened to "the dedication of a national
shrine."

Despite 3 months of rehearsal for the program and an $11 million invest-
ment in the park, all did not go smoothly on opening day. Audio and video portions of the program went dead intermittently, and the hosts had considerable
difficulty synchronizing their reporting with the pictures on the screen. The
park's drinking fountains did not work, leading to long lines at the concession
stands. Hot weather melted the freshly laid asphalt on streets and walkways,
causing women in high-heeled shoes to sink into the pavement and providing
small children with the opportunity to track footprints and leave rude messages
on the sidewalks. In an emblematic indignity, the dramatic appearance of actor
Fess Parker (dressed as his television character Davy Crockett) riding on horseback through Frontierland lost some of its intended drama when someone accidentally turned on lawn sprinklers, soaking Parker and his horse. One disappointed critic described Disneyland as being "like a giant cash register, clicking
and clanging, as creatures of Disney magic came tumbling down from their
lofty places in my daydreams to peddle and perish their charms with the aggressiveness of so many curbside barkers."

If everything seemed to go wrong for Disneyland on opening day, everything seems to have gone right for it ever since. By 1958, the annual attendance
at Disneyland surpassed the number of patrons at Yellowstone, Yosemite, and
the Grand Canyon combined. After 10 years of operation, one quarter of the
U.S. population had visited the park and Disneyland had earned $273 million

for the Disney Corporation. In the early 1970s Disney Enterprises joined the list of the 500 largest corporations in America, and by the late 1980s California's Disneyland and Walt Disney World in Florida accounted for 62 percent of the sales and 70 percent of the operating earnings for a corporation the annual revenues of which approached $3 billion each year.

Disneyland has been more than just a financial success story. It has exercised an influence on American culture that can scarcely be measured in dollars. Film maker George Lucas (the producer of *Star Wars*) says that Disneyland was his favorite playground when he was growing up. The pop singer Michael Jackson visits Disneyland frequently, and astronaut Sally Ride borrowed from the park's terminology when she described her first trip into space as "a real E ticket ride." Harry S Truman ceremonially received the Disneyland flag bearing the image of Mickey Mouse when the former president visited the park in 1957, and every U.S. president since has put in a personal appearance at the park, as have numerous visiting heads of foreign countries. Security con-

Walt Disney dons a straw hat and picks up a fishing pole as he poses for a photograph designed to provide publicity for the opening of Disneyland. Child actors pose as Mark Twain's characters Tom Sawyer and Becky Thatcher in a picture that presents Disney at the center of America's storytelling traditions. (Department of Special Collections, University Research Library, UCLA)

cerns prevented the Soviet Union's Nikita Khrushchev from visiting Disneyland in 1959, but newspaper photographs over the years have captured Egypt's Anwar Sadat shaking hands with Goofy and India's Jawaharlal Nehru piloting the jungle boat in Adventureland. "Oh, this is so much fun, father is having such a good time," enthused Indira Gandhi, Nehru's daughter and herself a future Prime Minister of India. "We looked forward to Disneyland as much as anything on our trip."

As the creator of Mickey Mouse and numerous other popular cartoon characters, Walt Disney Studios had become an American institution by the 1930s. But Disney's personal wealth never equaled his enormous prestige, and by the late 1940s both he and the studio he headed faced serious financial prob-

Vice-President Richard M. Nixon, his wife Pat Nixon, and their daughters Tricia and Julie visit Disneyland in 1955. This staged photo displays one function of the park—its role as a site for adult celebrities to show their "personal" sides. The smiles and postures of Mr. and Mrs. Nixon in this photo indicate that they understand this role very well, but their identically dressed daughters seem less at ease with their day at Disneyland turning into an opportunity for publicizing their father's career. (Department of Special Collections, University Research Library, UCLA)

lems. These financial pressures encouraged Disney to diversify into the amusement park business. At that time, amusement parks were not doing well financially, and few investors thought of them as places with a potential for profit making. He borrowed as much as he could from the Bank of America in California and the Bankers Trust Company in New York, but their skepticism about his chances of building a financially successful amusement park limited the amount of money they would make available to him. When Disney exhausted his credit with the bankers, he sold his second home at Smoke Tree Ranch in Palm Springs, California, and cashed in his life insurance policy in order to finance the amusement park. He took on a personal debt of over $100,000, confounding the bankers who expressed understandable skepticism about the likelihood of an amusement park repaying that kind of investment. Even Disney's brother Roy limited the financial investment of the studio in Disneyland to $10,000 because he considered the park to be just another of "Walt's screwy ideas."

Disney wanted to build a new kind of amusement park, one that broke with the traditions of the past. While planning his own park he inspected fairs and amusement parks all across the country to see what worked and what didn't. He was particularly depressed by the conditions at New York's Coney Island, which had been the first successful amusement park in the 1890s. One journalist reports that Disney found Coney Island "so battered and tawdry and the ride operators were so hostile that Walt felt a momentary urge to abandon the idea of an amusement park. But when he visited Copenhagen [Denmark] and saw that city's Tivoli Gardens, he proclaimed 'Now *this* is what an amusement park should be.'" He felt that most amusement parks had become unsavory places, that they placed too much emphasis on risk taking, danger, "thrill rides," games of chance, barkers, and concession stands.

Disney vowed to establish a park that replaced those sensations with "educational and patriotic values" transmitted through wholesome family fun. As a publicity brochure for Disneyland explains, "As a pioneer in the motion picture industry, Walt developed an intuitive ability to know what was universally entertaining. When his daughters were very young, Walt would take them on what he later called "very unsatisfying visits" to local amusement parks. He felt he could build a park at which parents and children could have fun together. He wanted Disneyland to be a place where "people can experience some of the wonders of life, of adventure, and feel better because of it."

Walt Disney wanted his amusement park to operate by the same principles as his motion pictures. "I hate to see a down-beat picture," he once explained, "so that when I come out [of the theater], it makes me feel that everything's dirty around me. I know it isn't that way, and I don't want anybody telling me that it is." That commitment to a wholesome and upbeat view of the world led Disney to take great pains with his creations. In the case of Disneyland, he wanted a park that would physically block out any view of the outside world, so that visitors could concentrate on the pleasant fantasies within its walls. He wanted to create a forum for fun, a public space free of danger, dirt, and depravity. To millions of Americans he succeeded magnificently, and they have repaid Disney and his heirs many times over with their patronage. But in order to accomplish all this he needed to raise large sums of money in a fairly short time.

It was Walt Disney's understanding of television that not only won him the financing necessary to build Disneyland, but also the resources to make it a success after it opened. Disney had produced a successful Christmas special in 1950, and he knew that the new medium of television was hungry for the sort of product that he could provide. He offered to produce a weekly series for television, but only if one of the networks would help finance Disneyland. ABC network officials agreed to invest $500,000 directly and to guarantee loans of up to $4.5 million for the amusement park in return for one-third ownership in the park and a weekly series titled "Disneyland."

During the construction of the park, Disney Corporation engineers transformed fields of orange groves and palm trees into an environment with many identities including the terrain along the Mississippi River. This photograph shows what Disney tried so hard to hide about the park—people doing actual labor in a real work place. (Department of Special Collections, University Research Library, UCLA)

Armed with this new infusion of funds, Disney commenced construction of the park. He commissioned the Stanford Research Institute (SRI) to identify a centrally located tract of land available at a reasonable price. Harrison "Buzz" Price, director of the Los Angeles branch of the Institute, recommended building the park in the vicinity of the main railroad station in downtown Los Angeles, but the cost of land in that location proved too high for Disney's budget. Disney rejected a proposed ocean-front location because he felt that the beach attracted unsavory individuals. Price and his fellow researchers noticed that residential growth in the Los Angeles area tended to follow the paths of new freeways heading east and south from the central city. They recommended several sites in suburban areas, but eventually settled on an Anaheim location because it received five fewer inches of rain per year than alternate locations in San Gabriel and in the San Fernando Valley. The SRI advised Disney to buy 65 acres of orange groves in Anaheim for $4,500 an acre; 10 years later the land was worth $80,000 an acre.

Disney cleared the orange groves and relandscaped them, sending his staff on scouting missions throughout Southern California to find "interesting" trees and shrubs for the park. He deliberately reshaped the terrain so that once inside Disneyland, visitors would lose visual contact with the surrounding area. "I don't want the public to see the world they live in while they're in the park," he explained to his design staff. "I want them to feel they are in another world." Yet financial considerations led Disney to include at least one part of the outside world in the park: advertising. As part of his efforts to raise money, Disney got 32 major corporations to lease concessions in the park, in effect paying him for the opportunity to sell their products and advertise their brands. The Bank of America opened up a small branch in the "Main Street" section of the park, and the Continental Baking Corporation paid for the privilege of having "Wonder Bread" designated as the "official white bread" of Disneyland.

Financial rather than aesthetic considerations dictated the connection between television and Disneyland. In his heart, Disney felt that television (then largely a black and white medium) was actually a poor vehicle for displaying the vivid colors and high production values of his cartoons and nature films. But he needed money for the amusement park, and he thought that the new medium could be very important as a marketing device, not just for Disneyland, but for all of his studio's other ventures. "We wanted to start off running," Disney later told *Business Week* magazine in regard to his decision to tie the amusement park to a television series. "The investment was going to be too big to wait for a slow buildup. We needed terrific initial impact and television seemed the answer." The Disneyland television program went on the air on October 27, 1954, with a full hour program previewing the opening of the Disneyland amusement park the following summer. Two other programs later in the season gave progress reports on the park.

The success of the Disneyland television series, and consequently the success of Disneyland itself, stemmed in large measure from a three-part episode broadcast during the 1954 to 1955 season about the frontiersman Davy Crockett. At first glance, the likelihood for success of such a series seemed slight. Popular tastes at the time in film and television had been moving away from

western and frontier stories. Furthermore, Crockett himself was, at best, an ambiguous historical figure—a man celebrated as a hero for his part in clearing the
wilderness, fighting Indians, serving in Congress, and dying in battle at the
Alamo, but one equally reviled as a villain for his destructive hunting practices
(killing 105 bears in one season, shooting six deer in a day and leaving five of
them to hang in the woods), the betrayal of his political supporters when he
turned against Andrew Jackson and joined the Whig Party, and his crude anti-
social behavior. To further complicate matters for Disney, the actor selected to
play Crockett, Fess Parker, was allergic to horses and hated the costumes his
role required him to wear. According to one account, Disney personnel had to
teach Parker how to ride a horse, and he disliked the leather breeches that he
had to wear so much that when out of camera range "he shied away from
them as if they were a bunch of poison ivy, swearing they would give him
'crotch rot.'"

Whatever shortcomings the story of Davy Crockett presented for purposes
of history or drama, it nonetheless offered an ideal marketing opportunity for
Disney executives. While the show was still in the planning stages, Disney merchandisers explored the possibilities for manufacturing and distributing coonskin caps like the ones Crockett would wear on television. Even though almost
no American homes had color television sets at that time, Disney producers
shot the episodes in color in anticipation of stringing them together and releasing them to theaters as a feature film.

Vince Jefferds, Disney's head of promotion boasted, "I could make a good
case that licensing of an article is more profitable than manufacturing it. I often
made money out of movies that were a loss at the box office." Shortly before
the first episode of the Davy Crockett trilogy was scheduled to air, producers realized that they did not have enough film footage to fill their entire program.
They asked the creative staff at the studio to write a song that would enable
them to bridge over some gaps in the story, and their creation, "The Ballad of
Davy Crockett," went to number 1 on the hit parade and stayed at the top of
the charts for 13 weeks. Merchandisers sold more than ten million coonskin
caps, making them out of rabbits and squirrels when they ran out of rac-
coon fur.

The filmed portions of the Davy Crockett series cost $700,000 to make
with only $300,000 in advertising revenue guaranteed for their dates on the air.
But when the episodes were spliced together for theatrical release, they made a
profit of almost $2.5 million even though they had already been seen by an esti-
mated 90 million viewers on television. The Davy Crockett phenomenon was
perfectly timed for the opening of Disneyland the following summer, each
episode not only enhanced the royalties from record sales and coonskin caps,
but they also served as advertising for the "Frontierland" section of the amusement park.

Television provided Disney with the money to finish building Disneyland,
and the shows he made for ABC in return worked to advertise his films and
amusement park. The second program of the 1954 to 1955 season was a promotional film about the making of the motion picture *20,000 Leagues Under the*

Sea, which was soon to be released by Disney Studios. Bolstered by the program-length commercial on the second Disneyland show, *20,000 Leagues Under the Sea* became the biggest grossing live-action Disney film up to that time, earning over $6 million in its first release. "The amazing thing is that nobody complained that we were doing publicity movies," recalls Disney executive Bill Walsh. "Far from it. Our '20,000 League[s]' documentary even won us an Emmy. *And* it brought in sponsorship for our programs, first from Coca-Cola and then from Johnson and Johnson." The deal benefited ABC as well. The network received one third of the profits generated by Disneyland until Walt Disney Productions exercised their option to buy back the network's one-third share of ownership of Disneyland in 1960 for $7.5 million, a sum 15 times the size of ABC's investment. In addition, the Disneyland television program established ABC as a competitive network for the first time, attracting a flood of national advertisers to their entire schedule.

Television gave Walt Disney the financial resources essential for the construction of Disneyland, and it also served as a marketing device crucial to the success of the park. The rides in the park advertised Disney comic books, cartoons, films, and television programs, and all of Disney's other entertainment and marketing efforts functioned as a commercial for the park. Customers paid money to enter Disneyland and to go on rides that advertised Disney entertainment. They bought souvenir merchandise that further advertised the characters and stories copyrighted by Disney Productions. Furthermore, they bought concessions from corporations that had paid money to Disney for the privilege of associating their products with the fun and frolic at Disneyland.

Walt Disney presided over every decision about Disneyland with an attention to detail that staggers the imagination. He often slept overnight in a small apartment above the fire station on Main Street, and he insisted on training sessions at what he called "the University of Disneyland" for all employees about how to treat the park's visitors. "Always smile," he ordered his staff. "Turn the other cheek to everybody, even the nasty ones. And above everything, always give them full value for their money. If a boat ride is supposed to last 12 minutes and they only get 11 minutes 30 seconds, they've a right to feel cheated. Thirty seconds shy, and they hate us for selling them short. Thirty seconds extra, and they feel they've gotten away with something. That's the way we want them to feel. Contented, even smug." Disney insisted that his staff completely clean the streets with high pressure hoses every night, and he ordered the installation of more than 45,000 signs to communicate with the public.

Most emphatically, Disney pursued uniformity and predictability in the Disneyland experience. He wanted everyone to enter at the same place and to see the same things. As one admiring journalist observed, "He saw the need for Disneyland to flow, as did a movie, from scene to scene." To maintain the "flow" of the Disneyland experience, Disney made sure that all visitors entered by the same gate and started their day with a view of Sleeping Beauty's Castle that served as a visual lure to pull them through the Main Street shops and into the rest of the park. Visual concerns dominated the aesthetics of a day at Disneyland. A corporate publicity brochure boasted about the park's visual clarity, its ability to present visual stimuli in a unified and coordinated manner, "Disneyland was the first to use visually compatible elements working as a coordinating theme avoiding the contradictory 'hodge-podge' of World's Fairs and amusement parks." To preserve the clean visual line of the park and to ensure that maintenance could take place outside the vision of park customers, Disney buried all water, power, and sewer lines beneath the street level. Each theme land (Fantasyland, Adventureland, Frontierland, and Tomorrowland) appeared completely self-contained and could not be seen from any of the other sections of the park. Costumed "characters" in each theme section traveled to their destinations in underground tunnels so they would never be seen in "inappropriate settings." Even on the jungle ride, Disney insisted on mechanical rather than real animals, "so that every boatload of people will see the same thing."

Opened at a time when human space flight had not yet taken place, Disneyland presented images of space travel in its Tomorrowland section. Yet the rapid pace of technological change has made this the part of the park most subject to obsolescence, as its futuristic fantasies sometimes came true in the present. (Department of Special Collections, University Research Library, UCLA)

Disney also thought of the park in transitory terms, like a television series that could undergo revisions over time. He complained about the permanence of films, about how they could no longer be changed once they had been released, and he talked longingly of making Disneyland a place that would change constantly. "The park means a lot to me," Disney explained to a reporter. "It's something that will never be finished, something I can keep developing, keep 'plussing' and adding to. It's alive. It will be a live breathing thing that will need changes."

No section of Disneyland carried as much of the burden of Walt Disney's ideals as did Main Street. In that part of the park, Disney drew on his youthful memories of Marceline, Missouri, as well as on the nostalgia for the Gilded Age evident in 1940s films like *Meet Me in St. Louis*. Disney scaled Main Street's buildings slightly smaller at the rear and top to give the illusion that they were bigger than they actually were, creating a perspective that enabled an adult to see the buildings through the eyes of a child.

In a press release, Disneyland's publicists described Main Street as "Walt's and anyone else's home town—the way it should have been." But unlike the real town squares of turn-of-the-century small towns, Disneyland's Main Street offered little space for leisure and none for work. Despite occasional parades by the Disneyland band and scattered benches in public spaces, Main Street's real social life depended on shopping, on funnelling (as rapidly as possible) enormous numbers of consumers into a "comfortable" environment for making purchases. Although buildings appeared to be distinct and separate on the outside, inner passages made it easy to walk from store to store (and difficult to walk back out into the noncommercial space of the street). The meaning of this was not lost on developer and retailer Mel Kaufman who observed that "Main's Street's purpose is exactly the same as Korvette's [a major department store] in the Bronx, but it manages to make shopping wonderful and pleasant at the same time. I'm sure people buy more when they're happy."

Although its prominence on commercial network television made Disneyland a national phenomenon, its success also stemmed from its strategic role in the cultural life of Los Angeles. Disneyland was most often described as a site specially designed for children, but most surveys showed that adults outnumbered children at the park by ratios of 3 to 1 or 4 to 1. Architect Charles Moore attributed Disneyland's success to its ability to provide Californians with a "public environment" in the midst of a region dominated by the private spaces of suburban subdivisions and automobile interiors. Just as Main Street functioned as the town square of Disneyland, Moore described Disneyland itself as the "town square of Los Angeles."

If there was ever a city in need of a town square it was Los Angeles in the 1950s. Home to the first and largest automobile-oriented highway program in the country, Los Angeles developed into a major metropolis as a scattered city with many well dispersed focal points. The city had experienced longer and more sustained population growth than any American city since the 1850s, and it enjoyed particularly enormous population growth during the 1930s, with 200,000 new migrants between 1936 and 1939 alone. Defense spending during and after World War II propelled an even greater expansion. Los Angeles became the second largest industrial center in America during the war (trailing only Detroit), and between 1940 and 1944 over 780,000 new immigrants entered southern California. This extraordinarily rapid growth continued after World War II. Between 1945 and 1955 more than a million and a half people moved to Los Angeles, a total then equal to the *combined* total populations of Pittsburgh and Baltimore. Figures from the 1950 census reveal that more than 50 percent of the residents of Los Angeles in that year had lived in the city for less than 5 years.

Workers came west to secure employment in Los Angeles's shipyard and aircraft industries during World War II, and massive defense spending for the Cold War in the postwar era fueled even further growth. During the war, Blacks, whites, Chicanos, Native Americans, and Asian-Americans worked side by side in the defense plants and traveled together on the city's efficient and effective streetcar and bus network.

Cultural interactions enlivened urban life. The city's vibrant popular music mixed Afro-American, Chicano, and Anglo forms in reflection of the increasingly heterogeneous culture of the city. Dances and concerts at El Monte Legion Stadium on the eastern border of the city attracted youths from diverse backgrounds who combined their styles of dress, dance, and speech to form an exciting multicultural youth culture. On the playgrounds and streets of inner city neighborhoods, in public parks, and commercial amusement centers at the Long Beach and Santa Monica piers the city's heterogeneous population enjoyed the exuberant festivity of public recreation.

But the growth of the postwar suburbs (largely subsidized by tax spending on new highways and the extension of city services including water, gas, electric, and sewer lines), encouraged new forms of isolation and segregation. Racial discrimination by private realtors and developers denied most African-Americans and Mexican-Americans access to the new suburbs, while the federal government's discriminatory home loan policies effectively subsidized the creation of all-white neighborhoods in the San Fernando Valley and Orange County. The newly dispersed population made public transit less efficient per mile and the numbers of automobiles driven by commuters further slowed the speed of trolleys and buses, thereby providing central city dwellers with even more reasons to move to the suburbs. In less than a decade, Los Angeles's diverse urban space became more segregated than ever, its effective rapid transit system collapsed, and the success of suburbs and freeways only contributed to ever increasing fragmentation, segregation, and dispersal of the city's population.

Disneyland's emergence corresponded with the increasing suburbanization of Los Angeles. Even though a majority of the park's visitors came from out of town, Disneyland firmly established itself as an important public space in Los Angeles—as the place one took visitors from out of town, as a site for special celebrations like high school proms, and as an emblem of a whole way of life built around suburbanization and the automobile in Southern California. The park provided an alternative to the heterogeneous public spaces of the city, and it powerfully projected its image of middle-class suburban consumer culture as a norm to which other groups should aspire. Massive in-migration and the city's dispersed physical form left Los Angeles without the kinds of geographic and focal points common to other cities. In addition, dependence on the automobile produced unhealthy and unpleasant smog and brought about traffic jams that inhibited access to the beaches, deserts, and mountains once within easy reach of most local residents. Disneyland came into existence as an easily reachable attraction conveniently located near new freeways in the midst of the region's largest locus of population growth. It redefined public space and culture, with its location and admission costs making it much more accessible to suburban white families than to ethnic minority residents of the inner city. But its appeal depended on more than accessibility; as a new kind of public space Disneyland contrasted sharply with alternative experiences in the Los Angeles area.

Visitors left their cars in parking lots with more acreage than the park itself, and entered a world with comfortable walkways and efficient rail public transit. The high price of admission and tickets attracted an economically homogeneous crowd and encouraged patrons to devote the entire day or evening to leisurely utilization of the park's facilities. The efficient movement of people through the park and the careful timing of rides and attractions worked against any feeling of overcrowding or stagnation, and the Disney philosophy of viewing visitors as an audience and park personnel as entertainers worked to effectively inculcate passivity in park patrons. A revealing phrase in a Disneyland promotional brochure identifies the kind of social space constructed in the park with startling precision:

> Up until now audience participation in entertainment was almost non-existent. In live theater, motion pictures and television the audience is always separate and apart from the actual show environment . . . Walt Disney took the audience out of their seats and placed them right in the middle of the action for a total, themed, controlled experience.

Disneyland also spoke to the break with the past that formed an important part of the lives of Los Angeles residents. In a city made up of migrants from all over the country, no common heritage served to underpin individual or collective identity. But by presenting images of familiar figures from television and motion pictures, Disneyland spoke to the commonality of experience made possible by popular culture. People came to Disneyland with a variety of experiences and beliefs, but the reach and scope of electronic mass media guaranteed that they all shared familiarity and knowledge about Disney stories and products.

Disneyland self-consciously promoted itself as an educational institution, as a place, among other things, for learning about the past. Many people admired its successes in that regard. The Freedoms Foundation at Valley Forge awarded Walt Disney its George Washington Medal, and California State Superintendent of Education Max Rafferty lauded Disney as "the greatest educator of this century, greater than John Dewey or James Conant or all the rest of us put together." When Disney died in 1966, California Senator George Murphy claimed that he knew of no individual "who has contributed more to the general welfare of mankind" than Disney did. But Disney himself explained his goals more modestly. "I've always wanted to do American history," Disney explained to an interviewer shortly before the opening of the park. "It's due. We have taken too many things for granted. I'm not really telling history, though. I'm telling about people; history happens to be going on at the time."

Disneyland showed Abraham Lincoln agonizing over the civil war, but not over slavery. Its "authentic" Frontierland Indians came from reservations in the desert southwest, and had to learn how to handle the "real Indian canoes" from non-Indian park personnel whose knowledge came from their experiences at summer camp. All of its "adventures" replicated the history of white Euro-Americans as they conquered the American or African frontiers. It looked at the conquests of the frontier and the jungle as the spread of European civilization rather than as the plunder of the possessions of indigenous peoples.

In some places, Disneyland's liberties with the past went beyond mere insensitivity. One restaurant featured an "Aunt Jemima" theme echoing the vicious "Mammy" stereotypes of black women that became a staple of popular culture after the Civil War, showing black women invariably as fat, nurturing, child-like, and totally devoted to their white masters. For years the jungle cruise encountered a "humorous trapped safari," which depicted "four red-capped porters, all blacks, who cling bug-eyed to a tree with their white client above them as a menacing rhinoceros stands below." These may seem like innocent errors, mere manifestations of the racism extant in the larger culture of which Disneyland was a part. But Disney's personal prejudices often guided his business practices. He never employed African-Americans as studio technicians, and did not allow them to work in Disneyland in *any* capacity until pressured to do so in 1963 by civil rights protests. Disney's anti-semitism was equally intense; as one writer well acquainted with the details of Disney's life notes "disappointment and resentment seemed to bring out his latent anti-semitism. He was often heard making snide comments about the Jews, whose success seemed to infuriate him." Disney tried to cloak himself in the American flag and to appropriate for his own purposes the patriotism of his customers. Yet his version of the national narrative was highly selective, prejudiced, and distorted. If his amusement park united its customers in a shared fantasy, it was one tailored to the economic and social interests of a small group of people and not one reflective of the larger shared experience of unity and disunity out of which the complex American nation and society have been forged.

Disneyland management has always tried to present the park as a world apart, as an island of fun in a serious world. Yet no multimillion dollar marketing effort is really cut off from the real world, much less one with the commercial and cultural power of Disneyland. Whether one looks at the lone individual who commented that his first trip to the Mississippi River reminded him of the first part of the Pirates of the Caribbean ride, or to the five high ranking members of the Nixon Administration who received their public relations training handling both the Disneyland and the Richard Nixon accounts for the J. Walter Thompson advertising agency, evidence of Disneyland's influence over American life and culture during the past 40 years has not been hard to find.

Over the years Disneyland has faced strikes ("Disneyland is a kingdom all right, and we're the serfs," complained a worker in a Br'er Bear costume during a 1970 work stoppage), lawsuits over a ban on members of the same sex dancing together, and repeated arguments over what constitutes appropriate attire at the park. One particularly vivid example of the links between Disneyland and the "real world" came on August 6, 1970, when 300 "yippies" marked the twenty-fifth anniversary of the dropping of the first atomic bomb on Hiroshima by staging a demonstration in Disneyland. The youths chanted anti-war slogans on the drawbridge to Sleeping Beauty's Castle, followed the Disneyland band down Main Street, and raised a Viet Cong flag over the fort on Tom Sawyer's

"Mouseketeers" from the syndicated "Mickey Mouse Club" television program visit Los Angeles City Hall. As a 5-day-a-week afterschool show, "The Mickey Mouse Club" extended the Disney Corporation's popular and commercial influence to the everyday experiences of children. The uniformity of the Mouseketeers' outfits (and ears) hides the symbols of youthful rebellion incorporated into adolescent dress and styles of the day. Adolescence itself disappears as the Mickey Mouse Club appears as a children's "gang" under wholesome adult supervision. (Department of Special Collections, University Research Library, UCLA)

island. They accused Disneyland of being "a plastic world of fantasy" at odds with the realities outside its walls. Over 100 uniformed Anaheim police officers equipped with riot batons eventually cleared the youths from the park, making nine arrests. Disneyland management closed the park 6 hours early and handed out refunds to 30,000 customers. The next day a *San Diego Union* editorial condemning the disruption of business at the park advised that "smaller folk who need an explanation for what happened at Disneyland Thursday might be told they saw a lifelike reproduction of the pre-historic world—before shaggy creatures with small brains gave way to the human race as we know it today."

In order to further secure the park and to control the nature of its experience, Disney officials began a rigid policy of dress and grooming codes, denying admission to the park any individuals whose hairstyles or clothing seemed inappropriate to park guards. This policy was based on the idea that there was only one respectable way for people to look and dress, that men should not have long hair or beards, that women should not wear sandals and "love bead necklaces," that black people should not have "Afro" haircuts or be allowed to wear African "dashikis." But as popular styles changed and allowed for more diversity, park guards found themselves facing a losing battle trying to stem the tide of rapidly changing subcultural styles and fashions. Similarly, the park's administrators enforced a policy against men dancing with men or women dancing with women on the grounds that "some patrons might find partners of the same sex offensive," until a lawsuit charging the park with violating the Constitutional rights of its patrons convinced them to drop the policy.

AN INTERPRETATION

Any cultural expression advances one view of reality, and in the process runs the risks of ignoring or erasing other ways of looking at the world. Any struggle over meaning influences struggles over resources, because cultural stories, signs, and symbols help determine what is legitimate and what is illegitimate, what is permitted and what is forbidden, who is included and who is excluded, who speaks and who is silenced. Like many other sites of commercialized leisure, Disneyland provides a useful site for the examination of these larger social questions.

Disneyland initiated and refined distinct cultural practices that characterize much of American society today. It created one of the most important public spaces in our society out of the imperatives of a private profit-making corporation. It redefined public recreation as primarily spectatorship and shopping, and carried the forms and logic of commercial network television outside the home. Its multilayered opportunities for profit-making mixed marketing, merchandising, and advertising into one unified activity, and it broke down barriers between media by blending film, comic book, and television references in the shared space of a theme park. It connected the personal memories of individual childhoods with carefully crafted narratives about the "childhood" of the nation, and it injected a profit-making corporation into the shaping of family life in an unprecedented manner.

In fact, Disneyland is such a microcosm of cultural practices in our society, it is sometimes difficult to view it as a carefully created and manipulated artifact. Like any good ideological cultural work, it seems to flow naturally from the consciousness of the audience and to demand no special investigation. To think of fun as consisting of shopping and spectatorship makes sense in a world of shopping malls and television sets, but these inevitably erode our collective memory of other more sociable, active, spontaneous, and creative ways to have fun. Disney's idea of a park that would always be in flux is a perfect expression of an economic system that is constantly in the service of fashion—changing clothing styles and automobile styles regularly to create "new" needs for what are essentially the same old products. Disney's success at creating a centralized site for recreation that standardizes stories for people around the world speaks powerfully about the forces of homogenization that have undermined localized ethnic and folk traditions that keep alive creative differences among and across diverse populations. Coming into existence at the same time that commercial network television and suburbanization changed the nature of culture and social life in America, Disneyland succeeded at least in part by recognizing that its visitors were likely to watch television and live in suburbs, and that consequently they expected a park that would conform with their other experiences.

Yet asking questions about Disneyland can help us begin to think critically about the world in which we live. It can help us to inquire into the relationships between commerce and art, between labor and leisure, between citizenship and spectatorship, and between our roles as consumers and our lives as community members, gendered subjects, and world citizens.

In 1955, Walt Disney and his corporation established their phenomenally successful amusement park in the wake of the popularity generated by their television films about Davy Crockett. More than 100 years earlier the historical Davy Crockett boasted that "Fashion is a thing I care mighty little about, except when it happens to run just exactly according to my own notion. . . ." Walt Disney created an amusement park, an entertainment empire, a version of American history, and an important element in the lives of many children by getting fashion to run exactly according to his own notion. We know that Disneyland's blend of commerce and art, its exclusion of those outside of mainstream narratives, and its insertion of cash transactions into the operative realities of family life have been the profitable thing, the successful thing, and the effective thing. But we need to think again about their consequences for what we think we know about the American past and for how we live the American present and future.

Sources: The Disneyland story has been told many times from many different points of view. From the wide range of secondary sources on the establishment and development of the amusement park in relation to the larger vision of the Disney Corporation, I have drawn repeatedly on the valuable information and insights presented by Herbert Schiller in *The Mind Managers* (Boston: Beacon,

1973), Michael Real, *Mass Mediated Culture* (New York: Prentice-Hall, 1977), Richard Schickel, *The Disney Version* (New York: Simon and Schuster, 1968), and Leonard Mosely, *Disney's World* (New York: Stein and Day, 1985). Also useful for descriptions and quotes were Randy Bright, *Disneyland: The Inside Story* (New York: Harry N. Abrams, Inc., 1987), and Bob Thomas, *Walt Disney, An American Original* (New York: Simon and Schuster, 1976). In journals and periodicals, the articles I found most useful were Richard Francaiglia, "Main Street USA," *Journal of Popular Culture* v.15 n.1 (September) 1981, Mark Gottdiener, "Disneyland: A Utopian Urban Space," *Urban Life* v. 11 n. 2 (July) 1982, and Paul Goldberger, "Mickey Mouse Teaches the Architects," *New York Times Magazine,* October 20, 1972.

12

THE BERKELEY FREE SPEECH MOVEMENT

W. J. RORABAUGH

When students set up card tables on the edge of the University of California's Berkeley campus in the fall of 1964, the action seemed harmless enough. But school administrators didn't see it that way, and their decision to ban the tables led to the emergence of a powerful student organization known as the Free Speech Movement and precipitated months of confrontation involving not just students and administrators, but faculty, police, area residents, and even the governor of California.

It was a curious confrontation, to be sure. At times, events at Berkeley seemed oddly removed from anything but the committees and procedures that were a part of a large, bureaucratic university. In W. J. Rorabaugh's account, the protesting students often seem more concerned with the quality of their Berkeley education—and with the nature of the institution that was dispensing it—than with civil rights, the war in Vietnam, or any other obviously political issue. Even the neat resolution of the controversy gives pause, for how could a moral and political struggle have been settled so quickly and so finally?

Yet Rorabaugh is certainly justified in claiming for the episode a larger significance. According to school officials, Berkeley's regulations on political activity were necessary to preserve the institution's political neutrality. When students in the Free Speech Movement refused to accept this analysis, and argued, instead, that the university was already deeply politicized (and committed to the conservative status quo), the stage was set for a struggle over a variety of issues that would be central to the 1960s: What was the proper role of the university vis-à-vis political and economic life? Could the universities—like the industrial unions of the 1930s—serve as centers of social activism and reform? What rights did students at Berkeley, workers in an automobile factory, or welfare recipients have to a participatory role in their education, their work, or the social welfare system? And how could ordinary people, whether students at Berkeley or blacks in a Mississippi small town, establish some measure of control over their lives?

If these issues were muted at Berkeley in 1964, it is partly because the early

1960s were not the "sixties"—that is, not the highly politicized era of confrontation and turmoil, and not the sixties of drugs and the counterculture—that often comes to mind when one uses the term. As late as 1963, the civil rights movement was still largely confined to the southern states, and Martin Luther King, Jr.'s dream of integration remained its central motif. Popular music ranged from Andy Williams's "Days of Wine and Roses" to Jan and Dean's "Surf City," and from the folk strains of Peter, Paul, and Mary to the rhythm and blues of Stevie Wonder. The United States had only 16,000 troops in Vietnam, and, officially at least, they were only "advisors."

In contrast, by 1965 the civil rights movement had moved north and west, sparking a race riot in the Watts section of Los Angeles that killed 34 people. Bob Dylan had alienated his folk music constituency and signaled a turn toward a more powerful rock music—and a new political era—by using an electric guitar for the first time. In February 1965, only 2 months after the regents had voted to bring the 1st amendment onto the Berkeley campus, Lyndon Baines Johnson ordered the bombing of North Vietnam; by the end of the year, Berkeley was a major center for anti-war protest.

The year 1964 was, then, a year of transition. In retrospect, the signs of the new order were there: the arrival of the Beatles; summer violence in the Harlem ghetto; in Vietnam, an August confrontation in the Gulf of Tonkin between U.S. destroyers and North Vietnamese patrol boats that led Congress to grant the president full authority to commit U.S. forces to Southeast Asia—and, in September, a few students at the University of California at Berkeley, fresh from registering black voters in Mississippi, setting up card tables along Bancroft Way.

In 1964 the University of California at Berkeley, like colleges and universities all over the United States, was bursting its seams. The first of the numerous baby boomers had reached college age, just as prosperity, parental pressure, new degree requirements for many jobs, and draft deferments for college men combined to spur enrollments. In 4 years Berkeley grew from 18,000 to 25,000 students. Rapid growth left one quarter of faculty positions unfilled, and graduate students called teaching assistants increasingly taught small undergraduate classes. Overenrollment forced hundreds of students in basic courses to watch lectures on remote television monitors. As History Professor Raymond Sontag observed, "I used to try to think of every student as made in the image of God, but when there are hundreds in a class I'm afraid they become just hunks of flesh."

Despite this deeply alienating environment, the university had no trouble attracting students. Fees under $100 a semester and high academic prestige were matched by Berkeley's reputation as an innovative, exciting community. Telegraph Avenue, just south of campus, provided fine bookstores and coffee houses. During the bland 1950s, when so many Americans watched "Father Knows Best" on television and embraced Eisenhower's cautious politics, residents of Berkeley and much of the San Francisco Bay Area refused to conform. Allen Ginsberg and other members of the Beat generation read their daring poetry in public, while the Kingston Trio's folk music satirized politics.

In the late 1950s a number of students at Cal organized a campus political party called SLATE. Its main goal was to get students to discuss serious issues. Administrators responded by disfranchising the SLATE-oriented graduate students and then banning the organization. In 1960, when the House Unamerican Activities Committee held hearings in San Francisco, Berkeley students protested.

President John Kennedy, who promised to get the country moving again, energized students by proposing to establish the Peace Corps and to land an American on the moon within the decade. More important, Kennedy's vigor appealed to young people. In 1962 the president visited Berkeley and was greeted warmly by 88,000 people in the football stadium. A few hundred radical students, however, protested nearby.

In the early 1960s local residents cared passionately about two great issues: peace and race. Cold War anxieties and fear of nuclear war, especially after the Cuban Missile Crisis of 1962, gripped young people, many of whom believed that they belonged to a last, doomed generation. At the same time, the largely southern, black civil rights movement, led by Martin Luther King, Jr., had gathered momentum from the boycott of segregated city buses in Montgomery, Alabama in 1955 to 1956 through the first sit-ins by black college students in the South in 1960 to the half million blacks and whites who marched together on Washington in August 1963.

Some Cal students, like white students all over the country, worked for civil rights. The issue had a special significance in Berkeley, which by 1960 was one-fifth black. Yet one seldom saw an African-American either downtown, where only one black was employed, or on campus, where more than 90 percent of the students were white and most of the nonwhites were Asians. Discrimination prevailed in schools, jobs, and housing. For example, the local newspaper routinely published "white only" housing rental or sales ads.

Throughout 1964 the Cal student chapter of the Congress of Racial Equality (CORE was the leading interracial nationwide civil rights organization) and its allies attacked job discrimination with demonstrations at Lucky's grocery stores in Berkeley, at the Sheraton-Palace Hotel and along auto row in San Francisco, and at the *Oakland Tribune,* the conservative Republican organ of William F. Knowland, a former U.S. senator. In the summer of 1964, when the Republican national convention met in San Francisco to nominate Barry Goldwater for president on a platform hostile to civil rights, Cal activists organized anti-Goldwater pickets.

Recruitment for these protests took place at card tables set up daily on city property along Bancroft Way at the edge of campus. There students passed out leaflets, solicited funds, and gathered names for demonstrations. This site for political activity had come about because in the 1930s, amid intense student interest in radical politics, the university had banned all political activity from campus. In the early 1960s the number of tables had grown, as had the number of blue-jeaned, bearded, and sandaled activists. Concern about the tables, the activists, and the causes they represented rose inside the campus administration.

Over the summer 30 to 60 Cal students, along with more than 1000 mostly white students from campuses across the country, had worked for civil rights in Mississippi. When these activists returned to Berkeley, they looked forward to recruiting students for vigorous civil rights activity. Suddenly, in mid-September of 1964, the university administration "discovered" that the 26- by 90-foot area in which tables had been placed was university property. (Years later the university conceded the property had always belonged to the city.) Officials banned tables or any political activity from Bancroft Way. When the activists sought an explanation, they could get no answers.

Clark Kerr, the brilliant but personally cold president of the statewide university system, had precipitated this crisis. A pacifist Quaker, a labor negotiator, a social scientist, and an active liberal Democrat who believed deeply that government programs could solve social problems, Kerr had first gained prominence in the early 1950s, when he led a faculty fight against the imposition of an anticommunist loyalty oath at the university. As president, he planned the university's expansion to nine campuses and coined the word "multiversity" to describe a large public university with multiple campuses and programs. Such a university, he argued, was necessary for a society based upon the "knowledge industry."

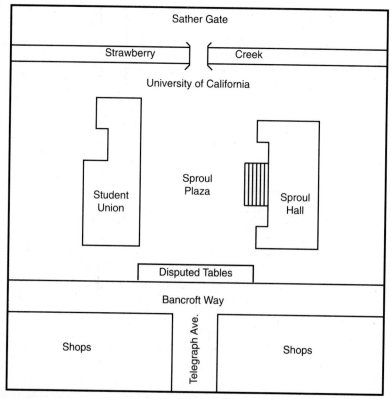

In 1964 thousands of Cal students each day crossed Bancroft Way at Telegraph Avenue, made their way through Sproul Plaza, and then entered the main part of the campus on the other side of Sather Gate.

Kerr's self-confidence masked his administration's problems. The president had strained relations with the university's wealthy, powerful regents, several of whom were suspicious, crusty conservatives, and with the Berkeley campus. The campus was run by a weak chancellor, the ironically named Edward W. Strong. A mere figurehead who did Kerr's bidding, Strong did not even have his own stationery. Nor had Kerr mastered the dual president's and chancellor's staffs through which he tried to run the campus. Neither group was liked. Berkeley's faculty members, long alienated by Kerr's inaccessibility and by the administration's endless flow of paper, called the president's bureaucracy "All State," because its actions resembled an insurance company's more than a university's.

Kerr did not wholeheartedly embrace the ban on the tables but declared, "There is to be no distribution of action literature on campus anywhere." For the president, tables along Bancroft violated the university's avowedly nonpolitical, intellectual mission. In public he said, "I just don't agree you have to take action to experience intellectual development. If that were so, why teach history? We can't live in ancient Greece." In private he was more blunt. "Activity had been getting rather wild and woolly and something had to be done," he wrote. "Handing out campaign buttons and bumper stickers is not essential to intellectual development!"

The activists were better prepared for war than Kerr. They demanded an end to the regulation of political activity on campus. This became known as free speech. "All we want are the rights guaranteed any American by the first amendment," said one supporter. "You'll never hear us ask for more, and you'll never see us settle for less." Many activist leaders were battle-tested veterans of the civil rights movement. "A student who has been chased by the KKK [Ku Klux Klan] in Mississippi," observed one student, "is not easily scared by academic bureaucrats."

The administration, in contrast, announced a series of shifting policies. First, tables were banned, but students could distribute literature explaining a political position so long as no particular *action* was advocated. Thus, a leaflet could announce an election issue but could not urge a yes or no vote. Then on September 21 the university allowed tables and the use of the steps in front of Sproul Hall for rallies but continued to deny the right of advocacy. A week later the university, under pressure from its attorneys, suddenly allowed advocacy literature, but there were still restrictions.

The exasperated dean of students wrote, "What is 'legal'? What is political? What is possible?" She noted that under the new rules a group might distribute literature on campus announcing an off-campus meeting for any purpose, but that same group could not meet on campus to plan the distribution of literature about the off-campus meeting. In practice, the regulations created bureaucratic nightmares.

Throughout September of 1964 activists intentionally defied the ever shifting regulations and were cited by irritated deans. The angry students escalated the conflict by moving their tables from Bancroft Way into Sproul Plaza in front of Sproul Hall in the middle of campus. Kerr told Strong, "We must maintain law and order." Strong declared, "We are going to enforce the rules." Kerr replied, "Right—Proceed." At a staff meeting the administration decided to "pick off [the activists] one at a time." On September 30 more students were cited, and these citations led hundreds of protesters to swarm inside Sproul Hall in what they called a mill-in and to the summary "indefinite suspension" of eight students.

Then, on October 1, university police went to the plaza to arrest a former student, Jack Weinberg, who sat at a CORE table. A native of the small Jewish community in Buffalo, New York, Weinberg had been a straight "A" student at Cal, and he had proved to be a brilliant tactician as leader of the campus CORE chapter.

The police drove a car onto the plaza to take Weinberg to be booked, and as Weinberg got into the car, someone shouted, "Sit down." Suddenly, several hundred students surrounded the car. The police did not know what to do, because they had never encountered such massive defiance. Kerr's bureaucracy became paralyzed.

For 32 hours Weinberg sat in the police car. Although students came and went, there were always at least several hundred and sometimes several thousand surrounding the vehicle. During the night students who disapproved of the sit-down—many from nearby fraternities—molested the protesters by tossing lighted cigarettes and garbage into the crowd. In a spirited display of defiance and solidarity, the activists sang civil rights songs, including "We Shall Not Be Moved."

During the sit-down the demonstrators gained police permission to use the roof of the police car as a podium to speak to the crowd. The most popular speaker was Mario Savio, a 21-year-old junior and one of the eight suspended students. The son of a devout Italian Catholic machinist, he had grown up in New York. In the summer of 1963 he had worked for a Catholic relief organization in rural Mexico, and that fall, after his parents had moved to Los Angeles, the former altar boy entered Berkeley as a junior. During the summer of 1964, he taught a freedom school for black children in McComb, Mississippi. Conditions there, he told the press, made him "very angry."

In 1964 the 6′ 1″, 195-pound Savio was proud and cocky, blazing, and defiant. He scowled beneath longish, sandy-red hair. He was not cool. Several times Savio carefully removed his shoes so as not to damage the roof of the car and climbed atop the vehicle to speak, energizing the crowd with his words. A reluctant celebrity, he was identified by the crowd as their leader. From then on Savio battled Kerr.

Part of his appeal came from his frank, humorous, and suggestive use of language. In calling the administrators "a bunch of bastards," he declared both their ancestry and their authority illegitimate. At the sit-down he said of the police, "They're *fam*-ily men, you know. They have a job to do!" He added, with reference to a well-known Nazi war criminal, "Like Adolph Eichmann. He had a job to do. He fit into the machinery."

Students, said Savio, were oppressed by "the organized sadism of the power structure." The university forced students to suppress their "creative impulses." As a result, he declared, "The university is well-structured, well tooled, to turn out people with all the sharp edges worn off." Indeed, taking away the right to place tables at the edge of campus had been an act of "emasculation, or attempted emasculation."

At one rally Savio noted, "The Bible says what knowledge is when it writes that a man knows a woman. Knowledge and action are inseparable." This comment provoked laughter. He then elaborated on the metaphor. "We want to be able to mount action on this campus," he said. This sexually suggestive wording was adopted by both sides as a description for the student demand to use the campus to plan off-campus civil rights protests. The administration declared its opposition to the use of the campus for "mounting" political activity.

While the police car was trapped, Kerr's bureaucrats dithered, and the activists came to believe that they could extract concessions in exchange for quietly ending the sit-down. Kerr pushed Strong aside and used his skills developed as a labor mediator to deal with the students. For the first time, some faculty

For 32 hours on October 1 and 2, 1964, protesters surrounded a police car in Sproul Plaza under the towering columns of Sproul Hall. This monumental architecture was dehumanizing, but it also suggested a Greek Forum for free speech. While arrestee Jack Weinberg sat inside the car, activists used its roof as a podium. (Courtesy University Archives, University of California, Berkeley)

members offered advice that encouraged both the administration and the activists to compromise.

The president offered the activists written terms that appeared to be generous. Jack Weinberg was to be released without charges, and two committees were to be appointed. One, composed of students, faculty, and administrators, would draw up rules for political activity on campus. The other, a faculty committee, would reconsider the penalties for the eight suspended students.

Kerr signed the proposal. Then he pressured the activist leaders to accept it by threatening to remove the protesters from around the captive vehicle by using hundreds of police officers, called to the campus from throughout the Bay Area. After a heated internal debate, nine student leaders, including Savio, accepted Kerr's offer and signed the agreement.

Savio then returned to the police car sit-down. He read the settlement aloud and concluded, "Now, I would like those who have taken part in this protest to accept this document and as soon as they have done so, rise quietly and with dignity, depart." The crowd left.

Many activists trusted neither Kerr nor the pact of October 2. On October 4, eight activists met to plot strategy. To encourage ordinary students to participate, they created an executive committee. Any campus organization could send one representative. The Executive Committee grew to more than 50 members. It met infrequently, and a steering committee, elected by the Executive Committee, exercised day to day control. Although the activists were a minority on the Executive Committee, they gained most of the positions on the Steering Committee, through which they controlled events. The next evening, at a meeting that ran until 1 A.M., the group picked a name. They rejected the United Free Speech Movement and Students for Free Speech in favor of the Free Speech Movement (FSM).

In addition to Savio, the FSM Steering Committee always included Bettina Aptheker, daughter of the communist theoretician Herbert Aptheker and herself then an undeclared party member; Suzanne Goldberg, a philosophy graduate student who later married Savio; Sydney Stapleton, a leader in the local Trotsky-oriented Young Socialist Alliance (Leon Trotsky, Stalin's deposed rival in the Russian Communist party, had advocated worldwide revolution); and Jack Weinberg, one of the most effective civil rights organizers, the FSM's chief strategist, and author of the statement, "You can't trust anybody over thirty." This remark was both generational and a sneer at aging communists leftover from the past.

In its early days the FSM Steering Committee also included leaders of civil rights groups, such as Brian Turner of the Student Non-Violent Coordinating Committee (SNCC), a civil rights organization; Art Goldberg, a passionate civil rights supporter and Mississippi veteran who planned an autobiography entitled *Commiejewbeatnik;* and Art's sister Jackie Goldberg, a longtime activist in Women for Peace and delegate to that organization's Moscow conference in 1963. As the crisis continued, the Goldbergs were eased out, the civil rights activists faded, and the FSM Steering Committee added several members, including Steve Weissman, a superb tactician; Mona Hutchins, a libertarian Young

Republican; and Michael Rossman, a math graduate student from an old leftist family.

Except for Savio, the most important FSM leaders were Jewish. This fact was never mentioned by either side, although it had much to do both with the FSM's style and with the administration's response. Jewish students had long resented the way in which fraternities, openly antisemitic and antiblack, had, with support from certain administrators, dominated student politics. In addition, the Jewish FSM leaders brought a playful aggressiveness, a kind of theatricality, to their cause. This style appalled or bewildered the university's prim, straight-laced, white, Anglo-Saxon, Protestant administrators.

In contrast, the administration freely commented on the activists' ties to the Left. Kerr was quoted as stating, "Among the demonstrators were many nonstudents who were followers of the Castro–Mao Tse Tung line of Communism." Although he later said that he had been misquoted, Kerr did nothing to remove the public impression that he faced a revolt of communist outside agitators.

While the FSM leaders did not deny their Left orientations, their radicalism was largely of a distinct type, which during the 1960s became known as the New Left. Rejecting both the rigid party structure and the revolutionary doctrine of the Old Left's communists and Trotskyists, New Leftists favored both socialism and democracy. They contemptuously regarded liberals like Kerr as unprincipled compromisers and strongly supported the civil rights movement, the tactics of which, including sit-ins, they adopted to try to bring social change without violent revolution.

While Savio had called for publicity, the California media scorned the FSM students as "witless," "insolent and unruly," and "wild and distinctly juvenile." Newspaper photographs of Savio were invariably unflattering. Hostile press coverage generated hate mail. The letters, many anonymous, poured in. One taunted Savio, telling him to join the still small but growing war in Vietnam. "Savio," read this postcard, *"Now* are you going to join our services and win *complete victory* as you call it??? Or will you let others do the *dying?* You get your way—But try to even *over-sleep* in the *army* and see how you come out. They make my boy *toe* the mark. So why shouldn't you serve for *freedom?"*

During October and November the pact of October 2 unraveled. Kerr tried to send the disciplinary cases of the eight students suspended prior to the capture of the police car to a committee that he controlled. The activists objected, insisting that the cases be sent to an *independent* faculty senate committee. After much wrangling, Kerr yielded. In late November this committee recommended that six students be reinstated with the suspensions expunged from their records and that Mario Savio and Art Goldberg, the most visible leaders, be suspended from September 30 to the date that Kerr accepted their report.

Chancellor Strong, acting on Kerr's direct orders and after Kerr had discussed the cases in detail with the regents, overruled the faculty committee and increased the recommended penalties. All eight students were suspended from September 30 to the date the decision was announced, while Savio and Goldberg were placed on probation until the end of the semester. The purpose of this probation was to allow the administration to discipline the two students for their activities after September 30. Already Kerr had privately informed Strong that Goldberg was to "remain suspended."

Meanwhile, the committee to negotiate permanent rules for political activity on campus had bogged down. After the activists won a battle over the committee's organization, the group deadlocked. The stumbling block was civil rights demonstrations. The administration proposed permitting all political activity on campus except the advocacy, organization, or planning of off-campus illegal acts. Activist students rejected this proposal, because it hindered the on-campus organization of off-campus civil rights protests. The problem was that civil rights leaders could never tell when a demonstration would produce arrests. The administration's proposal had the effect of banning any activity that *might* lead to arrests.

Faculty members and administrators then turned down an activist counterproposal that political rights be based on the U.S. Constitution's first amendment. The FSM wanted to open the campus to all speech, broadly defined, except that banned by the U.S. Supreme Court (e.g., shouting fire in a crowded theater). The activists rejected a conservative faculty compromise to permit political activity except *conduct* that led *directly* to off-campus illegal acts. This proposal would have left students liable to be punished for participating in a civil rights demonstration that had led inadvertently to arrests.

Kerr, wrongly convinced that support for the FSM was declining, calculated that delay would enable the administration to grant limited political rights satisfactory to the administration, the faculty, and a majority of students. The president did not understand the FSM strategy, which was to continue agitation to build wide student support for their position on political rights.

Jack Weinberg advised, "Don't let an escalation outrun our growing base of support, but likewise don't let our concern with out of control escalation over-ride the possibility of using rapid escalation if we do have a necessary base of support." Always, Weinberg emphasized, the larger purpose of broad student support had to be kept in mind. The FSM leaders recognized that students had little power, and they intended to use mass student support to force the faculty to choose between siding with students or with the administration. They intended, in other words, to bring the faculty into the activist camp on the FSM's terms.

The activists knew that the faculty's support for Kerr had declined over the years and that many faculty members sympathized with the civil rights movement. Because the issue of political activity on campus was seen as a question of how much civil rights protest would be permitted, the faculty could be drawn to support the FSM on that basis.

In order to gain student support, the FSM held rallies almost every day at noon on the steps of Sproul Hall. Large numbers of students passed through the plaza, and as many as 5000 students sometimes attended. During rallies the FSM leaders often led mass singing of either civil rights songs or union songs from the 1930s. The FSM also created its own songs, published a songbook, and made recordings, which generated funds. Most songs expressed the alienation of students forced to grapple with a large, impersonal university. In one song Malvina Reynolds, a professional folk songwriter and longtime Berkeley leftist, called the university a "robot factory." Another song, to the tune of "The Streets of Laredo," depicted the chancellor as unhappy because students did not act like children. Dan Paik's "Womb with a View" suggested that President Kerr wanted to change the students' diapers. Several songs defended the FSM against the charge that it was communist. "Don't know if I'm subversive, just want to say what I please," wrote Richard Kampf.

A number of songs satirized Christmas carols; the FSM sold 15,000 carol records. Jolly tunes contrasted with bitter lyrics. One sung to "Jingle Bells" went:

> Oski Dolls, Pompon Girls,
> UC all the way!
> Oh, what fun it is to have
> your mind reduced to clay!
> Civil rights, politics
> just get in the way.
> Questioning authority
> when you should obey.

Even with the rallies, the FSM leaders worried that Kerr's strategy of delay might cause their movement to crumble. So the group decided to resume setting up political tables on campus. Administrators usually ignored the tables, but one day they cited 65 students, and in a show of support more than 100 students then signed statements that they were equally guilty of violating rules. When the university mailed disciplinary letters to these confessing students, the FSM responded by sending 835 letters to the dean's office denouncing the administration's violation of constitutional rights. When teaching assistants—the graduate students who taught a majority of the university's small undergraduate courses—sat at tables, the activists noted that the TAs were not cited. The administration's double standard and fear of a TA strike disgusted the students.

In late November, 1964, with the disciplinary cases settled amid bitterness and the political rules committee suspended, Kerr moved, perhaps under pressure from certain regents, to punish the FSM leaders for their role in the events immediately preceding and surrounding the capture of the police car. The pact of October 2 had effectively granted amnesty for actions through September, but had excluded the seizure and holding of the car. Now, Kerr moved to suspend Savio and Art Goldberg on the grounds that on October 1 and 2 they had violated the terms of the retroactive probation that had been imposed by the chancellor, on Kerr's orders, in late November.

"They are trying to pick off our leaders one by one," said Steve Weissman, an FSM spokesman. History Professor Carl Schorske thought the suspensions "a renewed declaration of warfare by the administration." English Professor Thomas Parkinson called them "a real stupidity." The new disciplinary action rallied many faculty members and large numbers of previously uninvolved students to the FSM cause. The activists, in a spirit of rage, decided to confront Kerr with their ultimate weapon.

From the beginning the activists had considered a sit-in. The sit-down around the police car had spontaneously and serendipitously half fulfilled the desire, and now Kerr had created circumstances ripe for bringing the spirit of the civil rights movement to campus. Leaders believed a sit-in would galvanize, mold, and radicalize student opinion. Friends would join, and then friends of friends, and the feeling of camaraderie experienced in the sit-in would give the movement what it needed most: bodies.

The fellowship of a sit-in promised a vast expansion of the activist population on campus and the beginnings of a new community in Berkeley. Moreover, if a sit-in brought police, and the FSM leaders calculated that Kerr was not shrewd enough to avoid this outcome, then the bringing of police onto campus would alarm the faculty. Above all, the faculty, which included a number of

After negotiations between the Free Speech Movement and the university administration broke down, students defied regulations by placing card tables in Sproul Plaza. Campus Women for Peace, the most important women's organization in Berkeley in the early 1960s, set up this table on November 9, 1964. In this pre-Vietnam era peace groups focused on preventing nuclear war. (Courtesy Keith Denison. University Archives, University of California, Berkeley)

refugees from Hitler's Germany, could not tolerate the university run as a police state. Thus, the activists calculated that a large sit-in and police action would push the still largely silent faculty to act on the side of the FSM.

Both the sit-in and the administration's response were carefully planned. On December 1 the campus police sent a spy to an FSM mass meeting, where Steve Weissman predicted that 1000 to 1500 students would occupy Sproul Hall. He and Weinberg estimated that arrests would take 15 hours.

At a pre-sit-in noon rally on December 2, Savio spoke his most memorable lines. With anger restrained by resolve, the morally committed machinist's son said:

> There is a time when the operation of the machine becomes so odious, makes you so sick at heart, that you can't take part; you can't even passively take part, and you've got to put your bodies upon the gears and upon the wheels, upon the levers, upon all the apparatus and you've got to make it stop. And you've got to indicate to the people who run it, to the people that own it, that unless you're free, the machines will be prevented from working at all.

In these few words, similar to some thoughts of Thoreau, Savio calmly conveyed his strong feelings. The folk singer Joan Baez closed the rally with a funereally slow rendition of the civil rights song, "We Shall Overcome." Then, like Christian gladiators about to greet Roman lions, a large portion of the crowd, more than one thousand, walked into Sproul Hall.

The students occupied all four floors. Activities varied in different areas. Protesters prepared food in an alcove on the second floor. Elsewhere they studied for exams, watched old Charlie Chaplin films, attended a Chanukah service, or sang folk songs. The atmosphere was congenial, relaxed, and partylike. A few smoked marijuana, and two female students were said to have lost their virginity on the roof. Leaders used walkie-talkies to communicate. The students installed a public address system to broadcast to passersby and the press. Some brought sleeping bags and prepared to settle down for the night, or perhaps for several nights, while others expected the police to attack with tear gas at any moment.

Kerr was desperate. Painfully aware of the faculty's disdain for the use of police on campus, he did not want to be remembered for using police to make arrests and tried to keep his role in the unfolding events secret. Although the president later insisted that he had not authorized any arrests (and he may have been technically correct), Kerr and his administration had spent days preparing for this showdown. Throughout the crisis Kerr had consulted with the chairman of the regents, Edward Carter, and Carter in turn had frequently talked by phone with Governor Pat Brown, a liberal Democrat who had long been an admirer and supporter of Kerr.

The governor assumed responsibility for events on the campus. He received a phone call from the assistant county prosecutor, who was sitting in the campus police headquarters in the Sproul Hall basement. After hearing a false report that the demonstrators had broken into an office, the prosecutor had told the governor, "They're busting up the place. We have to go in." Brown then ordered the protesters arrested. The prosecutor who had made the call was Edwin Meese III, later one of Ronald Reagan's chief aides. As liaison between the police and the prosecutor's office, he supervised the arrests.

At 3 A.M., after many demonstrators had gone to sleep, Strong appeared with a bullhorn and, carrying out Kerr's directive, haltingly read a statement on each floor. When he declared that the sit-in had materially disrupted the operations of the university, the students applauded. He warned that the police were about to arrest anyone who remained in the building. For several hours entry into Sproul Hall had been blocked, but until this point students had been free to leave the building, and about 200 had done so.

Then the police came. The FSM leaders had urged students under arrest to force policemen to carry them from the building. The police obliged, although not gently. While females who refused to walk were taken down the elevator, males were tossed from officer to officer and hurled down the terrazzo stairs. "Take 'em down a little slower," advised one policeman, "they bounce more that way." Although some demonstrators complained about police brutality, few sought medical aid. The purpose of refusing to walk was to slow down the arrests so that students who walked past Sproul Hall in the morning could see how their classmates were being treated.

This tactic succeeded. Although 367 police officers took part, the building was not cleared and the last of 773 arrests made until 4 P.M. on the afternoon of December 3. It was the largest mass arrest in California history. After being booked in the basement of Sproul Hall, most of the arrestees were bused to Santa Rita, a county prison about 25 miles away. As news of the arrests spread, faculty sympathizers organized caravans of cars to go to Santa Rita to post bail and retrieve the students after they had been processed.

Who sat in? Survey data show about 85 percent were Cal students. Nearly half of the remainder were employees or former students. The overwhelming majority did not resemble the radical activists who led the FSM; in most respects the FSM followers mirrored their fellow students who did not sit in. Largely from middle-class families, the protesters had middle-class aspirations and values, were not particularly active in politics or civil rights, and might be described as liberal Democrats. Although many conservative students, including some Young Republicans, supported the goals of the FSM, few conservatives believed that the free speech issue justified illegal acts. Indeed, it was the willingness to break a law to protest injustice that most clearly set apart those who sat in from those who did not. "We teach the students liberal values," noted one professor. "They fight for them on campus, and the administration puts them in jail." Psychological data suggested that the arrestees were unusually independent, impulsive, and nonconformist.

Although Jews were somewhat overrepresented among the protesters, more came from Christian than Jewish backgrounds. The protesters were 36 percent Protestant, 6 percent Catholic, and 32 percent Jewish; Cal students as a whole were 44 percent Protestant, 15 percent Catholic, and 20 percent Jewish. Compared to students who did not sit in, however, those who sat in were less likely to attend religious services.

Those who sat in were concentrated in certain majors, notably speech, anthropology, philosophy, English, and history; not a single student from optometry or business administration sat in. One striking trait, which troubled Kerr, was that the protesters' grades were higher than average.

As a whole, Berkeley students were split. By December roughly one third supported both the FSM goals and the FSM's militant tactics. As many as 8000 students might be drawn into future protests. Another third supported the goals but rejected illegal tactics. Only the remaining third upheld the administration's view that politics had no place on campus.

The divisions strongly correlated with partisan politics. Democratic students favored the FSM; Republican students did not. In part, this split was due to the Republican party's nomination of Barry Goldwater for president in 1964 on a platform hostile to civil rights. The outrage of civil rights activists had led to the FSM, and few young people sympathetic to that cause in 1964 called themselves Republicans.

After the arrests, the FSM leaders called a student strike. The strategy was to mobilize students behind the FSM, paralyze the campus, and force the facul-

Following the massive sit-in in Sproul Hall on December 2 and 3, 1964, activists declared a student strike. On December 4, freshly scrubbed and well-dressed pickets marched at the edge of campus. Many classes were cancelled, and attendance was low. "Stand for What You Believe" might be considered an appropriate motto for the decade. (Courtesy University Archives, University of California, Berkeley)

ty, which still hesitated, to side with the students. The key to the strike's effectiveness was the support of the teaching assistants. TAs were poorly paid and shabbily treated, and they tended to identify more with the undergraduates whom they taught than with the faculty.

The strike, held on Friday, December 4, was surprisingly effective. Perhaps half of all students either stayed away from classes or had their classes cancelled. Administrators publicly called the situation normal but privately expressed alarm. Kerr decided to move boldly and announced a university-wide convocation at the outdoor Greek Theatre for Monday, December 7.

Over the weekend Kerr consulted with a number of faculty members, especially department chairs, and he intended to endorse the chairs' compromise proposal on political rights at the Monday meeting. This measure, which allowed political activity unless it led to off-campus illegal acts, paralleled a proposal that the FSM had rejected earlier. But Kerr's neglect of the faculty had hurt, and a large group of younger, more liberal faculty—they called themselves the Committee of 200—had already met and supported the FSM's demands. At the meeting in the Greek Theatre Kerr announced an amnesty in the four pending disciplinary cases, endorsed the chairs' compromise, and said that students arrested in the sit-in would not face separate university discipline. As the meeting ended, it appeared that Kerr had won some support among the 16,000 to 18,000 students and faculty in attendance.

But then Mario Savio jumped onto the stage and headed for the microphone. Almost immediately, campus policemen tackled him and dragged him backstage. A cry rose from the crowd: "We want Mario!" The president tried to salvage the situation by allowing the FSM leader to announce a noon rally, but the attack on Savio was all that most people remembered of the events at the Greek Theatre.

Some administrators urged Kerr to attend the next day's faculty senate meeting. A personal appearance and strong plea, they argued, might rescue the chairs' compromise. But Kerr chose not to appear. The long, raucous meeting began in Wheeler Auditorium late Tuesday afternoon. Sociology Professor Lewis Feuer, a militant anticommunist who had been a Marxist as a student in the thirties, warned, "As this resolution stands now . . . , it would allow a student Ku Klux Klan chapter to organize . . . actions for defacing Jewish synagogues. . . ." Remembering how Nazi students had led the attack inside German universities as well as how politics had a way of shifting over time, Feuer was afraid that total freedom of action could bear strange fruit in the future.

Speech Professor Jacobus Ten Broek, a beloved undergraduate lecturer and one of Cal's premier defenders of civil liberties, replied, "As to the substance of what men say, this place should be absolutely free." By this time most faculty members supported the pro-FSM proposal to base political rights on campus on the first amendment's broad provisions. After the faculty defeated several conservative amendments by wide margins, they approved the pro-FSM proposal 824 to 115. Conservatives charged that the vote was influenced by the presence of 5000 FSM supporters who listened to the debate on loudspeakers outside in the dark.

As the faculty exited Wheeler, the FSM supporters opened a corridor through their ranks and broke into applause. Savio told the press, "Our tactics caused the present success . . . ," and for the first time during the crisis, he had a grin on his face. It was his twenty-second birthday. Jack Weinberg observed, "A great big change has taken place. All of a sudden we're respectable. Now we're on the side of God and country. I'm not used to this." Kerr had been rebuffed by his own faculty and, in the process, had lost the war.

Although Kerr believed that the regents would never accept the proposal, a number of professors had talked with the regents and found them willing to settle on faculty terms. Several other universities, including nearby San Francisco State College, had adopted rules similar to those proposed by the Berkeley faculty. On December 18 the regents met and declared, "The policies of the Regents do not contemplate that advocacy or content of speech shall be restricted beyond the purview of the First and Fourteenth Amendments to the Consti-

At the campuswide meeting in the Greek Theatre on December 7, 1964, the Free Speech Movement leader Mario Savio listened intently to proposed university rules. Note that Savio claimed an essential equality with university administrators by wearing coat and tie. At the end of the meeting Savio attempted to speak from the stage microphone and was wrestled to the ground by campus police officers. (Courtesy University Archives, University of California, Berkeley)

tution." In other words, they endorsed the position first articulated by the FSM activists during the committee discussions in October. And so it was that a handful of civil rights activists energized a large number of students, persuaded an inert and alienated faculty to accept their position, and went on to win concessions from the wealthiest and most powerful people in the state of California.

AN INTERPRETATION

What, then, had the Free Speech Movement been about? At its simplest level students wanted to exercise constitutional rights on campus. But, as indicated by the contrast between free speech at Sproul Plaza rallies and the inability of students legally to set up card tables for political activity, the issue was more about political rights than speech. As Mario Savio once put it, the issue was *effective* speech. The FSM demanded the right not merely to say what they pleased, since speech in that sense was both unchallenged and ineffective, but rather to be able to organize, to collect funds, and to use speech to make changes in society.

The key issue was civil rights. The university, said Savio, "cannot tolerate the civil rights movement because it advocates things with consequences." Activists believed that their demand for political rights was opposed precisely because the effective exercise of those rights promised to bring far more changes in race relations than would the utterance of words in Sproul Plaza.

Both the activists and the administration understood that they were engaged in a battle over power. This fact explains the intensity and the bitterness of the struggle. The FSM pursued a strategy to gain power. As Jack Weinberg emphasized, agitation produced confrontation, confrontation led to repression, and repression generated converts. This is what made the large number of arrests inside Sproul Hall so significant. It also led to the slogan, "The issue is not the issue." In the final analysis, the victory for political rights on campus was less important than the number and solidarity of participants, who gained confidence in their own potency. "We learned," recalled Susan Druding, "you can beat city hall if you have 800 others on your side, and you're *right.*"

The emerging Berkeley activist community's robustness became the single most important fact in both the university's and the city's political life after 1964. Although liberals continued to dominate the university, activists strenuously opposed the Vietnam War and organized a local political party that took control of Berkeley. Activists also organized and gained power in Madison, Wisconsin, another city dominated by a large state university. The FSM inspired students at other universities for the rest of the sixties, but students elsewhere learned, often painfully, that the FSM's success was unique. With rare exceptions, the student activists of the sixties had only a minor long-term impact on either universities or governments.

The FSM's obsession for power was rooted, originally, in an overwhelming sense of powerlessness. For the students who participated in the FSM, the first thrill of having power occurred during the spontaneous capture of the police car, and power became an important theme in Savio's speeches. Savio also alluded frequently to sexuality. His most famous words, about stopping the machinery from working, can be read in terms of both power and sex. In that speech Savio calmly conveyed the deep anger, the anxiety, the frustration with modern life, and the sense of powerlessness that was the undercurrent of all the turmoil of the sixties. His remarks not only resonated with his audience on the day of the sit-in but became widely quoted and even appeared on a wall poster popular among alienated secretaries in the early 1980s.

The FSM, deep in its psyche, was not about campus rules; it demanded nothing less than a complete political and social rearrangement of society, with power flowing up from the bottom rather than down from the top. These demands struck terror into the hearts of opponents—and with reason. Governor Pat Brown understood this attack on authority and as a former prosecutor vigorously upheld law and order. Brown's high visibility in ordering the arrests in Sproul Hall, however, enraged the protesters, who might have been his allies under other circumstances, and failed to appease those Californians who came to consider Brown as part of the problem of Berkeley's disgrace. Many people saw the protesters as childish, selfish, and spoiled rich kids wantonly destroying a magnificent but expensive institution built with hard-earned taxpayers' dollars. As the public seethed, assistant prosecutor Edwin Meese III and his later mentor, Ronald Reagan, were waiting in the wings. In 1966 Reagan defeated Brown as governor and entered office with Meese as his chief aide. In the long run the FSM brought not radical reform but conservative reaction.

Clark Kerr was unfortunate. By experience a negotiator, by temperament a calculator of trends, and by training a social scientist with a love for order, Kerr more than met his match in the leaders of the Free Speech Movement. The activists' dogged, fixed principles exasperated Kerr, whose skill at mediation proved pointless when presented with the FSM's non-negotiable demand for first amendment rights. But Kerr, unlike Savio, had never been chased by the Ku Klux Klan in Mississippi. Nor, unlike Weinberg, had Kerr ever dared to cross William Knowland. The liberal president, like Lyndon Johnson, clung to his ground until long after the tides of fortune had all but swept it away. One of Reagan's first acts as governor was to have the regents fire Kerr.

Even Kerr's love for order betrayed him. The FSM leaders saw, correctly, that disorder—such as the illegal sit-in—could aid their cause. Their Jewish style, at once playful and aggressive, and harkening back to working-class, immigrant roots that suggested success came only to those who struggled against power and authority, grated against Kerr, a practicing Quaker pacifist, and the university's other white, Anglo-Saxon, Protestant administrators.

The order of the Free Speech Movement was the order of war in which strategy and tactics went hand in hand and, in a successful cause, were linked to moral values. "My social conscience," said Savio, "was formed by the Gospels, although I say it with some trepidation, because I don't belong to any church." The activists' moral fervor contrasted with the administration's pettiness and with the faculty's hesitancy to act. The university, long dominated by liberals like Kerr, was in trouble. "The moral collapse of such an institution and such a set of individuals," wrote the local radical activist Geoffrey White, "cannot but, for the students involved, sweep away much of the liberal myth in its wake." In the end, as evidenced by the mood at the beginning of the Sproul Hall sit-in, the FSM must be considered to be a moral crusade. Or as the newspaper columnist Ralph J. Gleason wrote, "Literature, poetry, and history are not made by a smooth jowl and a blue suit. They are made with sweat and passion and dedication to truth and honor."

Sources: This story is largely extracted from W. J. Rorabaugh, *Berkeley at War: The 1960s* (New York: Oxford, 1989), pp. 18–37. The book contains full documentation. Main sources are the Free Speech Movement Archives, the University of California President's Files, and the Berkeley Chancellor's Files, all in the Bancroft Library, University of California, Berkeley. Still useful is Max Heirich, *The Spiral of Conflict: Berkeley 1964* (New York: Columbia, 1971), although Heirich lacked access to official files. Primary documents are in Harold Draper, *Berkeley: The New Student Revolt* (New York, 1965); Seymour M. Lipset and Sheldon S. Wolin, eds., *The Berkeley Student Revolt* (Garden City, N.Y., 1965); and Michael V. Miller and Susan Gilmore, eds., *Revolution at Berkeley* (New York, 1965). Also useful is Mark Kitchell's *Berkeley in the Sixties* (1990), an Academy Award nominated documentary film.

13

WOODSTOCK AND ALTAMONT

MICHAEL FRISCH

When people today, especially young people, are asked what they know or remember about the 1960s, Woodstock and Altamont are always among the most frequently mentioned events: Woodstock—the monster rock festival in New York that verged on catastrophe but ended up demonstrating the youth culture's ideas of harmony and peace, and Altamont, its dark star opposite—the Rolling Stones concert near San Francisco that collapsed into violence between young rock fans and the Hell's Angels motorcycle gang, culminating in a brutal murder in the front of the stage, an ugly, depressing event that seemed to belie the naive hopes of the "love generation" of sixties "flower children."

Occurring in the closing months of the 1960s, Woodstock and Altamont came together in one story that presumably gave meaning to each festival, and to a decade of cultural change in the United States. That the story has not seemed to alter very much in the more than 20 years since the concerts suggests there may be more here than meets the eye. After all, interpretations of the 1960s have diverged widely, some viewing the decade as a lost dream and others as a happily forgotten nightmare. But the stories of Woodstock and Altamont have remained a shared legacy, perhaps because they combine both dream and nightmare images so neatly and conveniently.

Michael Frisch's recasting of these events evokes the older parable of Woodstock and Altamont as a tale of good and evil. But it does so in order to frame a very different perspective that at once uncouples the events from each other and yet provides ways of linking them that does not depend on a moralistic mythology of innocence and corruption. Setting aside the powerful dream–nightmare images that have so neatly "explained" the concerts after the fact, Frisch draws on the complex, individual histories of Woodstock and Altamont to tell a very different story. In this new version, Woodstock emerges not as symbol of pastoral simplicity and retreat, but as a veritable city, sustained by technology and engaged in a complex game of survival and collective, political experimentation.

Altamont receives less attention in the narrative, but it, too, is reinterpreted. Although hardly cleansed of the horrific violence that occurred there, Altamont becomes a more sympathetic and understandable event—even, in an odd way, a more intimate one—than the hallowed Woodstock. And for the vast majority of those who attended the concerts, the events that now seem polar opposites must have appeared to be very similar expressions of the musical culture of sixties youth.

At issue in this new interpretation of Woodstock and Altamont is more than a new set and arrangement of facts. The story asks us to think about important questions that have to do with stories themselves. Is the older version just an older story, a kind of instant history with enormous staying power? Or is it a myth? If it is a myth, is the myth any less real than "history," or any less useful in reconstructing the fascinating and tumultuous years of the late 1960s? If, as hindsight reveals, the optimism and exuberance of the "sixties" were fast eroding under the influence of an ongoing Vietnam war and a Richard Nixon presidency, were Americans so wrong in interpreting the tragic events in front of the Altamont stage as another harbinger of the end of an era?

On March 22, 1967, a small ad appeared in both the *New York Times* and the "Business Opportunities" column of the *Wall Street Journal:*

> Young men with unlimited capital looking for interesting legitimate investment opportunities and business propositions.

The unlimited capital came mostly from John Roberts, 21, whose family owned a major pharmaceutical firm and who was then an indifferent graduate student at the University of Pennsylvania. His partner was Joel Rosenman, 23, son of a wealthy orthodontist, recent graduate of the Yale law school, and bored junior attorney. The two had decided that life could be more interesting than graduate school or an uncle's law firm: They knew they had the money, connections, and talent to do something—but what? The advertisement was one way to ask the question. The Woodstock Music and Arts Fair ended up being the answer.

Two years later, a circuitous route had led the partners through some 7000 ad responses to a meeting with two young men seeking funds for a state-of-the art recording studio in Woodstock, New York, a town north of New York City that had become home base for folk and rock musicians like the already legendary Bob Dylan. Roberts and Rosenman sat down with the two, both also in their early twenties: Artie Kornfeld, a hard-driving hip young rock executive with Capitol Records, and Michael Lang, a counterculture figure with bell bottom pants, fringed leather vests, and a huge halo of long curly hair who had recently been the proprietor of a "head shop" and an active figure on the rock music scene near Miami Beach, Florida. When Lang and Kornfeld suggested that a promotional concert in Woodstock could inaugurate the planned studio, the two investors jumped on the idea, reversing the priorities—we'll finance the concert, they decided, and use the profits from that to build your studio. Woodstock Ventures, Inc. was born.

This was in February, 1969, and within weeks the four partners had assembled an impressive team to mount a 2 or 3 day festival. The key individuals were Mel Lawrence and Stanley Goldstein, friends who had worked with Lang on the big Miami Pop Festival and had extensive experiences in recording, festivals, and project management. Lawrence was put in charge of all site and facility preparations; Goldstein, a recording engineer, ended up handling anything and everything. "I had taken the position of Holy Ghost," he joked later, "no one knew what I did, but you knew you had to have one."

Each new recruit seemed to bring in others who had needed skills or experience. There was E. H. Beresford "Chip" Monck, later known to the Woodstock audience and to millions of movie viewers as the unflappable stage MC passing on calming messages about lost children and bad drug trips. But in rock circles he was "pretty much the best-known lighting tech around at the time . . . unflustered by anything." There was John Morris, former manager of the Fillmore East rock auditorium in New York, who was to handle artists, agents, bookings, and stage managing. Morris brought in Chris Langhart, who in his early twenties was already head of the theater tech department at New York University (NYU). The sound man, Bill Hanley, headed a company that was the best in the country at delivering quality music systems for large outdoor audiences. Jean Ward, one of the few women at the center of things, brought her husband Bill and a large group of art students from the University of Miami to literally sculpt the grounds and environment, as they had done at other major festivals. Other women had supportive roles at first, but some soon assumed leadership positions at command center, women like Penny Stallings, a recent Southern Methodist University (SMU) graduate, and all-around executive assistant Lee Blumer, who had worked for famed rock promoter Bill Graham at the Fillmore East.

And so it went—a team of experienced young professionals, most in their mid-to-late twenties, solidly grounded in the emerging rock music business. There was one striking exception: a tough ex-cop named Wes Pomeroy, placed in charge of security. In his late forties, Pomeroy had recently left a top policy position at the Department of Justice in Washington; he was one of the few law enforcement and crowd control experts in the country with both credibility among police and sensitivity to the culture of the young people who would be coming to the Festival.

For all the experience, energy, and expertise, it still would have taken a minor miracle to pull off such a complex operation in just a few months, with no wiggle room for unexpected problems. And there turned out to be plenty of problems, especially involving site and security.

The intended site, close to the actual town of Woodstock, vanished as soon as the landowner learned what was planned. John Roberts then found 600 acres in the town of Walkill, not too far away, a site that had good road and electricity access. The technical wizards and art students plunged into the challenge of bulldozing this ugly industrial park site into bucolic hills, trucking in old farm equipment for atmosphere. But the real problems were not so much physical as political, even spiritual.

In the late 1960s, it was a given that rural or small town America would not take kindly to an invasion of hippies. It didn't help that the recent hit movie *Easy Rider* had told a story of motorcycle-riding pot-smoking hippie dropouts in violent collision with rural culture and straight America. The promoters obtained early zoning board approval for the project, but only by soft-pedaling what was planned. As a small army of longhaired young people drifted in to work on the site, Joel Rosenman remembers, the local citizens "started to think, 'Maybe that's what was coming.' In fact it *was* what was coming."

A group called Concerned Citizens sprang up to block the festival, and the opposition snowballed. Finally, the town of Walkill set up deliberately prohibitive conditions and requirements. In the middle of July, the promoters found themselves with most of the bands contracted, with commitments for everything from an elaborate stage to 2000 portable toilets, and with nearly $750,000 spent and $600,000 in advance ticket sales—all for a festival to be held within the month that now had no site.

Frantically, Bill Ward and Michael Lang searched for usable land, helicoptering around the hills with a Texaco road map and swooping down to read the highway signs so they could know where they were. Finally, with no time to spare, the answer came to them, in the improbable form of a successful Jewish dairy farmer named Max Yasgur of the Catskill mountain town of Bethel. Mel Lawrence and Lang rushed out to see the farm, steeled for another disappointment. But this was different. Yasgur drove them to the top of a broad hill. "And there it is," Lawrence recalled:

> It's like a lake and a natural amphitheater and roads and woods. So we say, like, "Oh, and how much of this land is yours?" "It's all mine," he says, "all mine except the lake's not mine, but I know the guy . . ." *Whew.* And Michael and I looked at each other and said, "This is it."

Indeed, as Stanley Goldstein noted, "it would be very hard to have found a more ideal site than that."

Yasgur proved a tough negotiator when it came to money and contract details, but the key, Goldstein recalled, was that "he felt we had been mistreated, that people deserved to have their say and their moment, that we were entitled to that as folks." His determination and commitment only increased when one of his neighbors put up a sign saying "Don't buy Yasgur's milk, he loves the hippies."

There were some other last minute problems raising the specter of another Walkill, including a threatened holdup on building permits and a self-inflicted PR disaster: A week before the festival, the promoters invited local citizens to an "open house" to show the careful preparations being made. They asked a "street theatre" group working a nearby hotel to give a sort of "demonstration" of what the festival would be like. With everyone on best behavior, the troupe (whom nobody had actually seen perform) proceeded to strip naked and simulate an orgy, chanting something on the order of "Repressed Rednecks, Provincial Prudes, Loosen your Chains and Live!" It didn't help.

But this was not Walkill. Yasgur's support counted for a lot, and the setting was really very different—located close to the substantial "borscht belt" hotels of the Catskills, Bethel had a declining economy based on a few run-down bungalow colonies and struggling hotels, and farms run by exurbanites like Yasgur. There were quite a few people around who shared his principles, and others who could see how much the area needed the economic boost the Festival could obviously bring.

With only weeks to go, the pace became frenzied. At the site, wells were dug and water systems laid out, hundreds of phone lines installed, garbage and carting service arranged, and electricity run in. "It was like wiring a city up, actually," one worker remembered. "We probably put in a couple of hundred poles, strung wires. Then all of a sudden they realized they had to have a heliport." The stage was 76 feet across and deep, with a 60 foot turntable, eleven feet off the ground and served by an elevator, behind two tall barrier fences, and connected by a bridge to an imposing performer's pavilion. The bridge and pavilion were designed by the brilliant Chris Langhart, whose combination of counterculture daffiness and professional competence seemed characteristic of the overall effort:

> Well, I figured if Jimi Hendrix was running across that bridge and then chased by as many groupies as he could get on that bridge and they were all coming down on one foot at one time, what was the weight load for that bridge? Then I doubled it.

Farmer Max Yasgur delights his 500,000 guests by greeting them from the stage with a "peace" symbol. Yasgur became a counterculture hero not only for agreeing to lease his fields for the site of the Woodstock Festival despite great local opposition, but for regarding the young people with respect despite vast cultural differences. His appearance on the stage was a welcome sign that communication was possible across the "generation gap." Note, in contrast to the setting at Altamont, how the barrier fence and the height of the stage keep the Woodstock crowd at a safe distance. (Elliott Landy, Magnum Photos)

Indeed, the work spanned the cultural spectrum. "A lot of Woodstock was planned from U.S. Army field manuals," John Morris recalled. "Try to find out how many toilets you have to have for how many thousand people and how you set up food and how you do the rest of it—the only data was little brown U.S. Army field manuals." Meanwhile, Michael Lang was riding romantically through the fields on a horse, inspecting the work. If to some this suggested the offensive image of a hippie plantation overseer, to others Lang seemed a charismatic guarantee that the countercultural heart of the festival was still beating. "He just seemed to glow. He had this cosmic aura about him," one remembered, "this little smile on his face like he knew something that none of us knew. . . . He managed to glow a lot of things into existence."

One thing that could not quite be glowed was security, the other major problem area. Everyone understood the problems a large crowd camped for several days might present, especially with the expected widespread use of pot and LSD. The potential for confusion, panic, and violence was all too real. But these very circumstances made it just as clear that order could not be imposed by force without catastrophic consequences.

Nobody felt this more strongly than Wes Pomeroy, who used all his savvy to assemble a professional public safety force whose objective would not be law enforcement but community self-help. Early in the summer, Lee Blumer spent several days in a New York City armory interviewing over a thousand police officers, trying to select the several hundred who could maintain professional competence and cool while floating in a sea of pot-smoking hippies.

A secondary approach was more daring, and led Stanley Goldstein to the Hog Farm commune, a large and already legendary hippie group then based in New Mexico. Goldstein arrived attaché case in hand so there would be no misunderstanding that he represented a business venture needing solid commitments on clear terms. He more than met his match. The hippie dreamers agreed to run a free kitchen, to manage the camping areas and cleanup, and to provide overall coordinating and security assistance, for all of which they cut a hard bargain that included a free charter flight from Sante Fe for nearly 90 members with room for tepee poles and with free goat's milk provided en route.

Not a bad combination of straight professionalism and countercultural imagination, or so it seemed until the police commissioner of New York, just days before, barred his off-duty officers from working at the festival. On the eve of the event Pomeroy and his crew found themselves almost fully dependent on the Hog Farmers, who had created quite a stir when their goat's-milk express landed in New York on the way to Bethel. "My God, we're the cops! I can't believe it!" exclaimed their leader, Hugh Romney, a.k.a. Wavy Gravy. When a reporter asked him what he intended to use for crowd control, he replied "Chocolate cream pies and seltzer bottles," recalling later "and then I noticed they were all writing it down!"

Put-ons can be deceiving. Behind the scenes the Hog Farmers, with Roberts' funds, were trucking in tons of rolled oats, barrels of wheat germ, honey, onions, soy sauce, and 1500 pounds of bulgur wheat, chosen because it would cook faster than the brown rice then a symbol of counterculture cuisine.

And the communards had their own approach to security, whimsical on the surface and deeply serious underneath. Offered a hundred arm bands decorated with cheerful flying pigs to identify members of the commune, Wavy Gravy asked how many people were actually expected. "They say they're expecting a couple of hundred thousand," he recalled, "And we say, 'we'd like to have that many arm bands.' We just thought if everybody was a cop there couldn't possibly be a problem." He called this the "Please Force," rather than the police force; the idea, his wife Bonnie explained, was

> when we saw somebody who was taking responsibility in a really excellent way that we would have an extra arm-band in our pocket and would say, "You are part of the Please Force, help out where you can.

The last week or two was a race between things coming together and time running out. One focus was the great bowl itself, where the stage, pavilion, sound system, and medical areas were pretty much ready. Another was near the Hog Farm's encampment in the woods, where a five-acre Aquarian shopping mall had been set up with hippies selling leather goods and tie-died shirts and incense, and with tot lots, sandboxes, and even a small children's zoo complete with lambs, chicks, and piglets. The campgrounds were more or less ready, as were the adjacent fields and farms rented for parking lots. Huge banks of pay phones and Port-O-San toilets stood waiting.

But this still left hundreds of checklist items incomplete. When Joel Rosenman arrived at the site on Monday of the last week, he recalls, "everything was in a state of preparation roughly on target for a festival to be thrown sometime in November. But not for one that was supposed to begin within four days." Priority had to be given to the primary human support systems, and other things just had to be abandoned. Some didn't matter much—like plans for elaborate light-show screens. But others did, certainly from a business point of view, especially the detailed but unexecuted plans for fencing and 20 turnstiled gates through which ticket-holders could be admitted and the grounds cleared between each of the 3 days' shows. By Wednesday, some 50,000 people were already sitting in front of the stage; with the stream rising to a torrent by the hour, the promoters confronted the fact that they could never clear the bowl to collect tickets, that in fact they never would get the turnstiles or fences in place. They decided that one of the first announcements from the stage would have to be to declare Woodstock a free festival.

At this point, the crowds were so far beyond anyone's imagination as to make the distinction between completed and incomplete preparations almost beside the point. Rosenman and Roberts frantically tried to get the State Police to put into effect a traffic control system slated for Saturday, but they could not convince the authorities of the emergency. The result was that Route 17B leading to Bethel quickly became a 13-mile-long parking lot, and Route 17, the "Quickway" bisecting the Catskills, was rapidly backing up toward the New York Thruway. "The situation is hopeless," one trooper reported, "and getting worse." Too late, the police began to close roads and broadcast appeals to people to turn back. Although the 500,000 or so who eventually arrived at Woodstock dazzled the world and made this probably the largest mass entertainment event in history, some authorities estimate that as many as two million may have been trying to get to the Festival.

Who were all these young people, and why were so many on the road to Woodstock? One thing they weren't was a gathering of the flower-children tribes seeking a kind of hippie theme park, as the conventional image has come to suggest. What they were was a representative cross-section of largely middle-class white American youth, a broad spectrum that the promoters, succeeding beyond their wildest dreams, had explicitly sought to reach. Rosenman and Roberts sensed that by 1969 most young people were feeling the strain of a decade of diverse conflicts with parents, teachers, and politicians about hair, drugs, sex, race relations, urban crisis, and the war in Vietnam. And so their Woodstock ads barely mentioned the star musicians or the counterculture, speaking instead of "three days of peace and music." "Walk around for three days without seeing a skyscraper or a traffic light," the copy went on, "Fly a kite, sun yourself, breathe unspoiled air." Paintings would hang on trees, and

Route 17B, the road to and from the Woodstock Festival. For most of the weekend, the highway was jammed like this for some 13 miles. This photo, taken on Saturday, shows some disillusioned young people heading home after an uncomfortable, rainy Friday night, while in the background others are still moving towards the Festival. (Associated Press/ Wide World Photos)

"artists will be glad to discuss their work, or the unspoiled splendor of the sur- roundings, or anything else that might be on your mind."

But imagery explains only so much, and like most advertisers the Wood- stock promoters exaggerated its importance. Deep down, products matter; con- sumers buy because there's something that they want. And if the newspaper and magazine ads were projecting an image, rock music radio stations and record stores and head shops across the country were trumpeting the news that Woodstock would bring together the most sensational constellation of top musi- cians and bands ever seen at any festival. To understand why this massing of talent sent so many young people careening towards Woodstock requires a bit of attention to what rock music was and what it had become.

In the early 1960s, most American high schools were still complex quilts of visibly divergent subcultures—"hoods" who dressed in blue jeans and danced to rockabilly music, for instance, and "bohemians" who favored black clothes, coffeehouses, jazz, and folk music. The divide between rock music and the folk music revival of the early 1960s was particularly sharp, with fans of each seem- ing to have very distinct social and cultural roots: In 1965, concert fistfights broke out between Bob Dylan's folk followers and fans of his first great electric rock hits, neither group having previously been very aware of the other. For most kids the music that mattered most was music that helped signal and solidi- fy social differences rather than music that reached across them—music that told you who you were by distinguishing your group from others among your peers.

By the late 1960s, however, old divisions were breaking down. Musical in- fluences were flowing across every category in every direction. The numerous hit records of Creedence Clearwater Revival had the simplicity and heavy beat of 1950's rockabilly—but the lyrics were often countercultural. Iron Butterfly was a favorite counterculture group whose sound anticipated later heavy metal. The brooding music of the Doors fused black blues, the drug experimenting of the counterculture, and Jim Morrison's philosophical poetry. And the Beatles' epic album "Sgt. Pepper" brought together rock, popular balladry, traditions of music hall and theater, and experiments on the outer limits of studio produc- tion. These movements across borders of style suggest that rock music was be- ginning to define a new, inclusive youth culture very different from the frag- mented "teenage" cultures of previous years, which had never pretended to be more than a stage on the road to conventional adulthood.

In 1969, this emerging new rock music culture was by and large a private and small group experience. Young people shared albums, danced at parties, listened to "underground" FM radio, and indulged in the illicit marijuana and hallucinogenic drugs that were embraced as the doors to a new consciousness and a higher reality—and a sharp generational divider. Public concerts and fes- tivals attracted small and specialized audiences. But the musical lineup for the Woodstock festival promised a very different sort of public experience, on a new scale. It was spectacular not because it represented the great mega-stars of the rock revolution (neither the Beatles, the Rolling Stones, nor Bob Dylan were to be there) but because it so embodied just about every tendency and dimension of rock creativity, from folk to avant garde. Indeed, it was not until August 15, 1969, as those two million young people struggled to get to the Woodstock Festival, that it began to become apparent what the music of the previous few years was beginning to add up to for this generation.

For most of the young people at or on the road to Woodstock, the mood on that Friday was less one of exhilaration than of surprise, frustration, and annoyance. They found themselves in what one student recalled as a stream of initially frightening diversity, from "real hippies" to "teeny boppers" to clean-cut suburban college types, to bikers and rockers and even Hell's Angels, all bumping into each other with the frayed tempers sure to be found in any mammoth traffic jam. At the concert site, there was some excitement at discovering the fallen fences and the absence of gates, rules, regulations, police, or supervisors. But the realization that the situation was by that token beyond control contributed a dark undertone of anxiety for many, who wondered exactly what they had gotten themselves into.

Spirits lifted when the music got off to a good, if unplanned, start around 6 P.M. Among the first performers was Country Joe McDonald, who brought the crowd together with his famous "Fixin' to Die Rag," an anti-Vietnam War singalong, preceded by his even more famous call and response "Gimme an F . . . U . . . C . . . K" cheer—imposing when shouted by several hundred thousand kids realizing that there were no grownups around to disapprove or even be shocked.

But as night came on the mood darkened: Everything was so uncertain, from food to safety to shelter, and the parade of folksingers programmed for the evening, headed by Joan Baez, and curiosities like Indian sitar master Ravi Shankar, left much of the audience distracted and unmoved. Persistent rain dampened spirits further. As one youngster recalled,

> It seemed more like a war zone that happened to be peaceful at the moment. It was real strange and I didn't care for it. There was no question about the fact that I wanted to leave the next morning. And so we ended up hitchhiking out of the area back into New York City.

Saturday was a different story. Many spent the morning wandering around the fields, discovering the crafts area and Hog Farm compounds in the woods, and skinny dipping in the ponds. Meanwhile, streams of people were still arriving, and as the hillside bowl filled for the afternoon concert, the enormity of the crowd became visible and tangible for the first time, an immense human spectacle. One youth remembers that

> we walked from where we were in the woods to the stage and looked out and all of a sudden what had been what seemed to me a few thousand people had become this half million people and it all seemed to have happened on Friday night in the middle of the night . . . I was standing and thinking, "Oh my God, this is unbelievable."

This individual response quickly grew into a collectively shared sense that something momentous was happening, a realization assisted by commentary from the stage. A stream of announcements—by Mel Lawrence, John Morris, Wavy Gravy of the Hog Farm, and especially the calm-voiced Chip Monck—crystallized everyone's feelings and broadcast them back, amplified, to the crowd.

In this electronic dialogue, the pastoral vision of nature and rural harmony in the now irrelevant Woodstock advertisements gave way to an urban frame of reference. "Welcome to one of the biggest cities in the United States," Mel Lawrence boomed into the mike on Saturday morning. The image indeed fit: The density and variety of the immense crowd was generating the infectious excitement associated with city life at its best. But there was another side to the image: The environment was swiftly coming to seem a vast free-form museum of modern urban problems at their worst—litter and garbage, disintegrating communications, water and food shortages, and inadequate sewage and health care facilities. And looming in the shadows was the possibility of violence or chaotic rioting, with which urban America was all too familiar after the "long hot summers" of the 1960s.

In real cities, problems are handled bureaucratically, through administrative authority. But at Woodstock, administration did not survive the first day, and authority was nonexistent. In this situation, the promoters had no choice but to turn to the crowd. From the stage, spokesmen began telling vacationing kids, most of whom would have cheered the sixties slogan "Power to the People," that in fact they had the power—or rather, there was no power except what they, the people, chose to exercise. The genuine accomplishment of these voices was to help generate a sense of collective urban adventure, making everyone realize that they were a city not because of the exciting size or the real problems, but simply because they were so fully dependent on each other.

One motif epitomized the uniqueness and potential of this situation. Surrounding the stage were a number of huge scaffold towers for lights and cameras. During every set, some kids would climb up to enjoy the unsurpassed view from the towers' platforms, and invariably someone, usually Chip Monck, would patiently plead over the PA for them to come down. He would acknowledge politely that nobody could make them come down, but that they should anyway, because each person on a tower blocked the view of tens of thousands of others looking down from the hill. "There's a half a million people here," he said at one point, "and if we don't help each other we'll die. Come on, up there, join us!" The towers would usually clear after each of these sermons, although during the next set the kids, or different ones, would climb up again, producing another appeal and another sheepish retreat. It was almost as if some kids wanted the scolding, as a way to reestablish parental authority where none really existed and thus to decline the responsibility the situation was demanding that they assume.

There was even more at stake in the handling of other problems, particularly drugs. Widespread use of marijuana and experimenting with hallucinogenic drugs was a hallmark of the generation, viewed less as an escape than as an adventurous reaching to an alternative reality and a higher consciousness. But for most this was usually done with friends under familiar circumstances with known substances of reliable quality, precisely the opposite of conditions prevailing at Woodstock. The result was a great many unexpected reactions that could suddenly turn into terrifying "bad trips." Rumors that bad LSD was circulating made things worse—and presented organizers with a desperate dilemma. As Chip Monck said, "How do you keep them from taking it without freaking out those who already have?" His answer was a cool, hip voice that struck just the right note of reassurance and concern:

> You may take it with however many grains of salt you wish that the brown acid that's circulating around is not specifically too good. It's suggested that you do stay away from that. Of course, it's your own trip, so be my guest. But please be advised that there's a warning on that one.

In another risky stage decision, it was decided to share with the crowd the horror stories filling the national press and airwaves about the catastrophe taking shape at Woodstock—images of a drug-ridden anarchy careening out of control, and calls for the National Guard to step in. Sharing this news, a strategy Joel

Climbers on the light and camera towers at the Woodstock Festival. All the climbers appear to be young men—perhaps it seemed at first a macho challenge to scale these heights for a better view, regardless of how many thousands of others were thereby prevented from seeing the stage. (From the film *Woodstock*, Michael Wadleigh, Warner Brothers/Courtesy, Museum of Modern Art Film Still Archive)

Rosenman called "reverse information dissemination," challenged everyone to pull together and prove the authorities wrong.

Like the drug warnings, the images of crisis might themselves have provoked anxiety and panic. But the tactic worked: A remarkable ethic of mutuality and cooperation began to spread throughout the entire festival area. People willingly shared scarce food with strangers, helped those who were lost, shepherded those freaking out on bad drug trips to the medical aid stations, did what they could to gather in the rising tide of garbage, and linked into the chains of volunteer workers spiraling out of the Hog Farm. Throughout it all, the calm, encouraging voices from the stage, the public face of the community, magnified these efforts and made the instant city of half a million youngsters seem a tight knit community.

The other thing that made a difference on Saturday was the music itself—an incredible concert that began at 1 o'clock in the afternoon and did not end until well after dawn the next morning. For the first time it seemed as if all of rock's various streams were coming together, fusing diverse groups of fans into a single, public generational audience. The performers included the hard driving Creedence Clearwater Revival; the queen of acid rock blues, Janis Joplin; the experimental, theatrical British group The Who; the then virtually unknown Santana, anticipating the infusion of Latin rhythms into rock; and the quintessential San Francisco groups—the classic folk–rock–blues band the Grateful Dead and, closing out the long event after sunrise, the Jefferson Airplane, wellspring of a harder acid rock sound. But for most people, the peak came somewhere in the middle of the long night, with the black group Sly and the Family Stone, psychedelic rock grafted onto R&B (rhythm and blues) and gospel. As Sly Stone led the crowd in an ecstatic, almost religious call and response on the song "Higher," it seemed that rock music had finally become a kind of communal binding force.

It was not ecstasy, however, that kept music going all night—this was a decision of the organizers who knew that chaos was still a danger if the crowd were not kept focused and occupied. All day and night long, while the musicians played, they had been battling a ceaseless barrage of emergencies. Artists had to be helicoptered in, not to mention emergency medical and food supplies. Outside officials had to be persuaded that calling in the National Guard would be catastrophic. Outraged locals arrived waving lawsuits. Frantic parents were trying to call their children and desperate messages had to be passed on about lost friends who had needed medicine. And then some of the musicians refused to go on until paid up front: While the hillside was soaring on sound, John Roberts was frantically arranging to helicopter the local bank manager, in his pajamas in the middle of the night, to retrieve the needed cashier checks.

There were also problems with the more political activists from New York's East Village, especially Yippie leader Abbie Hoffman, who saw the festival as a plot to exploit the alternative culture for profit with nothing given in return. Early on, Hoffman had flatly threatened sabotage unless given $10,000 for community organizing and political work at the festival. A sort of deal was struck, and at the scene Hoffman threw all his formidable talents into organiz-

ing everything from a camp newspaper to emergency field hospitals. But he remained frustrated that political issues were so suppressed in the festival's public
voice and presence. Finally, he tried to seize the microphone while The Who
was playing, to rally support for John Sinclair, an activist who had recently
begun serving a 10-year jail term for possession of two joints of marijuana. A
whack from Peter Townshend's guitar sent Hoffman running, and seemed to
announce that his "political" approach to the festival was not welcome.

But what was happening at Woodstock *was* political. The counterculture
was demonstrating its capacity to solve problems in its own terms, and in ways
that advanced a broader vision of change. In the organization of the free kitchen
that fed tens of thousands and in dealing with the medical emergencies, the
Hog Farmers' "armband" approach reached its most inspiring heights, as Wavy
Gravy recalled:

> So there were these five doctors in white coats and shirts and ties and me. And this
> guy comes in screaming, "Miami Beach, 1944! Joyce! Joyce!" And this psychiatrist
> leans in and says, "Just think of your third eye, man." So I figured it was time for
> me to make my move. And the guy says, "Miami Beach, 1944!" And I said,
> "What's your name, man?" He says, "Joyce!" I said, "What's your name, man?"
> He says, "1944." I said, "WHAT'S YOUR NAME, MAN?" He says, "Bob!" I
> said, "Your name is Bob! Your name is Bob. Your name is Bob." And he is get-
> ting it, and he's getting it, and he's getting it. And when he's got it I say, "Guess
> what?" He says, "What?" I said, "You took a little acid and it's going to wear off."
> He says, "Thank God." They don't want to know about third eyes. They just want
> to know they're going to come down.
>
> And then—which is what made Woodstock unique—when he was near normal
> and ready to go back to rock 'n' roll, we said "Hold it. You see that sister coming
> through the door with her toes in her nose? That was you three hours ago. Now
> you're the doctor. Take over." And they'd take turns.

Sunday tested and deepened the intensity of Saturday's experience. It
began easily enough, someone reading the Sunday comics to the crowd and
Wavy Gravy announcing "breakfast in bed for 400,000," with the Hog Farmers
and hundreds of volunteers passing out paper cups of granola across the hillside. But soon after the music began in the afternoon, the skies suddenly darkened and a monster thunderstorm of near-tornado intensity broke over the unprotected hills and fields. "It was Dante's Inferno," John Morris recalled, "it
was all hell breaking loose, it was everything you could ever have possibly wrong
at one situation at one given moment."

He and the staff had good reason to be terrified. The crowd pressure had
exposed electrical cables; the whole stage complex was sliding slowly into the
mud; the electrified light towers were swaying in the gale like pendulums. Mass
electrocution was a real possibility, as was a tower collapse that could kill scores
and panic thousands more. It was imperative that the power be turned off—yet
the music and the medium of the stage PA were the lifeline keeping the huge
crowd from panic. In another desperate gamble, one mike was kept alive while

everything else was shut down. John Morris, alone on the huge stage, helped the crowd ride it through, talking kids down from the swaying towers in a voice calm enough to avoid panicking those huddled underneath.

Although the tension soon gave way to mudslide frolicking as the worst of the storm passed over, the emergency had been a dramatic reminder that Woodstock Nation was subject to larger forces, still enmeshed in a world beyond its own control. This was acknowledged ironically when the hillside multitudes chanted the demand "no rain, no rain" just as the immense thunderstorm was so obviously about to break. It was acknowledged respectfully in the way the young volunteers and organizers accepted the outside aid that began to make such a difference. One of the biggest cheers of the weekend came when a green helicopter swung in ominously over a crowd fearing a National Guard takeover, and John Morris announced with excitement, "Ladies and Gentlemen, the U.S. Army . . . Medical Corps!"

In the aftermath of the storm, kids skinny-dipped off the mud and thousands of others began to drift homeward. There was a growing sense of fulfillment and completion, a mood helped along by the final concert, also an all night affair that ended early Monday morning. This session featured the English singer Joe Cocker, launched to stardom by his Woodstock performance of "With a little help from my friends," a Beatles song especially appropriate to the situation; the new folk-rock based combo of Crosby, Stills, and Nash; the Band, Dylan's former backup group; and Blood, Sweat, and Tears, pointing mainstream rock toward a newer, broader 1970s sound.

But it was the closing of the festival early Monday morning, when a good part of the huge crowd had already left, that best brought the music and the meaning of the whole event together. The last performer was Jimi Hendrix, the enigmatic black superstar who was more a figure of the counterculture than of the black musical scene, his wild electric guitar style having propelled him to the frontier of experimental rock sounds. Hendrix closed the festival not with rock but with a long, meditative, almost tortured solo version of the Star Spangled Banner. The moment was very special, as one witness recalled:

> There was a sort of stillness and it really looked like those old photos you see of old Civil War battlefields, where you see a dead horse and these mounds of things that have been left. And there was Jimi Hendrix up there playing "The Star Spangled Banner" . . . I mean it was like a very strange, eerie close to the whole thing, you know. I just remember those two images together: him playing that song, and everything being so still while he played . . .

The image has become one of the lasting symbols of Woodstock—to some a flag-desecrating emblem of the counterculture's alienation, to others a more complex gesture of both respect and defiant pride.

Indeed, as it closed and even before, Woodstock was becoming a series of contested images. The process had begun in the first often-hysterical reactions to the crisis in Bethel, when a *New York Times* editorial called the whole thing "a nightmare of mud and stagnation" with "freakish looking intruders" who "had little more sanity than the impulses that drive the lemmings to march to their deaths in the sea. . . . What kind of culture is it," asked the *Times*, "that can produce so colossal a mess?"

Almost immediately, this posture gave way to grudging acknowledgments that the young people had been generally well behaved, cooperating with each other and with those who rushed food and medical help to their rescue. The *Times*'s next day's editorial, "Morning After at Bethel," generously pronounced Woodstock "essentially a phenomenon of innocence." But something more was going on in this shift of imagery: Woodstock's diverse cultural mix and complexity of interdependence was coming to be replaced, after the fact, by an image of a dreamy youth culture straight out of the "flowers in your hair/gentle people there" hippie stereotype born in San Francisco's Haight Ashbury district in the mid 1960s. And this was not just a response of the mainstream media. In the song that became a kind of "Woodstock Nation" national anthem Joni Mitchell sang, "We've got to get ourselves back to the garden." But the song was written after the Festival; Mitchell, in fact, had not even been there. In the fall of 1969, this Garden of Eden imagery seemed to be recapturing and transforming the meaning of Woodstock. And it also set the stage, in a kind of biblical drama, for the entrance of the serpent—at Altamont Speedway.

The great free Rolling Stones concert near San Francisco on December 6, 1969, would never have occurred had not Woodstock preceded it. The Stones and lead singer Mick Jagger were then at the height of their popularity, and somewhat jealous of the shadow that the August festival threw over their upcoming fall American tour. Knowing that a major documentary about Woodstock was being readied, they decided to have one made about their own tour, and began to toy with the idea of a huge free concert to provide its climax.

But it was not simply their idea, or even their choice. The tour had been grossing millions of dollars for the Stones in sellout appearances across the country. In New York City alone, a single advertisement brought requests for over 500,000 tickets. In the glow of the Woodstock spirit, the alternative community placed increasing pressure on the Stones to rise above profit, to return something to the community in the form of a free, public concert, especially considering the climax of the tour in San Francisco, the heart of the counterculture.

The Stones finally agreed, and the details began to be thrown together while their tour crisscrossed the country. If Woodstock needed years and only had months to prepare, this one day event needed months and had only weeks, and then only days. There was some of the same professionalism, including many of the same individuals behind the scenes—Chip Monck, for example, was in charge of the stage facilities—but no time or resources with which to work. After false starts and dashed hopes paralleling the Woodstock site location fiasco, land for this concert finally materialized with only 1 day to prepare. The grossly inadequate site was Altamont Speedway, a seedy drag strip 50 miles east of San Francisco offered by an owner hoping to put himself and his facility on the map. ("Please call it Dick Carter's Altamont Speedway," he kept insisting to the press, to no avail.) And where emergency security provisions at

Woodstock had come to depend on the Hog Farm commune, the Stones and their agents were persuaded to deputize a very different group: the Hell's Angels motorcycle gang. Given how catastrophically this turned out, it is hard now to appreciate how appropriate it seemed.

The Stones occupied then (and still do) an unusual place in the evolution of rock, encompassing within their own music and persona the kind of broad synthesis it took many different groups at Woodstock to represent. They had begun as blues purists, alienated middle-class English boys reaching beyond their backgrounds for what seemed a music of authenticity and power. In contrast to the genial Beatles, the Stones had fashioned themselves into the bad boys of rock, projecting an insolence, rebellion, and raw sexuality that flaunted their contempt for society's conventional values and institutions. Where the Beatles moved forward into experimental song forms and eclectic stylizing, the Stones deepened their hold on a hard-driving, R&B based sound that brought the full energy and spirit of black music into rock and roll. As they turned from performing their own versions ("covers") of black songs to writing their own material, the insolence became more culturally rebellious and even political. The Stones' music seemed increasingly to embrace violence and evil; their blatant sexuality became more excessive, taunting the mainstream with what appeared to be a kind of countercultural perversion. All these tendencies were at a

Mick Jagger and the Rolling Stones in performance, earlier in the tour that was to culminate in the concert at the Altamont Speedway. Note how Jagger's costume and gestures seem to combine both masculine and feminine sexual imagery—one of the things that made him seem so outrageous to "straight" society. Also note how close the crowd is to the stage and the performers, a pattern that was to prove so disastrous at Altamont. (From the film *Gimme Shelter,* David Maysles, Albert Maysles, Charlotte Zwerin; Maysles Films, Inc./Courtesy, Museum of Modern Art Film Still Archive)

peak in 1969, embodied in hit songs like "Sympathy for the Devil" "Street Fighting Man," and "Honky Tonk Woman."

As for the Angels, they had been a minor gang on the edge of dissolution when, in 1965, an incident or two led to a newsmagazine media blitz. Suddenly they were an overnight national phenomenon and began to live up to the image that had been created for them, roaring down the highway in huge convoys on a "run" to this or that location where locals cowered in fear. Said one of the Angels, almost as if he were speaking to an expectant public, "We're the one per-centers, man—the one percent that don't fit and don't care. We've punched our way out of a hundred rumbles, stayed alive with our boots and our fists. We're royalty among motorcycle outlaws, baby."

The motorcycle outlaw motif held particular fascination for a San Francis-co counterculture eager, in 1965, to identify with others who opposed authori-ty. "We're in the same business," LSD missionary Ken Kesey told the Angels when he met them, "You break people's bones. I break people's heads." Soon he had turned them on to acid and drawn them into the "love generation" scene, where they were embraced by poet Allen Ginsberg and other hip intellec-tuals.

The Angels themselves never quite knew what to make of all this—love, said their leader, Ralph "Sonny" Barger, is "the feeling you get when you like something as much as your motorcycle." And the hip romance burned off quickly; in October of 1965 the Angels beat up antiwar demonstrators trying to march from Berkeley to Oakland to shut down the Army Terminal there, a ship-out point for Vietnam troops. By 1969 there were few remaining illusions about the Angels and the violent threat their hostility could pose.

But it was this very realism that led to the request that the Angels serve at Altamont. The organizers were not thinking of general peacekeeping in a large temporary community on the order of Woodstock; they faced the narrower, classic challenge of rock concert security: protecting stars from overexcited fans. On previous tours, there had been repeated clashes between fans and police protecting the Stones, often ending in tear gas and indiscriminant beatings by police. And in San Francisco, pressure was guaranteed to be intense: Where the elaborate Woodstock stage had stood 11 feet off the ground and was protected by high barrier fences, the stage set up hastily at Altamont was at eye level, with the crowd able to press right up against it.

The Stones' managers and their San Francisco contacts thus knew that some sort of physical, visible, formidable protection would be needed at a huge free concert. But they feared, correctly, the provocation that uniformed police, armed or unarmed, would present. And so the Stones agreed to invite the Angels to protect them in exchange for the now legendary $500 in free beer.

On Saturday, December 6, the mood at Altamont seemed uneasy from the start, although not particularly because of the Angels, whom most of those attending never even saw. Perhaps it was the unpleasant, uncomfortable site, littered with junked cars, or the edge of counterculture violence in the air. (The previous week had seen the arrest of Charles Manson, a charismatic figure on the fringe of the hippie rock scene, for the horrific Tate–La Bianca murders, which themselves had taken place just before Woodstock.)

The concert got underway in early afternoon to the rhythms of Santana, the huge crowd of nearly 500,000 settling in for the long wait before the appearance of the Stones. Down in front were the Angels—sitting on the edge of the stage with their bikes parked nearby, hefting chains and cut-off, weighted pool cues, "dangling their legs over the side," Stones biographer Stanley Booth recalled with pointed irony, "like little boys fishing at a creek in the nineteenth century."

It might have worked, if so many of the Angels had not been so drunk or so hopelessly stoned. But with the crowd pressed tightly against the stage, the Angels, and their beloved bikes, the situation proved volatile almost from the start. Fights broke out again and again, brief flurries of violence that would erupt and then subside—defenseless, often stoned young people beaten with pool cues and stomped by crowds of Angels, in full view of the stage and the documentary movie cameras. Carlos Santana stopped playing and tried without

Hells Angels beating concertgoers with pool cues in front of the stage at Altamont. Most onlookers show no emotion, not because they are indifferent but because the events are unfolding so quickly and unexpectedly at a concert intended as a celebration of countercultural harmony. A few faces begin to register the horror of what is happening. (From the film *Gimme Shelter,* David Maysles, Albert Maysles, Charlotte Zwerin; Maysles Films, Inc./Courtesy, Museum of Modern Art Film Still Archive)

effect to calm things down. A while later Marty Balin of the Jefferson Airplane tried to break up a fight and was knocked unconscious by one of the Angels. Beyond the area in front of the stage, most people couldn't know quite what was happening, but a fitful mood of fear and anxiety began to spread back through the throng. On stage Stones assistant Sam Cutler was proving no Chip Monck at the microphone: Exhausted and frustrated, he scolded the Angels and the crowd like an unpleasant schoolmaster.

Finally the Stones took the stage, Jagger in his outrageous silver tights, black shirt, orange cape, and Uncle Sam hat. For the first few tunes it almost seemed as if the music would carry the mood beyond the reach of the Angels now massed at front of the stage. But as the band launched into "Sympathy for the Devil," the Angels resumed the savage pool cue beatings, enraged by what seemed to have been an attack on one of their motorcycles. The Stones stopped playing, trying to quiet things down: "Hey people—I mean, who's fighting, and what for? Why are we fighting?" a puzzled Jagger asked.

The Stones retreated to some "cool out" tunes, and Jagger continued to try to sooth the crowd between songs. But then the violence erupted again, as he began "Under My Thumb." In full view of the stage, a tall, black boy in an iridescent suit suddenly leaped up and was as suddenly set upon by a frenzied gang of Angels, stomped to the ground, and stabbed repeatedly with a long knife. The incident was over in a flash. Nobody beyond the immediate circle could see the blood from the youth's massive wounds or realize that indeed a murder had taken place in their midst, but the violence was still traumatic—including the fact that many *had* seen the young man, Meredith Hunter, 19, brandishing a pistol just before the Angels descended on him.

Cutler appealed for a doctor, and ineffectively tried to calm the crowd, as did another backstage figure who took the microphone—Michael Lang, the hippie promoter of Woodstock. Finally, announced Jagger, "It seems to be stuck down to me":

> All I can ask you, San Francisco, is . . . this could be the most beautiful evening we've had this winter, let's get it together, everyone, come *on* now. . . . You know, if we *are* all one, let's fucking well *show* we're all one. Everyone just sit down. Keep cool. Let's just *relax*, let's get into a groove. Come on, we can get it together, come on.

The emotional appeal was perplexing to most of the 500,000 who couldn't see what was happening down front. Meanwhile, with crazed intensity, the Angels continued to fulfill their assigned mission to protect the stage, mercilessly beating a stoned, naked girl trying to clamber up towards Jagger.

But in fact the groove did take hold. Perhaps Jagger's impotence in his spoken role inspired greater intensity in his singing. Many still say that what followed was one of the Stones' greatest performances ever; in the final analysis, its sheer power may well have made the crucial difference in preventing the horror up front from spreading and escalating into a catastrophic crowd panic. But the Stones were numbed by the effort and what they had seen. "I thought the scene here was supposed to be so groovy," Jagger commented soon after. "I don't know what happened, it was terrible, if Jesus had been there he would have been crucified."

AN INTERPRETATION

For most of those present, Woodstock involved struggle, process, and challenge. For 3 days, individuals were forced to relate to each other under great pressure, and to rise above circumstances that had somehow—to everyone's surprise—placed their destiny in their own hands. What made Woodstock exciting was how the emergency, the music, the linking of strangers in long voluntary chains of collective self-help, all served to create a political, cultural, and musical community where none had quite existed before. If those who kept climbing up the towers seemed almost nostalgic for a missing parental authority to challenge, the vast majority underneath were creating their own authority, discovering their capacity to take responsibility for the situation, and each other.

In all these ways, Woodstock epitomized the values of culture, politics, and community at the core of generational change in the 1960s. Abbie Hoffman may have wanted to move the assembled Woodstock Nation into a position of political confrontation, and the promoters may have imagined an apolitical, purely cultural celebration. But the real meaning of the experience—and of much of the sixties—was how these were merging, in new and not easily recognizable ways, becoming entwined in the experience of an increasingly unified, self-conscious generation.

To be sure, Woodstock also revealed how incomplete this community was, and how dependent it was on extraordinary circumstances—how hard it was for the same sense of unity, struggle, and spirit to survive for very long without confrontation, whether that confrontation involved the emergency of food and health care at Woodstock or the confrontation with the government over the war in Vietnam.

And it revealed something more as well: the power of cultural images as weapons in political, cultural, and generational conflicts, and how these can transform the meaning of experience—even seeming to become, after the fact, what is remembered as the reality of experience.

Woodstock, as advertised, had promised a pastoral garden, an opportunity for people to come into harmony with nature and each other. At the end of the rebellious sixties, with conflict and violence spiraling out of control even within the counterculture, this dream evidently had enormous appeal. And as we have seen, it is to this image of gentle innocence and simple harmony that images of Woodstock quickly and permanently returned, obscuring after the fact the deeper political and cultural experience of those who had been there.

Altamont played an important, even crucial role in this process—a process, at its heart, that involved a struggle to define at decade's end the meaning of the sixties. "Altamont was the killer of the dream," wrote one observer from inside the counterculture; said another: "On this day, hip jargon, flower power, and the Age of Aquarius were finished. The great sixties dream was washed up . . . all the beautiful fantasies of the sixties withered and died." Ralph Gleason, a mainstream San Francisco journalist who had done much to explain the rock world to his readers, wrote, "Is this the new community? Is this what Woodstock promised? Gathered here as a tribe, what happened? Brutality, murder, despoilation." Many concluded, as Vincent Canby was to say a bit later in the *New York Times,* that "Everything that the people feared would happen (but didn't) at Woodstock happened at Altamont."

Such statements say little about history and much about myth-making. There were four deaths at Altamont, true, but three were in accidents much like the one death that occurred at Woodstock. In either event, what is remarkable is how minimal was the conflict or disorder. The violence at Altamont remained restricted to a handful of Angels in a circle of several hundred people around the stage; horrific as this was, what needs to be explained is why the incidents have so generally been taken as emblematic of the experience not just of 500,000 concertgoers, but of the entire counterculture.

The explanation lies in the relationship between the two events—or, more precisely, in what the events at Altamont supposedly revealed about Woodstock. For Altamont was almost immediately embraced as proof of the fatal fragility of the Woodstock vision. If Altamont is the face of evil, then Woodstock must have been its opposite—the face of innocence. With the help of Altamont, Woodstock became remembered not for struggle, process, or community, but rather as a temporary Garden of Eden, inhabited by a naive generation. And—so the story goes—the Woodstock generation came to be (deserved to be?) expelled from the Garden for the dark, countercultural sins of Altamont. The story is an old one, of course, with proven appeal.

The dichotomy of blissful innocence and cruel, violent reality seems reasonable, but it is all too convenient and deflects us from the more challenging complexities of the 1960s. Indeed, the images might well be reversed, with Altamont understood as the more innocent, Woodstock the more real event. It was at Altamont, after all, that old-fashioned face-to-face confrontations led to violence, unprevented by desperate microphone messages from the stage that left a dazed Mick Jagger pleading for peace like a little boy. And so much of what was taken for innocence at Max Yasgur's farm was the product of those hallmarks of modern society, electronics and mediated communication: The blasts of music and the electronically amplified voice of folksy stage spokesmen combined to draw hundreds of thousands of distrustful strangers into sustained interaction with each other—into meaningful community and mutual responsibility.

Indeed, in broader cultural and political senses as well, it is Woodstock that offers the more complex testimony on young people in America at the end of the 1960s, when for many the challenges of the festival were just beginning to harden into wider confrontations with the policies and institutions of American society. Tom Law, a friend of the Hog Farm who gave the yoga demonstrations that seem so apolitical in the movie *Woodstock,* put it this way:

The thing I kept thinking when I look back on those times is, yes, you can say we were naive, but we were naive with a vengeance. What we were trying to avenge was the nastiness of what America had become in the Vietnam era. And I think that was the prevailing motivator: to do something different and to do something right. . . . Everybody was really pouring their time and energy into trying to heal this gaping wound, which, as you know, got worse and worse for the next three years . . .

The question is not "What happened to those of us who went to Woodstock?" It's "Where's the Woodstock for today's generation?" That's more important, because out of that sense of community comes the energy to go out there and actually participate in the process so that social change occurs.

Sources: The most valuable primary source for Woodstock is Joel Makower, *Woodstock: The Oral History* (New York: Doubleday, 1989). Most of this chapter's direct quotations from Festival participants are taken, with appreciation, from the extensive interviews in this well-edited collection. Also useful are the recollections of the festival promoters, wittily crafted by a professional writer: Robert Pilpel, Joel Rosenman, and John Roberts, *Young Men with Unlimited Capital* (New York: Bantam, 1989 [original edition 1974]); Abbie Hoffman's *Woodstock Nation: A Talk–Rock Album* (New York: Vintage, 1969) a spirited memoir–manifesto that Hoffman claims he wrote in a drugged frenzy immediately after the Festival; and a history based on many recent interviews with those who had been at Woodstock: Jack Curry, *Woodstock: The Summer of Our Lives* (New York: Weidenfeld and Nicolson, 1989).

There has been less written about Altamont, but I found Stanley Booth's participant–observer memoir of the Rolling Stones 1969 tour (at once a primary and a secondary source) the most helpful: *Dance with the Devil: The Rolling Stones and Their Times* (New York: Random House, 1984). The best documentation of the Altamont event is in the periodical press at the time, particularly *Rolling Stone.* A good example of mainstream reportage, with rich detail, is Ralph J. Gleason, "'Aquarius Wept': After Woodstock and Love Came Altamont and Disaster," *Esquire* 74/2 (August, 1970).

Finally, of course, there are the major documentary films of each event released in 1970 and still widely available in libraries and video rental stores: Michael Wadleigh's *Woodstock* (Warner Brothers) and *Gimme Shelter,* by David Maysles, Albert Maysles, and Charlotte Zwerin (Maysles Films, Inc.) These include primary documentary footage of each event, but each film is also a highly crafted interpretation—a version perhaps more valuable as a primary source for tracing cultural imagery than as a secondary source version of the event as history.

For broader background on the history of popular culture and music in the 1960s, the following were especially helpful in developing the interpretation I offer in this chapter: Jim Curtis, *Rock Eras: Interpretations of Music and Society, 1954–1984* (Bowling Green, OH: Bowling Green State University Popular Press, 1987); Morris Dickstein, *The Gates of Eden: American Culture in the Sixties* (New York: Basic Books, 1977); Simon Frith, *Sound Effects: Youth, Leisure, and the Politics of Rock 'n Roll* (New York: Pantheon, 1981); David P. Szatmary, *Rockin' in Time: A Social History of Rock and Roll* (Englewood Cliffs, N.J.: Prentice Hall, 1987); and Hunter S. Thompson, *Hell's Angels: A Strange and Terrible Saga* (New York: Ballantine, 1967).

14

THE IRANIAN HOSTAGE CRISIS

WALTER LAFEBER

*During the 444 days in 1979 to 1981 that Americans waited for the return of 76
American hostages, held by Iranian militants, they were entertained by a song by
country artist Kenny Rogers. It was called "Coward of the County," and it told the
story of a young man named Tommy and his efforts to deal with a menacing trio of
local punks called the Gatlin boys. Raised by his father to believe that one could
achieve manhood without fighting, Tommy had always walked away from trouble—
and, in the process, had become known as the "coward of the county." But when the
Gatlin boys gang-rape Tommy's girlfriend, Becky, Tommy takes his father's picture
down from above the fireplace, finds the Gatlin boys in a bar, and avenges Becky's rape
with a fury born of righteous indignation and "twenty years of crawling." Of course,
from then on no one called Tommy the "coward of the county."*

*It was a good song, and no doubt would have been popular under any
circumstances. But it had special appeal in 1980 because its parable seemed so closely
to parallel the American experience with the Iranian hostage crisis. To many
Americans, the conduct of the Iranian militants seemed no less barbaric and no
more explicable than that of the Gatlin boys; indeed, the holding of American
hostages seemed a violation as complete and horrifying as that Becky had
experienced. According to Rogers's story, Tommy's problem—and the American
nation's—was fundamentally one of the spirit, something inside Tommy, rather
than a matter of some exterior condition that Tommy was helpless to deal with. In his
July 15, 1979, television address, President Jimmy Carter had interpreted the
American condition in much the same terms: as a "moral and spiritual crisis," a crisis
of the "national will." And like Tommy, Carter and his advisors attempted to resolve
this spiritual crisis through action—the rescue mission of April, 1980—only to
discover that the world no longer yielded to the brawling barroom tactics of the wild
west.*

*Walter LaFeber's narrative confirms this view of the Iranian hostage crisis as a
moment in which an ignorant American people acted badly. But it also tells another,
more encouraging story, a story of a nation's first, begrudging adjustment to the
changing distribution of economic, political, and military power in the world. The
Carter administration was, of course, in charge of this process of adjustment, and the*

240

conflicts and disagreements over foreign policy that are apparent in LaFeber's account are indicative of the nation's divided sensibilities at a difficult moment in its history. To open a dialogue with the Ayatollah Khomeini or prop up the Iranian shah; to allow or refuse the shah access to the United States; to let the hostage crisis take its course or intervene militarily—at every turn, policy makers disagreed over what ought to be done. Carter, too—Carter, especially—appeared unsure and even confused, a champion of human rights toasting the leadership of one of the world's great tyrants.

Hoping to find a way out of its confusion, the nation turned in 1980 to Ronald Reagan. His foreign policy—a reinvigorated Cold War—seemed to give Americans a welcome sense of direction. But many of Reagan's initiatives, including the invasion of the tiny Marxist country of Grenada in 1983, failed to measure up to the Berlin airlift, the naval blockade of offensive weapons into Cuba, or other compelling moments in the epic of the Cold War. As Carter and then Reagan would discover, the post-Vietnam era of the 1970s and 1980s was no longer what Time magazine publisher Henry Luce had described in 1941 as "The American Century."

On November 4, 1979, 400 screaming Iranian youths stormed the stone walls surrounding the United States Embassy in Iran's capital city of Tehran. They then invaded the embassy itself, captured 100 people, including 66 Americans, and declared that the Americans would be held hostage for the crimes of "The Great Satan"—the United States—against the Iranian people. Elizabeth Montagne, an American working as an embassy secretary, soon faced an Iranian holding a gun. He put a single bullet into the pistol's chamber, pointed it at Montagne's temple, and demanded the combination to an embassy safe. When she replied she did not know the combination, he began pulling the trigger on the empty chambers one-by-one. There was one more click to go. "Do you think I'll pull the trigger?" he asked her. "We stared at each other," Montagne recalled, and then he put the gun down. "He said: 'OK, so you don't know the combination.' I just kind of collapsed."

Montagne's horror was relived in other ways by the American hostages during the 444 days they endured captivity. The world, especially tens-of-millions of Americans who followed the hostages' fortunes almost hourly on television, watched the ordeal with wonder and fear. Americans soon learned, however, that the story did not actually begin that rainy November afternoon in Tehran. Like all historic turns, it had deep, tangled roots. In this case the story went back to 1941 at least, when a thin 22-year-old, Muhammad Reza Pahlavi, became shah, or king, of Iran. He was made shah by the United States, Great Britain, and the Soviet Union, which removed his father from power because the old dictator had moved his strategically located, rich oil-producing nation too close to the Nazis. From the beginning, therefore, the young shah owed his kingdom to foreign powers. By 1946 he especially owed his throne to the United States, which that year forced the Soviets to leave Iran. The Americans then replaced the British as the dominant foreign power. When the shah's rule was threatened by a nationalist, antiforeign movement in 1953, the U.S. Central Intelligence Agency (CIA) played a key role in overthrowing the threatening movement. In partial thanks, the next year the shah allowed American oil companies to begin extracting the black gold for the first time.

By the mid-1950s the world and especially the Iranians, who had the best view, saw the young shah and the powerful Americans as political bedfellows. In 1964, the relationship was almost stretched too far. The shah agreed to a Washington request that U.S. troops stationed in Iran be liable only to U.S. law, not Iranian law—even if they committed a crime against an Iranian. The 62-year-old, bearded Ayatollah (or Islamic religious leader) Ruhollah Khomeini bitterly attacked the deal. The shah and the Americans, Khomeini declared, "have reduced the Iranian people to a level lower than that of an American dog." "The dignity of Iran," he concluded, "has been destroyed." Khomeini's influence, already immense in this nation that had followed the Shi'ite Muslims since the sixteenth-century, became even greater—so great that the shah's police threw the Ayatollah out of the country. Khomeini spent 15 years exile in Turkey, Iraq, and finally France. But whatever the distance, his influence continued to grow in Iran.

That was proven in 1970 when the shah announced that a group of visiting American investors, led by David Rockefeller of Chase Manhattan Bank,

The beginning of an ordeal. Within hours after Iranian militants stormed and occupied the U.S. Embassy in Tehran on November 4, 1979, American hostages are blindfolded and paraded by the mob outside the embassy. (UPI/Bettman Newsphotos)

would receive large investment opportunities. Anti-American riots erupted as Khomeini condemned the deal from exile in Iraq. One of his students, Muhammad Reza Sa'idi, publicly condemned the American group. Shortly after, the shah's dreaded secret police, SAVAK, tortured the young student to death. When other Islamic leaders mounted protests, the shah cracked down with arrests, more torture, and imprisonment of the protesters and their religious leaders. In 1974 the head of Amnesty International (a London-based organization that later won the Nobel Prize for Peace for its work on behalf of human rights around the world), announced that Iran had the globe's worst human rights record.

This announcement did not cool the United States relationship with the shah. By 1974 it grew even warmer because President Richard Nixon concluded he desperately needed Iran. Because of overspending (especially in Vietnam) and too many overseas commitments, the United States no longer had the resources to defend its allies everywhere. Nixon begged the shah to help protect vital U.S. interests in the Middle East. Americans' need for Iran, moreover, grew dramatically in 1973 and 1974, when Arab oil producers protested Israel's invasion of their ally, Egypt, by cutting off petroleum shipments to Israel's closest ally, the United States. The shah was willing to help Nixon, but for a price: almost unlimited access to the non-nuclear U.S. military arsenal. Nixon happily obliged.

With his immense oil wealth generating revenues that jumped five times to $20 billion in only a matter of months, the shah increased his defense spending seven times to nearly $10 billion between 1973 and 1977. He bought military goods, as one historian phrased it, "with the abandon of an alcoholic using a credit card in a liquor store." Thus at the very moment the shah used force against his country's powerful religious leaders, the United States was publicly sending him all the weapons he could buy. Then, in 1975 and 1976, Iran's oil revenues flattened out. The economy began to decline. The already wide gap between poor rural and well-off urban incomes greatly widened. As many resorted to criminal activities to make a living, corruption became so rampant that the shah was advised not to begin an anticorruption campaign because, as one adviser suggested, "people will laugh."

Conditions were ripening for revolution. The first small revolutionary bands had actually appeared in 1971. Between 1972 and 1975 the country endured more than 400 bombing acts of terrorism. Americans soon became targets. Three U.S. military officers and three American civilians had been murdered by late 1976. Even the U.S. Peace Corps office, as well as the U.S. Embassy, had been blasted by bombs.

When President Carter assumed power in January of 1977, he was determined to restore American moral authority at home and abroad by emphasizing human rights—supporting, in his words, "the idealism of Jefferson" instead of the right-wing monarchs and military dictators the United States had too long supported just as long as they were anti-communist. In Iran's case, however, Carter was trapped. If he demanded that the shah stop the arrests and torture, the Iranian ruler might be overthrown and the cornerstone of U.S. military policy in the Persian Gulf region removed. The president tried to escape the trap by continuing to talk publicly about human rights, but at the same time making over half of all American arms sales to the shah. The king was too important, revenue from the $5.7 billion in arms sales too vital for the U.S. economy, to anger the occupant of Iran's "Peacock Throne."

When the shah again cracked down brutally on protesters in 1977 and 1978, Iranians believed (wrongly) that it happened with Carter's consent, if not on United States orders. Their belief seemed confirmed when President Carter visited Iran on New Year's Eve of 1977, and delivered one of the most stunning, and unfortunate, banquet toasts in recorded history. "Iran, because of the great leadership of the shah," Carter began, "is an island of stability in one of the more troubled areas of the world. This is a great tribute to you, Your Majesty, and to your leadership and to the respect and the admiration and love which your people give to you. . . . We have no other nation with whom we have closer consultations on regional problems that concern us both. And there is no leader with whom I have a deeper sense of personal gratitude and personal friendship."

Within 10 days after Carter spoke those words, massive anti-shah riots, led by Islamic clergy and religious students, erupted in the holy city of Qum. The police killed at least 24 people, including religious leaders. The shootings ignited a chain-reaction of protests. By November and December, 1978, literally thousands of demonstrations were erupting. The death toll reached 10,000. Nearly all the dead were unarmed protesters whose only strengths were in numbers and the hot conviction that the shah had to be overthrown. "For more than a year," two close observers wrote, "literally millions of Iranians faced [the shah's] tanks and machine guns with little more than moral outrage."

Islamic religious leaders guided the demonstrators, but those leaders were divided. On one side was a small fundamentalist group that hated the shah's western friends. This group wanted to turn Iran into a fully religious state shorn of all possible western influence. A much larger and more powerful group of clergy wished to modernize Iran and bring it fully into the late twentieth-century, but under religious direction. These moderates were less opposed to the shah's vast plans to modernize (the "White Revolution" as it became known), than they were to driving peasants off their land and destroying communities; the changes that only made the rich much richer and the poor desperate; and the shah's ideas that seemed to be turning the country over to nonreligious, non-Iranian developers from the West, especially from the United States. These critics pointed out that even when the shah tried to meet some of their demands by reorganizing his government in 1977, his new advisers were Iranians who suspiciously held degrees from universities in California, Colorado, Nebraska, Kentucky, Utah, and New York.

This growing fear of western control even brought many educated Iranian women over to the anti-shah side. Their decision seemed especially remarkable because Islam required that they wear veils (*chadurs*) in public, and have a traditional, and inferior, role in society. But these women were first of all Iranian and aware of the shah's devastating policies. They were also young: Half the country's population was under 16 years of age, and two-thirds was under 30 years of age. As unemployment and educational problems increased, the young, both men and women, became more radical. As the protests grew, however, they cut across age, geographical area, and class. The Islamic clergy became the steering wheel but not the engine of the revolution. As one Western expert on Iran explained: "The causes of the revolution, and its timing, were economic and political; the form of the revolution, and its pacing, owed much to the tradition of religious protest."

Americans understood none of this. Most read little or nothing about Iran or other foreign policy problems. They received their view of world events from easily digested television programs. But in the 6 years of growing revolution between 1971 and 1977, the three United States television networks spent an average of only 5 minutes per year on events in Iran. The most respected national newspaper, the *New York Times,* closed its Tehran office in 1977. Not one regular U.S. reporter remained in Iran. American experts on Iran were few, and those few were either overlooked or ignored when they tried to explain the deep economic, religious, and anti-U.S. roots of the revolution.

The upheaval confused even some observant Americans. Throughout much of the twentieth-century, they had judged the anti-American sentiment of most revolutionaries by their communist ties. But Islamic fundamentalists hated atheistic communism. The revolutionaries' rallying cry was "Neither East Nor West!" Soviet leaders, sharing a 1600-mile border with Iran, and nervously watching millions of Muslims inside their own country, were nearly as fearful of the revolution as were Americans. The U.S. media, however, had long viewed the shah as a close anti-communist ally, so it began to characterize his opponents with other stereotypes—"religious fanatics," "Muslim fundamentalists," even "Islamic Marxists"—in order to discredit the revolutionaries. Columnist Meg Greenfield of *Newsweek* was one of the few exceptions. "No part of the world is more important to our well-being at the moment," she wrote in early 1979, "and no part of the world is more hopelessly and systematically and stubbornly misunderstood by us." She compared American ignorance of the Islamic Middle East with Columbus's ignorance when he landed in the New World and thought he was in India.

Greenfield and other close observers of President Carter also realized that confusion and ignorance paralyzed United States official policy. Carter's administration divided sharply between his secretary of state, Cyrus Vance, and the national security adviser in the White House, Zbigniew Brzezinski. Vance believed the problem was wholly Iranian and that the shah had to come to terms with the revolutionaries. His position would lead him to favor contact with Ayatollah Khomeini, who was now orchestrating the revolution from exile in Paris where he put his instructions on audio tapes that secretly circulated throughout Iran. Brzezinski, on the other hand, feared the shah's fall would have ramifications far beyond Iran: It could lead to a pro-Soviet Iran and a major U.S. defeat in the Cold War. Brzezinski urged that the shah establish a military regime that would ruthlessly crush the uprising. Carter could not make up his mind whether to follow Vance or Brzezinski.

By January of 1979, the shah himself could not make up his mind. Increasingly weakened by cancer of the lymph glands, which had been discovered several years earlier, and unable to destroy the revolution through either mass killings or political reforms, the king waited for advice and help from his long-time friends in Washington. But little of either advice or help appeared. Brzezinski continued to push a military solution. He even wanted to use force to prevent the plane carrying Khomeini back to Tehran from landing. But it was too late. The Iranian military, with its Muslim soldiers and its ranks infiltrated with Islamic leaders, simply disintegrated as a thousand and more troops defected each day.

On January 16, 1979, the shah and his family climbed aboard a blue-and-silver Boeing 707 and flew into exile in Egypt. Celebrations erupted on Iranian streets. On February 1, Khomeini landed in Tehran to be welcomed by two million followers. The United States, American Ambassador William Sullivan reported, was now linked in Iranian minds with "evaporating institutions." A new Iran was arising. On February 2, 45,000 U.S. citizens began to leave. Despite crowds that surrounded the U.S. Embassy shouting "Death to the Great Satan," Carter ordered 75 American diplomats to remain at their posts. Rumors spread through Tehran that the Americans were harboring hated agents of SAVAK. On February 14, Iranians, some armed, broke into the Embassy, seized 70 Americans, and demanded that Carter return the shah for punishment. The Americans, however, were quickly released.

Khomeini's role in all this was not clear. He seemed to hold ultimate power, although he did not occupy a government post. Khomeini despised the United States for its long friendship with the shah, but he did not want an immediate, possibly armed, confrontation with the world's most powerful nation. It was not clear whether Khomeini controlled the mob, many of whom were political leftists and not devout followers of the Islamic clergy. He also worked with a badly divided government. Several top officials, including the new Iranian president and prime minister, were moderates. They hoped to restore some relations with Washington because they believed Iran especially needed American spare parts and other help for the nation's wrecked economy. Other Iranian leaders, however, notably those among the clergy and in the streets, hated the United States. They hoped to use the Iranian fear of "The Great Satan" to gain control over the revolution and the country. In May of 1979, 50,000 marched to the U.S. Embassy shouting "Death to Carter!"

The United States had no contact with either the radical left or the religious right-wing in Iran. Americans talked only with the relative moderates at the top of the government, but these officials obviously did not control the street mobs. Washington knew too little about what was occurring. "We simply do not have the bios [biographies], inventory of political groups, or current levels of daily life as it evolves at various levels in Iran," the top State Department expert on the country, Henry Precht, wrote in July 1979. "Ignorance here of Iran's events is massive. The U.S. press does not do a good job but in the absence of [U.S.] Embassy reporting, we have to rely on inexperienced newsmen" for information.

Amid this "ignorance," Carter was touching a low point in his presidency during the autumn of 1979. The American economy was slipping badly, the victim of inflation and the loss of six million barrels of Iranian oil that were no longer available each day on the international market. Americans suddenly paid nearly twice the regular price for gasoline—or they did after sitting for hours in lines at the pumps. Carter's relations with both the Soviet Union and his own allies, as well as with Iran, steadily worsened. As prices jumped and gasoline supplies slumped, and both angry Democrats and Republicans circled Carter to wait for a political kill in the 1980 elections, the president escaped to his Camp David mountaintop retreat to ponder the American, and his own, decline.

He emerged to give a nationally televised address on July 15, 1979, that is unsurpassed in presidential messages for its pleading and pessimism. "It's clear that the true problems of our nation are much deeper—deeper than gasoline lines or energy shortages, deeper even than inflation or recession," he declared. "And I realize more than ever that as President I need your help." He spoke of "a moral and a spiritual crisis," a "fundamental threat to American democracy" that "strikes at the very heart and soul and spirit of our national will." The president became specific: "There is a growing disrespect for government and for churches and for schools, the news media, and other institutions." He noted the murders of John F. Kennedy, Robert Kennedy, and Martin Luther King, Jr., and how peoples' confidence in their economy had been shattered by "10 years of inflation" and the post-1973 years "when we had to face a growing dependence on foreign oil." Americans, Carter lamented, looked to the Federal Government for help but "found it isolated. . . . Washington, D. C. has become an island." After this litany of sadness, the president had few solutions to offer except a vague national energy plan and the hope that Americans would overcome their "crisis of confidence." Critics quickly responded that the problem was less in the American people than in their leader's confusion.

Amid this bleakest time of Carter's presidency, the shah urgently asked that he be allowed to enter the United States for treatment of his cancer. Brzezinski, supported by two close friends of the shah—former Secretary of State Henry Kissinger and Chase Manhattan Bank President David Rockefeller—pressured Carter to grant the request. At first the president refused and, as Brzezinski recalled, "made the prophetic comment that he did not wish the shah to be here playing tennis while Americans in Tehran were being kidnapped or even killed" by mobs tearing down the U.S. Embassy. Brzezinski noted that when he objected that "we should not be influenced by threats from a third-rate regime [like Iran], and that at stake were our traditions and national honor, both Vance and Carter . . . became quite angry" with him. Three months later Vance and Carter changed their minds.

The Brzezinski–Kissinger–Rockefeller pressure, and the realization that the shah's life depended on quick medical help, led the president to reverse himself. On October 22, 1979, the shah's Gulfstream aircraft roared to a stop in the darkness of New York's LaGuardia Airport. Carter had given in, however, only after high Iranian officials had guaranteed the safety of the U.S. Embassy in Tehran during the shah's temporary stay in New York. Brzezinski then went much further. He tried to open talks with the Iranian moderates. Flying to North Africa, he met secretly with top officials, including Prime Minister Mehdi Bazargan. The secret quickly leaked. Iranian mobs (and perhaps Khomeini), concluded that Bazargan was trying to make deals with "The Great Satan." On November 1, 1979, Khomeini issued a statement: "It is therefore up to the dear pupils, students and theological students to expand their attacks against the United States and Israel, so that they may force the U.S. to return the deposed and criminal shah."

At 3:00 A.M. Washington time (10:30 A.M. Tehran time) on Sunday, November 4, 1979, the Department of State's Operations Center's telephone rang. Voices in the U.S. Embassy in Tehran reported that a large mob of youths was storming the building. The mob was later estimated at about 400. The embassy was unprotected. The Iranian government had pulled its guard from around the building, but Carter was not concerned because he had been assured by Bazargan's government that the building would be safe during the shah's stay in the United States. Seventy-six Americans found themselves held hostage. Six others managed to escape and secretly lived in the Canadian Embassy until courageous Canadian officials helped sneak them out of Iran in January 1980. The mobs fell upon top-secret documents that the embassy staff had not had time to destroy. Other documents were found in small pieces in shredding machines. The Iranians painstakingly began to fit these together. Ultimately they had enough formerly secret U.S. documents to fill 60 published volumes.

More immediately, the documents revealed that since the shah had fled, the CIA had developed two operations in which it planned to work closely with the moderates. Within 48 hours after the storming of the embassy, Bazargan and other moderate leaders were driven from power. The new Iranian regime was more militant and anti-American, but neither it nor its spiritual leader, Khomeini, could fully control the youths who now occupied the embassy. Khomeini did convince them to release eight black Americans and five women (including Elizabeth Montagne) because of Iran's professed respect for "oppressed" blacks and women. Otherwise, Khomeini—who apparently had at first quietly disapproved of the occupation and then changed his mind when he discovered the widespread support for it—found that the occupiers included different leaders of competing political factions. They had few common goals except to humiliate both the United States and the Iranian moderates.

The militants succeeded far more than they had hoped. Television cameras quickly showed the world graphic pictures of triumphant Iranians leading blind-folded, apparently confused Americans through the streets as crowds shouted insults. As the militants discovered that a global audience, and especially the United States, seemed to be hanging on their every word, their every burning of a U.S. flag, and their every success at putting thousands into the streets shouting anti-shah and anti-American slogans, they also discovered how valuable the hostages had become for their cause. Americans who could not have located Iran on a map before November 4 now became addicted to watching such daily programs as ABC-TV's "Nightline," with Ted Koppel, a popular and influential late-night news show that was initially created to follow the crisis in the embassy.

Carter at first profited politically. As is usual during foreign policy crises, Americans rallied around their leader as they expressed fury and frustration. In

Denver three teenagers hurled a rock at a window of an Iranian; he fired a shot in return and killed one of them. The International Longshoremen's union ordered all members not to load vessels bound for Iran. A Kansas wheat farmer declared, "I'm beginning to think we should either seize [Iranian] oilfields or destroy them if we can." A New York truck driver concluded, "We might as well write off the hostages; they're going to be killed no matter what we do. We should bomb the hell out of the country so it will be a long time before anyone else does the same thing." Even the president's mother, Lillian Carter, was quoted as telling a New Hampshire men's club: "If I had a million dollars to spare, I'd look for someone to kill [Khomeini]." The men cheered. Carter's approval rating shot up from a lowly 32 percent just before the hostage seizure to 61 percent in December.

The president understood, however, that both his nation's honor and his own political future depended on freeing the hostages quickly, and certainly before the presidential elections only 11 months away. A Palo Alto, California, resident expressed the views of many Americans: "The political booby prize of

An American perspective on Ayatollah Khomeini. This poster, with the Iranian leader serving as a bull's-eye, became a best-seller in the United States as frustration grew after the Iranian seizure of the U.S. Embassy and hostages in November, 1979. (UPI/Bettman Newsphotos)

1979 should be shared by President Carter and Secretary Vance for giving a visa to the shah of Iran. . . . The United States cannot afford to have a president with such poor judgment." As one of his top aides later told the Phil Donahue television show, Carter developed an "emotional obsession" about the hostages, especially as he feared the Iranians might begin to execute one hostage each day until Carter met their demands. Those demands included the shah's return to stand trial, and the return of the shah's fortune that was variously estimated at $50 million to $250 million. The president had no intention of meeting either demand. He instead retaliated by cutting off imports of Iranian oil, froze Iran's assets (estimated at $18 billion) in U.S. banks, and ordered the aircraft carrier *Kitty Hawk* and five other warships to steam from their station in the Philippines to the Arabian Sea close by Iran.

As it became clear that the militants did not intend to surrender the hostages, American anger grew even more passionate. The *Wall Street Journal* urged a military solution that would use paratroopers and a helicopter attack to rescue the captives. Inside the privacy of the White House, Brzezinski also pushed again for military action. On December 27, 1979, however, he changed his mind when the Soviets suddenly invaded their neighbor, Afghanistan, to prop up a wobbly Communist regime. Carter was astounded and deeply angered by the invasion. He and many Americans believed it meant the Soviets were willing to use force to establish their dominance over Afghanistan and perhaps neighboring Iran. Brzezinski understood that using U.S. troops in Iran could possibly lead to a confrontation with the Soviet Union, so he reconsidered. But he and Carter, and to a lesser extent Secretary of State Vance, were now prepared to warn Moscow leaders that if the Red Army moved towards Iran and the oil-rich Persian Gulf, the United States was ready to respond with force. The president announced this "Carter Doctrine" in a nationally televised speech before Congress. Critics quickly claimed correctly that the United States did not have enough conventional power to stop any Soviet drive toward Iran. That realization led many to fear that the turmoil in Iran and the invasion of Afghanistan were setting the two superpowers on a dead-end course to nuclear war.

As tension grew, Iranian moderates recaptured some of their lost power when Abolhassan Bani Sadr was elected president. Determined to end the hostage crisis, on February 11, 1980, Bani Sadr set conditions for the captives' release: The United States must admit its "past crimes" against Iran and promise never to "interfere" again, while also recognizing Iran's right to seize the shah and recover his fortune. Carter continued to refuse to negotiate the fate of the shah, who by now had flown off to refuge in Panama. In any case, the militants were refusing to surrender the hostages to the moderate government. The Tehran power struggle became more heated. A United Nations Commission arrived in January of 1980 with the hope of negotiating the hostages' release. It was forced instead to view crippled and maimed Iranians tortured by SAVAK, was finally told by Bani Sadr that he sided with the militants, was threatened by street mobs, and finally decided to give up the mission.

Carter continued to seek a peaceful solution. His frustration, however, was becoming a torment. "What choices do we have," he blurted out to his close advisers in late January. "Those bastards have held our people for two months now. Nothing we have tried diplomatically has worked. The UN can't do anything, our allies have tried and struck out, everything imaginable has been attempted. We've got to take some risks." His popularity began to sink as the presidential primaries opened for the 1980 elections. "I say one thing," Carter bitterly remarked privately in March, 1980, "Khomeini says another—and who does the American press believe? Khomeini!" But by trying to use the crisis for his own political gain, he gravely wounded his own credibility. On April Fool's Day, 1980, the day of a key primary in Wisconsin, Carter faced powerful opposition for the Democratic Party nomination from Senator Edward Kennedy of Massachusetts. Early that morning, Carter called an unusual early morning press conference to announce that the hostages were about to be transferred from the militants to the more moderate Bani Sadr government. He implied this could lead to their release. Actually the prisoners' situation did not change, and Carter knew nothing about any possible release, but he scored a victory over Kennedy in Wisconsin. The president soon learned that the transfer of the captives to Bani Sadr's care had been vetoed by Khomeini. As one White House insider observed, now "there was a sense that the diplomatic route was closed." Carter angrily broke diplomatic relations with Iran. He vowed not to leave the White House to campaign until the hostages were released.

On April 11, the beleaguered president summoned his National Security Council to discuss a rescue plan. It had begun to be developed by Brzezinski and U.S. military leaders just 48 hours after the hostages had been seized. Vance condemned the plan. He believed that Khomeini, for his own interests, would not allow the hostages to be killed, but that they could be shot during a rescue attempt. Vance also feared that the use of U.S. military power would not only endanger American interests throughout the Islamic world, but anger close allies in Western Europe and Japan who were now willing to squeeze Iran economically, but wanted no use of military force.

At the decisive April 11 meeting, Vance was absent. He had flown off for several days of rest in Florida. His top aide, Deputy Secretary of State Warren Christopher, did attend. As Brzezinski viewed it, only three options existed: Continuing "negotiating ad infinitum, even if the Iranians gave no indication of a willingness or ability to accommodate;" undertake a major military operation to punish Iran severely—a strike that could, however, lead the Iranians to kill the hostages or perhaps even ask the Soviets for help; or, finally, try a quick but highly risky rescue mission. Christopher outlined possible nonmilitary options. He was quickly overruled by Defense Secretary Harold Brown and Vice President Walter Mondale. Both of them favored the rescue mission. Brzezinski himself argued that it was time "to lance the boil." After a discussion lasting 1 hour and 50 minutes, the president announced, "We ought to go ahead without delay." Convinced the plan would not work, and that the attempted use of force could deeply injure relations with allies, Vance believed he had to resign. He became the first secretary of state to resign on an issue of principle in 65 years. Brzezinski, however, privately concluded simply that Vance "is the ultimate example of a good man who has been traumatized by his Vietnam experience."

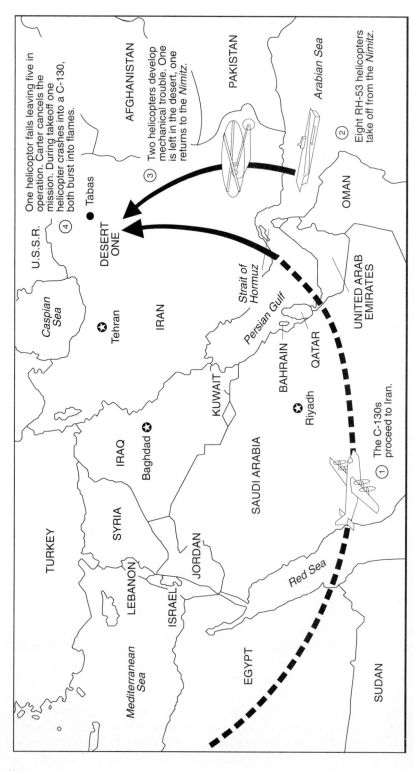

This map of the Middle East shows Iran and the routes of the attempted U.S. rescue mission in April 1980. Note the proximity of the Soviet Union and also of Afghanistan, which Soviet troops had invaded four months earlier.

At a press conference a week later, Carter indirectly revealed one reason for his secret decision. He announced that reports had been received that Khomeini would not release the hostages until after the U.S. presidential election. Carter would not elaborate on the reports, but he reemphasized his determination not to apologize to Iran for U.S. relations with the shah.

The president had triggered a rescue plan that was as dramatic as it was dangerous. Six giant C-130 transport planes were to carry 130 army Green Berets, Rangers, drivers, and Iranian translators, along with 50 air crewmen, from an Egyptian air base to a secret landing strip in Iran—"Desert One"—260 miles from Tehran. At Desert One this force would be joined by eight Sea Stallion helicopters that had left 3 hours earlier from the U.S. aircraft carrier *Nimitz* sailing in the Arabian Sea. The troops were to transfer to the helicopters, fly to "Desert Two," a secluded mountain 50 miles from Tehran, then board trucks for a ride into the capital. Just before midnight, some would storm the compound where the hostages were held, while others would break into the Iranian Foreign Ministry where three other Americans were hostages. Forty minutes later they were all to board helicopters flown into the embassy compound or, if the compound was insecure, into a nearby soccer stadium. If mobs threatened the operation, two C-130H Spectre gunships, circling overhead, were to use any necessary force. The helicopters would then rendezvous with transport planes south of Tehran, the helicopters were to be destroyed, and everyone would fly off to safety in Egypt.

The Delta Force, as the special troops were called, had undergone special training since 1977 to combat terrorists. Colonel Charles A. Beckwith, better known to his military colleagues as "Chargin' Charlie," would lead Delta Force. Fifty-one years old, former University of Georgia football player, a veteran of the wars in Korea and Vietnam, Beckwith had become a legend among his fellow soldiers. In Vietnam he had survived a supposedly fatal chest wound. On his desk was a sign: "Kill 'em all. Let God sort 'em out."

Carter had emphasized that he wanted to "avoid wanton killings" in the rescue. The president lost sleep over the possibility of hostages dying. Beckwith held a different view: "When we went into that embassy, it was our aim to kill all Iranian guards . . . and we weren't going in there to arrest them; we were going in there to shoot them right between the eyes, and to do it with vigor!" As a military expert later observed, Beckwith's men were trained to kill anyone with a weapon, and "there would be no time for recognition of any hapless American holding a gun in the shadows." Carter wanted the hostages' lives saved, this expert continued, but "he had authorized a raid in which there was a good possibility that some of them might die."

The president's caution vividly appeared 24 hours before the attack was to begin on April 24, 1980. Brzezinski had urged that the rescue be accompanied by an air force strike against Tehran. The strike would either help the mission or, if the rescue failed, the United States would at least have punished the Iranians. Carter, however, pulled back the air attack because he wanted no needless killings and feared it would severely hurt U.S. relations with other Middle East states. Brzezinski nevertheless wrote in his journal at the last minute: "I feel good about [the mission]. I realize that if it fails I will probably be blamed more than anybody else, but I am quite prepared to accept that. If it is a success, it will give the United States a shot in the arm, which it has badly needed for twenty years."

During early dawn of April 24, Delta Force reached Desert One. But two of the eight helicopters from the *Nimitz* never made it. One suffered mechanical problems. The others ran into a dust storm that one pilot likened to "flying into a bowl of milk." A helicopter used too much gas avoiding the dust, had mechanical difficulties, and returned to the *Nimitz*. Only six helicopters remained, the minimum number Beckwith demanded for the mission. Then, after they landed at Desert One, another helicopter was disabled by an hydraulic system failure. With only five choppers left, Beckwith radioed that the mission had to be aborted. His words were relayed to Carter, who was monitoring the operation minute-by-minute in the White House. He approved Beckwith's decision. Now, Beckwith recalled, "the only thing on my mind was, 'We've failed, and I've got to get my soldiers out of here.'"

As a helicopter pilot lifted away, his spinning rotor sliced through the fuselage of a C-130 loaded with troops. Beckwith "looked out to my left and a C-130 all of a sudden exploded. It was one hell of a fire. . . . The munitions went off. The heat from the [burning] aircraft forced the helicopter pilots out of their cockpits." Three Marines on the helicopter and five Air Force crewmen in the transport plane died instantly. Beckwith quickly decided that the intense

The end of a failed rescue mission. At "Desert One" charred remains of Americans lie among the wreckage of C-130 transports and the destroyed U.S. helicopters on April 27, 1980. (UPI/Bettman Newsphotos)

heat, along with the rising sun, that made it probable the Iranians would soon discover his force, made it impossible to stay until the eight bodies could be recovered. The survivors climbed into the remaining C-130s and flew off. Beckwith put his head in his hands and cried.

Carter went on television at 7:00 A.M. to reveal the disaster. Republican presidential candidates George Bush and Ronald Reagan, as well as Edward Kennedy, supported Carter and asked for national unity. By a margin of 4 to 1, Americans backed the president's decision to try the rescue. But the failure helped seal Carter's political fate. Detroit Mayor Coleman Young, who led the president's campaign in Michigan, declared flatly, "Unless the hostages are rescued, it's a no-win situation for Carter." Publicly, the closest U.S. allies in Western Europe and Japan sympathized with the president. Privately some were seething. They had reluctantly gone along with U.S. demands for squeezing Iran economically in the belief that Carter would not then resort to military action. Now they feared their Middle East oil supplies could be endangered by angry Arab producers. A top West German official declared privately (and was soon quoted in *Time* magazine): "The incompetence that permeates this Administration is incredible."

In Iran, Khomeini declared that the president had "lost his mind," and that the disaster proved whose side was favored by heaven. On April 26 the charred, unrecognizable bodies of the dead Americans were publicly displayed in Tehran. The government announced that the bodies would be returned to relatives, but through an organization such as the Red Cross, not through the U.S. government. The Iranians had also captured secret maps, photographs, and lists of radio frequencies that had been left behind in the abandoned helicopters. As for the hostages, the Iranians separated and moved some of them outside Tehran so another rescue mission would not be attempted.

Negotiations for their release went into a dead stall. The lack of movement was due partly to the rescue tragedy, but it was especially due to turmoil in Tehran. In what a French reporter called a "witch-hunt atmosphere," militants conducted a feverish search for moderates, "CIA agents," leftists, rightists, anyone suspected of having cooperated with the rescue plans. In early July, the hostage number dropped to 52 as Richard Queen was released because of illness; the Iranians had clearly decided they wanted no hostage to die in their hands. In late July, the shah passed away in Cairo. Tehran radio rejoiced that "the bloodsucker of the century has died," but quickly added that the hostages would nevertheless continue to be held until the United States delivered both apologies and as much as $24 billion.

Carter defeated Kennedy for the Democratic presidential nomination in August, but public opinion polls showed an astounding 77 percent of the voters giving Carter a negative rating. By 79 to 19 percent, they also condemned him for his handling of the Iranian crisis. There had been an incredible negative swing of 47 points in just 7 months over his handling of the hostages. The president, one congressman believed, "couldn't get the Pledge of Allegiance through Congress."

Republican presidential nominee Ronald Reagan declared that he would never "negotiate with terrorists," but otherwise he stressed Carter's economic failures and said little about the hostages. He did not have to say much; television kept the suffering of the hostages and their relatives in the United States before millions of viewers every night. The Republicans did worry about published reports that the Iranians and Carter were preparing an "October surprise:" The hostages would supposedly be released on the eve of the election to ensure the president's victory. Republicans were especially worried about this after Carter's attempt to spring his "April Fool's Day surprise" against Kennedy during the Wisconsin primary. Nine years later, British reporters found evidence that the Republicans had sent former President Richard Nixon on a secret mission to the Iranians to prevent such a "surprise."

In April 1991, Gary Sick, who had been Carter's White House expert on Iran, dropped a bombshell. Sick announced that his investigations had turned up evidence to suggest that Reagan's campaign chair, Willam J. Casey, had met secretly with Iranians in July and August, 1980. Casey, so witnesses told Sick, had sent $150 million of arms to Iran in return for the Iranians' assurance that the hostages would not be freed until Reagan was safely elected. Reagan and his advisers heatedly denied Sick's allegations. (Casey could not respond. He had died of a brain tumor just as the Iran-Contra scandal broke in 1986—a scandal in which he, as director of the CIA, had secretly sold arms to Iran in 1985 in return for the release of several other hostages. Throughout the 1980s, Reagan publicly denied that he would ever deal with terrorists who held hostages.) Evidence and public outcries nevertheless built up until, in 1991, Congress had to begin investigating the possibility that 11 years before, a small group of campaign officials had seized U.S. foreign policy and kept 52 men hostage for 5 extra months so Reagan could be elected president. Whatever Nixon's and Casey's activities, the hostages were not released. Reagan won a landslide victory, taking 44 states. "The voters," Carter recalled, "expressed their disgust with our nation's apparent impotence in the face of several disturbing problems— Iran foremost."

After early November, the defeated president no longer faced a political timetable for producing a settlement. It was becoming clear to the Iranians that a deal could be struck with Carter. As the hostages were losing their political value to Tehran officials, talks became serious in December, 1980. As one Iranian diplomat declared, "The hostages are like a fruit from which all the juice has been squeezed out." Another reason for the release, however, also now existed. In September, 1979, Iraq attacked Iran to begin a struggle to decide which nation would control the Persian Gulf area. The conflict turned into one of the longest and bloodiest in the post-1945 era. Iran needed at least relief from U.S. pressures and even, if possible, western help.

Tehran officials suggested, and Carter accepted, that Algeria become an intermediary to help in the talks. Deputy Secretary of State Warren Christopher flew to Algiers and on January 18, 1981, a settlement appeared. Iran had demanded $24 billion, but finally accepted Carter's offer of $5.5 billion, released out of frozen Iranian assets, in exchange for the hostages. The remaining frozen assets and the American counterclaims against Iran were to be decided through arbitration.

Throughout the night before he was to surrender the White House to Reagan, Carter remained awake in his office surrounded by his close advisers. He prayed that Iran would release the hostages during his presidency. Khomeini, however, squeezed out the last drop of "juice:" The hostages became free shortly after noon on January 20, 1981, just minutes after Reagan took the oath of office.

AN INTERPRETATION

The hostage crisis was not only one of the most frustrating and embarrassing chapters in American history. It encapsulated major themes of the 1970s that mark the decade as part of a turning point in the nation's experience as a great world power. Between 1945 and the 1970s the United States controlled world affairs in a manner unmatched by any nation in history. In the 1970s, however, Americans finally lost the war in Vietnam, realized that the Soviet Union had the capacity to destroy them in a nuclear exchange, and had to tolerate the rise of a radical Sandinista government in Nicaragua (a country long considered by the United States to be in its "backyard"), and, of course, lost the shah's cooperation, oil resources, and military intelligence listening posts in Iran. As Christopher declared in 1978, the "absolute power" of such great nations as the United States "is growing," but "the relative power of any single nation has been reduced."

Americans had to come to terms with that relative decline during the hostage crisis. In a real sense they had to understand that the 1945-to-1970 years were aberrations, an era never to be repeated because the unique conditions that made the United States so powerful after World War II would never—if human civilization is fortunate—be repeated with another such war. In the 1970s, history began to return to normal as a more multipolar world emerged, the kind of world that more closely resembled the pre-1939 or even pre-1914 years than 1945 to 1970.

Americans also discovered that although they had spent trillions of dollars developing weapons that could destroy all civilization, they could not negotiate a quick political settlement, or mount a successful rescue mission, to release Americans held in chains by a much weaker nation. Power other than simply military was working in the world. Indeed, the religious belief embodied in Ayatollah Khomeini's cause not only was organizing a new Iran, but neutralizing vast U.S. military and economic power. Vaunted American technology, which the nation had proudly paraded since the days of Samuel Colt's revolver and Henry Ford's Model-T, even came into question. The nation was suffering disastrous unfavorable trade balances with Japan and Western Europe because Americans were having difficulty competing in tough world markets.

The nation's most basic assumptions about how the world worked became so fundamentally questioned that its educational system, as well as its top decision-making apparatus, became suspect. Most Americans knew nothing about Iran or its neighbors, although these same Americans utterly depended on these distant nations for an energy supply. Those in the press and government who did think they knew Iran too easily assumed, as Frances FitzGerald pointed out, "that the shah was the only person who counted . . . ; that the country, being underdeveloped, had no politics in the sense that advanced countries do; and that Iranians, being apolitical, would simply accept a dictatorship as necessary and good for them. The [U.S.] foreign-policy establishment," FitzGerald emphasized, "has traditionally made similar assumptions about almost all Third World countries."

Americans' assumptions about how easily they could burn up energy were also undermined. Since 1945 they had burned or melted about 40 percent of the world's non-renewable materials. The world consumed 30,000 gallons of petroleum each second; with 6 percent of the world's population, the United States burned 10,000 of those gallons. In 1973 and 1974, and again in 1979 and 1980, severe energy shortages not only inconvenienced American motorists, but increasingly expensive petroleum made costs skyrocket until the United States found its goods less competitive on the world market and millions of its people newly out of work.

A psychological, as well as an economic, depression also set in. "For the first time in its history," influential *Business Week* magazine declared in late 1979, "the United States is no longer growing in power and influence among the nations of the world. In fact, the United States is now in steep decline." Ronald Reagan rode that pessimism into power. Three of four Americans polled in 1980 believed Reagan would ensure that the United States would be respected by other nations. The hostages were indeed released minutes into his presidency.

From 1990 to 1992 President George Bush led a U.S.-dominated coalition that waged war during another Middle East crisis. But this crisis, triggered by Iraqi dictator Saddam Hussein's invasion of oil-rich Kuwait, ended with a massive victory for Bush and the coalition's half-million troops and thousands of high-technology weapons. Republicans noted sarcastically that 11 years earlier Carter could not even get "eight helicopters across a desert." The victory of 1991, however, did not lessen the importance of learning from the events of 1978 to 1981. Saddam Hussein's threat was a more traditional military aggression that the United States and its allies could overwhelm with superior firepower. Americans did not need to understand his culture to repulse his aggression. But the Iranians had posed a more subtle threat that could not be dealt with by conventional forces and high-tech wonder weapons. The Ayatollah represented a cultural and religious force in a world increasingly shaped by cultural pluralism and non-military power. Neither the Ayatollah Khomeini's ideas nor the hostages' situation could have been dealt with successfully by military weapons, no matter how high-tech. What the United States needed was an understanding of the Iranians before 1979, the limits of U.S. military power, and the new international arena in which the United States had to act. Whether the basic conditions that led to the hostage crisis and its intense frustrations have fundamentally changed remains a central question of today's United States.

Sources: The best scholarly treatment of the background is Gaddis Smith, *Morality, Reason, and Power: American Diplomacy in the Carter Years* (New York, 1986). Especially useful for understanding the crisis and its backdrop are three revealing memoirs: Jimmy Carter, *Keeping Faith* (Toronto, New York, 1982); Cyrus R. Vance, *Hard Choices* (New York, 1983); and, most notably, Zbigniew K. Brzezinski, *Power and Principle* (New York, 1983). A number of fine studies on post-1973 U.S.–Iranian relations have appeared that focus on the hostage crisis: James A. Bill, *The Eagle and the Lion: The Tragedy of American-Iranian Relations* (New Haven, 1988); Gary Sick, *All Fall Down: America's Tragic Encounter With Iran* (New York, 1985); William H. Sullivan, *Mission to Iran* (New York, 1981), by the embattled U.S. Ambassador. Paul Ryan, *The Iranian Rescue Mission: Why It Failed* (Annapolis, 1985) is a good analysis of that tragedy. The Iranian background is in R. K. Ramazani, *The United States and Iran* (New York, 1982).

15

BERNHARD GOETZ: SUBWAY VIGILANTE

JAMES GILBERT

In 1984, on a New York City subway car, Bernhard Goetz shot four black teenagers who he believed were threatening him. For much of the rest of the decade—through a 1987 trial and subsequent appeals—the incident remained an important sounding board for American opinions on crime, race, the inner cities, and the value of the nation's liberal institutions and heritage.

In the days that followed the shooting, when little was known about Goetz, the "subway vigilante" was widely proclaimed a hero: It seemed to many Americans that someone, finally, had stood up for the defenseless victims of rampant urban crime. Later, as it became increasingly apparent that Goetz had overreacted, only a small minority of Americans continued to believe that Bernhard Goetz was a figure of heroic proportions.

Although this reevaluation of Goetz's act was certainly sensible, the original judgment—of heroism—was probably of greater significance as a marker of the nation's attitudes and values. As James Gilbert explains in this story, the legal proceedings against Goetz necessarily reduced and confined the issues involved in the case to the relatively narrow ones of fact and interpretation of statute. Meanwhile, the American public indulged an insatiable hunger for fictional, screen heroes that resembled Goetz in certain fundamental respects. Dozens of 1980s films—among them Bladerunner, *the* Rambo *series,* Batman, The Running Man, Total Recall, *and two versions each of the* Robocop *and* Diehard *spectacles—featured isolated protagonists, often alienated and seeking revenge, in an unrelenting war against crime, social disorder, America's declining role in the world, and the uncaring and incompetent bureaucrats who are at best incapable of acting. Many of these films, including the critical success* Bladerunner, *were set in a chaotic, anarchic, threatening postcatastrophic environment of public space that resembles the New York subway system. For a while at least, before the facts intruded on the fantasy, Americans seemed to have found in Bernhard Goetz the vigilante hero they wanted.*

Gilbert's story also develops the other side of this vigilante dream: the perception that liberalism had failed. Republican presidential candidate George Bush had raised the issue in a televised 1988 debate with Democrat Michael Dukakis, accusing his opponent of being a "liberal." Dukakis hemmed and hawed, but ultimately failed to come to the defense of a label that had once stood for government's ability to contribute to an economically and socially just society. For many reasons, a majority of Americans no longer had much faith in liberalism. Some believed that liberals were too "soft" on crime. Others believed that liberal social programs had helped create a population of dependent, lazy, and threatening poor people, many of them black. From a very different perspective, another group of Americans were critical of liberalism for being too timid, for not having done enough to educate or house the poor or to maintain decaying systems of urban mass transportation.

Bernhard Goetz may have believed all these things, but he also, no doubt, lacked the conviction that there was any obvious political solution to the nation's problems. Anxious, confused, and cynical like many of his fellow citizens, he resolved to take personal control of a little bit of his world—not by voting, but by carrying a gun.

Bernhard Hugo Goetz walked quickly toward the entrance to the IRT subway at 14th Street in New York's Greenwich Village. A slight man 37 years of age with lank blond hair and wire rimmed glasses, he wore jeans, a green plaid shirt and a blue windbreaker. It was a Saturday afternoon (December 22, 1984)—not a busy time underground.

Picking a token out of his pocket, Goetz walked down the dingy steps of the entrance. Greeted by a warm bath of stale air, acrid with ozone, he scuffed rapidly along the gritty corridor, lined with gleaming, chipped tile, looking at, but hardly seeing advertisements for current Broadway hits. When he came to the turnstile, he shoved the brass-colored token into the slot and pushed his way through the clicking barrier. He thought about sitting down, but didn't: The seats were dirty and unpleasant and besides, there was something vulnerable about their position. A blurred beam of light in the distance, the squeal of metal wheels, and the rhythmic, crashing roar of the train, caused him to turn, to step back and pause. The weight of the .38 caliber revolver under his left arm, nestled in its quick-draw holster, which he always carried, reinforced his sense of danger and anticipation.

On the train, four teen-age boys were lounging in the portion of the car they had appropriated from other passengers. The men and women sharing the ride had retreated to the other end. The boys put their feet on the plastic seats or scraped them along the grainy tile floor. The floors were scuffed and dirty with use and poor maintenance. The walls of the car were afflicted with graffiti: swollen hearts with anonymous initials linked at the center, scrawled in black magic marker. Some markings announced or denounced racial and sexual tastes and preferences; others were just names—as on a memorial to obscurity. Spray paint, smeared over the greasy plastic map of the subway system, hid any clue to the destination. But the boys certainly knew where they were going: to Coney Island where they intended to force open video coin machines. The tools they planned to use were simple: screwdrivers, hidden in their pockets. Traveling down all the way from the Claremont Village housing project in the Bronx, the four boys—Barry Allen, James Ramseur, Darrell Cabey, and Troy Cantry—were bored and restless as the train plodded through dark tunnels and dim stations.

The coaches pulled heavily and noisily into the station and the doors sprang open. Goetz looked into the starkly lighted car as he entered. The situation was immediately apparent: For whatever reason most of the passengers were obviously shunning the four young black boys. Nonetheless, Goetz slid into a seat near the entrance opposite them. It was, perhaps, a dangerous thing to do and Goetz could feel the tension that his arrival created. Troy Canty, slumped on the seat, greeted him with a curt, "How are ya?"

The train shrugged to a start and plunged into the tunnel on its way to the next stop at Chambers Street. What happened in the next 30 seconds has been blurred by countless retelling and interpretations. Canty stood up and moved

Right before the IRT train entered Chambers Street Station, Bernhard Goetz fired on four youths who accosted him. This typical train, smeared with grafitti, was like the one on which the incident occurred. Dimly lighted, dirty, and fiercely utilitarian, this station, like most on the system, was constructed decades earlier. (Allan Tannenbaum/SYGMA)

toward Goetz and demanded: "Hey man, you got five dollars for me and my friends to play video games?" Goetz stood up awash in a wave of fear and anger. The "arrogant manner" of the four boys enraged him. "I have five dollars for each of you," he snapped, and yanked his nickel-plated, Smith and Wesson pistol out of its holster. Taking aim at one boy, then another, he fired, four shots in rapid succession—two of them dumdum bullets. Three of the boys were obviously hit and slumped to the floor, Canty with a shot to the center of his body; Ramseur hit in the arm, the chest and the spleen; Allen, who had turned to flee, wounded at the base of his neck. The fourth, Cabey, seemed unhurt. Goetz spoke excitedly to him: "You seem to be all right; here's another," and shot Cabey, the bullet piercing both lungs and his spinal cord.

The conductor on the train, hearing the shots, pulled the emergency cord and the train screeched to a stop in the middle of the tunnel. Goetz walked to the end of the car and tried to comfort two women who were cowering in fear. Were they hurt he wanted to know? Had the bullets strayed? Then the conductor asked him, "Are you a cop?" Goetz replied quickly. "No, I don't know why I did it. They tried to rip me off." With these words, Goetz moved swiftly through the connecting doors of the coach, into the next, and then out the doors, vanishing into the tunnel.

Moved quickly by ambulance to the hospital, the four boys told their story to police and witnesses recounted as best they could a drama that they had only watched distractedly. The story, however, became an instant sensation in a guise that took its few known facts and pumped them up into myths and stereotypes. Four black teenagers, threatening a white man, had been shot. Enraged by this assault, the man had taken the law into his own hands. He was a vigilante—an ambiguous stock character from American history. The word so quickly applied to Goetz could refer to the frontiersman who preceded the forces of law and order, who protected his family and community from outlaws. But vigilantes could also be lynchers who enforced the rigid separation of black and white in the South during the period of intense and violent racism that followed the Civil War. Which kind of vigilante Goetz represented depended on who described him and the opinion of those listening.

The dramas of retribution against criminals, pictured in endless television and film presentations, worried over by politicians, and recognized by most Americans to be fictionalized answers to frustration, seemed suddenly fulfilled in real life. The very anonymity of the perpetrator, the scarcity of facts, made the fictionalized version of a revenge shooting stronger and more apt. Not knowing anything about Goetz tempted—even forced—the press to speculate about an unknown character. Indeed, the true Goetz would only with difficulty emerge from the fictions surrounding the shootings. Not so the four boys, some of whose background became quickly known to the New York public.

The immediate reaction of the city was seasoned by sensationalism, misinformation, and myth. The tabloid presses blazed the story in gigantic headlines, immediately dubbing Goetz, because his identity was a mystery, the "Subway Vigilante." Along the heavily traveled East River Drive, some graffiti read: "Power to the Vigilante; N. Y. Loves Ya!" Motorists passing by honked or made a fist—from the insulation of their cars. The police department released information indicating that the screwdrivers found on the boys were sharpened and, therefore, dangerous weapons. Furthermore, reporters quickly discovered that all four of the boys had arrest records for offenses ranging from disorderly conduct and receiving stolen property to attempted assault and armed robbery. The case laid before the public seemed clear enough. An unknown white man was assaulted by four black criminals and he shot them in self-defense.

Other New Yorkers joined in to laud—or "understand"—the actions of the Subway Vigilante: Callers to radio talk shows praised him; the Guardian Angels (a group of predominately black and Hispanic young men organized to patrol the subways and suppress violence and crime) supported him; and Roy Innis of the Congress of Racial Equality praised him as an "avenger for all of us." Conservative newspaper columnist Patrick Buchanan wrote bluntly: "Far from being a manifestation of 'insanity' or 'madness,' the universal rejoicing in New York over the gun man's success is a sign of moral health."

A later song by Ronny and the Urban Watchdogs, "Subway Vigilante," had the following lyrics:

> He's the subway vigilante
> The brave subway vigilante
> Where law and order can't
> He showed us how to take a stand
> He had enough and came out fightin'
> Drove the rats back into hidin'
> Let's cheer the subway vigilante
> He's one special kind of man.

Certainly not all the leaders of public opinion jumped on this careening bandwagon. Jimmy Breslin, columnist for the *New York Daily News,* pressed a number of obvious points about the dangers of vigilantism and eventually forced the New York Police Department to acknowledge that the screwdrivers were not, in fact, sharpened. Governor Mario Cuomo of New York denounced the practice of vigilantism. Mayor Koch, never known to shy away from the opportunity to play the street-wise, law-and-order politician, termed the shooting "animal." "A vigilante," he said, "is not a hero."

While the press and the public debated the merits of his assumed actions and spun out tales about his possible identity, Goetz himself remained in hiding in New Hampshire. After he left the stalled subway train, he had walked to the Chambers Street station along the empty tunnel, where he emerged from the subway. By 3 o'clock that afternoon, he had rented a car and was speeding on his way out of the city. He headed toward New England—as he said later, "heading North is the way to go if there's a problem." This cryptic comment is not hard to understand. His family had settled in upstate New York, so this was friendly, or at least familiar, terrain.

During the next few days the search for the unknown subway shooter preoccupied New York police who set up a special "Vigilante Task Force" on December 23 and a telephone hot line. An informant tipped them to Goetz's identity and detectives visited his apartment and left him a note asking him to

"Please contact the police A.S.A.P. [as soon as possible]." They weren't sure he was their man, but they had strong suspicions.

Then, during the evening of December 28, Goetz decided to call a neighbor. Obviously distraught, lonely, unsure of himself, and burdened by the enormous public attention that only he knew was directed at himself, he needed to talk to a friendly voice. Myra Friedman was, in some respects, an odd choice for a contact. She was a friend, or better, an acquaintance who knew Goetz because they had nearby apartments in the same building. She had observed him in a hundred small ways—in the fashion that city dwellers get to know, by indirection, the habits and traits of people whose lives intersect with theirs. But she was not particularly close.

When Goetz called, he immediately asked her if she could get a car and a tape recorder and bring some of the Guardian Angels for a meeting off Interstate Route 95 in New England. He had decided to tell his story. Perhaps the request for a tape recorder set her suddenly thinking, for Friedman switched on a nearby recorder and then preserved most of the rest of the conversation when Goetz called back 5 minutes later. What she preserved was a remarkable few moments of self-revelation.

After telling Friedman about the shooting, Goetz began to talk on three points at once, jumbling his train of thought, but following several ideas. He had already developed a particular way of telling his story that would remain his explanation throughout the next several months. "I have a good possibility of perhaps being able to live a normal life," he proclaimed, defensively. He would repeat variations of the same notion throughout the conversation.

What he meant was his intention to explain to someone—the Guardian Angels, Friedman, even the police—what had happened in exchange for a promise of anonymity: a chance to be, by his own definition, normal. He also meant that the myths developed to describe him in the press and on the radio fit very badly onto the narrow shoulders of his self-image. "Now the city, they can drag me through the dirt," he exclaimed, "by showing how savage and vicious I was and by not releasing the whole truth, even on the technical things that happened. . . . I know the truth. Those guys know the truth. The people are looking for an easy answer. They're looking for a good guy defending himself or a Clint Eastwood. Or if they want to condemn it, they're looking for someone who was looking for trouble." What Goetz wanted most was to seize his self back from the public by explaining his motives, and then return to obscurity.

A second train of thought was his explanation of the shooting. "Myra, I responded viciously and savagely. It's a state of mind that you're not familiar with. If you corner a rat and you are about to butcher it, OK? The way I responded was viciously and savagely, just like that rat." This justification was a "technicality," by which he meant that he had acted in self-defense. Unaware precisely what self-defense meant in legal terms, Goetz had already, nonetheless, erected a story in which he was excused, because he had been compelled to act as he had. As he explained:

> Myra, in a situation like this, your mind, you're in a combat situation. Your mind is functioning. You're not thinking in a normal way. Your memory isn't even working normally. You are so hyped up. Your vision actually changes. Your field

of view changes. Your capabilities change. What you are capable of changes. You are under adrenaline, a drug called adrenaline.

Goetz also pursued a third line of thought, about coming home. He promised Friedman that he would return very soon. He had lots of things to do: checks to write, laundry to do, his apartment to clean, work to finish for his electronics repair company, the Electrical Calibration Laboratory—the million and one mundane details that in some respects he must have known he could not do, but that he needed very much, desperately, even, to accomplish. With this confused explanation, he hung up.

The next day Goetz returned—Myra Friedman saw him on the way to do his laundry. Then, a few hours later, he knocked gingerly at her door and pushed quickly inside when she answered it. He took the chance to explain himself again. He railed against the criminal justice system that let criminals out on bond or failed to convict them. Yet, he hesitated, the boys who harassed him were also victims—of poverty and bad schools. "I don't know, Myra," he said, "the whole thing's hopeless." Then suddenly he jumped up and left the apartment.

When he returned less than an hour later he was carrying a paper bag. "Would you keep this for me for a couple of days?" he asked and then, hardly waiting for an answer, he left. In fact, he left the city and returned to New England. In the paper bag were Goetz's other pistols.

The next day, he called again, from New Hampshire. Fearful that the police knew his identity and stung by continued media discussions of the character of a "subway vigilante," he told Friedman that he planned to turn himself in to the New Hampshire police, or possibly, the Guardian Angels. Once again he talked about a deal—the truth in exchange for anonymity. "I'll tell them *everything* that they want to know." But just as suddenly he contradicted himself, promising to fight yet hoping that the police would release him without bail. In parting, he promised to be in touch and to turn himself in to the police.

On December 31, 9 days after the subway shooting, Bernhard Goetz walked into the police headquarters of Concord, New Hampshire, at around 12 noon, and gave himself up to Watch Commander Lt. Robert Libbey. In the course of the next several hours, he recorded a long, fitful confession.

After contacting the New York police department, the New Hampshire police released Goetz to the New York authorities, who questioned him first and then transported him back to New York. At last the public would be able to judge the character of the man who had occupied their imaginations for almost 2 weeks. Charged by the City with several felonies, Goetz was then released on $50,000 bail, which he raised himself. He returned home to his apartment.

During the next few months, the public learned a good deal more about the five men whose fates were twisted together by the events on the subway that had made them unwilling comrades of fortune. Not all of the boys who accosted Goetz recovered quickly. The extent of their injuries was sobering. James Ramseur had to undergo two operations to remove obstructions created by his chest wound. And Darrell Cabey fell into a coma after several days in the hospital and remained dangerously ill. When he finally regained consciousness on

March 7, it became apparent that he had suffered serious brain damage. Had he died, Goetz could have been charged with murder. As it was, Cabey remained paralyzed from the waist down. While all of the assailants were known to have police records of one sort or another, their intentions toward Goetz became less clear when it was revealed that the screwdrivers were only ordinary tools, not sharpened and dangerous weapons. Furthermore, when Goetz's confession became known, the public realized that the boys had not even brandished the screwdrivers—he could not have known of their existence.

Yet the issue before the public was never really the motivations or the personalities of the four boys. They were taken as given: high school drop-outs, youngsters from the huge Claremont Village housing project in the Bronx, a poverty and crime infested part of the city. Their identity was only known because they had threatened a white man on the subway. They could never really emerge from these categories nor their implicit assumptions of guilt. Even those who might sympathize with them sometimes cast them in the role of victims of society—of poverty, of discrimination, of broken families. The press of the city by and large ignored them. During all of 1985 there were, for example, only about 10 stories about Cabey in the *New York Times* but over 75 devoted to Goetz. In this respect the boys remained invisible; they were only important as

Shown here on January 3, 1985, Goetz has just returned from New Hampshire under arrest by the New York City Police. (AP/Wide World Photos)

catalysts for the story of Bernhard Goetz and foils for the agonizing scrutiny of his motivations.

When the *New York Daily News* printed a poll on January 6, it revealed a curious and divided set of attitudes:

Asked about Goetz's reactions:

49% "tended to approve"
58% disapproved of his being charged with attempted murder
78% said he was not a hero.

Shortly after this, *New York Times* columnist Sydney Schanberg printed excerpts from the mail he had received about Goetz. Obviously, he intended the sample to shock—and it did. One writer noted: "People have been running scared. Here's someone who struck back." Another loudly proclaimed: "Bernhard Hugo Goetz makes me proud, P–R–O–U–D, to be a white, male American! At long last we can hold our heads up again." But perhaps the most poignant reaction came somewhat earlier from Mrs. Cabey, whose child lay in a coma: "I'm not angry," she said, even after receiving a stack of anonymous hate mail. "A lot of people have been victims and are boiled up to the boiling point. I am hurt, though, that people would take this time to be so mean. Time is so precious these days."

In this context of intense public fascination with the case, with obviously conflicting signals about public opinion, and yet tremendous pressure either to convict Goetz of attempted murder or to exonerate him as a hero, entirely justified in his actions, the decision of how to proceed fell into the hands of the city district attorney, Robert Morgenthau. At 65 years of age, he had been New York DA for 10 years, yet this was perhaps his hottest case. If he asked a grand jury for an indictment for minor offenses such as illegal gun possession, he would be damned, particularly by black leaders who had begun to demand a stiff penalty for Goetz. If he went for a tougher indictment—such as attempted murder—he would incur the wrath of a large and vocal section of the press and population that supported Goetz. In an atmosphere in which crime had become a political vehicle, a fear that had proved crucial in several local and national elections since 1968, a dispassionate decision was probably impossible. During the next several months, Morgenthau actually secured two separate sets of indictments. The trial finally began in April, 1987, in Manhattan Supreme Court. By this time the charges had become serious: four counts of attempted murder, four counts of assault, criminal possession of a weapon, and reckless endangerment (13 felony counts in all).

In some respects, the evolving seriousness of these charges reflected growing public disenchantment (or puzzlement) over Goetz. In part it also reflected a response to that sector of public opinion that demanded more serious punishment. So Morgenthau decided to replace the earliest charges, secured on January 25, that indicted Goetz only on three counts of illegal gun possession. A new grand jury agreed that there was sufficient evidence to indict on several felony charges.

What the public learned in the 2 years between the event and the trial, and even during the trial, was sobering as well as confusing. Goetz had been right from the beginning: He was no hero. Even when he responded to the temptation to become a more public figure by supporting anticrime crusades or vigilantism or armed self-defense, even when he consented to appear on television, he always drew back into his other, much more retiring role.

Furthermore, his own past became the subject of public examination, and it too suggested contradictory interpretations. Goetz reported that he had been the victim of a previous subway mugging, in 1981 in the subway station at Canal and Varick streets. Carrying some electronics equipment for his business, he was approached by three black men who seized his parcels. Breaking away, Goetz ran out of the subway station pursued by one of the three men. Luckily a policeman was standing nearby: "The police officer saw him strike me, knock me down," Goetz testified at a gun permit hearing in 1982. "He attempted to push me through a plate glass window. I still have a minor permanent injury from that mugging."

The other two thieves dropped the equipment and the police officer approaching Goetz took his assailant into custody. What happened next infuriated Goetz. At the police station, he was detained for 6 hours. But his attacker was questioned for 2 hours and then released. The injustice of this was a scar as deep as any he received in the attack. Although the mugger was later convicted and sentenced to prison, Goetz did not know this. Instead, after the event, he damned the police department for its incompetence and the legal system for allowing criminals to remain at large. When his request for a permit to carry a revolver was denied in 1982, he secretly armed himself, carrying a revolver almost every time he went out.

While knowledge of this previous crime certainly disposed New Yorkers to understand why he armed himself, there were troubling aspects of Goetz's personality that began to emerge. A long story published in *New York Magazine* by his neighbor, Myra Friedman, disclosed that Goetz had evaded the Vietnam draft during the 1960s by feigning insanity. Furthermore, her obvious attempt to distance herself from him by suggesting his oddly obsessive behavior about the dangerous neighborhood he had chosen to live in was telling. Even worse for his case, his New Hampshire testimony, when made public, contained a sort of confession: He intended to "do anything I could do to hurt them. . . . My intention was to murder them, to hurt them, to make them, suffer as much as possible."

When the trial began, Goetz had hired two clever and energetic lawyers, Barry Slotnick (an attorney known for defending Mafia figures) and Mark Baker. After the laborious and difficult selection of jurors (over 300 were dismissed), the team quickly revealed its strategy. It would plead self-defense, arguing that Goetz had every right to believe he was being attacked and every reason to shoot the four boys. The prosecution, on the other hand, contended that Goetz had not acted reasonably—as defined by New York state law—and hence could not plead self-defense. But to prove their case, they had to enlist the aid of the four boys because almost no one had really witnessed the action. And to persuade the boys to testify, the District Attorney had to grant them immunity from prosecution, something he was not inclined to do.

While the public saw the case in its broadest context—as a symbol of the violence and broken-down social relationships that swirled around them—the courtroom increasingly narrowed the meaning of the trial. Goetz could not be tried for what the action seemed to mean, but only on the narrowest of grounds: Could his response be seen as a reasonable action in the circumstances? In effect, the trial would not satisfy either side nor would it settle any larger social interpretation of the event. It all hinged on the subtle point of his motivation. And while many of the larger echoes of the case may have played on the minds of the jurors, they too, had to confine their judgment to this narrow path of consideration.

The definition of self-defense in New York State has three essential elements that must be satisfied for a successful plea. The danger must be imminent; the response must be necessary and proportional to the danger; and the intent must be self-protection, not injury or revenge. The defendant in such cases must "reasonably believe" in the probability of an attack. Clear enough in law, this created a complex issue that required difficult deliberations. The most important problem was finding some agreement between subjective and objective standards. Simply put, the subjective standard involved Goetz's feeling that he believed himself under attack. In addition, his response had to be measured against the objective standard that asked how a reasonable citizen would act under the same circumstances. It was the task of the defense lawyers to make the jury believe Goetz: his motivations and the need for his actions. This meant, in effect, putting the four boys themselves on trial. As Slotnick said, "I'm going to prosecute these four."

When the prosecuting attorney, Gregory Waples announced he would call James Ramseur as a witness, Slotnick saw his opportunity. By antagonizing Ramseur through hostile questioning, he infuriated the witness, who then refused to answer, bringing on himself a citation for contempt of court. Through this and other strategies, Slotnick built a plausible case for Goetz's behavior. He was on "automatic pilot"; he fired shots in "rapid succession"; and consequently was only acting in self-defense. Another of the boys, Troy Canty, also testified, but his words did little to aid the prosecution. In fact the appearance of these two boys allowed Slotnick to flail away at their credibility and build a verbal portrait of their behavior. They were "thugs," "hoodlums," "predators," "savages." Goetz, on the other hand, never went to the witness stand.

When the jury reached its verdict, it vindicated Slotnick's strategy. The 12 men and women, black and white New Yorkers, convicted Goetz only on one count: Third degree criminal possession of a lethal weapon. Three months later, on October 19, 1987, Goetz was sentenced to 6 months in jail, a $5,075 fine; 4½ years of probation, and 280 hours of community service, plus psychiatric counseling by someone of his choosing. The jury and the judge had, in fact, exonerated Goetz of most of the charges; they accepted his story and convicted him only of illegally carrying a dangerous weapon. Nonetheless, Goetz still appealed this single conviction.

While the trial confined the meaning of the subway shootings, the public saw it in a much broader context and gave it far deeper, more representative meaning. The writer of one letter explained how the event touched most New Yorkers' lives:

> One problem is that the subways are used only by little, unimportant, uninfluential people. We really don't count much to politicians. The mayor, council president, governor all have big autos supplied at our expense. They don't have to use subways to be at work on time. Our local government is not doing the job; that's why the guy with the gun is a hero.

At issue in these words was something important—the perception that ordinary people were forced to use public transportation. Poor and working-class New Yorkers who rode underground were the special victims of crime, of crowding, of unpleasantness that could be avoided by wealthier, more powerful citizens. Evidence of this angry backlash by New York's "little" people could be seen in the tone of stories written for the newspapers (the *Post* and the *Daily News*) most read by this segment of the population. Full of lurid headlines and vengeful prose, these papers construed the public they served as Goetz's fellow victims. The *New York Times,* on the other hand, deplored vigilantism and reminded readers that the boys who accosted Goetz were themselves victims of poverty and racism. The African-American press generally called for severe punishment of Goetz.

James Ramseur, one of the four teenagers shot by Bernhard Goetz, is pictured here, outside his home on March 18, 1985, before the trial of the "Subway Vigilante." (UPI/Bettmann Newsphotos)

These different opinions suggest conflicting perceptions attributable to social class and race. Such distinctions were confirmed, in part, by Gallup polls,
both before the trial and after the sentencing, which showed whites and blacks
divided to a considerable degree (whites by 83% favored the outcome while
only 45% of blacks did).

Perhaps the division of New Yorkers between those who had no alternative to the subway and those with other means of transportation—taxi cabs, lim-
ousines, private cars—was even more important in generating the angry public
defense of Goetz. For if the city was divided between those who traveled underground in one of the world's largest and most crowded public spaces and those
who traveled above in one form or another of private transportation, this issue
went to the heart of what had happened to the American urban experience during recent history.

Still, there is a certain irony to the public attention to crime in the subway
during these years, for, according to statistics, subway muggings and other
felonies had decreased somewhat in the years prior to the shooting. Police also
claimed that the crime rate inside the subway was not as high as it was in some
of the areas above the subway on city streets. Yet many New Yorkers believed
that subway crime was growing rapidly, and they poured out their resentment
against the degradation of the trains, the service in which they were trapped,
and their fears, into sympathy for Goetz. It was not just crime, but, in effect,
the entire ambience of the system that New Yorkers deplored. They too defined
themselves as victims of the degeneration of public order of which crime was
the most obvious and dangerous symbol. They had learned from experience not
only what offered danger in the subway; they also thought they knew who.

This was a deplorable end to the story of a great engineering feat. When it
was completed in the early years of the twentieth century, the New York subway system became the spine of the city's commerce. It linked the four princi-
pal boroughs—Brooklyn, Queens, the Bronx, and Manhattan—with a service
that brought workers and shoppers into and out of the special commercial,
manufacturing, and residential districts of the city. Its peak service was reached
during the 1930s. After World War II, with increased suburbanization and the
loss of jobs and retail stores from Manhattan, ridership began to shrink. The
city government responded in two ways. It raised fares, several times by the
1970s and early 1980s, and it allowed service to deteriorate. As ridership became more and more confined to the poor, to new immigrants to the city
(blacks and Hispanics), support for subway expenditures among politically
powerful groups in the city shrank.

By the 1970s, the system had hit bottom. Equipment, safety, inspection,
and reliability all declined. For example, in the period 1975 to 1980, a growing
number of passengers and employees were killed in accidents. In 1980, 17,000
passengers claimed injuries. Of the 460 miles of track, 137 miles of tunnel,
10,000 signals, and 6,500 subway cars, many were in disrepair. The most visible sign of deterioration, however, was the rapid spread of graffiti both inside
and outside the trains. By 1984, 93 percent of all interiors and 12 percent of exteriors were defaced by graffiti.

This visual transformation occurred in two forms. Exterior graffiti was often the work of budding young artists who used the decaying metal exteriors of the subway cars as canvas for their works. Elaborate, colorful, and inventive, these designs often drew the praise of other artists or social commentators who declared them to be a sort of people's art. Most of the work was by young men in their early teen-age years. They invaded the railroad yards at night with spray cans of paint. The next morning, they could watch their work lumber through the subway stations. Inside the cars there was a wholly different sort of graffiti, most of it written in black magic marker with no pretense to art.

However one might assess the occasionally interesting piece of exterior design, this was clearly public art in a form that the public rejected. In fact, graffiti became a despised symbol of a system out of control. With its small budget, the Metropolitan Transit Authority could muster only feeble attempts to clean off the writing and painting, and shelter cars at night.

By the end of the 1970s and the early 1980s, the subway system had reached a crisis and sunk even further. Incompetent management, a lack of capital investment, and general aging of the system provoked widespread anger from customers. Dirt, overcrowding, disrupted schedules, and, especially, crime disturbed passengers. As one person told the *New York Times:* "I tolerate discomfort, but I can't tolerate terror."

By 1984, a group of citizens called the "Straphangers Campaign," organized to monitor subway service, declared that the system had become noticeably worse. This was true, it seemed, despite the fact that New York state had appropriated $5.7 billion for the period from 1982 to 1986 to purchase, among other things, 1300 new air-conditioned subway cars that were built of materials that could be easily cleaned. Furthermore, the legislature demanded that the MTA draw up a strategic plan of action.

During this same period there was a more intensive campaign to control crime underground. The police followed a number of strategies, deploying a canine corps in 1980 and then, beginning in 1982, running sweeps of the system. At the same time, the service began a program of planting decoys—usually dressed as the typical victim, a young urban professional or a female shopper. The transit police also advised passengers to change their behavior. They should not engage in any "flamboyant" display of jewelry or money; they should avoid riding in empty cars; and they should wait in designated and surveyed areas of platforms and not at the isolated ends. To measure their efforts, the transit police recorded in their 1985 official report:

Arrests	27,595
Felony Arrests	8,364
Summonses	355,055
People ejected	10,197
Homeless removed to shelter	3,500
Truants picked up	7,000

At about the same time the New York Criminal Justice Agency completed an exhaustive study of the nature of crime in the system. Its findings were, in most respects, anticipated. Fridays and Saturdays saw the highest incidence of robberies in the system. Weapons used included fists (47.9%), guns (24.4%), and knives (22%). The ages of those robbed or intimidated were primarily between 20 and 40 years and a large majority of complainants were women. A great many of the perpetrators were young (16 to 19 years of age) and in a great many cases they attacked in groups. More often than not they were black. In fact, the average profile of the attackers of male passengers would have described the four boys who accosted Goetz. The study also disclosed that crime in the subways since 1981 had diminished somewhat, although the rate in 1983 was still over twice as high as it had been in 1970.

In attempting to control crime on the subways the transit police and the managers of the system recognized the extreme difficulty of their task. Their advice to passengers—to change their behavior, to be suspicious and guarded — was, in fact, a recognition of the decay in this immense public space and an admission of their failure to protect those who entered it. Given the explicit recognition that passengers could not expect normal behavior from others, this was only a public acknowledgment of what passengers had already known for a long time. Under these tense conditions, any different or threatening behavior could summon images of crime and violence, and invoke prejudice, either

Pictured here in late April 1985, Bernhard Goetz receives the "Good Samaritans Award" from Frank Borzellieri, president of the Queens Good Samaritan Committee, at the New York State Rifle and Pistol Clubs annual Luncheon. (AP/Wide World Photos)

racial, class, or ethnic, that had become part of the repertory of self-protection. Thus the breakdown of civic order encouraged patrons to act on their prejudices and fears. As Goetz himself put it with heavy irony:

> Why shouldn't we get ourselves beaten up without a whimper? We have already given up the streets, the trains, the city to criminals: it's only a matter of time before we give up our houses.

This sentiment is what conservative politicians hoped to use to convince the public to "get tough" on crime, to give up efforts to alleviate poverty through public assistance programs, and to defame liberals whom they attempted to picture as defenders of criminals and opponents of such desperate vigilantes as Goetz. The issue of the subway shooting thus entered an intense public debate during the 1980s about the nature of government that reached into presidential and congressional races. Should government attack criminals, or should it attack the sociological causes of crime? There was nothing inherent in the complex Goetz case to provide any clear answers. But there were all the factors present to make a society act on its worries about what was happening to public spaces.

AN INTERPRETATION

The Bernhard Goetz case raises several interwoven and complex problems of historical interpretation. These require several preliminary distinctions to be made. Like a great many other criminal cases in the United States, the trial settled only the question of the guilt of the perpetrator and the punishment he would receive. Inevitably, the confined drama of the courtroom excluded from consideration some of the larger implications of the shooting, the significance that provoked contemporary observers and fascinates students of history.

What a great many New Yorkers responded to was, of course, the racial confrontation inherent in the subway incident. Goetz was white and his assailants were black. While this complexion may well have fit the profile of many subway muggings, Goetz's actions changed it from an incident in which he was the victim into one in which he became the aggressor. By shooting all four boys—the last with apparent deliberation—Goetz reacted in a way that forced the court and the city to scrutinize his motives. Was he a racist? Some believed that he was. There were stories in the press to bolster this charge that recounted his expulsion from a local community organization for his extreme attitudes. But a more subtle problem has to do with the public reaction to him. Was it favorable because he was a white man who "fought back"? While opinion polls found a great deal of sympathy for him (or at least his situation), they also showed distinct differences according to the race of the person speaking.

A fair question, which many commentators asked, was whether or not a black victim accosted by whites would have received the same outpouring of sympathy. There is little evidence to indicate that he would have. Crimes against black New Yorkers (the most common victims) were underreported in the large daily newspapers. Studies of punishment for crimes indicate that black criminals often receive stiffer sentences than do whites; black killers of whites are executed more often than black killers of blacks, for example. This suggests the problem of the double bind of race. If, in a city like New York, blacks are more likely to commit robberies, so are they also more likely to be punished and to be victims.

In the racially supercharged atmosphere of the mid-1980s, the shootings evoked commentary that crackled with animosity. A generation removed from the struggles and triumphs of the civil rights movement, African-Americans had increasingly been stigmatized as the perpetrators of crime and the creators of social disorder—the source of urban problems, the feared casualties of failed social engineering policies. The subway shooting tapped the energy of such accusations and appeared to legitimize a new form of racism cloaked in the rebirth of vigilantism, of getting tough on crime, of striking back. Perhaps not directly linked to this incident, a rise in crime on the subways during 1990 led to several other dramatic episodes of vigilantism and a further decline in ridership.

Goetz (as he readily admitted) and Cabey, Ramseur, Allen, and Canty were all victims who played out their fate in the degraded confines of the subway. The confrontation occurred in a shared public space—but not one visited ordinarily by all New Yorkers. Columnists tirelessly pointed out that a great many of those who rode the subways had no choice, while those who could avoid them moved in other conveyances. This division between privileged and less privileged, a vague dividing line in a city like New York, nonetheless intensified the reaction of political and social claustrophobia so characteristic in expressions of support for Goetz. Those compelled to share the subway, forced to ride with muggers and criminals, believed themselves callously ignored by politicians who allowed the system to degenerate so badly that they themselves refused to ride on it. Whatever community feeling existed was probably generated by a fellowship of inconvenience and danger. As New York Senator Alfonse D'Amato told the U.S. Congress about the subway system: "I'm afraid to get in that subway system even when I'm with my bodyguard, and my bodyguard is afraid."

While politicians of the city and the state of New York allowed the subway system, indeed, public transportation in general, to decline, there were some who hoped to exploit the Goetz incident and others like it for political purposes. This strategy could run in two directions. In the first place, the clamor of support for Goetz convinced many black politicians that they needed to make sharper demands on the city and to ask for more help for the hopeless poverty into which many of their constituents had fallen. Their case was a plea for the four boys who had accosted Goetz.

On the other hand there were those who hoped to turn the enormous anger generated by the incident into a reprimand for liberals who predominated the city and state government. While it certainly played no immediate role in national politics, this incident became part of the backlash exploited by conservatives, who blamed liberals for being soft on crime, for seeking social programs instead of prisons and harsh sentences, for explaining crime rather than punish-

ing it. The Goetz case thus fit neatly into the emerging American political debate about crime, race, and social welfare that began in the late 1960s and
erupted into the presidential elections of 1984 and, especially, 1988 in which,
perhaps, it decided the result. The difficulty of using this case in such a debate,
however, was its complexity, and the dubious character who had been elevated
by public opinion into a vigilante. Very early on Goetz had said he was no hero.
Indeed, he was not. He was a very lonely man, frightened of the world he had
to share with others, prey to his own fears and actions as well as the dangers
that the city had forced on him and the underclass to which Cabey, Ramseur,
Allen, and Canty belonged. It is deeply sad that what he appeared to treasure
most was his invisibility in a place in which the breakdown of community made
him a victim.

Sources: The sensationalism of the Goetz case inspired a number of instant histories as well as reasoned accounts of the trial. The most thoughtful of these is Lilian Rubin's *Quiet Rage: Bernie Goetz
in a Time of Madness* (1986), a book that takes a very critical look at the "Subway Vigilante." A fascinating look at the conduct of the trial and its issues is George Fletcher's *A Crime of Self-Defense:
Bernhard Goetz and the Law on Trial* (1988). A juror's account is by Mark Lesly, *Subway Gunman:
A Juror's Account of the Bernhard Goetz Trial* (1988).

   One interesting feature of the episode is the dispute over the political implications of the
shootings. The conservative *National Review* took a position that in many respects supported Goetz,
while the liberal *Village Voice,* and columnist James Breslin in the *New York Post* were skeptical of
his motives. This discussion is continued in legal journals such as the *National Law Journal* (June
29, 1987) and the *Yale Law Review* (February, 1988).

   Original sources are particularly important in reconstructing what happened on the subway.
Interviews with Goetz, such as carried by the *New York Post* on March 22, 1985, as well as Myra
Friedman's article, "My Neighbor Bernie Goetz," in *New York Magazine* (February 18, 1985) con-
tain important information and impressions. Of course Goetz's "confession" is a crucial, if dubious,
account.

   Finally, the story of the New York subway and its decline may be found in a series of articles
in the *New York Times* series by M. A. Farber (July 30, 31, and August 1, 1984). Other important
sources for information are the police reports and internal documents of the New York City Transit
Authority issued throughout the 1980s and testimony before the New York State Senate (1981).